NTC's
Dictionary
of
MEXICAN CULTURAL
CODE WORDS

Boye Lafayette De Mente

D0029643

NTC *Publishing Group*
Lincolnwood, Illinois

Library of Congress Cataloging-in-Publication Data

De Mente, Boye.
    NTC's dictionary of Mexican cultural code words / Boye Lafayette
    De Mente.
        p. cm.
    ISBN 0-8442-7959-5 (alk. paper)
    1. Mexico—Social life and customs—Terminology.   2. National
characteristics, Mexican—Terminology.   3. Spanish language—
Provincialisms—Mexico—Glossaries, vocabularies, etc.   I. National
Textbook Company.   II. Title.
    F1210.D38   1996
    972'.003— dc20   96-3871
                                                              CIP

Published by NTC Publishing Group,
4255 West Touhy Avenue, Lincolnwood (Chicago), Illinois, 60646-1975 U.S.A.
©1996 by Boye Lafayette De Mente.

2 3 4 5 6 7 8 9   BKM BKM   9 0 9 8 7 6 5 4 3 2 1

Dedication

This book is dedicated to my wife, Margaret Warren De Mente, for a lifetime of support and contribution to my efforts; and to Mario ("Mike") De La Fuente of Nogales, Sonora, Mexico—a romantic, sportsman, bullfight impresario, businessman, author, member of the University of Texas Longhorn Hall of Fame, mentor and friend who represents the promise of Mexico—for his goodwill and help.

CONTENTS

Contents

Contents

GUIDE TO KEY CULTURAL THEMES

PREFACE

BEHIND THE MASK OF MEXICO

Most Americans and Canadians in general are not knowledgeable about the cultural heritage and character of their Mexican neighbors to the south. When they think of great cultural accomplishments, they think of Europe. When they think of the exotic, and perhaps the erotic, they think of the Orient. Unknown to them, they have overlooked on their own doorstep one of the most unusual and fascinating countries on earth.

Many people see Mexico as a culture of tacos, tortillas, over-sized sombreros, leather sandals, bullfights, ancient ruins and revolutionary art. But these are only minor manifestations of Mexican culture. Far more significant and important are the intangibles—the fundamental values, the shared attitudes and the deeper, more complex forms of behavior that are the heart and soul of the country.

Mainstream Mexico combines elements of Europe, the Orient and the "New World" in a unique culture that is a blend of historical influences in some parts but startlingly pure Indian in others. "Indian Mexico," often referred to as "Remote Mexico," has remained virtually unchanged for more than four centuries. In broad terms, industrial Mexico is Western European, intellectual Mexico is Oriental, spiritual Mexico is Indian and erotic Mexico is a unique hybrid.

The average visitor to Mexico generally leapfrogs from one city or resort to another, seldom looking beyond the facade of everyday life and historical monuments into the body and soul of the country.

Mexican writer Carlos Fuentes says the culture of his country is "far more intricate and challenging to the North American mind than anything in Europe; a country at times more foreign than anything in Asia." Others have described Mexican life as a combination of ritual and disorder, of the spiritual over the material.

Outsiders must make an effort to discover who the Mexicans are, what they are really like (when they are not reacting to foreigners) and what compelling factors determine their characteristic attitudes and behavior.

The paradoxes of Mexico—the omnipresent trappings of Catholicism, the pagan soul of the people, the savage brutality of the criminal and the rogue cop, the gentle humility of the poor farmer, the warmth, kindness and compassion of the average city dweller, the perverse masculinity cult, the sensuality of the culture—are glimpsed and touched only in passing, and if considered at all are usually misunderstood.

The most direct and easiest route to understanding Mexicans and interacting effectively with them is through their language—and more precisely, through key words in their language.

Virtually all linguistic and philosophical authorities agree that the language of a people influences their thought and culture in the deepest and most fundamental ways. In fact, they hold that one cannot think coherent thoughts without language, that *all* thinking takes place within language.

Not only is language the medium of thought, it also controls and channels thought, and the thoughts people are capable of having are determined by the language they use, whether it is their mother tongue or a second or third language. The older a language and culture is the more powerful the influence the language has on the people who speak it.

Thus, like all ancient societies, Mexican culture, in all of its social, economic and political nuances, is bound up in key words that identify its historical, philosophical and psychological roots and explains the attitudes and behavior of the people.

These special words, both Spanish and Indian, are like genetic codes which serve as windows to the heart and soul of the country. When combined, they become a map to the character and personality of the Mexican people.

Boye Lafayette De Mente

ACKNOWLEDGMENTS

I am deeply indebted to the following people for reading the manuscript of this book and making many suggestions for its improvement: Jorge Carrera, Spanish Language Professor at the American Graduate School of International Management (Ret.); Mario de la Fuente M., Publisher, *Diario de la Frontera*; Lorenzo de la Fuente M., Director, Television por Cable del Norte de Sonora; Gilbert Jimenez, Senior Vice President, International Banking, First Interstate Bank of Arizona; Geri Canalez de Jimenez, entrepreneur; Milena Cuellar de Astorga, teacher; and Alberto A. Medina, international marketing executive.

INTRODUCTION

MEXICO: THE UNKNOWN COUNTRY

Mexico has a short history as far as written records are concerned, but archaeologists and anthropologists tell us that the country has been the home of human beings for at least 30,000 years. The true figure is probably well above that.*

In any event, there is ample evidence to prove that thousands of years before the appearance of any of the modern people of Europe, a number of sophisticated, highly refined civilizations had risen and fallen in the central and southern portions of Mexico. Altogether the sites of more than 10,000 pre-Columbian cities have been identified in central Mexico alone.

Among other things, the Mayan civilization, which flourished until about A.D. 300, discovered and began utilizing the vitally important principle of the zero more than a thousand years before it became known in Europe.

Mayan astronomer-mathematicians measured a year at precisely 365.242 days hundreds of years before the Arabs were able to accomplish the same feat. The pyramid of Tepanapa in Cholula, built around A.D. 400, is said to be the largest pyramid in the world.

In Mexico, as in many other early civilizations, it was obsessive religious fervor that provided the creative impulse for scientific advances and the building of great pyramids, temples and palaces.

Yet when Europeans stumbled upon the Americas in 1492 the wonderful civilizations developed by such ancient peoples as the Olmecs, Toltecs and Mayas had faded into myths. Their magnificent cities and many of their arts had already been abandoned.

By A.D. 1500 virtually the sole successors to the genius of these long dead people were the Aztecs and a few nearby nations.

When Spain's Hernán Cortés and his band of fortune hunters landed on Mexico's southeastern coast in 1519 (101 years before the Pilgrims landed at Plymouth Rock), they found the country inhabited by 149 distinct tribal nations, each with its own language and traditional customs.

---

*One of the most remarkable anthropological finds in Mexico are the remains of a now-extinct people who had flat tibia or shin bones in their legs, something the anthropologists had never seen or heard of before. However, the Ainu, the indigenous people of Japan, of whom some 15,000 are still alive, also have flat shin bones, which suggests a possible link between these two ancient peoples. The Ainu of Japan are Caucasoid, not Mongoloid.

In the century before Cortés's arrival, most of these tribal states had been brought under the military hegemony of the Aztecs, whose capital Tenochtitlán (now Mexico City) was located in the Valley of Mexico. (The Aztecs called themselves *Mexica*.)

According to Aztec tribute records, there were around 17 million people in the so-called Aztec empire at the time of Cortés's arrival. Another eight or so million people lived outside the realm of Aztec influence, giving Mexico a total population of around 25 million. (Spain at that time had about eight million people.)

Many of the tribal nations in the fairly loose-knit Aztec confederation lived a primitive existence, but others lived in highly organized, affluent societies in which architecture, art, astronomy, literature, mathematics, music, sports and other forms of entertainment were essential parts of their lives. (The bouncing rubber balls used in some of the Indian games fascinated Europeans.)

Before Tenochtitlán was destroyed by the invading Spaniards and their Indian allies, it was one of the largest and most beautiful cities in the world at that time. According to the testimony of the Spaniards themselves, Tenochtitlán was so splendid they were tongue-tied with awe when they first came upon it. They also testified that well-to-do citizens lived amidst luxurious comfort and beauty far surpassing anything they had seen in Europe, or even dreamed about.

Within two years after the arrival of Cortés all of this was gone. The Spaniards and their Indian allies slaughtered large numbers of the Aztecs, systematically destroyed Tenochtitlán, then went on to subjugate and enslave most of the rest of Mexico. (A few Indian tribes, in remote jungles and mountains, were too far away and/or too fierce for the Spaniards to bother with.)

The libraries of books and public records (written on bark paper and deer skin) kept by the more advanced Indian nations of Mexico were also systematically destroyed, first by Spanish soldiers and then by Spanish priests, whose aim was to totally eradicate the Indians' traditional religious beliefs and customs and convert them to Catholicism.

Mexico's advanced Indian civilizations simply vanished with the death of their priests, scientists, scholars and military leaders, and the destruction of their traditional way of life. Today, the Aztecs are primarily remembered because human sacrifices were part of their religious rites, not because of their many virtues and worthwhile accomplishments.

From this distance it is difficult to see much difference between the ritualistic sacrifice of men and women to their gods by the Aztecs, and the wholesale slaughter of people by the Catholic Spaniards in the name of their god.

Officially, the Spanish regime began in Mexico in 1521 and ended in 1821, almost exactly 300 years later. During this long period, Mexico was ruled by a succession of 61 Spanish viceroys, of whom two are said to have been capable and just rulers.

With their Moorish traditions going back to A.D. 800, the Spaniards introduced into Mexico the latest in Oriental despotism, including holding the native Mexicans in perpetual bondage as slave laborers.

Serfdom and slavery were ancient in Mexico, but because the conquerors of Mexico took away the religious foundation of the Indian societies, the Indians could not cope with the new system introduced by the Spaniards, and their society literally disintegrated.

Prior to the arrival of the Spaniards the Aztecs and other Indians mined gold in fairly substantial amounts. Some 30 years after the Spaniards arrived, huge deposits of silver were discovered in Taxco, Guanajuato, Querétaro and Zacatecas. Within a few decades Mexico was the largest producer of silver in the world, which changed the whole character of the administration of the colony.

Hundreds of thousands of Mexico's Indians were worked up to 16 hours a day in Mexico's gold and silver mines. Others were used as farm laborers and construction workers. The luckier ones were used as household servants.

Every three to five years a fleet of Spanish galleons would ferry the Crown's share of the silver to Madrid, a voyage of considerable danger. Some of the fleets fell prey to pirates and others to hurricanes, but enough of them made it through to make Spain one of the world's richest nations. Eventually, the Colonial administration in Mexico began to mint silver dollars, which soon became the coin of the world.

During the first generations of Spanish rule, Indians received no pay for their work and were subject to whatever punishment or indignity that struck the fancy of their Spanish masters. About the only barbaric brutality not imposed upon the helpless Indians during the Spanish reign was the full force of the Inquisition.

In their arrogance, Spanish priests assumed that common Indians were not mentally responsible for their actions. Those who were killed or stripped of their property and exiled by the church immediately after the conquest of Mexico were mostly members of the former nobility.

Despite this attitude, the Spanish overlords were zealous in "converting" Mexico's native peoples to Catholicism, usually by means of sprinkling thousands at a time with water and giving them Spanish names.

Cortés, his soldiers and the first higher-ranking Spaniards settling in Mexico after the conquest were given large grants of land, which included all the Indians living on it, and any industry made from it. Cortés's grant, for example, consisted of 25,000 square miles of territory. This included 22 towns and over 100,000 Indians. His grant, which was in perpetuity, was gradually increased over the centuries and by 1823 included a city, 157 towns, 119 farms, 5 ranches, 80 haciendas, 15 villas, and 150,000 Indians.

One of the Spanish government stipulations was that estate grant holders without wives had to marry within three years or lose their grants, a measure designed to make the holders permanent settlers. This resulted in a number of them marrying their Indian mistresses and others taking Indian wives.

These estate grants were known as *encomiendas*.[†] In this system Indians were required to pay tribute to local landlords, as well as to provide them with free labor. Later historians say this system so demeaned and demoralized the Indians that it, more than anything else, eventually destroyed those societies that were under the direct control of the Spanish overlords.

Three of the first *encomiendas* were awarded in perpetuity—the one that went to Hernán Cortés, and two that went to daughters of the last Aztec emperor, Moctezuma. Because these latter two estates assured that the families of the two princesses would be wealthy, the daughters were immediately sought after as brides by Spaniards, and the estates quickly passed into their husbands' hands.

Encomiendas granted in perpetuity could not be broken up and were passed down from one generation of owners to the next. Eventually, several of the grants came into the hands of the European relatives of the original holders, allowing them to live in luxurious splendor.

Italian relatives of Cortés, none of whom ever visited Mexico, received a large yearly income from his grant for several generations. (Cortés's own direct line of descendants died out in the fourth generation, but the grant was not rescinded until 1910.)

From the beginning of the Spanish period in Mexico the Spaniards made a valiant effort to impregnate as many Indian women as possible, a policy that was to have a fundamental impact on the history of Mexico thereafter.

Blacks, imported as slave laborers to replace the Indians dying from overwork and disease (and mostly confined to Veracruz, Guerrero and Acapulco), were also allowed to interbreed with Indian women. European diseases brought into Mexico by the Spanish swept across the country several times, altogether killing some 80 percent of the Indian population.

As the generations went by, the number and complexity of the mixed-blood combinations began to assume national importance. At first three broad classes were recognized: Euromestizos, or Spanish-Indians who were

---

[†]Spain applied the *encomienda* system to all of its colonies in the Americas. Many overseers of Indians subjected to the *encomienda* system treated them as animals who understood only the whip. Within some three generations, the Indian populations of the Caribbean islands had been totally exterminated (many died from European diseases).

culturally Spanish; Indomestizos, or Spanish-Indians who were culturally Indian (the largest group); and Afromestizos, or mestizo-black mixtures.

Eventually, the Spanish overlords established a detailed caste system that recognized 16 "breeds," which thereafter became a key factor on every level of Mexican society. These caste classifications were:

1. Mestizo: Spanish father and Indian mother
2. Castizo: Spanish father and Mestizo mother
3. Espomolo: Spanish mother and Castizo father
4. Mulatto: Spanish and black African
5. Moor: Spanish and Mulatto
6. Albino: Spanish father and Moor mother
7. Throwback: Spanish father and Albino mother
8. Wolf: Throwback father and Indian mother
9. Zambiago: Wolf father and Indian mother
10. Cambujo: Zambiago father and Indian mother
11. Alvarazado: Cambujo father and Mulatto mother
12. Borquino: Alvarazado father and Mulatto mother
13. Coyote: Borquino father and Mulatto mother
14. Chamizo: Coyote father and Mulatto mother
15. Coyote-Mestizo: Chamizo father and Mestizo mother
16. Ahi tan Estas[‡] (Coyote-Mestizo father and Mulatto mother)

The Spanish viceroys of Mexico as well as all of the larger land-grant holders maintained their own armed guards and small private armies, and in close collaboration with the Catholic Church, ran Mexico as a virtual prison colony.

Not all of the second generation of conquers were satisfied with the spoils they had gained, however. Several of them, including Don Martín Cortés, son of the hero Hernán Cortés (and his Indian mistress), conspired in a half-hearted way in the mid-1500s to overthrow the Spanish administration. Several of the young conspirators, who many said were just having a lark, were arrested, tortured and executed. Don Martín was excused because of his illustrious father.

Catholic priests began arriving from Cuba and Spain in large numbers shortly after the Aztec empire fell to Cortés. Most of these Catholic missionaries were humane if not Christian, and several dedicated themselves

‡*Ahi tan estas* translates as "Remain there," or "There you are."

to trying to prevent the Indians from being worked, starved and beaten to death.

The king of Spain, to his credit, lent these few compassionate souls a sympathetic ear and issued royal decrees aimed at protecting the Indians. But the Spanish overlords of Mexico were not about to give up their slave kingdom, and generally ignored the king's orders.

During the first several decades of the colonization of Mexico, the Spanish priests set up schools in cities, towns and villages, and made a genuine effort to educate as many Indians and *mestizos* (Spanish-Indian mixed-bloods) as possible in Spanish and in the tenets of the Catholic Church.

However, by 1600 wars and political changes in Spain, combined with the near extinction of the Indian population of Mexico, had brought an end to these relatively enlightened efforts.

For the rest of the 300-year Spanish reign in Mexico, and the following 100 years of rule by home-grown dictators, most of the surviving Indians and mixed-bloods were kept in ignorance, brainwashed in race hatred, fanaticism and corruption, and punished at the whim of their masters.

Until the last few decades of Spanish rule in Mexico the Spaniards did their best to keep the country isolated from the rest of the world. Trade with other countries was banned, while Spain alone exploited its silver and gold, piling up the largest hoard of treasure the world had ever seen.

Trade restrictions were so tilted in favor of Spain that the colonists were forbidden to raise their own grapes and olives, or to maintain mulberry trees and silk worms for the production of silk.

During the 1600s and 1700s there were periodic riots and small rebellions by Indians, *mestizos* and black slaves, but they were savagely quelled. The Gulf coast area also experienced raids from pirates. In 1683 one thousand pirates captured and looted Veracruz, then sailed away.

By the early 1800s the long rape of Mexico had just about run its course. The mixed-bloods had blended into a new race which outnumbered the Spaniards. Records published in 1808 show that Mexico had approximately 80,000 residents who had been born in Spain (so-called *peninsulars*), one million pure-blooded Spanish residents who had been born in Mexico, and 1.5 million mixed-bloods.

By this time the pure-blooded Indian population had increased from a low of around one million to an estimated 3.5 million; most of whom lived in remote areas, continued to speak their own languages and were virtually untouched by European civilization.

Throughout the Spanish era the government of Spain kept absolute control of Mexico, which it called New Spain, by assigning only native-born

Spaniards as administrators of the colony and stationing its own troops there to enforce its policies.

Mexican-born Spaniards, called *criollos*, or Creoles, could inherit the wealth of their *peninsular* fathers, but could not participate in the government of the colony in any way. (A few sons of viceroys born in Mexico but sent back to Spain for their education succeeded in becoming viceroys themselves—three in the 17th century.)

Spain's war with England in the late 1700s resulted in the Spanish Crown recalling most of its Spanish garrisons and top commanders from Mexico, leaving the military there in the hands of *criollo* officers with mostly *mestizo* troops, an action that was to contribute significantly to the war for independence that began in 1810.

From 1776 on, American and French ideals of personal freedom, human rights and democracy began to penetrate the thinking of a growing group of *criollos* and a few mixed-blood intellectuals. Technically and socially, Mexico had hardly changed in nearly 300 years, and these new ideas found fertile ground among a small but growing group of Mexican-born Spaniards, particularly those who lived on the northern frontier of Bajio Basin (later to become known as the cradle of Mexican independence).

However, wealthy Mexican-born Spaniards in Mexico City, no longer willing to accept their status as second-class citizens, were the first to flirt with freedom from Spain. In 1808 a conspiratorial group of them imprisoned the reigning viceroy, deported him and set their own man up in his place.

Yet it was a humble priest in the little town of Dolores and *criollo* stalwarts in Bajio led by Captain Don Ignacio Allende, owner of the town of San Miguel, who began the revolution.

Some time around 1808 this unlikely group formed a secret "literary" society to talk about breaking away from Spain, and from there planned a coup to be carried out in December 1810.

Of all people, Napoleon Bonaparte, the emperor of France, provided the first spark for the fire that was to set Mexico free from its Spanish overlords. He invaded and captured Spain in 1808, forcing King Charles IV to abdicate. Napoleon than imprisoned the king's son, Ferdinand VIII, and put his own brother, Joseph Bonaparte, on the throne of Spain. (None of Spain's other Latin American colonies wanted to be a part of the French empire, and at this time rebelled. By 1824 all of them, including Argentina, Bolivia, Colombia, Peru and Venezuela, were independent.)

It was the lowly village priest, Miguel Hidalgo, a second-generation Spanish Mexican, who took the torch lit by Napoleon and set the country ablaze on September 16, 1810. Hidalgo (1753–1811), born into a well-to-do *criollo* family and educated for the priesthood, was a natural rebel who was more of an outspoken macho heretic (with a mistress and all) than a priest. In 1800 he was called before the Inquisition board of judges because of his reputation for blaspheming the church, criticizing the king of Spain, and advocating sedition, but none of the allegations stuck and he was freed.

After he was put in charge of the small parish in Dolores, Hidalgo spent most of his time helping local Indians and *mestizos* improve their livelihood. Among other things, he introduced wine-making and silk culture to the Indians, both illegal activities. Troops were sent in to destroy the winery and cut down the mulberry trees that fed the silk worms.

By the summer of 1810 Hidalgo, Captain Allende and other members of the secret society had completed their plans for an insurrection to overthrow the Spanish regime. But in early September, Captain Allende, who had organized a clandestine army, was warned by the wife of one of the royalists that the viceroy had gotten word of their planned uprising.

On September 13, 1810, the authorities began arresting people identified with the society as well as others suspected of being disloyal. Allende and a few of his men hurried to Hidalgo's church in Dolores, arriving there shortly after midnight.

Allende was inclined to postpone the revolution and go into hiding. But Hidalgo said their only choice was to start the revolution immediately by attacking the local Spaniards and seizing their gold, supplies and arms.

Around 2 A.M. on the morning of September 16, 1810, Hidalgo, Allende and their small band first captured the local prison and released all of the prisoners.

Returning to the church with the released prisoners and others picked up along the way, Hidalgo preached an impassioned sermon that has been immortalized in Mexican history. In his speech, Hidalgo coined the phrase that was to become the slogan of the revolution: *El Grito de Dolores, Mexicanos, Viva Mexico!* ("The Cry of Dolores, Mexicans, Long Live Mexico!") The crowd, growing as it moved, then marched on the homes and businesses of the local Spaniards. Meanwhile, alarmed by the raid on the prison, all of the Spanish residents of the town had taken refuge in the local granary.

Hidalgo, who was anything but a general, suddenly found himself the nominal head of a revolution. Almost immediately, the rebellion turned into an orgy of burning, killing and looting by the downtrodden Indians and *mestizos*. All of the Spaniards in the town were killed outright. (Another slogan quickly adopted by the rebels was *Mueran los Gachupines!* "Death to the Spaniards!")

Soon after the insurrection began the rebels adopted a graphic rendition of Our Lady of Guadalupe (an Indianized version of the Virgin Mary) as its banner as a means of attracting both Indians and *mestizos* to the rebellion.

The movement quickly escalated into a full-scale war. The enslaved Indians and most of the *mestizos* were motivated as much by smoldering anger and hatred as anything else, and did not distinguish between the ruling *peninsular* Spaniards and Spaniards born in Mexico.

Armed with machetes, miners' picks and rock slings, these social outcasts begun a brutal rampage that shocked the Mexican-born Spaniards, most of whom soon withdrew their support. Battles between royalists and rebels became a long series of atrocities in which men, women and children were slaughtered by both sides.

Hidalgo lived to lead the revolution against Spanish rule for only six months. He was betrayed to the Spanish authorities, captured and executed. Other leaders, including Captain Allende, were also captured and shot. (Their heads were cut off and put in an iron cage on public display outside of Granaditas in Guanajuato for the next 10 years.)

After Hidalgo, Allende and the other *criollo* leaders were killed, the revolution turned into guerrilla warfare on a national scale. In his magnificent book, *Fire and Blood—A History of Mexico*, author-historian T.R. Fehrenbach described some of the actions that followed as "casual executions and sadistic reprisals." Castration and burial alive in quicklime were just some of the savagery that was inflicted upon revolutionaries captured by royalist troops.

But the fire Hidalgo had started burned inexorably. When he died the cause was taken up by others in turn. The most outstanding of these second-stage revolutionaries were José Maria Morelos (1765–1815), who was a *mestizo* priest, Vicente Guerrero and the opportunistic and brutal Augustín de Iturbide, both Mexican-born Spaniards.

By 1813 Morelos, described by later historians as a political and military genius, and his forces had captured most of the country. But his liberal reform proposals horrified the Catholic Church and most of the *peninsulars* and Mexican-born Spaniards, who rallied their forces to capture and execute him in 1815.

Augustín de Iturbide (1783–1824) began his career as a royalist army officer but after some 10 years of fighting and killing rebels by the tens of thousands (he followed a take-no-prisoners policy), he suddenly switched sides and was soon commander-in-chief of all the rebel armies.

Iturbide entered Mexico City in September 1821 as the paramount power in the country. His administration officially ended Spanish dominion over Mexico on September 27, 1821—300 years, one month and two weeks after it began. After 11 years of wholesale slaughter, treachery and plundering, Mexico was politically free from Spain. But the revolution had been captured by Mexican-born Spanish leaders of the army and church who were just as unscrupulous and savage as their former *peninsular* masters.

Soon after entering Mexico City, Iturbide had himself crowned as the emperor of Mexico. Less than a year later there was a rebellion against him. The soon-to-be famous Santa Anna (1794–1876), one of his generals, took up arms against him, forcing him to go into exile in Europe. (Many of Santa Anna's contemporaries described him as being as evil as any human can be.)

A short time later, Iturbide surreptitiously returned to Mexico, thinking he might be able to regain power. He was recognized soon after landing in Veracruz and was captured and executed by a local military garrison.

Iturbide was succeeded by Guadalupe Victoria as the first president of the new republic of Mexico. Victoria turned the presidency into a dictatorship. The army and clergy dominated all government functions, and like their Spanish predecessors, were concerned almost exclusively with enriching themselves and their friends.

Mexican independence from Spain was thus followed by a savage free-for-all among rival generals, top clergy, *criollos* and wealthy mine and *hacienda* owners. None of them had any experience in self-rule, and both ethics and morality were virtually nonexistent.

Immediately after the successful revolt against Spanish rule most of the European-born Spanish residents were stripped of their property and driven out of Mexico. The Indians and mixed-bloods, who made up four fifths of the population, got nothing and were to remain outcasts and slaves in all but name for another 100 years.

While low-echelon priests like Hidalgo and Morelos had been the firebrands of the revolution, the bishops and canons of the church had supported the royalists, earning the wrath of the new leaders. But the church was so politically powerful that all efforts to reduce its influence failed.

Between 1822 and 1855 Mexico had 25 presidents. During this period the country outside of Mexico City was actually run by state governors and regional *caudillos* (chiefs), who were the Mexican equivalent of China's warlords.

In 1838 the French blockaded and bombarded the Port of Veracruz in an effort to force the Mexican government to pay some back debts, but the next chapter in the history of Mexico was to be written by Americans.

In 1821 an American pioneer in the Southwest named Moses Austin obtained a concession from the Mexican general in charge of the garrison at Monterrey to settle 300 Catholic families in the Texas portion of the state of Coahuila.

Moses died shortly afterward and his son Stephen became the leader of the mass immigration into Mexican territory. All an immigrant had to do to qualify for permanent residency and full citizenship rights was to claim to be Catholic and promise to obey the laws of Mexico. Each family was to receive a seven-year exemption on customs duties and a 10-year exemption on Mexican taxes.

Stephen Austin began offering land in Mexico to American colonists free of charge, waiving the six cents per acre that was in effect at the time. Other groups of Americans quickly obtained similar concessions, and over the next several years the stream of Americans immigrating into Mexico became a flood.

Each American immigrant over the age of 21 could buy 640 acres of land for himself, 320 acres for his wife and 160 acres for each of his children—at a few cents per acre. If he brought slaves with him he could buy 80 acres for each of them. Families who agreed to raise cattle were eligible for one square league of land—4,428 acres.

By 1827 there were 12,000 Americans in the Texas portion of Coahuila, and only 5,000 Mexicans. In 1830 there were 30,000 Americans and 7,800 Mexicans.

Although the American immigrants had promised to integrate themselves into the state of Coahuila as citizens, they remained totally separate, and soon began to complain about having to obey the laws of Mexico. They staged several little rebellions in 1830.

In 1832 American residents of Texas came out in support of the Mexican general Santa Anna, who had launched a full-scale rebellion against the then president-dictator Bustamente.

In return for their support, the Americans asked Santa Anna to abolish the Mexican customs houses and border patrols along the U.S. frontier. Santa Anna refused and sent troops into the area to make sure that regulations governing trade between Mexico and the United States were obeyed.

The American Texans banded together and drove Santa Anna's troops back across the Rio Grande (which Mexicans called Rio Bravo). This infuriated Santa Anna. He assembled a much larger army of troops, recrossed the Rio Grande and defeated the Americans at the Alamo. (Prior to the beginning of the battle, Santa Anna ordered his bugler to play the *Deguello*, a battle call to a fight to the death, first used by the Spanish in their battles to expel the Moors from Spain. Only six of the 180 men defending the Alamo survived the battle. Although all of these were wounded, Santa Anna ordered their immediate execution.)

Two months later a freshly recruited army of Texans, led by Sam Houston, surprised, defeated and captured Santa Anna. Houston freed Santa Anna after he had signed a document—many say at gunpoint—recognizing Texas as an independent country. (Santa Anna later became the president-dictator of Mexico 11 times for a total of 30 years.)

However, the Mexican government at that time refused to honor the document signed by Santa Anna, who was no more than a rebel general and regarded by many as a traitor. But Texas was to be a republic from 1836 to 1845.

During the next several years as one Mexican "general" after another rose in rebellion against the Mexican government, the Texans were afraid they might be reconquered, and repeatedly asked the United States to annex them. Because of dissention over whether Texas would be a "free" state or "slave" state, Congress didn't make up its mind until it appeared that the British were going to come to the rescue of the Texans.

Then, Mexico offered to guarantee Texan independence if the Texans would not go through with their move to join the United States. But the offer came too late. In 1845 the United States annexed Texas and President James K. Polk sent General Zachary Taylor there to establish army patrols along the new border. In 1846 the United States also annexed New Mexico.

In April 1846 Mexican troops fired on an American calvary patrol encamped on the Rio Grande. History records show that President Polk then went before Congress, and in a totally fabricated story, announced that the United States had exercised every option to steer clear of war with Mexico but that it could no longer be avoided.

Congress approved a declaration of war. Within little more than a year U.S. troops had captured and occupied a wide swath of northern Mexico, comprising what is now Arizona, Nevada, part of Utah and California, as well as Mexico City itself.

Following the signing of a peace treaty that gave all of northern Mexico to the United States (the U.S. government later paid a token sum of $18 million for the huge area), American troops were withdrawn from Mexico City. This annexation left Mexico only about one fourth the size of the now greatly expanded United States.

For what it is worth, the original southern boundary of Texas was the Nueces River, not the Rio Grande. The American troops that the Mexicans fired upon were *in* Mexico, and it was they who were in violation of international law.

A young Abraham Lincoln denounced this aggregation by American troops (see the *Congressional Record*) as did Henry Thoreau, who refused to pay taxes to support the "unjust war" and was jailed for his action.

As far as Mexicans were concerned, the United States had taken over more than half of their national territory by foul means. Thereafter it was taught in Mexican schools that the United States was an imperialistic despoiler, scheming to swallow up the rest of the country.

A number of American politicians contributed to this image by constantly proclaiming that that was exactly what the United States should do.

The Hearst newspapers editorialized that the United States should overrun Mexico and plant the American flag in Panama.

Discrimination against Mexicans who suddenly found themselves living in the United States was intense. In 1856 the new American administration in California passed an antivagrancy statute that referred to "former" Mexicans as "the people known as Greasers."

Hundreds of Mexican citizens living along the new border were gunned down by American border patrols, police and ruffians merely because they were "greasers"—a derogatory term taken from the common use of a heavy hair pomade by Mexican men. No one was ever punished for these crimes.

American agents worked openly for the annexation of the remaining northern states of Mexico. Under these circumstances, Mexicans came to distrust and hate all foreigners, especially Americans.

It was not until 1858 that Mexico was to have a president who was both capable and honest. This was Benito Juárez, a Zatopec Indian who is still regarded by most Mexicans as the greatest statesman the country has produced. (Juárez was an Indian in race only, having been raised and educated from the age of 12 as a white man.)

Some of the reforms proposed by Juárez included separating the church and the state, abolishing the special privileges traditionally enjoyed by the military and the clergy and introducing education for the masses.

In late 1861 a consortium of English, Spanish and French troops landed in Veracruz, ostensibly in a showdown move to force Mexico to settle old debts. But the Catholic Church and opposition leaders who hated President Juárez had conspired with Napoleon III to remove Juárez from office and replace him with the Archduke Maximilian of Austria (the younger brother of Franz Josef, the emperor of Austria), who was led to believe that Mexicans wanted a foreign emperor.

Taking advantage of the Civil War in the United States, the greatly expanded French forces quickly defeated Mexico's ill-armed and disorganized army and occupied the whole country. Juárez escaped execution by fleeing to the United States.

In 1864 Maximilian accepted the throne. But much to the dismay of the church and the other anti-Juárez forces, Maximilian turned out to be a liberal who approved of Juárez's reforms. His reign was therefore opposed not only by the forces backing Juárez but also by those who had brought him to Mexico.

When the Civil War in the United States ended, America began pressuring France to withdraw its forces from Mexico, and liberally supplying arms to Mexican rebels who were against the occupying French army.

By 1867 it was obvious to France that it could not hold into Mexico, and its troops were withdrawn. A few months later Mexican forces backing ousted President Juárez captured Maximilian and executed him. His wife Carlota, a Belgian princess who had gone to Europe to persuade Napoleon III and the pope to support her husband, escaped the wrath of the rebels (but went insane and died in a mental institution in 1927). Juárez resumed the presidency and died of a heart attack in 1872 while still in office.

In 1876 a young general named Porfirio Díaz[1] led a rebellion against the government and installed himself as the new president-dictator. After four years in office he chose Manuel Gonzalez as his successor. Gonzalez's four-year reign was an orgy of theft on a grand scale. When he retired in 1884 as a multimillionaire, Díaz returned to power and ruled Mexico with an iron fist for the next 26 years.

Díaz maintained his power and kept order in the country by means of the *Brevi*, a secret police organization, and the *Rurales*, an elite mounted police corps mostly recruited from former bandits, which was infamous for its sadistic brutality.

Díaz created the *Rurales* primarily to rid the countryside of bandits, but they then became a rural police force that in effect replaced the bandits, charging farmers and villagers for whatever protection they might provide them.

The *Rurales* tortured and killed tens of thousands of people, the innocent and guilty alike, during the Díaz reign. One of their favorite methods of disposing of people and entertaining themselves at the same time was to bury their victims in standing positions with only their heads exposed above ground, then to race their horses over the victims until their heads were crushed.

Díaz divided huge portions of Mexico up into "hereditary fiefs" and gave them to relatives and friends—much as the Spanish Crown had done 350 years before. He opened the country up to foreign investments, and gave foreign firms and foreigners outrageous privileges and advantages over Mexicans.

The big winners in Mexico, in addition to Díaz and his friends, were Americans like John D. Rockefeller, J.P. Morgan, William R. Hearst and Daniel Guggenheim and his six brothers. Among them they virtually monopolized the oil, mining, sugar, coffee and cotton industries. The Guggenheims alone owned farms, ranches, mines, factories and other businesses all over the country.

---

[1]Porfirio Díaz's full name was Porfirio Díaz Mori. His grandfather, Mori, was one of many Japanese who had immigrated to the state of Oaxaca, where they became noted for being ambitious, hard workers and skilled fighters. Some Oaxacan military troops wore head bands patterned after the Japanese *hachimaki*, traditionally worn by Japan's samurai warriors (and Word War II kamikaze pilots) as a symbol of courage and power when going into battle.

Historians record that at the end of the Díaz reign foreign individuals and foreign companies owned around half of the total wealth of the country, and dominated every productive category except agriculture and handicrafts.

The most notorious example of the Mexican family-owned business empires during Díaz's era was that of the Terrazas family. Don Louis Terrazas owned 50 *haciendas* (huge farm-ranches) totalling seven million acres, plus railroads, sugar mills, mines, and dozens of other companies.

Workers throughout Mexico were forced to toil 11 to 12 hours a day, seven days a week. Employees of factories and *haciendas* were required to spend all of their income in company-owned stores (*tienda de raya*), which kept them permanently in debt. The debts of parents were passed on to their children.

Díaz allowed the Catholic Church to reclaim property confiscated by the Juárez administration in the 1860s. Prior to this the church had owned approximately one half of all the real estate in Mexico. He also allowed several thousand Spanish and other European immigrants to enter Mexico during his reign.

Americans in Mexico could get by with almost any crime, including murder. Díaz was, therefore, very popular among the foreign community living in Mexico, and was hailed by the world press as a great leader and the savior of his people.

Díaz's own controlled press liked to proclaim that Mexico was the safest country in the world. Historian Ernest Gruening pointed out later that the country was indeed safe for foreigners, but not for 90 percent of its own people. Mixed-bloods and Indians were routinely arrested and imprisoned for such things as speaking in a loud voice in public places.

Personal accounts by American travelers in Mexico during the late 1800s and first decades of the 20th century note that most of the Indians and poor *mestizos* lived in utter squalor, in makeshift huts, under conditions that were worse than what their ancestors had faced more than 5,000 years before.

During Díaz's reign Mexican Indians could not appear on the main streets of Mexico City or in the city's public parks. Most towns of any size had segregated squares for Indians.

One of the most draconian laws of the Díaz government was the *Leva*, under which military garrisons stationed around the country could arbitrarily conscript men and women into the army to fill their numerical quotas, without warning or documentation.

The first taken were criminals, followed by troublemakers and vagabonds. When there were none of these available, people were taken from their homes and off the streets; in the case of the latter, without their families ever being officially notified.

In 1909 writer Andres Molina Enriquez published a book titled *Los Grandes Problemas Nacionales*, in which he said that the only true Mexicans were the *mestizos* and that they would be the inheritors of Mexico, a concept so shocking and powerful that it would forever change Mexico.

Molina pointed out that the *criollos* were still Spanish/French in their thinking and ways, while the *mestizos* of Mexico were a new national type, a totally new race, with a new culture of their own, and that they were the majority in Mexico.

Finally in 1910, after nearly 400 years of cruel bondage, the dispossessed, the poor, the forgotten and the tortured of Mexico rose in another great rebellion. Díaz was forced to resign and went into exile in Europe.

Mexico's civil war was started by an obscure intellectual priest named Francisco I. Madero, but it was to be finished by lean, tough young men from the northern states of Chihuahua and Sonora—Pancho Villa, Abraham Gonzalez, Venustiano Carranza, Alvaro Obregón and Plutarco Elias Calles—with Indian and *vaquero* troops, and in the south by Emiliano Zapata and his peasant armies.

In 1910 there were 1,150,000 pure or nearly pure European Mexicans, eight million mixed-bloods and around six million Indians. Historians say that some 75 percent of the population at that time were illiterate, had no sense of nationality or nationhood and were what Mexico's famed writer Octavio Paz was later to refer to as *pelados*, or "plucked ones."

Madero, the first leader of the civil war, served as president from 1911 to 1913. In 1913, reportedly with the connivance of the American ambassador to Mexico at that time, Henry Wilson Lane, and U.S. oil interests, Madero was deposed and murdered.

From this point on, the revolution became a series of battles between competing generals. For the next several years Mexico was drenched in one blood bath after the other as such figures as Victoriano de la Huerta, Pancho Villa‖, Venustiano Carranza, Alvaro Obregón and Emiliano Zapata# burned and killed their way across the pages of Mexican history.

In April 1914 the United States blockaded the gulf ports of Mexico to prevent European arms from entering the country. A short time later the U.S.

‖ Pancho Villa, whose real name was Doroteo Arango, began his career as a bandit who specialized in cattle rustling.

In real life Emiliano Zapata, an honest and selfless man, was far more handsome and commanding in presence than Marlon Brando, who immortalized him in the movie *Zapata*. In addition to the Spanish language, Zapata also spoke fluent Nahuatl, the language of the Aztecs, and regularly used that language when talking to his Indian troops. In 1919 he was tricked into attending an ambush set up by Venustiano Carranza, then the president of Mexico, and was riddled with rifle bullets.

Navy shelled and then occupied Veracruz. Then the United States began actively supporting Pancho Villa in his efforts to overthrow the government.

When Villa's fortunes began to wane, the United States switched to Venustiano Carranza. Villa paid American gunrunners in advance (in gold coins) for a shipment of arms, but the Americans reneged on the deal. In retaliation, Villa had 18 American engineers at Santa Isabel shot, and in May 1916 raided Columbus, New Mexico.

America's soon-to-be-famous General "Black Jack" Pershing was ordered to follow Villa into Mexico and punish him. American troops entered Mexico and did not withdraw until February the following year. They never did find Villa.

One of the landmark good deeds accomplished by the administration of Venustiano Carranza, president in 1914 and again from 1915 to 1920, was passing the *Constitution of 1917*, which was primarily the work of a 31-year-old general named Francisco Mugica.

The Mexican civil war officially ended in December 1920. It brought an end to the official caste system that had been severely enforced in Mexico for more than 300 years, but the class system had hardened into stone. And there was to be one more rebellion, in 1923, before an uneasy, harsh peace settled over the prostrate country.

For the first time since the beginning of the Spanish era in 1521, the majority of the population of Mexico, the previously ostracized and degraded mixed-bloods, began to think of themselves as the true Mexicans.

Still, for the next several years assassinations and political murders on a mass scale were commonplace. Most men who were not farmers carried guns, and farmers carried machetes and knives. Daily killings, many of them sublimely senseless, were routine.

Plutarco Elias Calles became president in 1924, and in the next four years distributed eight million acres of land to small farmers. In 1929 he founded the Institutional Revolutionary Party (PRI).

Lázaro Cárdenas, elected president in 1934, distributed 49 million acres of land to peasants. He also began a program to provide basic education to Mexico's masses.

In 1938 the Mexican government, acting under orders from President Cárdenas, seized all of the American and British oil facilities in the country. The United States and Great Britain accused the Mexican government of having gone communist, and quickly imposed a boycott on Mexican oil.

Mexico just as quickly began selling oil to Germany, Italy and Japan—all militantly anti-communist countries. When World War II broke out, the United States and England gave up their boycott, and Mexican oil subsequently played a major role in the Allied victory. In 1942 Mexico agreed to pay the oil companies $120 million for their property.

As overall peace endured year after year, the lust for violence and blood so characteristic of Mexican males gradually subsided, but most men carried guns at all times until the 1950s.

The "Revolutionary Party" that took control of Mexico in 1929 maintained itself at the expense of both democracy and the people. (Just before the Olympic Games in Mexico City in 1968 hundreds of students who had gathered in the Plaza de Tlateloco to protest the policies and practices of the government were massacred by *Granaderos*, an elite antiriot force maintained by the government.) In the 1970s a new generation of more enlightened leaders began the slow and painful process of following up on reforms first proposed by President Benito Juárez in the 1860s.

By that time the racial and cultural changes began by Cortés in the 1520s had come full circle. Less than five percent of the population was fully Caucasian. Some 10 or 12 percent were full-blooded Indians, most of whom lived in remote central and southern regions of the country and still had not been integrated into the mainstream of Mexican life.

Today people of mixed blood, mostly Indian and Spanish, make up more than 60 percent of the population, and are typical Mexicans. African, Arab and Chinese blood have also been mixed into this gene pool, and it is this mixture of people and cultures that give Mexico its special character and strength.

Finally, after more than 400 years of stagnation and suffering, there are growing signs that Mexico is on its way to becoming one of the great nations of the earth.

Abrazo

(Ah-BRAH-zoh)

"Ritual of the Embrace"

Mexicans are an exceptionally emotional people, expressing themselves in a variety of ways which have become an integral part of their culture, from their songs and dances to every aspect of their interpersonal behavior.

In fact, it might be said that the whole of Mexican culture is an exercise in emotionalism, whether it is in harmonious communion with each other or the spirits and nature, or in self-flagellation and outbursts of violence.

The emotional character of Mexicans was forged in a caldron of physical, intellectual and spiritual oppression and abuse over a period of many centuries—the type of experience that brings out the best and the worst in people, producing artists, poets and philosophers, as well as people who are totally amoral with no respect for life.

When at peace with themselves and the world at large the typical Mexican is a paragon of goodwill, hospitality and personal warmth that is unsurpassed, a factor that adds a special dimension to life in Mexico.

For people who are not used to expressing their emotions so openly, Mexico takes some getting used to, but once newcomers have accepted the Mexican way it takes hold of them and never lets go.

One Mexican custom that has a subtle but profound influence on personal relationships, which nurtures friendships and helps fulfill the deepest emotional needs, is the *abrazo* (ah-BRAH-zoh).

Most people are familiar with the theory and practice of "touch therapy," a physical contact technique designed to break down psychological walls and help people open themselves up to full communion with others. A natural "touch therapy" is an integral part of the lives of most middle- and upper-class Mexicans, a practice that has long been institutionalized and ritualized in the custom of the *abrazo*, which means "embrace"—to clasp another person in your arms in a demonstrative hug.

The *abrazo*, brought to Mexico by the Spanish, is recommended in the New Testament and was part of an early Christian liturgy used as a symbol of spiritual fraternity. When priests received their habits and knights their swords and armor during the Middle Ages the ceremonies were ended with an *abrazo*.

When the Spanish conquistadors brought the semireligious custom to Mexico it became a part of their courtly religious and social etiquette. In addition to being a demonstration of friendship, the *abrazo* was also used to seal political alliances.

As practiced by Mexicans (and other Hispanics) today the *abrazo* has been formalized for convenience. Your right arm goes over the left arm of the other person. Your left arm, in turn, goes under the other person's right arm. Both persons tilt their heads to the left, so they are looking over the other person's right shoulder. The embrace is accompanied by patting the other person's back with the right hand.

Among middle- and upper-class Mexicans, the *abrazo* is the common form of greeting by friends who have not seen each other for a while, and it is often followed by a handshake.* The higher social class of the people, the more often they engage in the practice.

The special value of the *abrazo* is that it merges the outer dimensions of the "soul" with that of the other person, allowing for an intimate exchange of warmth, sympathy, joy and spirit, and in the process recharges one's own "batteries."

The *abrazo* is not only an emotional and spiritual stimulus, it is sensual as well, and thus touches on the three wellsprings of our mental and physical health. Mexico's *abrazo*, in a minor way, is something like "plugging in" to the master spirit of the cosmos. It is a small but important affirmation of the spiritual brotherhood of man in the deepest, most profound sense.

When entered into deliberately, enthusiastically and wholeheartedly, the *abrazo* raises one's awareness of this common bond, brings a warm glow of goodwill and love and also satisfies a deep craving that all people have to be accepted and loved, to express affection and appreciation in a way that is much more meaningful than words.

There is an outstanding passage in the book *I Like You, Gringo—But!* written by Mario ("Mike") De La Fuente of Nogales, Mexico, that captures the power and promise of the *abrazo*.

The setting is the bullring in Nogales. De La Fuente, the impresario, had just presented a spectacularly successful bullfight and the emotional pitch of the fans was at a high fever. He wrote: "Something extraordinary began to happen. I became aware that a great number of people (had entered the ring and) were coming across the arena toward my box. I could feel their eyes on me. When they reached the front of my box they shouted at me to come

---

*Mexican shake hands more often than most other people. Lovers meeting secretly may shake hands before kissing. When a Mexican man shakes hands with an attractive woman he wants to impress, the action is more than a greeting. It is a ceremonial caress.

down into the arena. The eight-foot climb was difficult for me but my *may-ordomo*, Don Nacho, was right below me and helped me down. The crowd engulfed me in an air of extraordinary intimacy. *They wanted to hug me!*"

The *abrazo*, or hug, is the oldest and most powerful means human beings have of expressing kinship and love, for showing joy and pleasure at happy times and sorrow at sad times. Yet in most non-Latin societies its practice among adults is rare.

Mexicans cannot feel really close or intimate with people until they engage in the *abrazo*, so it especially behooves businesspeople from other countries who want to establish good relationships with their Mexican counterparts to wholeheartedly adopt this custom.

Adulación
(Ah-doo-lah-cee-OHN)

"The Importance of Flattery"

Social harmony in Mexico has traditionally been a very fragile thing because it was based more on emotional reactions than on studied reason and such principles as equality. As long as Mexicans conducted themselves according to a precisely established etiquette things went smoothly and, in fact, had a formal and dramatic essence that was very attractive. But this harmony was instantly shattered when anyone failed to follow the prescribed rules.

A number of the most fundamental and conspicuous elements in Mexico's traditional etiquette are products of the hierarchical authoritarian political system that prevailed in the country until recent decades.

As is typical of all such authoritarian systems, government officials on every level tended to be arrogant and extraordinarily sensitive to real and imaginary slights, and did not allow inferiors to question or criticize them. Punishments for disobeying or displeasing the authorities were severe.

In order to survive within this system Mexicans had to develop ways of protecting themselves from the corruption and excesses of those in power. This included exercising extreme caution in their behavior toward their superiors, catering to them in a variety of ways and using respect language and an obsequious form of body language.

Another of the key facets in this culture of pandering to the emotions and egos of superiors was the use of *adulación* (ah-doo-lah-cee-OHN) or "flattery" to help ward off any kind of negative reaction from them.

As time went by it became symptomatic for Mexicans to use effusive flattery to everyone, regardless of their social relationship, further reducing the motivation of people in general to set and maintain higher standards for themselves. It thus became characteristic of Mexicans to avoid criticizing and correcting others, and to flatter and praise them no matter how incompetent or unproductive they might be, all in the interest of harmony.

This excessive use of *adulación*, itself a symptom of an unjust and inefficient system, fed on itself, further corrupting the system, and taking people further and further away from rational reality.

Today the effusive use of *adulación* is still a primary feature of typical Mexican behavior. Flattery is still an oil that makes the society function as smoothly as it does. Face-to-face public criticism of people is still frowned on and can be dangerous, especially if it involves less educated men who are highly protective of their self-image.

It is particularly important for foreign visitors and businesspersons in Mexico to be wary of creating enemies by making critical remarks about Mexicans or Mexico, even when they are obviously well deserved.

Overall, *adulación* to most Mexicans, especially those in the middle and upper classes, is gradually becoming more of a social indulgence than a matter of survival. The most dramatic signs of this change occurred during the first two years of the administration of Ernesto Zedillo (1994–2000), when President Zedillo took the lead in criticizing individual politicians, jurists and bureaucrats, along with all three branches of the government. However, it will no doubt be a generation or more before most Mexicans can break the deeply entrenched custom and give honesty and common sense precedence over flattery.

Algo Sucedió
(AHL-go Soo-say-dee-OH)

"Something Came Up!"

When ordinary Mexicans go to the United States for business and other professional reasons they are profoundly shocked to discover that there is little or no social content in business and other professional affairs.

They have been programmed to believe that the personal and social aspects of business and professional relationships are as important as their purely economic aspects, and to conduct all of their affairs on that basis, something that is also true in most Asian and in some European countries.

While most Asians and Europeans who take up residence in the United States find that being released from the restraints imposed upon them by their own culture is like being freed from a mental straightjacket, that is generally not the case with Mexicans. Mexican culture carefully defines interpersonal relationships and gives them precedence over purely pragmatic matters, but unlike Asian cultures this adds to, rather than subtracts from, the emotional, intellectual and spiritual contentment of Mexicans. Mexicans in the United States eventually adapt to the American way of doing things, but they never lose a deep longing for the personal and social content that is so important to business relationships in Mexico.

Because Americans in particular do not think in terms of basing their business activities on social factors—in fact, the traditional approach in the United States has been to *de*-personalize business affairs—those who go to Mexico on business invariably encounter attitudes and behavior they regard as impractical as well as irrational. The objective, materialistic and time-is-money approach of Americans to business and life in general is directly opposed to the traditional Mexican rationale.

Unlike Americans, Mexicans have never been driven by some deep-seated compulsion to be constantly busy, to produce more than what they need. In the Mexican cosmos life is to be enjoyed, not blindly worked away. Part of this traditional Mexican view of the world at large was that it was irrational to always be in a hurry, to set deadlines for anything, to count passing time, to be the bearer of bad news or to upset anyone at any time for any reason.

This philosophy led Mexicans to try at all times to avoid disappointing people by agreeing with whatever they said, by saying whatever they thought the other party wanted to hear, by seldom if ever saying no and by giving ambiguous rather than clear responses. Not surprisingly, this characteristic behavior regularly got people in trouble and was just as regularly met with the stock phrase *algo sucedió* (AHL-go soo-say-dee-OH) or "something came up."

Today *algo sucedió* is something like the national excuse in Mexico. It is automatically used by people when they are confronted by something they promised to do but didn't. And, of course, in the Mexican context of things, the other party is supposed to accept this excuse.

There is no quick, easy way around the propensity of Mexicans to make commitments or promises that they do not take seriously, particularly where time is concerned.

In work situations about the only recourse is to try to come up with personalized incentives that will encourage the people concerned to treat the project, or whatever it is, differently, and then to diplomatically and regularly follow up to make sure the program is working. The stronger the personal relationship that one has with Mexican employees, suppliers and government personnel, the more likely that any work or business transactions will be done within a reasonable amount of time.

Of course, there are growing exceptions to this *algo sucedió* type of behavior, particularly in the northern parts of Mexico, where the people are more influenced by American attitudes and conduct. But it is not likely to disappear completely even in these regions because Mexicans do not want to be like Americans.

Another factor growing out of the strong social content of business in Mexico is that businesspeople are used to making commitments simply by giving their word and shaking hands, which they have traditionally regarded as more binding than a written contract. But since large-scale international business is usually complicated by both cultural and legal factors that often cannot be controlled by personal relationships, detailed contracts with Mexican business partners are essential.

Alma
(AHL-mah)

"Inner Versus Outer Qualities"

Mexican and American views of self-worth and the inner qualities of others are often almost exactly the opposite, creating differences in attitudes and behavior that range from subtle to blatant.

Americans pride themselves on their independence and individuality, but in reality they are conformists at heart. They expect everyone to behave more or less as they do, and in business and political situations they are made uncomfortable by people who "follow a different drummer." Americans also tend to view the world in concrete terms of black and white, and to measure the worth of individuals by their accomplishments.

In fact, Americans generally go out of the way to avoid judging people on the basis of their innate character. Instead, they often concern themselves only with attitudes and actions of the moment and the surface qualities that people exhibit.

Americans are thus led to tolerate and even admire people who are utterly immoral and who routinely behave in the most disreputable way as long as they are successful, especially if they occasionally do something positive. This is one of the reasons—probably the main reason, in fact—why people from other cultures typically accuse Americans of being culturally shallow.

Mexicans, on the other hand, see the world in mixed hues, and are more concerned with the inner qualities of people than with how hard they work, what skills they may possess or what extraordinary feats they may accomplish. Despite the conformity demanded by Mexican etiquette, it is the individuality and the intellectual and emotional uniqueness of each person that they prize the most.

In fact, Mexicans regard the innate *alma* (AHL-mah) or "spirit" of the individual as the most important of all human qualities, and their culture is fashioned around this concept.

Alma is manifested in the national character of Mexicans in many ways, and colors their character and personality. It is the foundation of many of the primary elements in their Mexicanness, and is especially important to the sense of personal dignity that imbues Mexicans. *Alma* influences—and sometimes compels—Mexicans to do things for the sake of their image and emotional well-being that range from wonderfully nurturing to irrational, and oftentimes dangerous as well.

Among the *alma*-influenced things for which Mexicans are famous—or infamous, depending on their nature—are their highly stylized personal etiquette, their close family ties, their fascination with bullfighting, the penchant for men to drive recklessly and taking violent revenge for some real or imagined slight.

Because of their spiritual and emotional orientation, Mexicans are generally uncomfortable with American-style systems or programs that are highly structured and which reduce or eliminate the "human" element that Mexicans hold so dear.

While Americans are conditioned to repress their personal feelings, to thrive on facts and abstract reasoning and to do things "by the numbers," Mexicans have long been taught to ignore numbers and abstractions and let their spirits guide them.

Not surprisingly, most outsiders wanting to do business with Mexico naturally begin with an approach that is based on facts and logic, only to discover eventually that they must first resolve spiritual and emotional issues in order to achieve lasting success.

Foreign businesspeople who are tempted to regard the *alma* factor in Mexican culture as a handicap should keep in mind that Mexicans themselves view it as one of the most admirable facets of their lifestyle, and they believe that people who live in more mechanistic societies are being deprived of much of their humanity.

The spiritual element in Mexican culture is certainly not all negative, even from the outsider's viewpoint. It is the source of the artistic and poetic impulses that are characteristic of Mexicans, including their obsession with music. It is also the wellspring of the special warmth and hospitality that Mexicans typically extend to friends and guests, as well as most of the other facets of Mexican culture that outsiders find so beguiling, from their long midafternoon lunches to their festivals.

5

Amigos
(Ah-MEE-gohs)

"Counting on Your Friends"

One of the facets of Mexican cultural that newcomers, particularly North Americans, need to become familiar with is what the word *amigo* (ah-MEE-goh), or "friend," means to Mexicans, particularly when it is used in reference to men and to business.

North Americans use the word "friend" in a variety of ways—to describe people they have just met and really don't know at all, as well as in reference to people they have known for years or all of their lives and with whom they have close, intimate relationships. This casual-to-formal use of "friend" by North Americans is indicative of the typical American character—informal, flexible, arbitrary and personal, with a tendency to be aggressively presumptuous and culturally insensitive. North Americans generally make and discard "friends" with the greatest of ease because there are no substantial ties binding them. They can literally get by without them.

Mexicans, on the other hand, tend to be exceptionally sensitive to every nuance of human relations. They are formal and avoid getting personal with people they do not know well. They also use the word *amigo* in a significantly different way because they cannot get by without friends.

In its male Mexican context, *amigo* has traditionally been used in its deepest and broadest sense; specifically in reference to relationships that have been carefully nurtured over a period of years and which play an important role in the lives of men.

Family and personal relationships became the foundation of Mexican life during the first years of the Spanish colonial era because there was no body of law to protect or support the people. Their only recourse when they needed any kind of help was to depend upon family and friends. In this atmosphere, which prevailed for more than 400 years, having sincere, caring friends who were absolutely loyal, no matter what else they might be, was essential for survival and for any progress one might make in business or any of the professions.

Members of one's family could more or less be counted on automatically to be loyal and supportive—to act as *amigos*—without any special effort.

But for men to maintain a full *amigo* relationship with non-family members required an extraordinary amount of involvement and nurturing.

Various aspects of the distinctive lifestyle developed by Mexicans, from long afternoon lunches to the custom of gathering in the evening after work for drinking and partying, were based in great measure on the fundamental need to nurture relationships with friends.

The overall cultural legacy inherited by Mexicans has conditioned them to feel lonely and spiritually hungry if they do not have intimate friends with whom they can spend substantial amounts of time in affectionate communing, whether or not they need any specific help or support at the time. This need among Mexican men for emotional and spiritual communion generally has a higher priority than working, and is one of the factors in the behavior of Mexican workers that productivity-oriented outsiders have traditionally found frustrating.

In contrast to the cultural rituals designed to serve the emotional and practical needs of men, Mexican women were traditionally kept in a different world.

When young and while they were still single, Mexican girls carried on intensely emotional friendships with other girls. But an equally intense effort was made to prevent them from developing any kind of relationship with males until they were allowed to accept the attentions of suitors for marriage.

Once married, it was the custom, particularly among the poorer classes, for women to stop seeing their childhood friends and thereafter devote their lives to their husbands and their children. Many husbands were so paranoid about their wives having affairs that they prohibited them from having any friends, even from leaving their homes without an escort.

For generation after generation, the only emotional solace for most Mexican women came from their children, and the only spiritual communion they had was in the smothering arms of the church.

The role of *amigos* among Mexican men has changed very little in modern times. Getting things done and staying or getting out of trouble is still primarily based on who they know and the closeness of their relationships. Establishing and nurturing the necessary relationships to make the system work still takes up a great deal of their time and energy.

However, beginning in the 1960s changes for Mexican women in the middle and upper classes have been dramatic. Fewer and fewer of them are kept in virtual isolation by their husbands, and most of them have their circle of female friends. Some have male friends as well.

Foreign businesspeople stationed in Mexico will find that going out of their way to make friends and thereafter cultivating the friendships the way their Mexican counterparts do will make life a lot more fun and things will get done a lot more easily.

The feminine form of *amigo* is, of course, *amiga*. In addition to meaning "female friend," *amiga* may also be taken to mean "lover" when used in conjunction with the possessive "my"—*mi amiga*. The way around this is to say "a friend of mine" (*una amiga mia*).

6

Amistad
(Ah-me-STAHD)

"The Boundaries of Friendship"

The institution of *amistad* (ah-me-STAHD) or "friendship" in Mexican culture, which includes the philosophy as well as the rules and parameters governing relationships between *amigos* or "friends," is one of the keys to understanding how Mexican society functions.

The basis for Mexican-style *amistad* is mutual need and reciprocity, a fundamental factor that grew out of the political and religious systems that existed in Mexico before and after the arrival of the Spanish conquistadors in 1519.

Mexico's pre-Spanish Indian societies were hierarchical and collective. People were divided in vertical ranks according to their class, and were collectively responsible for producing their own livelihood, paying tribute in labor and goods to their overlords and obeying both civil and ecclesiastical authorities. If an individual failed in any of these obligations, everyone in the family, including relatives, was considered to be responsible and subject to punishment. Death was the punishment for many offenses that today would not warrant a lecture. This made wholehearted cooperation among family members, relatives, villages and other groups absolutely essential for survival.

The system established by the Spaniards after they took over Mexico in 1521 was also hierarchical, with gradations based on race and family background, but it was not universally collective in the case of punishment. It was, however, far more destructive to the spiritual, emotional and physical welfare of the people than the Indian regimes had been because it was permeated by personal avarice, racial discrimination, malicious cruelty, religious bigotry and contempt for the lives of the Indians.

In this setting, the Indians who survived the slaughter and diseases that accompanied the conquest of their homeland, and the growing number of mixed-blood Spanish–Indian offspring who came to be treated as outcasts, could depend only on themselves and friendship networks.

This system continued virtually unchanged for some 400 years, during which time the concept and practice of *amistad* became a vitally important facet of Mexican society.

The process of creating *amistad* relationships was the same as in other societies—exchanging favors, eating and drinking together, gift giving and the like. But in Mexico the need for friendships was so great that the relationships were nurtured with extraordinary intensity in order to make the bonds tighter and more lasting. Sincerity (*sinceridad*) and loyalty (*lealtad*) became highly valued.

In Mexico today *amistad* networks remain a vital aspect of life in private as well as public or business matters. Much of Mexican society still operates on the basis of personal relationships and actions, as opposed to an objective, mechanical system in which things get done because they are prescribed by law or custom. Particularly in matters involving government offices or agents on any level, it is difficult or impossible to get things done efficiently without the personal element of friendship or money.

Social class and family background play a key role in *amistad* networks. Obviously, the higher the social class and the more illustrious the family, the easier it is to establish and maintain powerful connections and to gain benefit from them. It is the personal nature of politics and business and the auxiliary *amistad* factor that has led to the wealth of Mexico being concentrated in the hands of a few families, and remaining there from one generation to the next.

The national pooling of political power and wealth in Mexico was repeated on every regional level, with each state and city having its coterie of politicians and businesspeople who controlled the bulk of the wealth, assuring that the chasm between the rich and poor remained wide and deep.

While *amistad* remains a vital factor in the functioning of Mexican society whether one is rich or poor, a growing number of political and economic reforms are adding to the overall wealth of the country, as well as offering new opportunities for more of the poor to join the middle class.

Still, when foreign businesspeople approach Mexico with any kind of project in mind, they are almost always directed toward a small group of people, often individual families, who have the necessary political and economic clout to make things happen. Doing business in Mexico therefore remains very much a personal undertaking based on establishing and maintaining an *amistad* network with key individuals in government and the appropriate industry.

Insiders say that the types of relationships that are characteristic of Mexicans, and within which they feel the most secure and comfortable, result from the "fusion" of their interests and needs; that is, instead of separate entities that have strong ties, they literally merge and become one with extended parts. Most foreigners hold back from such merging of their personal as well as their business interests, but to succeed in Mexico it is usually necessary to go at least half way.

Many of Mexico's most enlightened and progressive-minded businesspeople and political leaders say that the traditional concept and practice of *amistad* remains a crucial element in Mexico today because it is essential in carrying out the reform process and making sure that the end result remains "human."

Some list *amistad* as the third most important word in Mexican society.

(See **Amor, Libertad, Motivación, Respeto, Reto, Solidaridad.**)

Amor
(Ah-MOHR)

"Love Mexican Style"

Mexicans point out that love is not a natural thing as far as mankind is concerned. It is manmade and subject to being subverted and perverted at any time by any number of things. They also say it is not a matter of choice; that it is dictated by social approval or disapproval and the Christian concept of sin.

Christian-oriented societies equate love with marriage and the production of children, whereas in truth love is not related to either one. Generally speaking, the demands of society frustrate love and society punishes people for falling in love.

Mexicans have traditionally treated romantic love as a falsehood and as the betrayal of one's inner self to another, which leads both men and women, but especially men, to exaggerate their passion to an extraordinary degree in order to overcome the feelings of vulnerability that result from putting their emotional selves into other people's hands.

Still, sociological studies in Mexico reveal that Mexicans on every social level regard *amor* (ah-MOHR) or "love" as the bedrock of their culture. They are quick to point out that it is the presence of love that distinguishes Mexican society and makes it superior to many other societies, particularly that of the United States.

There are all of the usual forms of love in Mexico—parental love for children, the love of children for their parents, love between a man and woman, love of country, and so on. And not surprisingly, each of these forms of love has its own unique Mexican character.

For Mexicans the most important form of love is almost always "family love"—the deep, overriding emotional ties of a person to their family as a primary social unit, rather than to individuals in the family. One of the key reasons for the extraordinary importance of family ties in Mexican culture is that until well into the 20th century the people could not depend on any outside institution for their survival.

Neither the government nor the church gave priority to the survival, much less the prosperity, of the people. Both of these institutions were predatory by design, living off the the labor of the people while returning as little as possible, and often nothing at all.

For most of the history of Mexico, the lives of ordinary people were in constant danger from government troops, the police, rural bandits, city criminals, violence-prone drunks and machismo-obsessed men. Their only choice was to take refuge in their families.

Within families, love ties centered around mothers and children. Mothers sacrificed themselves to their children in such a way that lifelong bonds were created. Fathers doted on their young children but their attachment to their wives was not exclusive.

The attitudes and behavior of both fathers and sons toward female members of their families had a strong Oriental flavor with a harem mentality. Generally speaking, men demonstrated unselfish, romantic love toward women only in the courting stage. Once the relationship was sexually consummated, with or without marriage, men reverted to their potentate mentality, treating women more like property than love objects.

Mexican women, primed in sexuality and romanticism from a young age, typically had to give up both once they were married or living in "free union" with men. Thereafter, the only women who continued to have romance and passionate sexual encounters in their lives were those who had the courage and opportunity to engage in affairs with other men, something that put them in mortal danger.

In its American context love is closely associated with sex because of religious conditioning that the only legitimate sex—sex that is not sinful—is within love-based marriage. Americans have an optimistic view of love and equate it with happiness, security and peace.

Mexicans, on the other hand, do not directly relate love with sex, which is more a matter of passion, and generally view love as a source of unhappiness, insecurity and conflict. (Mexican love songs and poetry about love tend to be sad.)

Male–female relations in Mexico are gradually evolving away from the traditional forms, but the process is very slow and is primarily occurring among those in the upper classes, who are more exposed to outside influences.

Studies of Mexican families in which the attitudes and behavior of the husbands have become conspicuously more Western than Oriental indicate that they now enjoy the best of the old and the new. Love within these families remains exceptionally strong but it has become much more individualized and unselfish, providing the members with the benefit of strong, positive emotional ties that contribute both to their level of happiness and to their economic security.

On a totally practical level, Mexicans who are leaders in the reforms and positive developments now occurring in Mexico rank *amor* right up there with motivation, a cooperative spirit, respect and other cultural elements that they regard as essential to the kind of society they are trying to build.

Said one: "You cannot have a peaceful, positive-minded, cooperative society without love—love for yourself, for your family, your co-workers, your community and your neighbors."

(See **Amistad, Libertad, Motivación, Respeto, Reto, Solidaridad.**)

8

Apellidos
(Ah-pay-YEE-dohs)

"Getting Names Right"

Getting the "last name" right in Mexico, and other Hispanic countries, can be confusing. Mexicans generally use two "last names"—their paternal surname as well as their maternal surname, with the paternal surname placed first, appearing like a "middle name" to those who are unfamiliar with the Latin system.

If Maria Carrera Lopez marries Juan Garcia Alvarez, she becomes Mrs. Maria Carrera de Garcia, which translates as "Maria Carrera the wife of Garcia."

Another variation and in contrast with the practice in North America, Mrs. Garcia Carrera is never referred to as Mrs. Juan (husband's first name) Garcia (husband's last name). She is Señora Maria Garcia Carerra, Señora de Garcia or La Señora Maria Garcia.

A child becomes Pablo or Paula Garcia Carerra. The official *apellido*, or "last name," is Garcia, the father's surname.

Some Mexicans, particularly the upper class, use both the paternal and maternal last names as their surname, connecting them with a hyphen: Garcia-Carerra. In writing their name, some also use only the initial letter of the maternal surname: Juan Garcia C.

Just as in most other societies, Mexicans customarily diminutize long first names to make them shorter and more personal, as well as changing them completely to what are called *nombres hipocoristicos* or "pet names." Antonio, for example, is commonly shortened to Tono; Carmencita to Carmen; Guadalupe to Lupe; Francisco to Paco and so on.

Apodos, or "nicknames," are also common in most societies, but none more so than in Mexico, where they make up a distinctive feature of the culture. Most Mexican nicknames refer to the physical appearance or characteristics of the individual, or to their birthplace, workplace or some other identifying factor. Many *apodos* have become institutionalized.

Two of the most common nicknames for the thousands of "Jesuses" in Mexico are "Chuy" and "Chucho." (The original meaning of the latter word refers to dogs and calling dogs. In Chicano jargon *chucho* is also used to mean "stool-pigeon," or someone who has bad manners and likes to fight.) Plump people are invariably called *Gordo* (fatty).

As is obvious, nicknames in Mexico are often anything but flattering. Those that are really derogatory are not used directly to the individual concerned unless it is meant as a criticism or insult. However, it is common for friends to address each other by unflattering nicknames which other people generally consider insulting.

Visitors in Mexico should not address people who are older or senior to them by the nicknames that their friends use without asking permission and/or being invited to do so. Of course, anyone in a superior position may assume the privilege if the person concerned is quite young.

Dealing with first names in Mexico is usually a very simple matter because the majority of them are names of saints taken from the Bible. On the

Mexican calendar every day of the year has its own saint or saints. It has long been the custom to give infants the names of their birthday saints.

Another common practice is to give the first son the father's name and the first daughter the mother's name, with the result that juniors and junioresses abound in Mexico.

It has also long been a custom in Mexico to address men as José and women as Maria, from the biblical Joseph and Mary, when one does not know their real names.

9

Apología
(Ah-poh-loh-HE-ah)

"The 'Social Oil' of Mexico"

The role that the apology plays in Mexico is similar to what one finds in Japan, China and other traditionally autocratic societies in which those in authority had the power of life and death over ordinary citizens, and in which personal etiquette of a very high standard was equated with morality.

In such societies making any kind of mistake in the eyes of a superior, whether it was doing something or saying something that was considered wrong, out of place or whatever, could have extremely serious consequences.

These factors had a fundamental influence on the psychology and behavior of the people involved, making those in powerful positions arrogant and often cruel, and those without power passive and obsequious— until the social and political restraints on their behavior were suddenly removed, at which time they were prone to outbursts of extraordinary violence.

Traditionally in Mexico the powers of government officials, the military and the police were practically unlimited. Ordinary people could not demand anything of them, and typically were afraid to ask even in the politest terms because those in power did not see themselves as public employees with an obligation to serve the public. In this environment, the only manner that was open to ordinary people—if they did not have powerful connections of some kind—was as apologetic supplicants. It thus became second nature for

Mexicans on all levels of society to be constantly apologizing to those above them whether they were guilty of anything or not.

Another institutionalized practice, especially among the higher social classes, was to apologize and attempt to end confrontations by saying something like, "Let's pretend it never happened."

Today the apology (*apología*) is still of special importance in Mexico, for real transgressions as well as a preventive "oil" to make things run more smoothly, because it is so deeply embedded in the etiquette.

Said a Mexican friend: "The apology has traditionally been invoked by people on all social levels as a way of escaping responsibility; for not knowing something, or not having done something they were supposed to do. As long as they apologize there is no guilt. When the apology is used as an excuse there are no idiots."

Changes are occurring, however. Because of the political reforms instituted by the administrations of Salinas and Zedillo in the 1980s and 1990s, speaking up and demanding various rights and services from the government is no longer life threatening.

For the first time in the history of the country, people can both criticize the police, the military, government employees and government officials, and demand things of them without jeopardizing their freedom or their life. Because of these changes, people are no longer forced to be so circumspect or servile in their behavior, and the traditionally apologetic attitude that has been characteristic for centuries is slowly but surely being replaced by a positive, aggressive spirit that is more conducive to genuine understanding and cooperation.

However, foreigners interacting with Mexicans should continue to be especially sensitive to the traditional role of the apology in Mexican culture. When used in a positive manner, it still serves an important role in interpersonal relations of all kinds and on all levels of society.

Ayuda
(Ah-YOO-dah)

"The Good Samaritan Syndrome"

The traits that have long been associated with Americans are individualism, independence, an entrepreneurial spirit, a willingness to take risks and a willingness to help other people when they are in trouble.

Mexicans admire these traits in an intellectual sense, but emotionally they tend to react strongly against all of them, except the willingness to help others. However, in this area as well, *ayuda* (ah-YOO-dah) or "help" has a subtle but important Mexican twist to it.

Whereas Americans are culturally conditioned to help others in emergency situations and on other special occasions that occur now and then, to Mexicans the concept of *ayuda* covers emergency situations as well as ongoing help during normal times in all matters, routine and otherwise, without end.

Ayuda in its Mexican context is a holdover from earlier times, when people lived in small communal groups in which virtually all effort was marked by what anthropologists label as collaboration, cooperation and sharing.

In the case of Mexico this ancient custom survived because the political, social and economic systems imposed upon Mexicans during the 300-year-long Spanish regime practically prohibited individual, independent effort. Furthermore, the colonial administration did not provide for social welfare or governmental assistance, and, in fact, generally demanded more taxes and tribute in kind than common people could afford. Even more pressure was brought on ordinary people to look out for themselves because both the civil and ecclesiastical governments that dominated Mexico for so long were essentially designed to exploit rather than support the people and their efforts, and both governments were corrupt beyond reason.

In this environment it was essential for Mexicans on all levels of society to do everything they could to protect themselves from the government, to deal with it effectively when they had no choice and to do whatever they could on their own to survive and prosper as much as possible.

Mexican-style *ayuda*, therefore, played a key role in the lives of the people for more than four centuries, and today continues to be a vital part of the culture. Generally speaking, Mexicans cannot automatically depend upon the police or other public institutions for the kinds of protection and service that are taken for granted in the United States and elsewhere. They have to have help from family, friends or connections with influence; or they have to pay what amounts to bribes.

One of the most admirable qualities of Mexicans is, in part at least, an outgrowth of the overwhelming need for *ayuda* in coping with the government and other handicaps they have traditionally faced. This need for *ayuda* conditioned Mexicans to regard the practice as the highest form of social morality, and to take great personal satisfaction in helping others. Mexicans seem to be at their happiest when they are coming to someone's aid, and especially when they do so voluntarily.

But there is a catch to Mexican *ayuda*. It is limited to one's own circle of family, relatives and friends, and in small communities, to one's neighbors. About the only general exception to this rule are friends of friends.

Foreigners living and working in Mexico who are the most successful (the most contented, the happiest and the most productive) are invariably the ones who come to understand and follow the Mexican way of *ayuda* in both their business and private affairs.

Newcomers just approaching Mexico would be well advised to begin their relationships with the importance of this cultural factor firmly in mind. The rewards can be overwhelming.

Aztecas

(Ahz-TAY-cahs)

"The Romans of Mexico"

Life in pre-Columbian Mexico was just as varied as it is in many countries of the world today. There were the rich who enjoyed all of the amenities money could buy. And there were the poor and the enslaved, to whom a day's leisure and a full meal might have been the most they could ever hope for.

When the first Spaniards arrived in 1519 the customs of Mexico's 149 tribal nationalities differed in both substance and form. Some were honest and upright citizens with a refined sense of public and private morality, others were addicted to intrigue and deception. Some were stolid introverts, others were gay extroverts who loved festivals, parades and other public displays.

The Aztecs, the largest and most powerful of the Indian nations during the 15th and 16th centuries, believed that they had to offer human sacrifices to their sun god to ensure that day would follow night. Time was a living thing to the Aztecs and was tangibly represented by the rising and setting of the sun each day. All life was dependent upon the sun rising each morning, and the sun god had to be fed with the hearts and blood of human sacrifices.

The Aztecs also followed an ugly custom of skinning some sacrificial victims, donning their skins, and performing religious dances.*

The gods of most pre-Columbian Mexican Indians are described by anthropologists as "monsters," which might account for the blood-letting rituals the people created to placate the gods. To the Aztecs and other Indians who sacrificed humans in their religious rituals, the victims were "god food." Their need for sacrificial victims was what made most if not all of Mexico's Indians warlike.

Many of Mexico's Indian wars were fought for the specific purpose of capturing victims to be sacrificed—the so-called "Flower Wars," which were arranged by the two sides and ended when the two parties had captured their quota of victims.

The ancestral home of the Aztecs is believed to have been Aztlán, which is where the name Aztec comes from. But the Aztecans called themselves *Mexicas*. (The Nahuas people called themselves *Mexicanos*.)

Aztlán is a Nahuatl word meaning "place of water." Historians say it may refer to valleys in one of the northwestern states of Mexico (Sinaloa, Sonora or Nayarit) which are watered by streams from the Sierra Madre Occidental mountains, or even to an area along the Salt River in what is now Arizona, or along the Rio Grande in present-day New Mexico.

Azteca was a militaristic caste society ruled over by autocratic kings and priests, and was therefore not that different from Spain, its eventual colonizer. Society was highly stratified in absolute hierarchies. Children were conditioned to obey their parents and elders, and severely punished if they disobeyed or questioned their superiors.

*Years after the conquest of Mexico by Hernán Cortés, a Spanish writer noted that the Aztec custom of sacrificing humans to their gods was more humane and less murderous than the Spanish custom of torturing and burning people for their religious beliefs. The Aztecs, he pointed out, killed their victims with one quick thrust of a sharp obsidian blade, while the Inquisition's Spanish priests inflicted the most savage torture on their victims over a period of days and weeks before finally subjecting them to one of the most painful of all deaths, burning at the stake. At the time of his writing, the Spanish Inquisition had killed over 400,000 people by torturing them to death or by burning.

21

Unmarried females were chaperoned. Sexual promiscuity was prohibited among the common people. Punishment for breaking the sex taboo was normally death, yet upper-class men were allowed to have harems.

The elaborate etiquette of the Aztecs far surpassed the stylized manners of the *Gachupín* and *criollo* Spaniards. Bad manners in public was a crime. Punishment for any kind of crime was collective. A man who refused to obey orders was executed and his family enslaved. Aztec judges practiced the "two strikes and you're out" philosophy. Second-time offenders were almost always executed.

At the same time there were among the Aztecans profound philosophers, poets and artists of the highest order. Aztecs were taught humility from birth, and as they grew older, respect for temperance and moderation in all things.

However, while they were young, Aztec men were passionate, scheming and often unscrupulous. It was only after they passed middle age that they became philosophical and kind.

The Aztecans, like the Romans of old, were imbued with a driving will to be in power, while at the same time they cultivated the senses of aesthetic appreciation and practiced a refined system of manners.

Like Moorish Spain, *Azteca* was a man's world. Women were instruments of utility and pleasure. In recognition of the role of sex in human life, the Aztecs had adopted the old Huaxtecan goddess of carnal love, and it appears that it was one of their favorite divinities. Sex played an important role in a number of religious rites.

Victims of most Aztec sacrificial ceremonies were enemies captured for that purpose, but there were certain ceremonies at which Aztecans themselves were immolated, which attests to the importance of the ceremonies.

One of these ceremonies involved young men who were selected for their physical beauty and good character. For a full year before they were killed these young men were entertained and treated as gods on earth. Four months before their date with death each man was simultaneously married to four of the most beautiful girls available.

It is said that these young men went to their deaths on the sacrificial altar willingly, believing it to be the supreme honor to die for their gods. What with rich food, daily entertainment and conjugal obligations every night that were no doubt taken seriously, the victims were probably on their last legs anyway.

It was accepted in Aztec society that men were born to fight, but not all young men could pass the rigorous standards of the army. Separation of the men from the boys was done while they were still in school.

At school, which was compulsory, boys were taught civics, religion, a trade and the martial arts. Those who excelled at the arts of war became soldiers. The others generally became tradesmen or priests, although some of them were enslaved or executed.

Courtesans were assigned to the young men who went into the army. Those unable to become soldiers generally took mistresses but they had to be discreet about it. Only nobles could live openly with mistresses before being officially married.

Once married, Aztec men could have as many concubines as they wanted and could afford, but each man was restricted to one legal wife. The punishment for adultery was death by stoning or strangulation.

No Aztec man was permitted to marry until he reached the age of 20. Girls could marry at 16. Young men had to have been graduated from school and have the permission of their former school masters before they could marry.

All Aztec girls were consecrated to the temple and were instructed in female occupations until they married. Go-betweens arranged the details of marriages, if the participants could afford the fee, but the young people had a say in the matter of choice.

It was good manners for the parents of a would-be bride to claim that she was stupid and unworthy.

Weddings staged by wealthy Aztecans were magnificent affairs lasting five days. Those with less means did what they could to emulate the rich. The very poor who could not afford any kind of ceremony just set up house-keeping, which is still common is present-day Mexico.

As members of a warrior society, Aztec soldiers enjoyed certain privileges with women (as did the Spaniards who replaced them). Every August, soldiers who had been successful in battle (captured an enemy alive) participated in a sacred dance that included sex with the women who served as companions to the unmarried soldiers.

Aztecans were dedicated gamblers. It was common for men to gamble away all of their property and then sell themselves into slavery to raise money for one last wager.

When young, Aztecans were thoroughly conditioned in stoicism to prepare themselves for an austere, severely disciplined life. But their existence had a light side. Festivals were held regularly and they were among the world's most sports-minded people.

Like all other Mexican Indians, Aztecans learned to dance as naturally as they learned walking. Many of their formal dances were elaborately costumed and staged rituals of great artistry and beauty.

Singing and dancing played such a vital role in the lives of the Aztecs that it was mandatory that all children attend *Cuicacuilli* or "Houses of Song" from the age of 12.

These song and dance studios were generally located in the vicinity of temples. They prepared Aztecans for participation in the many religious ceremonies built around singing and dancing. To them, singing and dancing was a way of communicating with the gods who controlled their lives. The importance of music in Aztec rituals is indicated by historical records noting that musicians who made mistakes were subject to being put to death.

Spanish priests, who arrived in Mexico two years after the fall of the Aztec empire, had all of the *Cuicacuilli* destroyed, and prohibited the Indians from performing any of their traditional songs and dances.

Dancing is still the heart of many festivals held in Mexico, however. One pre-Cortés Indian dance that has survived in only slightly altered form is the spectacular *voladores* or "flying pole dance." In this mysticism-laden ritual, a long pole with a round platform on top that is large enough to hold five people is inserted into a hole in the ground and pulled erect.

Ropes are tied to the top of the pole and wound around it. Five men, one a musician and the other "fliers," climb to the top of the pole on a ladder provided for that purpose.

While the musician plays and dances, the four men tie the loose ends of the ropes around their waist, then leap out into space. The height of the pole and the number of times the ropes are wound around it are carefully calculated so that each "flier" will make 13 revolutions around the pole on his way down. Thirteen represents one quarter of the 52-year cycle that made up an age or epoch, after which the world was renewed. The "fliers" usually dress in spectacular costumes, or wear a crest of feathers.

Most of the Aztecs who escaped slaughter by the conquering Spaniards and their Indian allies, primarily women and children, later succumbed to disease and mistreatment. Today about the only things that remain of the once powerful Aztecs are stone artifacts of their remarkable culture.

12

Braceros
(Brah-SAY-rohs)

"The 'Arms' of Mexico"

Prior to 1836, when Texas broke away from Mexico, and the U.S.-Mexican war in 1848, the northern territory of Mexico included what is now Arizona, California, New Mexico, Nevada, Utah and part of Colorado.

Military *presidios* (forts) and *haciendas* (huge farms) that supplied the military outposts with food were scattered throughout this vast territory. (Some of these forts and haciendas grew into towns and cities, such as Los Angeles.)

Santa Fe, the first non-Indian city in what is now the United States, was founded by Mexicans in 1610, 10 years before the Pilgrims landed at Plymouth Rock. (When the Spaniards arrived in the area, the site was a thriving Indian town that had existed for centuries and was a noted spiritual center.)

For more than 200 years, Mexican cowboys, craftsmen, farmers, laborers and shopkeepers were recruited from the more populated areas of central and southern Mexico to work in these far northern territories.

After the northern half of Mexico was annexed by the United States in 1848, the flow of Mexican workers into these areas stopped—only to begin again in the 1860s when Americans began recruiting Mexican laborers to work on the great network of railroads being built to span the country.

As Americans swarmed into the former Mexican territories and established their own large farms and ranches, the demand for agricultural workers from Mexico continued.

The outbreak of revolution in Mexico in 1910 and the beginning of World War I in 1914, during which time agricultural production in the American Southwest was vastly increased, resulted in more than 220,000 documented Mexican workers entering the United States.

In 1921 the American Congress passed laws establishing immigration quotas and the U.S. Border Patrol. But Mexicans were so much in demand as agricultural workers throughout the American West that they were exempted from the quotas. All Mexicans had to do to cross the border and work in the United States was pay a head tax. American farmers, ranchers and others advertised heavily in Mexico for workers.

All of this ended when the Great American Depression began in 1928. Thousands of Mexican workers were deported, and efforts were made to prevent them from returning to the United States illegally.

Then World War II broke out and once again American businesses of all kinds, this time throughout the country, began vying for Mexican workers. In 1942 the U.S. government signed the International Agreement of Migratory Workers with Mexico to officially allow Mexican *braceros* (brah-SAY-rohs) to enter the United States as needed to work seasonally on farms and ranches.

Over the next 22 years, 4.8 million *braceros* legally entered the United States to work, and an unknown number of others—millions according to unofficial estimates—came in illegally, establishing a tradition that continues to this day.

The government-run *bracero* program ended in 1964, but the influx of Mexican workers did not. Working in the United States had become an integral part of the existence of millions of Mexicans living in central and northern Mexico. Virtually every village and rural family in those regions of Mexico had at least one family member who worked periodically or full-time in the United States.

By 1986 there were so many Mexicans living full time but illegally in the United States that the U.S. Congress passed a new law allowing some three million of them to obtain American citizenship.

Over the years, critics of the *bracero* program, aided by news media reports that did not tell all of the story, have generally given the impression that Mexican workers were not wanted in the United States; that it was totally a one-way street that benefited only Mexican workers at the expense of Americans.

History shows, however, that officially as well as unofficially, the majority of *braceros* who have entered the United States since the mid-1800s have done so at the urging or invitation of the American government and American businesspeople, and that they have traditionally played a key role in making the agricultural industry in the United States the envy of the rest of the world.

(See **Coyotes, Los Pollos.**)

13

Buena Gente

(BWAY-nah HANE-tay)

"One of the Good Guys"

Generally speaking, in order to succeed in Mexico the foreign businessperson must be accepted as a *buena gente* (BWAY-nah HANE-tay) or a "good person," a challenge that is not as simple or as straightforward as it might seem to the uninitiated.

Until the 1970s and 1980s, the newly arrived foreign businessperson was first of all judged by his or her personal behavior, not by educational background, professional experience or technical competency. Mexicans were more interested in people's humanity than in their pedigree. Now, newcomers are judged on both their background and character.

The very first priority for businesspeople newly assigned to Mexico should be to take all of the time necessary to become personally acquainted with any Mexican executives, managers and supervisors they will be working with, as well as with as many rank-and-file employees as possible.

Among other things, *buena gente* are the kind of people who make a dramatic point of calling on friends and employees who are sick or injured to bring gifts and to express their sympathy.

Generally speaking, Mexicans work well only for people they like and trust; people they regard as at least friendly if not personal friends. Foreigners can be *buena gente* without speaking Spanish, but not being able to speak any Spanish at all, and not making any effort to learn, is a major mistake. In addition to reducing the incidence and degree of culture shock, being able to speak some Spanish adds immeasurably to enjoying the Mexican experience, whether it is for pleasure or business.

In general terms, being a *buena gente* means not taking oneself or one's job so seriously that it precludes spending time with friends and family and having fun.

Regular two- and three-hour lunch breaks at restaurant featuring *mariachis* and margaritas are falling victim to a much faster pace and a more focused dedication to business these days, but they still have their place. Such an afternoon spent with fellow employees, customers or suppliers is almost always far more effective in nurturing good relations and bringing in more business than lectures, exhortations or typical sales calls.

One thing that invariably separates *buena gente* from *mala gente* (bad people) is how superiors react toward their subordinates when the latter have some kind of personal or family emergency or misfortune. It is unforgivable for a superior to ignore such a situation and do nothing. The only acceptable protocol is for the superior to express personal condolences and make some kind of contribution to help remedy the situation. This contribution may be money, time off from work, the use of a car or truck for transportation, material gifts or all of these things.

Newcomers to Mexico who are not intimately familiar with the cultural nuances that determine correct and beneficial behavior should quickly establish mentor relationships with older Mexicans from whom they can seek advice on how to handle the personal side of their business affairs. Of course, the same suggestion applies to taking advantage of mentors for ordinary business matters as well. Obviously, one key source of such mentors are other foreign businesspeople who have been in Mexico for many years and have learned—usually the hard way—the insider ways of doing things.

Often the best approach for newcomers and those with less experience in Mexico is to have both foreign and Mexican mentors, because there are invariably occasions when a well-placed, well-respected Mexican can do things that are impossible for foreigners.

In any event, foreign businesspeople assigned to Mexico should take all of the cultural differences seriously, no matter how minor or insignificant they might seem to be. Minor things add up, and as the accumulation grows they often fester. Things that newcomers consider minor may be of vital importance to Mexicans, and might spell the difference between being accepted as a *buena gente* or as just another insensitive, profit-driven foreigner.

14

Caballeros
(Cah-bah-YEH-rohs)

"The Gentleman's Gentlemen"

There are many images of Mexican men, including the peon-farmer in loose white trousers and sandals, the bandit swathed in gun belts, the bandit-general-patriot also heavily armed, soldiers in ill-fitting uniforms, suave businessmen, romantic playboys, somber musicians in huge hats and *caballeros* (cah-bah-YEH-rohs)—upper-class men who wear highly stylized cowboy attire and are known for their refined manners and good deeds.

Mexico's famous *caballeros* have their origin in the character and customs of the European- and Mexican-born Spaniards who were the ruling class in Mexico until the early 1920s.

Caballero, which literally means "horseman," is an old word, dating back to the Middle Ages in Spain, when it came to mean a man of high social rank who fought on horseback—a knight, in English terms. *Caballero de Cuantia*, or "Knights of Rank," were required to fight for the king at their own expense, in exchange for favors from the throne.

Much of the life of the Spanish overlords in Mexico (1521–1821) revolved around horses, elaborate costumes and a highly refined and formalized style of etiquette that distinguished them from mixed-bloods, who by 1810 made up the bulk of the non-Indian population of Mexico.

During the early generations of the Spanish era, only Spaniards could own and ride horses, and they referred to themselves as *caballeros* because they looked upon themselves as knights in the service of Spain.

As time passed, *caballero* came to be associated with the etiquette affected by the Spaniards, and eventually *caballero* took on the meaning of "gentleman" in reference to both the manners and character of Spanish men in general, whether they rode horses or not. Of course, the morality implied by the term was strictly according to the Spanish definition.

With the passing of more time and the gradual emergence of mixed-bloods as the predominant racial group in Mexico, the term *caballero* was absorbed into their culture as well. In the process, however, the standards of character and conduct originally associated with the term were changed to reflect more of their world.

Today, the word *caballero* is readily applied to men who are a cut above the average in character and behavior, and is also often used more as an honorary title or as flattery than as a genuine description of a person's beliefs and behavior.

Problems in interpretation arise because *caballero* does not necessarily mean the same thing in its Mexican context as "gentleman" does in English. Mexican men who consider themselves the epitome of *caballeros* may be anything but "gentlemen" by other standard, particularly when dealing with women.

However, the definition of a gentleman in Mexico today is not that different from the way the term is used in the United States and elsewhere in its common colloquial sense, such as concealing information to avoid embarrassing someone, and so on. Mexican *caballeros* have a significant advantage over "gentlemen" in most other countries, however, because there is much more form and style to their manners. They "act" more like gentlemen in the idealized sense of the word than most of their foreign counterparts.

Mexican *caballeros* can be especially impressive to foreign women whom they want to impress. Their behavior in such instances is often the epitome of gallantry and generosity. In most cases, the older and more affluent the Mexican man the more gentlemanly and generous he actually becomes when in the presence of foreign women, especially attractive foreign women.

When a tall, immaculately dressed, handsome, middle-aged or older Mexican man strolls through a hotel lobby, spies a group of pretty teenaged American girls at the cashier's counter trying to figure dollars to pesos, spontaneously pays their bill for them, then bows and continues on his way, the girls are naturally going to be impressed.

In the past, and for lack of a better comparison, Western observers have described the highly refined behavior of *caballero* Mexicans as similar to the knights of old Europe. While the comparison may not be as complimentary as intended, there are, in fact, many Mexican men whose character as well as manners make them *caballeros* in the best sense of the word.

It is still high praise to describe a Mexican man, or any other man, as *muy caballero*; it means "very gentlemanly" or "very polite." For a foreign man in Mexico to be described as a *caballero* means that he has been accepted.

However, in judging the character of Mexican *caballeros*, particularly in business and political settings, it is necessary to keep in mind that in order to be accurate the judgment must be made within the context of the culture.

Personal morality and business ethics in Mexico are based more on circumstances and necessity than on any Christian or universal principles. Mexicans know what is moral or right by these standards, but historically neither the government nor the church upheld any of these principles, which left the people no choice but to fend for themselves as best as they could.

Throughout their history life has been mean and mostly bitter for most Mexicans. It says a great deal for their spirit that they made the most of a harsh existence by creating another reality in which their spirits could soar.

Most Mexicans, particularly those who are poor, continue to be keenly attuned to the mystical and spiritual aspects of life, and are practical and concrete only when they have to be. They take a philosophical view of everything, including fate.

It helps to understand that Mexicans, on all social levels, tend to think of themselves as artists and poets, not that the majority of them paint or write poetry, but in the sense that they have the poet and the painter's outlook on life.

Cabrón
(Cah-BRONE)

"The Ultimate Disgrace"

Mexican women in all social classes have traditionally lived a much more restricted and disciplined life than Mexican men. In middle- and lower-class families, young girls were put to work early, keeping house and waiting on male members of the family. They were at the bottom of the pecking order, and were subject to being punished for real as well as imagined transgressions by their fathers, mothers and often older brothers as well. The poorer the Mexican family the harsher the conditions under which young girls lived.

In addition, girls were teased about sex from an early age. Their noses were rubbed in it. Many began participating in courting rituals before they were in their teens, but their parents shrouded them in taboos designed to prevent them from engaging in any kind of sexual activity.

As a result of this perverse conditioning, by the time Mexican girls got through puberty they were as attracted to sex as moths are to light. Boys began making passes at them in the streets by the time they were 11 or 12 years old.

Once married, the typical Mexican woman was outwardly reserved, quiet and obedient. Yet behind her mask of beautified resignation, she had a will and temper, and could be as scheming and often as violent as Mexican men.

Despite the obvious dangers, Mexican women just as obviously admired men who were very macho, but at the same time they lamented that machismo made Mexican men irresponsible and vicious. They regarded completely submissive women as fools, and were always ready to help other women in conspiracies against men.

When a Mexican woman wanted to get revenge against a man, whether it was her father, husband or lover, she went for the jugular vein. She had sex with some man. This was the sweetest revenge a Mexican woman could take against a man, and it was often the first thing that she thought of doing when a man displeased or hurt her.

Because typical Mexican men were so aggressive in their pursuit of married as well as unmarried women, they naturally harbored extreme suspicions about their own wives and sweethearts and were extraordinarily careful in guarding them from other males.

After marriage, Mexican men generally discouraged and often prohibited their wives from having female friends for fear that they would help them arrange meetings with lovers. Men also tended to give up inviting their male friends to their homes because they were afraid the men would seduce their wives.

Mexican men equated completely passive women with virginity and saints. They believed that wives should be secretive about sex, and should never become sexually aroused even when faced with an erotic situation.

Many husbands therefore avoided any word or action that might arouse the passion of their wives. Their romantic charm and lover techniques were reserved for outside affairs. They believed a frigid wife was more apt to remain faithful. They also tended to believe that any wife, frigid or not, would be unfaithful if the opportunity arose.

Some husbands were so suspicious and jealous of their wives that they were constantly accusing them of having lovers. Since the husbands themselves spent a great deal of time and energy pursuing other men's wives—with considerable success—their attitude toward their own wives was understandable.

The status of women in Mexico has changed significantly in the past few decades, but the world of male–female relations is still primarily controlled by the male concept of hypermasculinity.

Says Mexican writer Frank Gutz [a pseudonym], "According to the code of *machismo* the worst disgrace that can befall a man is for him to be cuckolded—to be made 'an ox' and wear the classic horns.

"But disgrace and surveillance notwithstanding, unfaithfulness on the part of Mexican women is common. It is just not acknowledged. Women often take advantage of this situation to get revenge against husbands or lovers and make them suffer.

"Like Frenchmen, Mexican men will put on a big front and insist that their wives couldn't possibly be unfaithful to them, despite all the evidence to the contrary.

"If Mexican men admit that they have been cuckolded and do nothing about it, they have been disgraced. Proper punishment for one or both of the offenders is generally a 'bloodbath' to wash away the *sin*. The amorous triangle (sometimes even a pentagon) is classic and recurring in Mexico."

The common term for a cuckolded man or unfaithful wife in Spanish is *cabrón* (cah-BRONE), which literally means "big goat." It is also used in a weaker sense in reference to men whose masculinity doesn't measure up, and as a good-natured dig among friends. It also has a number of other nuances.

Men who are close friends often tease each other with the *cabrón* label as a way of male bonding rather than as a slight on their masculinity. *Es muy cabrón!* translates as "He's a real stud!" In *pachuco*-ese, *Orale, cabrón!* is the equivalent of "Hey, mother-fucker!" A *cabronazo* is a man who pimps for his own wife.

Other versions of the same word: *cabrona* (cah-BRO-nah), which is the English equivalent of "bitch"—a decidedly unflattering term used in reference to women—and *cabrones* (cah-BRO-nehs), used in reference to men who are regarded as jerks or as mean s.o.b's. It may also be used in a joking sense among male friends.

Outsiders who are tempted to use the term *cabrón* or any of its derivatives in their relations with Mexican friends should be sure of the level of their friendship before doing so.

Generally speaking, it is better to avoid using the word.

(See **Machismo, Mucha Mujer, Mujeres.**)

16

Calentada
(Cah-len-TAH-dah)

"Warming Up Prisoners"

Mexican history is a graphic demonstration of the axiom that oppression and brutality go together. The more oppressive a political regime, the more brutality that is necessary to maintain it. Oppressive regimes are invariably even more brutal when race and religion are primary factors, as they traditionally were in Mexico.

It is also axiomatic that oppressive regimes create cultures in which the people are stoically passive most of the time but explode in extreme violence when their frustration becomes unbearable and when the power of the regime becomes vulnerable for some reason, and this too was precisely the case in Mexico.

As in all oppressive societies, Mexico's military and police have been the primary agents of oppression and brutality, with the police being the most pernicious.

The brutal side of Mexican police has long been epitomized by a routine interrogation procedure that is commonly known as *calentada* (cah-len-TAH-dah), or "warming up." *Calentada*, also diminutized to *calentadita*, which can be translated as "little warming up," actually means the act of disturbing or hurting someone, a very common occurrence throughout Mexican history.

When used in ordinary conversation, *calentada* and *calentadita* refer to torture systematically used by the police to get information or confessions from people they have arrested and jailed.

The usual "warming up" procedure consists of tying victims to chairs, then forcing alcohol or soda water impregnated with pepper down their nostrils until they are bloated and in extreme pain.

When soda water mixed with chile powder is used, the favorite brand is said to be the nationally famous Tehuacán, resulting in this particular torture technique being known as *tehuacanazo*, which means something like "the system (or institution) of Tehuacán."

If this doesn't work, interrogators may punch victims in the stomach, which usually results in vomiting—and often broken ribs. The process is usually repeated until the victim "confesses" or dies.

Other torture techniques traditionally favored by the police include touching the tongue and testicles with electric prods.

Beginning in the 1980s successive government administrations have come out against the use of torture in police interrogations, and there are indications that the situation has improved. But there is also personal testimony by prisoners and former prisoners, as well as occasional newspaper accounts, that the practice of *calentada* continues. According to some reports in some regions of Mexico, particularly border areas, it is as common as ever.

Calidad
(Cah-lee-DAHD)

"Who's in Charge of Quality Control?"

As mentioned elsewhere, there are many similarities in the cultures of Mexico and Japan, particularly in their highly stylized etiquette and the role playing that is required by their authoritarian, vertically structured societies. The emotional response of Mexicans and Japanese to any behavior or comment that they regard as disrespectful is also very much the same.

In normal situations both Mexicans and Japanese are the epitome of politeness and good behavior, but they are also subject to sudden outbursts of violence when the normal social restraints are dropped or when they are pushed beyond the limits imposed on them from the outside.

There are also cultural attributes where Mexicans and Japanese are as different as day and night, and one of the most conspicuous of these has to do with the quality (*calidad*) of handmade and manufactured products.

For at least a thousand years, the Japanese have literally been obsessed with striving for the ultimate in quality in everything they produced. In practical terms, their obsession with quality verged on a cult-like fanaticism. Thus the concept and practice of producing high-quality goods in Japan became an institutionalized part of the culture; something that everyone took for granted and strived for endlessly.

In Mexican culture, on the other hand, quality as such remained a personal standard, and therefore varied enormously with the individual artist, craftsman or workman. The acceptable standards of quality that more or less became universalized were therefore quite low.

A key reason why neither *calidad* nor quality standards became a factor in Mexican culture was because the system of interpersonal relationships that developed in Mexico simply made it impossible.

It was culturally taboo to closely monitor the work of another person, to criticize their efforts or to give them detailed instructions on how to do something and then make sure they did it.

The culturally acceptable procedure was for people in superior positions to give orders to employees and then leave the results up to them. Upper-level managers seldom if ever had any contact with employees. They used middlemen to deliver their orders, and that was that.

This system made it inevitable that the overall quality of goods manufactured in Mexico would vary greatly, and that deadlines and other goals would generally not be met because there was no coordinated control of the overall process of designing, engineering and fabricating.

It was not until the entry of large numbers of foreign-managed *maquiladora* (mah-kee-la-DOR-rah) factories in Mexico that the concept of *el control de calidad* or "quality control" became a major topic of concern in Mexico, and practice of the concept is still alien and "anti-Mexican" to most Mexicans.

Generally, foreign companies going into Mexico must first educate their Mexican managers and foremen in the concept of *el control de calidad* and then work with them to develop ways of incorporating the concept into practice in their manufacturing systems.

This means introducing the concept of teamwork and mutual responsibility to the work force, from the ground up, and thereafter working closely with both managers and factory employees.

Another aspect of the problem of quality control in *maquiladora* plants in Mexico is the extraordinarily high turnover among employees, making it necessary for management to continuously train new employees in their quality-control systems.

(See **Maquiladoras.**)

18

Campesinos
(Cahm-pay-SEE-nohs)

"Caldron for Revolutionaries"

One of the images of Mexico, etched in the minds of North Americans and others by movies depicting periods of revolutionary turmoil and the depredations of brutal bandits, is of its *campesinos* (cahm-pay-SEE-nohs), or "farmers," living in abject poverty with only their religious faith to sustain them.

Throughout the history of Mexico it has been the *campesinos* who carried the burden of the country on their shoulders; they fed themselves—and the urban masses—and provided cheap labor for industry.

During the 300-year period of the Spanish reign in Mexico and the following 100 years of dictatorial rule by generals, Mexico's *campesinos* had no hope of changing their fate. Passive and peaceful until driven to desperate, violent actions, they endured from one generation to another, now and then producing a rebel of extraordinary character and spirit who led them in revolution against the ruling classes.

Like the peasants of China, whom the late Mao Zedong, founder of the People's Republic, compared to grass which is repeatedly mowed down only to spring up again, the poor peasant farmers of Mexico have been a permanent part of the rural landscape.

For generations the majority of Mexico's *campesinos* were attached to *haciendas*, large agricultural/ranching operations usually owned by absentee landlords, many of whom were foreign, or *ejidos* (eh-HE-dos), small farms of communal lands surrounding villages with populations of up to 300 or so.

The poor Mexican village in the classic Western movie *The Magnificent Seven* was an authentic depiction of both the appearance of such villages and the lives of the people inhabiting them from the 1700s until the 1950s, including the depredations by gangs of brutal bandits.

Mexico's rural areas are no longer infested with mounted bandits but nearly half of the population of the country, particularly the 30 percent or so that is Indian, remain tied to small plots of land where they scratch out a bare existence, very much the way their ancestors did two and three hundred years ago.

Among the more conspicuous examples of the latter are Mayan Indians, whose ancestral home is in the mountains of Chiapas State, in southwestern Mexico.

A few paved roads were built into the rugged mountains, plateaus and jungles of Chiapas in the 1970s and 1980s, but most of the Indian inhabitants of the state remain isolated in the vastness of its hinterlands. In the 1990s most of them still lived in huts made out of odd pieces of wood, with dirt floors and no modern facilities.

In the mid-1990s these conditions led to a rebellion by several thousand Chiapas *campesinos*, resulting in the death of over 300 in one clash with federal troops. In sharp contrast to earlier times, this rebellion received both national and international news coverage, and the Mexican government quickly pledged itself to meeting some of the demands of the rebels.

Critics of the government noted, however, that the promises of improvement were based more on concern for the international image of the country than on the welfare of the people of Chiapas; adding that the farmers of Chiapas had been voicing the same complaints since the revolution of 1910–1921, and that the government had been making the same promises.

The lives of *campesinos* in central and northern Mexico are gradually improving, as the combined effects of more education and political and economic reforms work their way down into the masses. But poverty in all of its various forms is still the rule in both rural and urban areas in the northern states and there are occasional outbreaks of violence against landowners and local authorities in those regions as well. (Large numbers of farm villages in central and northern Mexico survive today only because many of their members are in the United States as either documented or illegal workers.)

The ongoing plight of Mexico's *campesinos*, particularly those who are racially and ethnically Indian, is based on a number of historical and cultural factors that contradict all democratic ideals.

From the beginning of the Spanish era in Mexico in 1521 Indians were treated as both outcasts and slaves, and for generation after generation were kept outside of the social, economic and political mainstream of the country.

The vast majority of the mixed-blooded offspring of the Spanish colonials were also relegated by law and custom to the bottom rungs of society. Virtually all mixed-bloods who lived in rural areas became Indianized and like Indians survived as subsistence-level farmers.

From the early 1600s to the middle of the 20th century it was the official policy of most of the powerful Catholic bishops of Mexico that Indians and poor mixed-bloods should not be educated, and should not be encouraged or helped to improve their condition. (Until the civil war of 1910–1921 the Catholic Church controlled all education in Mexico.)

The overwhelming majority of Spanish administrators and the elite class of Mexican-born Spaniards agreed with and colluded with the policy of the church to keep Indians and *mestizo* farmers "in their place."

All Mexicans were so conditioned to this belief that it was acccptcd as natural by most people. Those who disagreed were few and far between, and when they protested they were either eliminated or ground down even further. It was not until the middle of the 20th century that Mexico's *campesinos* began to be thought of and treated like full-fledged citizens of the country.

A *peón* (pay-OHN), another key term in the history of Mexico, refers to someone who works for daily wages, usually farm labor.

(See **Coyotes, Los Pollos, Maquiladoras**.)

Casa Chica
(CAH-sah CHEE-cah)

"Little House of Love"

Mistress-keeping has been institutionalized in Mexico since the days of the Spanish conquistadors, a custom that was fueled by a masculinity cult which made men obsessed with having sex with as many women as possible, and kept women in a state of sexual bondage to men.

Another major factor in the widespread practice of mistress-keeping was a taboo that generally prevented a middle-class woman who had been widowed, abandoned by her husband or divorced from remarrying.

Throughout the 300-year Spanish period in Mexico and the following 100 years of rule by *criollo* Spanish-Mexicans, the death rate among mixed-blood Mexican men and Indians was very high. Over half of the married women in these groups were widows or abandoned by the time they were in their early 30s.

Generally, the only sexual relationships available to these women were as mistresses or prostitutes. (In the early 1900s records show that 12 percent of the women in Mexico City between the ages of 15 and 30 were registered to work as prostitutes.)

Another custom that contributed to mistress-keeping in Mexico was the traditional courting system that prevented young men and women from getting to know each other before their marriage. In effect, most marriages were arranged between virtual strangers, so there was no emotional bond between the couples.

Until recent decades, virtually every bachelor one met in Mexico City had an "arrangement" with a relatively young widow or divorcee.

Explained one bachelor, "It is difficult for a middle-class woman to remarry, but having once been married and being used to having men they cannot give up sex and male companionship so easily. So they become mistresses.

"Such women are usually very emotional and have very strong sexual appetites, but they are not pushy or demanding. They generally will never mention marriage for fear of frightening their patrons away. As a result, such women are not adverse to their patrons being married or keeping other mistresses."

Lower- and middle-class Mexican men who have mistresses visit them in their own apartments or homes or at outside trysting places. Some men take special pleasure in carrying on affairs with married women in their homes, the danger making the adventure that much more exciting.

Affluent Mexicans who have mistresses commonly set them up in *casas chicas* (CAH-sahs CHEE-cahs), or "little houses" (as opposed to their main or "big" homes). Another term, *quinta* (KEEN-tah), refers to a "weekend house" maintained by a well-to-do man as a place to take paramours of the moment.

Mexican men who are married seldom spend all night with their mistresses (except when they take them with them on trips), and they almost never visit them on Sundays. Sundays are religiously reserved for their families, and are usually marked by picnics, visits to parks and restaurants and so on. Visiting foreign writers who have observed Mexican fathers on Sunday outings with their families have awarded Mexican men the highest honors for being "devoted husbands and fathers."

Well-known political figures in Mexico still occasionally appear in public with their paramours, but the days when newly rich politicos would maintain half a dozen or more mistresses and flaunt them in the most fashionable places went out with the 1910–1921 civil war.

However, public displays of passion, once utterly taboo in Mexico, are commonplace. Young couples hold hands, walk arm-in-arm and kiss in public. In shadowy lounges and similar places it is common to see men in their 30s and 40s and young women obviously not their wives engaging in passionate kissing sessions that would arouse the envy of many American teenagers.

Traditionally, the custom of keeping a *casa chica* was not just to satisfy large sexual appetites. It played a key role in providing men with a superior public identity that derived from having more than one wife and additional sets of children. It was a concept that went back to ancient times, throughout the world, when men in power had wives plus concubines, and sired dozens to hundreds of children.

The custom of mistress-keeping in Mexico continues as a male prerogative, but it is less prevalent than what it was in earlier times, and will no doubt continue to decrease as Mexican women achieve greater degrees of economic independence and social and political equality.

Another element in the gradual reduction of mistress-keeping in Mexico is the simple fact that many men between the ages of 40 and 70 years who can afford to maintain mistresses, and were traditionally the most likely to so, now work so much they don't have time to keep up two households.

Mistress-keeping has also been fairly common among more affluent Mexican-American men, but Chicano men are more likely to have independent lovers than to kept mistresses because it is more expensive to keep a mistress in the United States than it is in Mexico, and because of the influence of American cultural values.

Some Mexican-American men who keep mistresses in *casa chicas* may refer to them as *nestos* or "nests" when talking to their buddies.

Ceviche
(Say-VEE-chay)

"Have a Little Aphrodisiac"

In most if not all societies, the role and importance of sexual potency in males has led to the use of various foods and drinks as sexual stimulants.

In the dark past, the need for such stimulation was no doubt considered from a strictly objective viewpoint. Mortality rates were very high and if men could not perform, the survival of the society was threatened.

But as time passed and populations grew, the use of aphrodisiacs became more of an indulgence than a necessity. As a result, the so-called civilized world lost much of this ancient lore.

Mexican Indians of pre-Columbian times had a variety of supposed aphrodisiacs which are no longer readily available. These included dried hummingbird hearts and crocodile testes.

Today, the idea of a modern-day lothario preparing for an evening out by fortifying himself with either of these two concoctions stimulates the wrong area. However, that does not mean the highly educated and sophisticated Mexicans of today have given up on the idea of aphrodisiacs. A variety of common foods and drinks are especially popular because of their reputed aphrodisiacal qualities.

Ceviche (Say-VEE-chay), one of the most common of Mexico's restaurant dishes, is highly reputed in upper-class circles as a sexual stimulant. In its original form *ceviche* consisted of a smorgasbord of raw but marinated seafood. Some restaurants now cook the fish prior to marinating it because its freshness cannot be guaranteed.

Said a Mexican bachelor of my acquaintance who often orders this dish for his dates with American women, "American girls, particularly those from the inland states, are seldom aware of the stimulating effects of certain seafood.

"Many of the girls I date have never eaten seafood other than perhaps fish and shrimp. When I take them to an attractive restaurant and order *ceviche* it makes them feel very sophisticated and they really get turned on."

(It should be noted that in less than first-class restaurants *ceviche* has long been known as a catch-all dish of seafood scraps that couldn't be used in any other way, not as an aphrodisiac.)

Other Mexican experts in stimulating women say the same results can be obtained from a popular seafood soup called *levanta muertos* or "wake up the dead." Abalone and turtle eggs are also considered aphrodisiacs by Mexicans, and eaten for that purpose.

Of course, the efficacy of *ceviche* as an aphrodisiac is open to debate, but it nevertheless occupies a tiny but interesting niche in male–female relations in Mexico, and is therefore worth knowing about.

Foreign men in Mexico who date Mexican women can add a lot of psychological spice to the relationship by asking them if they would like to have *ceviche* as an appetizer before the main course in some romantic place. This sends an unmistakable signal that the foreigner knows all about the reputation of the concoction, and whether or not the Mexican lady believes in *ceviche* as an aphrodisiac, she is certainly going to react to the implications of the scenario.

If the lady declines the suggestion, calling in a *mariachi* band might do the trick. There is much more to *mariachi* music than meets the eye.

Another reportedly sure-fire way of revving up either male or female sex hormones is having a few swigs of the popular Mexican drink *licor de damiana*, made from a substance that has been in use in Mexico as a medicine and aphrodisiac for thousands of years.

(See **Mariachis, Peyote, Toloache.**)

21

Charritas / Dichos / Indirectas)
(Chah-REE-tahs / DEE-chos / Een-dee-RECK-tahs)

"Adding Spice to Spanish"

The Mexicans style of speaking distinguishes them from North Americans and others with Anglo-Saxon backgrounds. Mexicans love their language and they love to talk, privately as well as in public. They exalt in flowery, flamboyant expressions, in poetic and literary *dichos* (DEE-chos) or "quotations," in witticism and in insults—both humorous and serious.

Charritas (chah-REE-tahs), or "short jokes," make up a significant amount of the verbal interplay between Mexicans during informal social gatherings. Among males, sex jokes are especially common.

In sharp contrast to the average American, most Mexicans, including those in the lower classes, naturally learn how to speak their language with considerable eloquence.

The American who attends virtually any kind of Mexican social function, such as a wedding, learns a major lesson, not only about the way Mexicans express themselves, but also about the broad swath of Mexican culture. All of the courtesy, protocol and pomp that is characteristic of Mexican behavior is on display on such occasions. There are eloquent speeches and singing and dancing. In fact, all Mexicans tend to be good public speakers and practically all Mexicans, including men, can sing quite well.

Mexicans also speak and sing their language with great emotion. The words they use and their manner of expressing them are charged with passion and cultural context that puts virtually everything on the level of a great drama.

To understand and communicate effectively with Mexicans it is necessary to be aware of the language in all of its cultural implications, in song as well as in speech.

It is also characteristic of Mexicans (and other Hispanics) to speak in circumlocutions, literally zigzagging all over the place rather than getting right to the point in as few words as possible, something that non-Hispanics often find confusing and sometimes irritating. The North American custom of speaking directly and succinctly, laying everything on the line and expecting a similar response, is therefore alien to Mexicans and can be equally upsetting to them.

Mexicans have made the use of *indirectas* (een-dee-RECK-tahs), or getting their meaning across by the use of "indirect comments," into a fine art. It requires a great deal of insight and experience to "translate" this form of speech into the kind of communication that North Americans and others can understand.

Becoming irritated or angry because of *indirectas*—a common reaction of people who are not culturally conditioned to accept and deal with this kind of communication—just makes things worse.

Like their Asian cousins, Mexicans have an aversion to jumping right into business. Their way is to get acquainted, put everything on a personal basis and then discuss the big view, the grand view, leaving the details to be gradually introduced over a period of time. Unaware of these cultural factors, foreign politicians and businesspeople alike routinely talk over the heads of their Mexican audiences. Obviously, if they are going to communicate effectively with Mexicans they must talk on the same cultural channel.

Presuming that Mexicans, on whatever level, will understand and accept messages in a foreign cultural context is arrogant, dumb and dangerous.

Virtually all aspects of Mexican culture, the mainstream culture as well as all of the regional variations, are changing, and on both a social and economic level these changes are in the direction of the United States. But the Indian–Asian aspects of Mexican culture are thousands of years old and deeply imprinted on the psyche of the people. The changes that are occurring are mostly at the top of the society. It is a slow process which will be ongoing for many generations.

Mexicans expect businesspeople to have interests and skills that go beyond business. They expect them to have knowledge of at least one art and be informed about literature and philosophy, and for this cultural side to balance the time they spend on business.

One of the best ways for outsiders to exhibit this important side of one's character is to demonstrate a sincere interest in learning as much as possible about Mexico, its cultural as well as its political and economic history, and the language. Anyone who is going to spend more than a few days in Mexico should learn some Spanish. Those who are going to work there or be involved in business with Mexico should make a serious effort to learn as much of the language as possible. Although learning how to speak Spanish in its full cultural context is a difficult challenge, the mechanical side of it is relatively easy for English speakers.

Whatever the case, making a serious effort to learn Spanish is, by itself, enough to gain the respect and appreciation of business associates and others, and will totally change one's Mexican experience for the better.

Note: In Mexico it is customary to begin speeches with an appropriate *vocativo* or "saying" rather than a joke, as in the United States, or an apology, as in Japan.

22

Charros
(CHAH-rohs)

"Mexico's Urban Cowboys"

Long before Columbus discovered the Americas, Spanish noblemen had made horsemanship into a virtual cult; horses were used not only as instruments of war but also in the various social and political ceremonies of the times.

Horses subsequently played a key role in the early successes of the Spanish conquistaᵈ ᵣs in their campaign to conquer Mexico. The Indians of Mexico had never seen horses before, and were both amazed and frightened when they first encountered armored soldiers fighting on horseback.

Realizing full well the advantages that horses gave them, the Spanish quickly made it the law of the land that Indians could not own, ride or use horses in any way, an edict that was severely enforced during the first century of the 300-year Spanish reign. The penalty for breaking this law was death.

In the meantime, the leisured class of Spanish men born in Mexico, the *criollos* (cree-OH-yohs), gradually expanded on the "cult of the horse." They adapted the highly stylized attire that was traditionally used by bullfighters who fought bulls from horseback to create their own "uniform." They also added aspects of the stylized etiquette of the matador to their own behavior.

Criollo men who followed the way of the horse also made a ritual out of idolizing women when in public, treating them as princesses, queens and saints.

Most important, they became master horsemen, superbly skilled at riding, roping, bull throwing (by riding alongside of running bulls, grabbing their tails, and swing them down) and hitting targets with their lances while riding at full gallop.

The men who followed this fashion and lifestyle came to be known as *charros* (CHAH-ros), which literally means "horsemen." In public as well as in private *charros* represented the idealized form of Mexico's famed machismo—manly, brave, courteous and protective of women.

By the time the revolution of 1810–1821 ended Spanish rule in Mexico, many of the *charro* traditions established by the rich Mexican-born Spaniards had permeated the whole of *criollo* society and greatly influenced the attitudes and behavior of the *mestizo* mixed-bloods, who by that time made up the majority of the population.

As the cattle industry spread in the northern regions of Mexico in the 1600s, the *charros* also became role models for North America's first cowboys, known as *vaqueros* (vah-KAY-rohs). They set the style of dress and behavior that was associated with ranching and cattle raising in general.

Both *charros* and *vaqueros* were forbearers of the bandits who became synonymous with Mexico in the 19th century, and the bandit-rebels (such as Pancho Villa) who played leading roles in the second revolution in 1910–1921 which finally wrested power from the *criollos* and the church.

Traditions of the *charros* survived Mexico's civil war (1910–1921) and are alive and well today, carried on by a small group of well-to-do urban and rural men, somewhat like service clubs of the United States.

Charros participate in parades, festivals and other public events, and are noted for their civic efforts and for upholding the traditional etiquette of Mexico's upper classes.

Today, the term *charro* is sometimes translated as "cowboy." But a Mexican *charro* is more of an urban cowboy than one who rides the range in the fashion of the cowboy and gunfighter of the American West.

It is important to keep in mind, however, that the first cowboys in the American Southwest, including Texas, New Mexico, California and Arizona, were Mexican *vaqueros*, who were there long before the United States became a country.

All that is now a part of the cowboy legend of the American West—from the cattle drives out of Texas to Buffalo Bill, the sheriffs of Dodge City and Tombstone and Billy the Kid, to the boutique shops of Scottsdale and Sedona in Arizona which feature cowboy art—originated with the *charros* and *vaqueros* of Mexico.

(See **Corridas, Vaqueros.**)

23

Chicanas
(Chee-CAH-nahs)

"Slowing the Wheels of Justice"

Mexico Business ("The Magazine of Business in Mexico"), published in Houston, Texas, once carried an article titled "Law and Disorder" which described the judicial system in Mexico as "inefficient, ineffective and corrupt," and traditionally a tool for the rich and powerful. Written by contributing editor Sallie Hughes, the article went on to detail what amounts to the first comprehensive reforms taking place in the country's judicial system since it was instituted in the 16th century.

The reform package, announced by the new president Ernesto Zedillo in January 1995, required that all of the Supreme Court justices sitting on the court at that time retire. The number of justices was reduced from 26 to 11, and their term in office changed from life to 15 years.

Zedillo's judicial reform package also made it mandatory that nominees to the Supreme Court had to appear before the Senate in open hearings and be approved by a vote of two thirds of the Senate. Prior to that, membership on the Supreme Court was by presidential appointment.

Another key part of the reform package eliminated the right of the Supreme Court justices to appoint all lower court judges. That authority was relegated to a newly created selection committee made up of representatives from the executive, legislative and judicial branches of the government.

In a further reduction of the incestuous power of the presidency, the reforms also made it mandatory that the president's nominee for attorney general appear before the senate and be approved by a minimum of 50 percent of the members for confirmation.

Although widely praised as a long overdue first step in bringing genuine justice to Mexico, critics pointed out that the reforms did not go far enough and would not eliminate the weaknesses of the judicial system or its age-old corruption.

Mexico's minimal qualifications for both judges and lawyers are a major part of the problem. Judges are required only to be lawyers and at least 35 years old. Lawyers need only a bachelor's degree. There are no bar examinations and no review systems of any kind. This, critics add, makes it inevitable that Mexico's legal profession will attract unsavory characters whose only purpose is to accumulate as much power and make as much money as possible.

Another ongoing problem within Mexico's judicial system that has traditionally made it virtually impossible to obtain justice within a reasonable amount of time and at a reasonable cost is the use of *chicanas* (chee-CAH-nahs) or "delaying tactics" to keep matters from being decided by the courts. It is reported that *chicanas* of one kind or another are used in some 95 percent of all cases filed in Mexico, and even the simplest legal proceedings can take several years. All either side in a lawsuit has to do to delay the proceedings for up to six months is to challenge the right of the opposition lawyer to act as counsel.

The use of *chicanas* is particularly onerous for businesses because circumstances can change so dramatically over a period of months and years that the negative results of "justice delayed" are greatly magnified.

Chicanas remain a favorite ploy of defense lawyers in Mexico because there are few if any sanctions against using them. Among other things, it is customary for judges to allow lawyers to ignore the court's orders to present their case three times without any sanctions. On the fourth time, they may be fined a nominal amount.

In addition to *chicanas* the judicial system in Mexico is rife with *mordida* (mohr-DEE-dah) or "bribe." Virtually every document copied or filed requires a payoff to some clerk or minor official to prevent them from sitting on it for days, weeks or months.

For the most part, the efficiency and fairness of the justice system in Mexico remains directly related to how effectively the wheels and cogs are "oiled" with money.

24

Chicanos
(Chee-CAH-nohs)

"The Mexican Americans"

North Americans of European extraction are inclined to forget that when the United States took over Texas, New Mexico, Arizona and California in 1840s these areas were part of Mexico and had been populated by Mexicans for more than 200 years. Much of the character and color of these states that Americans of European descent find so attractive today is a legacy of their Mexican history, and that history is not yet over.

The Mexican-American population of the United States is now one of the fastest growing racial and ethnic groups in the country, and is having a growing economic and cultural impact. Yet many of the same apartheid-type barriers that were erected in the mid-1800s by North Americans to keep Mexicans in a separate sphere still exist today, and new ones have been added, sometimes inadvertently by Mexican Americans themselves.

One of the linguistic cultural barriers that originated in the Mexican-American community is the term *chicano* (chee-CAH-noh), meaning an ethnic Mexican born in the United States and therefore an American citizen.

The word *chicano*, a takeoff from *Mexicano*, apparently first came into limited use in the early 1900s as a nickname for Mexican Americans; a slang term that was created and used by young Mexican-American boys, not adult Mexican Americans.

Chicano began as an in-group word that was used to indicate and foster peer fellowship and pride among youths who did not like being called "Mexicans," "Mexican Americans," or "Greasers," and who were especially vulnerable to violence within their own group as well as from the outside. Violence against Mexicans who crossed the border legally or illegally was endemic.

A 1916 edition of *World's Work* noted: "The killing of Mexicans throughout the border area over the last four years has been incredible. There is no penalty for killing [Mexicans] for no jury along the border would ever convict a white man for shooting a Mexican."

Most of the killings, the publication continued, were done by police and border patrols. Such killings were common until the 1970s, and it was

1977 before the first American police officer was convicted of the unwarranted killing of a Mexican.

During this long period, the news media in the United States generally portrayed Mexicans as criminals or bandits, contributing to if not condoning both the harassment and killing, and blackening the image of Mexican Americans.

At first the term *chicano* was very controversial among adults in Mexican-American communities. Then, over the next several decades, particularly in the 1960s, young politically active Chicanos begun using the word because it gave them something relatively neutral to call themselves other than "Mexican Americans," which seemed both redundant and insulting.

But the word did not remain neutral very long. Anglo-Americans, encouraged by the mainstream North American press, soon began using the word with negative overtones, imputing into it many of the prejudices that had traditionally been applied toward the terms *Mexicans* and *Mexican Americans*.

This bias was quickly picked up by racially and culturally prejudiced North Americans living in the Southwest, particularly those in areas with a high percentage of Mexican-American residents, illegal immigrants and undocumented seasonal workers.

Today Mexican Americans still face discrimination from Mexicans as well as from other Americans. Some Mexicans accuse Mexican Americans of having rejected their Mexican heritage.

Chicanos, like their *mestizo* ancestors, typically find themselves ostracized by both European-descent Americans and Mexicans. Some Americans either ignore them or treat them as outsiders. Some Mexicans treat them as cultural traitors and criticize them for not being able to speak contemporary Spanish fluently and not following Mexican customs.

Said one Mexican businessman who is very sympathetic toward the plight of the Chicanos: "They are no longer Mexicans and are not yet Americans. All they retain of their Mexican culture are their beans, tacos, music, two or three annual celebrations and their outdated memories."

Discrimination by North Americans against Chicanos begins with skin color. The darker the skin the deeper and more pervasive the discrimination. Dark-skinned Chicanos are frequently treated like blacks, particularly by police and other law enforcement agencies. Witness after witness has detailed that police harassment against Chicanos, and the degree of brutal treatment, is based on "how Mexican" the individual looks.

Mexican Americans began to organize on a national basis in the 1920s, and in 1929 founded the League of United Latin American Citizens, known as LULAC for short. The letters of this acronym stand for:

*L*ove of country (the U.S.!) and fellowmen

*U*nity of purpose

*L*oyalty to country (the U.S.!) and principles

*A*dvancement of a people

*C*itizenship, true and unadulterated.

During the 1960s and thereafter, a number of Mexican-American organizations met in study groups and at conventions to draw up action plans designed to improve their understanding of the Chicano experience. Eventually these planners began using *La Raza* or "The Race," a phrase coined to mean the new Latin Americans race made up of people with mixed European and Indian blood, along with *Chicano* in references to their aspirations for the future.

Major political, economic and social crusades were begun in a mass effort to improve the circumstances of Mexican Americans, including labor strikes in the agricultural areas of the American Southwest, and marches in cities. Some of these marches, particularly in Los Angeles, were treated as revolutionary rebellions by the police, who routinely used deadly force to break them up.

But like their *mestizo* ancestors, second- and third-generation Mexican Americans persevered, and their members are now represented in the highest echelons of business and government in the United States from state legislators and governors to congressional representatives and senators.

Mexican Americans now incorporate dignity, self-worth, pride and cultural uniqueness into Chicanoism. The more negativism and abuse they encounter, the stronger the appeal of Chicanoism, which emphasizes consciousness of the best of Mexico's cultural heritage, including the ability to speak Spanish.

However, first-generation Mexican Americans are especially handicapped if they are poor and uneducated, and if they do not speak English; both men and women are locked out of the mainstream of American society. Parents cannot participate in school activities with their children or join in any activities outside of those involving other Mexican families. This linguistic barrier is compounded by cultural differences that range from food and religious festivals to male-female relations.

Mexico's notorious masculinity cult also continues to be a significant element in the lives of poorer Chicanos. *Machismo* contributes to domestic violence, the existence of youth gangs and juvenile delinquency. Most of the excessive drinking and murders in Chicano communities derive from a compulsive desire among young Mexican males to prove their courage, manhood and superiority in a society that still often disparages and disdains them.

It should not be too long, however, before the term *Chicano* itself is relegated to the "dustbin of history" in favor of the more universal and neutral word *Latino*—or *Hispanic*, a term favored by a growing number of influential Mexican Americans.

Syndicated columnist Roger E. Hernandez (King Features Syndicate Inc.) is one of those who advocates the use of "Hispanic" in reference to Mexican Americans. He points out that *Hispano* is a very old word referring to Spain and that it is the Spanish element that unites all people of "Latin" America; that it is the one cultural component that gives all Latin Americans something in common.

(See **Cabrón, Machismo, Mestizos.**)

Chingar
(Cheen-GARR)

"The Strongest Word"

Chingar (cheen-GARR) would surely be included on any list of important slang words in the Mexican vocabulary. It is one of the most used words in the Mexican language, and is the only word to have a whole dictionary devoted solely to its many forms and uses.

Some authorities say *chingar* comes from an Aztec word, *chingaste*, which means residue or sediment, and a number of its uses are associated with drinking or drinks of one kind or another. Some form of the word is common throughout Latin America, as well as in Spain.

The meanings of *chingar* range from to drink, to molest, to penetrate by force, to violate, to hurt, to hate, to screw (in the sense of to take advantage of), to destroy, to make a fool of, to fail and to have sex with. When used in the sense of sexual intercourse it refers to rape, not consensual sex. (A similar but less offensive word is *joder*.)

In addition to being used as a verb, *chingar* is also used as an adjective and as a noun. In its root noun form *chingar* is used in a colloquial sense as a "mess" or "fuck-up."

Chingón, another noun form of the word, has the meaning of someone who is powerful, overbearing, clever or good at something, and is often used in the sense of a kind of lowdown compliment. *Qué chingón!* means "What a faker!" (What a guy!). The feminine form of this is also used: *Que chingona!* (What a gal!).

Chingón also denotes superiority and power gained through having sexual intercourse often and with many women. Mexican men generally regard themselves as more *chingón* than English or North American men.

Chingón is the male, the raper; *chingada* is the female, the raped. *Chingaderas* are people who commit acts of violence that create confusion, terror and destruction. Mexicans say that in life you are either the *chingón* or the *chingada*.

Both the male and female noun forms, *chingado* and *chingada*, are used in the vulgar sense of "fucked up." *Ella esta chingada*, "she is fucked up" (but in the noun form it is common to use the less offensive *jodida* or *jodido*).

When *chingar* is used in conjunction with someone's mother (*madre*) it is one of the strongest insults in Mexican culture. In this case "mother" is meant in both a personal as well as a symbolic sense; it refers to all the mothers of Mexico now and in the past, to the Virgin of Guadalupe (who is viewed as the "mother" of all Mexico) and to everything else Mexicans hold sacred.

In earlier times when a great many Mexican men went about armed, the combination of *chingar* and *madre* was such a powerful insult that it frequently resulted in bloodshed. The words represented the dark and most unstable side of the Mexican character, and were considered unspeakable in polite society.

The most famous and most powerful cry in Mexican history was *Viva Mexico! Hijos de la chingada!* "Long Live Mexico! Sons of Mothers Who Were Raped!"—a reference to the fact that throughout the Spanish colonial period, Spanish men routinely compelled Indian girls and women to have sex with them. In this usage, mothers and Mexico are virtually synonymous.

Another saying, popular until recent times, was that the Constitution (*La Constitución*), which is feminine in gender, was the most raped female in Mexico.

By the 1990s *chingar* and its most potent derivatives had been degraded to the point that they were often heard in use by taxi drivers and other ordinary people who got involved in verbal disputes. Mexico City taxi drivers in particular had long since became masters at sounding out the worst *chingar/madre* insults onomatopoeically on their car horns.

The use of *chingar* and mother in insults has made Mexicans extraordinarily sensitive to the word *madre*, which was already a semi-sacred word in the first place. Using them in the same sentence, even though innocently, can be serious.

The *chingón* concept has always been a significant factor in the world of Mexican men, and Mexican fathers have traditionally had two images—the all-good, all-wise, all-powerful patriarch who took care of the family, which mostly applied to middle- and upper-class families, and the *chingón*, the machismo-driven, heartless, cruel man who stifled and punished his wife and children and abandoned them on the slightest whim, and was mostly associated with lower-class men. In reality, the record shows that there has always been, and still is now, some *chingón* in most Mexican men, regardless of their social class.

Unless one is perfectly fluent in the Spanish language as well as in the Mexican culture, it is wise to avoid using the word *chingar* in any of its forms. The possibility of such use creating a situation that cannot be handled successfully is simply too great to risk.

Anyone who uses the very common phrase *Chinga tu madre!*, "Rape your mother!" (or "Fuck your mother!") should be ready to fight. A typical response to this is *La tuya!*, literally "Yours!" but figuratively, "The same to yours!"

Foreigners who are on the receiving end of *chingar* insults don't necessarily have to grin, but it is usually the better part of valor to bear it.

Foreigners should be aware that some Mexicans will try to teach them how to use *chingar* in some of its many forms, advising them to use it to show friendship. But it is better to avoid using it altogether even if one is trying to sound funny or show off fluency in Spanish.

26

Chistes
(CHEES-tehs)

"Laughing at Pain"

There is a dichotomy in Mexican culture that emphasizes one of the most astounding things about the human spirit; something that seemingly contradicts common sense, but without which Mexicans (as well as the rest of humanity) would be a totally different kind of people.

Apparently, humans have an innate compulsion to not only make the best of bad situations but to make light of them, and in the process gain strength and character.

The history of most Mexicans, specifically the Indians and those of mixed blood, from shortly after the beginning of the Spanish colonial era in 1521 until the last decades of the 20th century, was marked by a degree of oppression and discrimination that might be expected to have turned them into a hopelessly dour and mean-spirited people. However, for reasons that are difficult to understand, the frustrations and hatreds that built up in the Mexican people by centuries of abuse and pain were leavened by a sense of *humor* (YOO-more)—albeit often macabre—and a spirit of goodwill that belies the suffering they were forced to endure.

Humor is, in fact, one of the main pillars of Mexican culture, and colors the whole spectrum of Mexican life, helping to hold it together by neutralizing many of the stresses that have constantly threatened to tear it apart.

For many generations, *humor* was the only antidote available to Mexicans to counteract the poison of racial bigotry, political and religious abuse that was practiced as official policy and such self-imposed cultural abuses as machismo.

Mexicans, like Jews and many other traditionally oppressed people, learned a long time ago that a well-turned *chiste* (CHEES-teh) or "joke" could help diffuse frustrations and keep anger below the boiling point, and often deflate the ego and arrogance of their enemies as well.

Because Mexicans were confronted daily with institutionalized abuses and frustrations which they could not change or escape from, they became masters at focusing on the weaknesses and pretensions of individuals as well as the government and the church, and using humor to make them bearable.

By the 1960s, this mastery of the humorous putdown had become an important weapon for the Mexican people in their efforts to eliminate the worst political and economic abuses. Yet it was not until the initial political reforms of the 1980s and 1990s had guaranteed ordinary people a greater measure of security from reprisals from the government that the use of humor as a political weapon came into its own. Now, Mexico's news media is replete with cartoons and jokes that unmercifully skewer politicians and government institutions, puncturing their pretenses and leaving them roasting over fires of laughter.

Mexicans will not be fully free of the terrible legacy of their past, however, until they lose some of their insecurity about "face" and image, learn to laugh at themselves with gentle humor and accept the same kind of casual joking from foreigners.

Mexicans (and others) can learn something from the American state of Hawaii, where people of diverse cultures have learned to mix and merge, to enjoy not only their diversity but also an open and wonderfully reassuring cross-racial and cross-cultural sense of humor.

27

Chueco
(Choo-WAY-coh)

"Avoiding Crooked Deals"

When young General Porfirio Díaz took over as president of Mexico in 1876 he came under the influence of a group of bankers, financiers, industrialists and lawyers known as *cientificos* or "scientists," because of their familiarity with modern business methods. They advised him to open the country up to foreign investments and foreign companies. The new program resulted in a virtual stampede of major American corporations, individual investors and deal makers into Mexico.

For the next 40 years these companies and individuals treated Mexico more or less as their private colony—paying their Mexican employees starvation wages, forcing them to work under hazardous conditions and helping to perpetuate the traditionally enormous gap between the country's rich and poor.

The Mexican civil war of 1910–1921 and subsequent political reforms ended many of these unequal business concessions, but foreign interests continued to take advantage of Mexico's economic weaknesses at every opportunity, making Mexicans especially wary of doing business with *gringos*.

Passage of the North American Foreign Trade Agreement (NAFTA) in 1994 resulted in a new influx of foreign companies and foreign deal makers into Mexico. Some of them offered legitimate, mutually beneficial business propositions, while others sought to benefit only themselves. Among this latter group were large numbers who had no money of their own to invest and who began approaching well-to-do Mexicans to finance their deals.

According to Mexican sources, the overwhelming majority of these deals were what Mexicans describe as *chueco* (choo-WAY-coh), which means "turned around," or "crooked," and therefore unacceptable. (The original meaning of *chueco* is "bow-legged." It is also used in reference to false immigration documents used in attempts to enter the United States illegally.)

Said one Mexican businessman: "The arrogance of many of these individuals is incredible. They come to Mexico with the attitude that all Mexicans are stupid and will agree to anything that they propose.

"Some of them are outright *coyotes*—charlatans trying to get their hands on somebody's money and then run with it. Others have done no research at all and know nothing about Mexico, socially, economically or politically, and are so naive it is laughable."

Because such proposals are so common, the typical first reaction of Mexican businessmen to any proposal from foreigners is, *De a como?*, "How much is it going to cost me?"

In addition to doing their homework on Mexico and their particular area of interest, foreigners wanting to go into business with Mexican partners should become familiar with the words *derechito* (day-ray-CHEE-toh) and *parejo* (pah-RAY-hoh).

Derechito, the diminutive of *derecho*, which means "straight," refers to business deals that are not *chueco*; that are honest and clean. *Parejo* means "even," referring to business deals in which both parties have an equal opportunity to profit.

Because of their long history of having been continuously "raped" by everyone with any kind of power and misled by promises that were never kept, Mexicans who are honest and trustworthy are especially wary about going into business with anyone outside of their family or circle of friends.

The only way *gringos* can overcome the sensitivity and wariness of potential Mexican business partners is by taking the time and making the effort to develop strong personal relationships that are based on their own integrity and on their ability to follow through on commitments.

Of course, representatives of large, well-known foreign companies have an advantage in attracting Mexican partners, but ultimately the success of partnerships on this level as well almost always depends upon the strength and viability of the personal relationships forged between executives and managers on both sides.

Nurturing of personal relationships with Mexican partners must be continuous. North Americans in particular habitually assume that once a contract is signed, the hard part is over and thereafter everything will go smoothly of its own accord. In actuality, the hard part begins after the contract is signed and the honeymoon is over. There are always enough differences in understanding, opinions, motivations and goals to create permanent gaps between the two sides. The only way these gaps can be kept narrow enough so that they can be bridged, and the two sides can continue to communicate and cooperate, is for both parties to constantly work at keeping the bridges in good shape.

It is therefore of vital importance that foreign managers and executives stationed in Mexico have necessary qualifications to deal effectively in cross-cultural personal and business relations.

In addition to language ability, these qualifications include a high degree of tolerance for cultural differences and a special talent for achieving consensus and cooperation across the cultural borders.

Comida

(Coh-ME-dah)

"Communing Over Meals"

Like most other people, Mexicans generally eat three or four times a day. But unlike most non-Hispanic people, Mexicans eat their main meal of the day, called *comida* (coh-ME-dah), which means "food," "meal" or "dinner," in the middle of the afternoon.

Breakfast (*desayuno*) in Mexico tends to be rather late in the morning, and ranges from light to heavy, depending on the habits of the individual. Lunch (*almuerzo*) is usually eaten as a very late breakfast or as an early lunch.

It may be heavy if eaten as a late breakfast and light if eaten as an early lunch, again depending on the habits of the individual.

At restaurants, *la comida* may start as early as 1 P.M. and last until around 4 P.M. At home, *la comida* is generally served between 2 and 3 P.M. and lasts for around two hours.

There are two kinds of meals after the main midafternoon meal. One, called *merienda*, which means "snack," is a light meal that may be eaten as early as 6 P.M. in some parts of the country and as late as 10 P.M. in other areas. The other type of evening meal, *cena* or "supper," is a heavy banquet-like meal usually associated with a social event.

La comida has traditionally been the time that the entire Mexican family, sometimes with friends or visiting guests, gathered to socialize and commune with each other, and to reconfirm the social relationships between the various members of the family.

Each family member—the grandparents, the parents and the children—had his or her specific hierarchical place and role to play in the serving and eating, and in the *sobremesa* or "over the table" conversation that followed.

The grandmother, as the senior woman in the house, had the role of serving the family members during the meal, and was the family storyteller. After everyone had finished eating, she would tell stories about the history of the family and their community, and recite the legends and myths that made up the cultural heritage of the people. It was also a time for catching up on current events and gossiping.

The English word "lunch" does not do justice to the traditional midday meal in Mexico. Even the popular American-invented phrase "power lunch" suggests only one element of the Mexican *comida*, which is a multifaceted cultural experience.

Well-prepared and tasty food is important in a traditional midday meal for the affluent in Mexico. But it is the overall ambience of the setting, the individuals making up the party, the conversation, the interplay of humor, and the emotional and philosophical communion that counts.

These long afternoon rituals of eating and drinking provide the foundation for the all-important personal and business relationships in Mexico. Generally, it is impossible to consummate a business deal in Mexico without first going through this ritualistic stage of bonding.

Sandy Sheehy, author and contributor on social and business themes to *Money, Forbes, Town & Country,* and other publications, writes that wining and dining people in Mexico is a necessity, not a luxury, and that the foreign businessperson in Mexico trying to cut a deal who "flunks lunch" might as well go home.

The formality of family *comidas* has decreases substantially in recent times, but the midafternoon meal in a Mexican home is still a special time for many people. The big thing in Mexico today is the long, midafternoon business "lunch."

Business *comidas* at restaurants differ from the "power lunches" that are popular in the United States and elsewhere in that generally they last longer and are not all devoted to business talk. In fact, the social element is just as important as—if not more so than—the business side. Mexican businesspeople use *comidas* not only to get acquainted with new contacts and to discuss the details of business, but also as an occasion to relax and enjoy themselves, regardless of how anxious a foreign guest (or host) may be to get on with business.

The first hour or so of a *comida* is devoted to small talk, usually about personal things, and eating and drinking. After the meal is finished, the conversation generally switches to national events, literature, philosophy, art and so on, depending on the individual interests and tastes of the participants. Business talk usually takes up the least amount of time at a *comida*, and generally occurs in the last half hour or so.

Foreign businesspeople hosting a *comida* with topics they want to discuss should follow this protocol, unless, of course, their Mexican guests themselves bring up business earlier, something that is becoming more common as Mexican businesspeople adopt faster-paced international practices.

Introduction of the business topic by the Mexican side depends upon any number of factors—if they feel comfortable with the foreign party (how well the visitors have "performed"), how anxious they are to make a deal and so on. Of course, more and more Mexican businesspeople have been educated abroad and/or have had extensive business experience abroad. These people—readily identifiable—are fully at ease in dealing with foreigners in a more direct give-and-take manner.

Foreigners planning on going to Mexico to initiate business dialogue should include finding out as much as possible about the individuals they are going to be meeting as a key part of their preparations. Such knowledge can be as important as what they know about the companies concerned.

More and more Mexican businesspeople also routinely hold breakfast meetings, especially if they already know the individuals they are meeting and if the purpose is to continue business discussions that are under way. Mexicans who have adopted the American way of doing things—giving work precedence over virtually everything else—are especially likely to prefer breakfast meetings because they take up less of the workday.

As the business scene in Mexico becomes more international, another custom that is becoming more and more common is for businesspeople to meet for an hour or so after work at a bar or lounge, before they go home for the usual late-evening supper with their families.

Foreign visitors who invite Mexican contacts out for breakfast, lunch or after hours meetings should be aware that Mexicans are generally aggressive in paying restaurant and bar bills; it is part of their image. Visitors should be equally aggressive in making sure that it doesn't happen. This means staying alert and signaling the waiter or waitress as they approach with the bill, or making sure the server gets the word in advance. Failure to make any such move—and mean it—can result in a very negative image.

Foreigners who are conditioned to quick, all-business lunches often find it very difficult to adjust to the much slower, laid-back pace of the Mexican *comida*, but those who can't adapt to them are not likely to succeed in Mexico in the first place.

On the other hand, some foreigners who adapt to the *comida* and the following *sobremesa* often come to prefer the Mexican way in other things as well. Visitors who are in Mexico for whatever reason should plan on participating in the custom of *sobremesa* because it is one of the secrets to getting to know and enjoy Mexico. Foreign businesspeople should be cautious about being the first to bring up business subjects during *sobremesa*, however. Older, more traditionally minded Mexicans (who are not Americanized) may be offended.

29

Compadres / Comadres
(Com-PAH-drays / Co-MAD-drays)

"The Co-Father / Co-Mother Connections"

Historically in Mexico personal rights based on principles of equality and justice, supported by fairly and efficiently enforced laws, simply did not exist. Generally, authority on whatever level was primarily used for the personal benefit of those in power. The public at large came last, if at all.

This fundamental factor resulted in a society in which people had to depend upon personal relations in order to protect themselves, as well as to engage in business and deal effectively with government authorities.

Bribery, kickbacks and other forms of corruption were a natural out-growth of this kind of system. Given the hierarchical nature of the society, people in each level of authority fed off of those below them. The lower people were in society, the less likely they were to have high-level connections and the more likely they were to have to make some kind of payoff in any kind of official act.

In the middle and upper classes another element in this system was that the ability to use personal connections in lieu of monetary payoffs depended on the connections being on the highest level, since people in lower levels of company management or government agencies generally had limited, if any, real authority. One of the results was that people who had a wide range of top-level connections, regardless of their own abilities or accomplishments, were often among the most powerful and sought-after people in the country because they could get things done.

The need for connections thus became one of the most important factors in survival and success in Mexico, and gave birth to a number of institutions that were to give Mexican society much of its character.

One of the key elements in this personalized world of Mexicans was the institution of *compadres* (com-PAH-drays) and *comadres* (co-MAH-drays) or "co-fathers" and "co-mothers," the custom of appointing outside friends—not relatives—to be co-parents of one's children.

From the first years of the Spanish regime in Mexico in the 16th century, the *compradrazgo/comadrazgo* system, which had its origin in medieval times as a kinship ritual, became the core of Mexican society.

The co-father and co-mother ties included a spiritual bond that made them responsible for influencing the children's upbringing and behavior, so they would become good Catholics and good citizens. They participated in baptisms, confirmations, marriages and other important events, often resulting in a "client relationship" that included both personal and political alliances.

If anything happened to the birth parents, co-parents were obligated to take their godchildren in and raise them as their own.

Compadres and *comadres* were generally arranged before children were born. Of course, before desirable co-fathers and co-mothers could be approached, people had to already have some kind of connection or relationship with them, particularly since the ideal co-parents were on a higher social level.

At the same time, the roles of co-father and co-mother brought prestige and honor, and were frequently sought after. People often vied for the privilege (and the responsibility), and would approach expectant parents before the birth of their children and implore them to "give me your child." So the custom was both a way of strengthening existing networks and gradually expanding them.

The co-parenting system is still an important part of life in Mexico. Well-placed compadres, especially, take a personal interest in the welfare of their godsons, and become key figures in the network of connections that are vital to accomplishing things.

The higher the social level of the people involved the more important the co-father/co-mother relationships, because they serve to perpetuate the status of the families. A great deal of the corporate world in Mexico is run by families, close relatives and people who have co-parenting relationships. (It is widely reported that the bulk of the industrial wealth of Mexico is in the hands of just 25 families, some of whom have interlocking godfather and godmother ties.)

Once the co-parenting relationship is established, the birth father thereafter addresses the co-father as *compadre* at all times, and the birth mother addresses the co-mother as *comadre*.

To the children concerned, the co-father becomes their *padrino* (godfather) and the *comadre* becomes their *madrina* (godmother), and they are addressed by these titles. Ordinary friends will also often address each other as *compadre* or *comadre*, either as a sign of respect or as a bit of flattery.

Madrina and *padrino*, similar to their English equivalents, incorporate the role of "protector," a responsibility that is usually taken very seriously.

Generally, the more successful a Mexican man the more common it is for him to act as mentor and godfather to a number of young men, whether or not they are officially his godsons—a custom that greatly benefits both parties. The young men have the benefit of the advice and influence of their mentors, and the older men in turn can count on the loyalty and support of the young men as they rise in their own business or political careers.

Foreigners in Mexico are generally not eligible for formal godfather relationships, but it is possible for them to be informally "adopted" by older, successful Mexican businesspeople or politicians with whom they have developed a truly close personal friendship; these men will subsequently act as their mentors and as conduits into the inner circles of Mexico. Such relationships are, in fact, fairly common and play a significant role in the success of the foreigners who are lucky enough to have them.

While it makes very good sense for newcomers to Mexico to make developing such relationships a high priority, it should be kept in mind that they must be based on true friendship, not one-sided opportunistic motives.

When treated with courtesy and good will, Mexicans on whatever level respond enthusiastically, typically going beyond what is normal in non-Latin countries.

———————————— 30 ————————————

Comprención
(Cohm-prane-see-OWN)

"Understanding Mexican Style"

Similarities between the cultures of Japan and Mexico are often astounding, especially given the dramatic economic and social contrasts between the two countries. Yet in their response to human relations Mexicans and Japanese are very much alike.

One aspect of Japanese culture that continues to mystify and frustrate uninitiated foreigners is the concept of *rikai* or "understanding." When the Japanese use this term it means a lot more than intellectually grasping something.

In Mexico exactly the same concept, with all of its attendant nuances, is bound up in the word *comprención* (cohm-prane-see-OWN), translated as "comprehension" or "understanding." *Comprención* in its Mexican context incorporates not only an understanding of the hard facts of a proposition or situation, it also includes an intellectual and sympathetic acceptance of the situation. This acceptance goes well beyond just passive believing in, approving of or agreeing to something. It calls for a positive response. This response may involve taking some action, or stopping some action that is in process.

In both Japan and Mexico "understanding" in this sense means to become an advocate of the other's viewpoint and goals, and doing whatever is possible to help the other side achieve those goals.

Both Japanese and Mexicans believe that most of the criticism that is directed toward them as a group, and toward their way of doing things, results from their critics not understanding the "facts" involved. They also believe that as soon as critics fully understand their viewpoint and their way of doing things the critics' opposition will disappear and they will join with them in the enterprise.

Finally, there is a conspicuously affectionate as well as a protective attitude that comes with *comprención*, an emotional factor that is especially meaningful to Mexicans which can cause ill will if it is inadvertently or deliberately ignored. Mexicans have a deep-seated desire to be understood and to be liked, because during most of their history they were reviled, misused, abused and ostracized from higher society, making them extremely sensitive and emotional about who they are and where they fit in. Much of the personal violence that has plagued Mexico for centuries is a manifestation of this extreme sensitivity—plus the constant struggle of Mexican men to live up to an exaggerated image of themselves. This sensitivity remains very much a part of the character of Mexicans today, and the lower one is on the social scale the more apt it is to lead to open confrontation and violence.

In higher society perceived slights to one's image, or to Mexicans in general, are more likely to result in some kind of subtle, covert revenge.

It is important for foreigners to keep in mind that *comprención* in its Mexican context includes a strong element of mutual trust and caring that precludes critical attitudes and harmful behavior. It presumes unqualified support, regardless of the circumstances.

One of the results of the *comprención* factor in Mexican life is that it frequently leads to attitudes and actions that outsiders regard as illogical and as barriers to efficiency and progress. This naturally leads to the outsiders becoming frustrated, and unless they are especially perceptive and skillful in dealing with cross-cultural problems, they often exacerbate rather than mitigate the problem.

It is therefore important that when dealing with Mexicans, foreigners keep in mind that when they say they "understand" something, the implication is that they also approve of it; further clarification is necessary if this is not the case.

Confianza
(Cohn-fee-AHN-zah)

"Living on Trust"

Historically, life in Mexico was not based on a rational, objective concept of right and wrong, or on laws founded on such concepts as equality and justice for all. Laws were primarily designed—and always enforced—to preserve and protect the religious and civil authorities in power, which meant they were generally used to oppress attitudes the authorities considered threatening, and to control all behavior judged as dangerous to the state and church.

Because both the church and the state were adversaries of the people, the only viable choice the people had was to turn inward, to depend upon their families, close-knit groups and connections, not only to protect themselves but also to do things they could not do as individuals.

In this context, the sense of family and community became especially strong. Conformity to the mores of the group was essential for maintaining good relations. A stylized etiquette based on the careful recognition of age, sex and social status became an integral part of the system, essentially replacing the universal concept of right and wrong as the prevailing morality.

The personal characteristics needed to make this system as humane and as effective as possible were a strong sense of dignity and carefully programmed respect within families and groups. Because of the importance of group relationships, conforming to the prescribed etiquette often took precedence over what one actually did. This did not necessarily mean that individuals had to be scrupulously honest and candid in their dealings with each other or with outsiders. It meant only that they were expected to conform to the etiquette prescribed for each situation.

These traditional attitudes and behaviors are still characteristic of most Mexicans, and one of the keys to making the system work as well as it does is *confianza* (cohn-fee-AHN-zah) or "trust." Because both business and professional connections in Mexico are primarily based on personal relationships, the trust factor must be especially high for people to make commitments and to follow through on them.

Foreign businesspeople approaching Mexico for the first time invariably have to go through a period of building *confianza* on a personal level. Having a good product or service, charging good prices and offering good deals are important, but without the *confianza* factor such deals are not likely to get off the launching pad.

Building confidence with Mexican authorities and companies should not be taken lightly or be unduly hurried. It should be as well planned and as conscientiously carried out as any marketing program would be.

Of course, the key to building *confianza* in Mexico is to respect the customs as well as the feelings—and fears—of the people concerned, to conduct oneself in a dignified manner, to be honest and fair and candid, etc.

As a general rule, every foreign company approaching Mexico for the first time should employ the services of an experienced and reputable Mexican consultant to advise it on how to be culturally correct enough to succeed.

32

Corridas
(Coh-REE-dahs)

"The Truth About Bullfights"

The term "bullfight" is a misnomer, a mistranslation from the Spanish word *corrida* (coh-REE-dah), which means something like "the running of the bulls." When Mexicans use the word *corrida* (or when they use "bullfight," which they often do), they do not have in mind a "fight" in the English sense of the word.

In its Mexican context, *la corrida* is "a demonstration of human (read 'masculine') courage and skill against a wild animal." It is not meant to be a competition between two opponents, well-matched or not. It is a sacrifice; a blood ritual to demonstrate raw courage, fearlessness in the face of death and other manly virtues.

Foreigners who are not culturally conditioned in this concept generally find it difficult or impossible to understand or appreciate bullfighting, and most are appalled by what they perceive as the cruelty of the ceremony.

Modern-day psychologists have added a new twist to the traditional *corrida* ritual. They say that the bull is the masculine symbol, the horns representing the male organ. They say the bullfighter is the female symbol.

This may come as a surprise to many women who have viewed the spectacle, particularly to those who swoon over the bullfighters' masculine appearance and display of courage. But it is not a surprise to the bulls!

Bulls used in the fights are bred and trained for the ring, and are much larger, stronger and more fierce than ordinary bulls. They are never allowed to mate with cows but are deliberately teased by having cows near them, and go into the rings as frustrated virgins. Mario De La Fuente, who was impresario of the bullring in Nogales, Mexico, for many years, quipped: "That's why the bulls get so damned mad and try to gore the toreador!"

De La Fuente, who featured the greatest Mexican and Spanish bullfighters in his ring, bought his bulls from famed fighting bull farms in Jalisco, Estado de Mexico and San Luis Potosí.

On one occasion, when the toreador was famous and De La Fuente had made a point of getting an especially large, strong bull, the bull became ill the night before the fight. The next morning when De La Fuente went to the ring early, as was his custom before a bullfight, the bull couldn't get to its feet.

In a panic, De La Fuente telephoned his mayordomo, Don Nacho. He explained that every seat in the ring had been sold and that none of the other bulls were of sufficient quality to offer the famous fighter. He feared that the whole day was going to be a disaster if something couldn't be done.

Half an hour later Don Nacho showed up at the ring with a large bucket filled with water into which he had crushed and stirred several marijuana plants. He poured the whole contents of the bucket down the sick bull's throat.

Continued De La Fuente: "About three minutes later the bull rolled over onto its feet, snorted, got up and began attacking the stall walls. That afternoon we had one of the best *corridas* ever staged in Nogales!"

Bullfighting was introduced into Spain by the conquering Moors in the 12th century, and brought to Mexico by the conquering Spaniards in the 16th century. The earliest forms of the custom apparently originated on the island of Crete in ancient times.

In the first centuries of bullfighting in Spain it was an amateur "sport" and only the aristocracy were allowed to act as matadors. But so many of them were maimed and killed that in 1567 Pope Pius V issued a warning that any prince who allowed bullfighting in his territory would be excommunicated. Of course, the warning was ignored.

The first bullfight in Mexico was staged in Mexico City on August 13, 1529, only eight years after Hernán Cortés and his Indian allies destroyed the great capitol of Tenochtitlán, and with it the Aztec empire. By the mid-1700s bullfighting in Mexico had become an established profession and the national blood-sport.

Bullfights are always held in the late afternoons on Sundays. Apprentice bullfighters do their practicing on Thursdays, known as *Jueves Taurinos* or "Bullfight Thursdays."

Plaza Mexico, the bullring in Mexico City, is the largest bullring in the world, with seats for more than 50,000 people.

Visitors to Mexico who have a bullfight on their itinerary should keep in mind that it is not an entertainment sport in the sense of baseball or football, where the best team wins and the loser survives to play again another day.

In one sense *la corrida* is a duel between two highly trained antagonists. In another sense it is a blood sacrifice of a living creature; a ritual such as those traditionally practiced by priests in most of the world's religions. The religious custom of scourging one's self with needles, knives and various other objects, practiced in many Catholic countries around the world, is also akin to *la corrida*.

Most Mexican men often fantasize that they are toreadors or bullfighters, especially in their relationships with women. While they ordinarily—of course—do not kill women, they use them to demonstrate their courage,and masculinity, and expect women to sacrifice their lives to them and their children.

Like the matadors, Mexican men often put their lives on the line for their dignity and their honor, both of which derive from their maleness, a combination that often leads to individual as well as gang violence.

Despite foreign criticism, bullfighting continues to be one of the most popular spectator events in Mexico because it provides psychological release and fuels the cultural spirit of Mexicans by reaffirming their identity and stoking their pride.

There are some 150 cattle ranches in central and western Mexico that raise *ganada bravo* or "brave bulls" for the ring. From the day of their birth potential fighting bulls are kept isolated from people so they will react aggressively when finally confronted by them. Those that do not demonstrate a sufficient degree of fighting spirit are weeded out. Only the most aggressive bulls survive.

Inexperienced fans who applaud moves that real pros consider amateurish or cowardly are referred to as *villamelones*, literally "village melons," a nickname coined by one of Mexico's most famous matadors, who became a radio commentator on bullfights after retiring from the ring.

Diehard male fans who are angered by bad performances may show their disapproval by urinating in paper cups and throwing the cups at the matadors.

Cortesía
(Cohr-tay-SEE-ah)

"A Superior Side of Mexicans"

From 1521 until the 1960s, the common people of Mexico were physically oppressed, abused and otherwise mistreated by an arrogant, cruel government, and intellectually, emotionally and spiritually oppressed and abused by an equally arrogant and often cruel church. The concepts of fairness and justice were turned into tragic farce, making corruption in government the rule. This brainwashing and abuse on a national scale created a wide variety of contradictions in the character and personality of ordinary Mexicans.

It made them passive most of the time, but also subject to explosive outbursts of violence which were often even more senseless and cruel than what had traditionally been inflicted upon them by their government and religious overlords.

The same system created an overall view of male–female relations as romantic to an extreme degree. Women were bound to standards that would crush a saint. At the same time it charged the men with an irrational degree of sexuality, which often made their lives, as well as the lives of their wives and daughters and other women in general, a kind of hell, with women suffering the brunt of this warped cult of masculinity.

Over the generations, the mixed-blood descendents of Spanish–Indian interbreeding emulated the behavior of their Spanish forbearers, adopting their courtly manner as well as their sexist attitudes and behavior toward women, and toward all people lower then themselves.

Yet among the many legacies bequeathed to modern-day Mexicans by the Spanish, the courtly side of the Spanish culture was one of the few things of which the Spaniards could be proud.

In Mexico today, *cortesía* (cohr-tay-SEE-ah) or "courtesy" plays a central, vital role in the lives of people on every level of society, including poor urban males—the famous *pelados*—who carry their special brand of etiquette to extremes in desperate attempts to protect their masculine image. Just as *cortesía* means more than common courtesy to the poor *pelados*, it also means a great deal more to ordinary Mexicans, and grows in importance as one goes up the social scale.

In its full sense, *cortesía* means a high standard of refined, stylized manners, effusive hospitality to guests and a gentle and generous nature—all things that directly contradict the violent side of the Mexican character. When Mexicans are at peace with themselves and with others, it is this courteous and dignified face that they demonstrate to the outside world, and there are no warmer, finer people on earth.

The dignified courtesy that is typical of Mexicans contrasts sharply with the loose, casual behavior that is characteristic of many Americans, and creates some friction. Most Americans newly arrived in Mexico go through a period of feeling a bit awkward, and sometimes very ill at ease, in contending with the traditional *cortesía*.

The hospitality of Mexicans, including those who are pitifully poor, is often so generous that it can be disconcerting to more sensitive visitors. In the poorest of homes and under the worst of conditions, welcoming guests with drinks, and often food, and treating them with ceremonial politeness is built into the character of Mexicans.

At the same time, the unrefined and, from the Mexican viewpoint, frequently discourteous behavior of foreigners lowers them considerably in the eyes of Mexicans.

It is important to keep in mind that proper behavior in Mexico includes polite speech, the correct use of the language and a high standard of formalities such as hand-shaking and the *abrazo*.

Yet like the Asians, Mexicans in crowded urban areas follow a strict form of courtesy only when the situation is personal. Mexican men in particular can be rude, callous and uncaring where the general public is concerned—witness typical behavior in the streets and in drinking places.

Foreigners whose image of Mexicans is based on movies, the news media and experiences along the U.S.–Mexican border invariably have an image that does not apply to most Mexicans. For those who go beyond the border and the popular image of Mexicans, exposure to the tradition of Mexican *cortesía* can be one of the most emotionally and intellectually satisfying experiences possible. *Cortesía* adds a dimension to life in Mexico that exercises a subtle but powerful magnetic force to the culture which, once experienced, is never forgotten.

Cortesía extends to dress also. To the Spanish conquistadors, formal dress was the mark of a gentlemen. As colonization and miscegenation progressed hand-in-hand, the wearing of a coat and tie by the *gachupines* and *criollos* became a cult, a mark of caste.

Over the centuries the custom spread downward to include all men who had any pretensions of social status. Today middle- and upper-class Mexican men are noted for being unusually fashion conscious.

Of course, Mexican men, particularly young bachelors, have been dramatically affected by Mexico's ongoing social revolution. Their behavior has changed, along with what they typically wear. A more casual approach to male attire began to creep in during the 1960s and 1970s and it is now common to see affluent men, particularly young men, in public without ties or coats. These days middle- and upper-class young Mexicans dress very much like Americans.

The famed resort city of Acapulco was a leader in introducing informality in men's wear back in the 1960s, posting signs saying "Go Casual" in a program to make casual wear the uniform of the day for everyone.

But wherever one is in Mexico, the level of courtesy is high, and should be followed by visitors.

Coyotes
(Coh-YOH-tehs)

"The Border Spirits"

In 1986 the U.S. Congress passed a law making it possible for some three million Mexicans who were in the country illegally to become American citizens. Most of the Mexicans covered by this law had been in the United States for many years, in some cases for two generations.

Shortly after this new law went into effect, Mexicans coming into the United States illegally in search of work went from a flood to a tidal wave. A huge network of border-crossing guides, "safe houses" and other clandestine operations, generating millions of dollars a year in income, were spawned as a result.

Guides who specialize in smuggling illegal immigrants and undocumented workers across the border are known as *coyotes* (coh-YOH-tehs) in Spanish because of their knowledge of the back trails and their ability to operate virtually under the noses of immigration officials and border patrols. These "people smugglers" came into existence in the 1920s when the border was closed to casual crossings.

Use of the word *coyote* to describe the people smugglers has deep significance to Mexicans. In Mexican mythology *coyotes* are cunning creatures that have supernatural powers which allow them to pass in the night without being seen, and to transport people into their dimensions.

The sudden increase in demand for illegal crossings in the 1980s turned the profession of the *coyote* into a growth industry. By the early 1990s there were thousands of them, ranging from teenage boys to grandparents.

The *coyotes* not only smuggled illegal job searchers into the country through tunnels and holes in fences and via out-of-the-way trails in desert and mountain areas, many became as sophisticated as professional espionage agents, preparing fake identification papers of all kinds, from birth certificates and marriage licenses to work permits.

Many *coyotes* have become so brazen that they are no longer discreet about offering their services. Dozens of them can be seen and heard daily; they line the streets outside of border immigration offices, shouting out to Mexicans who have been turned away by immigration officials because they have no work permits, or their documents were not valid and so on.

Not surprisingly, the demand for *coyotes* and the amount of money that could be made in a few hours (fees go up to what are astronomical figures for poor Mexicans when "delivery" is to a distant inland city) also attracted a criminal element that includes robbers and killers who prey on the trade.

The evil side of the genuine *coyote* is the *ratero*, literally "rat" but in this usage "robber," who specializes in taking advantage of victims by misleading, then robbing and sometimes killing them. The *rateros* are often small-time criminals, with connections to larger criminal groups. Some deal in drugs as well as human flesh. (It may be the term *ratero* came into use because in the early days the most common way of getting into the United States illegally was via rat-infested tunnels.)

Many *rateros* gather at bus stations in the interior of Mexico, where people start their journey to the United States, and con their victims with lies and exaggerated claims about their ability to get workers across the border.

Some *rateros* have been known to collect their fees from their human cargoes and then deliver them directly to U.S. Immigration officials.

There are American *coyotes* as well, but they are far fewer in numbers. The "legitimate" ones usually handle clients who have documents of one kind or another, and are attempting to come into the United States by passing through Immigration.

American *coyotes* generally prefer to help people who are flying to their destinations, because it is usually easier to get through airport immigration than it is through border posts.

Some American *coyotes* limit themselves to picking up the illegals after they cross the border, and driving them to their destinations. One of the requirements of these drivers is that they have newer, clean-looking cars so there will be less chance of them being stopped by immigration officials or the highway patrol.

Mexican *coyotes* who live in the border towns where they operate often become known to the Mexican police, and regularly pay them off to avoid being arrested.

More professional *coyotes* continue to operate behind the scenes through a network of contacts that extend deep into Mexico and into the United States and Canada. They don't advertise themselves. Their "customers" come to them through introductions.

The city of Juárez in the state of Chihuahua, across from El Paso, Texas, has its own version of *coyotes*. These are young men called *pasadores* or "guides," who help Mexicans cross the Rio Grande illegally. Until a human blockade of U.S. Border Patrol agents was established in 1993, most crossings took place only a hundred yards away from the legal immigration checkpoint.

Guides in Juárez say they call themselves *pasadores* because they work only during the day, and they never take people through mountains or across deserts, as the *coyotes* do in other areas.

Clients of the *pasadores* are people who don't want to get themselves or their clothes wet crossing the river—businessmen, office workers and others crossing for appointments or some other purpose. They are ferried across on rubber boats, rafts and sometimes inner tubes. Operators of the boats and rafts are called *lancheros* or "ferrymen."

Until 1993 as many as 10,000 people a day crossed illegally into El Paso from Juárez. Most of these were residents of Juárez who had jobs or family in El Paso. Others included people from Central and South America. In 1993 the U.S. Border Patrol established a 24-hour blockade, stationing agents within sight of each other along a 20-mile section of the Rio Grande; as a result the number of illegal entrants has been reduced to an estimated 1,000 a day.

Pasadores take some of the illegal entrants only as far as the railroad tracks on the river side of El Paso. Other entrants who speak no English and can afford the cost retain *pasadores* to accompany them to their final destination, wherever it is in the United States or Canada.

Pasadores say they do not get paid until they have delivered their customers to their destinations safely, so there is no way they can cheat them.

A number of *pasadores* claim that in earlier years they were the victims of sting operations conducted by undercover Mexican-American immigration agents who crossed into Mexico, got the guides to take them to some inland city (at the expense of the guides) and them arrested them.

Most of the *pasadores* have been picked up by *migra* (short for *migraciones* or immigration officials) any number of times. "As long as you don't run or cause them any kind of trouble they just hold you for an hour or so and then haul you back across the border," said one.

Illegals who cannot afford to pay for the services of *pasadores*, or don't want to pay them, have traditionally waded across the Rio Grande when it was low and swam across it when it was high—thus the term *mojados* or "wet ones," i.e., "wetbacks." Another term used in reference to illegal entrants is *alambistas*, literally "wire ones," from the wire fences separating Mexico and the United States in many inhabited areas.

In the mid-1990s by some estimates there were as many as five million Mexicans crossing into the United States illegally each year, many of them making the crossing several times each year to visit their families or to take care of emergencies, and when they were in between jobs.

Many illegal entrants literally commute back and forth. All are at the mercy of their employers and any contacts they might make. Said one: "Mexican border police also steal from those returning without papers. They know they have them in a vice."

Most Mexicans who are in the United States illegally say they are there just for the money, that they are Mexicans, will always be Mexicans, and will go home permanently as soon as they can find jobs in Mexico that will pay enough for them to live on.

In addition to its "people smuggler" context, *coyote* is also commonly used in reference to businessmen who cannot be trusted, and to people who are clever but sneaky in the way they do things, and always hungry.

During Mexico's colonial period under Spain (1521–1821), the offspring of parents with a 13-part combination of Spanish, Indian and African blood were officially designated as *coyotes*. In later years anyone with mixed blood was sometimes referred to as a *coyote*.

(See **Los Pollos.**)

Criollos
(Cree-OH-yohs)

"People of Color"

The Spanish era in Mexico officially began in 1521, less than 30 years after Columbus returned to Spain with stories of the amazing new world he had discovered.

Over the next several decades the government of Spain established a system to administer the huge land that had fallen into its hands. At the time of the conquest of Mexico by Cortés, Spain had a population of about eight million, while Mexico was inhabited by some 25 million people. Mexico was also considerably larger than Spain in land area.

In a carefully calculated move to ensure the loyalty of its colonial administrators in Mexico, the Spanish government followed a strict policy of appointing only European-born Spaniards to all of the key posts in "New Spain," as Mexico came to be called.

Thus, with two exceptions during Spain's 300-year reign, Spaniards born in Mexico were automatically excluded from succeeding their parents as the elite of New Spain. Mexican-born Spaniards could inherit the wealth of their fathers but could not hold political power. (The two exceptions were the sons of viceroys born in Mexico during their fathers' tours of duty. Both were raised and educated in Spain and were later appointed to the prestigious position their fathers had held.)

Before long, Spain's political discrimination against Mexican-born Spaniards became social as well. In order to distinguish between European-born Spaniards and Spaniards born in Mexico, the latter came to be known as *criollos* (cree-OH-yohs), or "Those of color"—in this case, white* (to distinguish them from the growing number of mixed-bloods and the surviving Indians).

Most of the *criollos* of Mexico were born into wealth. The men were generally haughty, vain and contemptuous of both work and anyone outside of their own group. They spent their time in idleness, intrigue and the pursuit of pleasure. Historians say the important things in the lives of the *criollos* were sex, highly stylized etiquette, resplendent uniforms, vendettas, cards and bullfights.

Many *criollos*, often more so than European-born Spaniards, discriminated against the mixed-blood and Indian population of Mexico with special vehemence in an effort to distance themselves from these downtrodden people.

After a number of generations the *criollos* began calling themselves *Americanos* in order to further distance themselves from the various class labels and from Spain as well. Therefore they were the first people on the North American continent to be known as Americans, although the label was unofficial.

By the end of the 18th century, when the coffers of Spain had become depleted by wars and corruption was rampant in both Mexico and Spain, rich *criollos* began buying titles and public offices for themselves, but they still had no political power. Even mixed-bloods who had money could buy certificates from the king of Spain which legally recognized them as "white."

By 1810 there were an estimated one million *criollos* in Mexico, as opposed to some 80,000 European-born Spanish administrators. And in the

---

* The original meaning of *criollo*, "Creole" in English, was any person of European descent born in the West Indies or Spanish America. It later came to be applied to people descended from the original French settlers of the southern United States, especially Louisiana. Later, it was applied to people culturally related to the Spanish and Portuguese settlers of the Gulf states. Eventually, it also came to mean mixed European and black Africans who spoke a Creole dialect. When written with a small "c" it also applies to cooking with a spicy sauce.

almost 300 years that had passed since the beginning of the Spanish era, Spain had become as remote to most of them as any other foreign land.

Inspired by the American and French revolutions, the *criollos* of Mexico began to talk of freedom from Spain. Finally, after Napoleon conquered Spain in 1808, a small group of more militant *criollos* made the first coordinated move. They kidnapped the ruling Spanish viceroy and put him on a ship bound for Spain.

A full-scale rebellion against the Spanish administrators, led by a second-generation *criollo* priest named Miguel Hidalgo, broke out on September 16, 1810. Hidalgo was quickly betrayed to the Spanish authorities, however, and was executed. But the rebellion continued, at first led by both mixed races (*mestizos*) and *criollos*.

Over the next 11 years Mexico was drenched with blood. By the time the last of the Spanish overlords and their armies had been defeated, the rebellion had been taken over by *criollo* leaders of the rebel armies and church leaders.

Mexico was politically free from Spain, but the lives of the majority of the population—the *mestizos* and the Indians—changed hardly at all. They were to remain slaves in all but name to their new *criollo* overlords for another 100 years.

Today, Mexicans whose racial ancestry is pure Spanish account for less than two percent of the population.

Culpa
(COOL-pah)

"Blaming the Spirits"

Mexicans take special pride in the fact that their culture emphasizes a casual, laid-back approach to life and a preponderance of personal pleasure, which they attribute to the superior nature of their culture.

On the other hand, cynics might be inclined to credit a failing in Mexican culture rather than its superiority for this and other distinctive features of the Mexican lifestyle. These cynics are likely to point out that

Mexicans have traditionally been less than ambitious, and overly attached to talking, singing, dancing and festivals, and otherwise using up time in "non-productive" ways because they were conditioned to believe that the gods and spirits were responsible for their lives; that everything that happened was preordained.

The other side of this belief was that they could not be blamed for "bad" things that they did, that they caused, or that they allowed to happen; that there could be no *culpa* (COOL-pah) or "fault" because all things were in the hands of unseen, uncontrollable spirits.

Over the centuries, this rationalizing away of *culpa* was a key factor in the destructive and otherwise harmful behavior that took place in Mexico, on an individual as well as an institutional basis. Where there was no *culpa* there was no guilt.

Men abused women and had their way with them because they were compelled to do so by the nature of their sexuality, so there was no *culpa*. Drivers speeding on crowded streets and unsafe highways had accidents but did not blame themselves because they were expressing their god-given nature. Whether or not there was any human agency involved, things happened "by themselves."

This philosophy is at the root of the political, economic and social evils that have historically plagued Mexico. It helped make people passive and patient. It discouraged them from being critical and from taking constructive action to prevent future mishaps.

Lack of a strong sense of *culpa* is still a significant factor in the lives of Mexicans today. The inertia that it creates is a tremendous drag in both business and politics, making it doubly hard for managers and officials to achieve their goals.

The one big change from earlier times is that businesspeople, workers and politicians generally blame other people rather than spirits for their failures.

There are occasions when foreign businesspeople in Mexico are less handicapped by the traditional no-fault syndrome than their Mexican counterparts, because Mexican employees who go to work for foreign enterprises expect to change their way of thinking and doing things, and are therefore more amenable to being reprogrammed.

Veteran expatriate managers in Mexico advise newcomers to take advantage of this situation by having all new employees go through a training and reorientation program which emphasizes the role and importance of everyone accepting responsibility for their own actions. A main point in these reorientation programs is that reacting to *culpa* in a positive way will be rewarded rather than punished.

Culpa / Vergüenza

(COOL-pah / Bayr-GWAIN-zah)

"Guilt Versus Shame"

Most people raised in the beliefs of the Christian Church live in "guilt cultures," meaning that they have been conditioned to obey civic and ecclesiastical laws because of an abiding sense of personal guilt. This sense of guilt has its origins in the Christian tenets that those who disobey the laws of God and man will be damned to eternal punishment in Hell. In some people the sense of guilt is so strong that they suffer terribly for even minor offenses, and oftentimes for things that should not be regarded as offenses in the first place. The suffering inflicted upon so many people, especially women, for centuries over guilt feelings caused by sex taboos is one of the great tragedies of the Christian (and Muslim) worlds.

As horrible as guilt cultures can be, they have some advantages over other types of cultures because the threat of psychological suffering they impose upon people becomes a powerful internal governor which compels them to do the "right thing" even when no one is watching and when there is no danger of them being found out and punished by earthly powers.

Surprisingly, Mexico has a "shame culture" rather than a "guilt culture," despite the omnipresence and omnipotence of the Catholic Church from the beginning of the Spanish period in the 1520s until the 1920s.

The only ready explanation for this remarkable fact is that both the beliefs and practices of the overwhelming majority of the Catholic priests, who virtually ruled Mexico for some 400 years after the Aztec empire fell to Spanish conquistadors, were so corrupt, so unjust and so anti-human in general that guilt became meaningless to those who set the cultural standards as well as to those they ruled over.

The Catholic Church was not the only corrupting influence on Mexican culture. Historians say that all but two of the 51 Spanish viceroys who ruled Mexican in tandem with the Catholic Church from the 1530s until 1821 were either incompetent or corrupt, or both, and generally speaking, the values and morals of the Spanish colonials as a whole were anything but Christian.

In any event, the twin authoritarian regimes established in Mexico by the Spanish administrators and the Catholic Church resulted in a society in which *vergüenza* (bayr-GWAIN-zah) or "shame" was a far more powerful factor than *culpa* (COOL-pa) or "guilt."

In a guilt-based society, individual conscience counts the most. In a shame culture, appearances are what count. As long as a person is not shamed by his or her own behavior or by the behavior of someone else, he or she does not necessarily suffer any remorse based on personal moral judgments.

Thus, generally speaking, Mexican morality has traditionally been based on face, image and reputation rather than Christian concepts of sin or man-made laws. What people said and how they presented themselves often took precedence over what they actually did. Mexicans feared social humiliation more than anything else.

Therefore, morality came to be equated with abiding by strict rules of etiquette, which left an enormous gap in actions that were not limited or restrained by any moral conscience. The important thing was social consequence.

Sociologists say that present-day Mexicans have virtually no concept of a bad conscience or guilt feelings; that as long as they fulfill their responsibilities to others they are not plagued by a guilty conscience no matter what they do. In other words, say the sociologists, the Mexican conscience does not act as a watchdog, or punish them for wrongdoing.

Within Mexico's shame culture, what can be *seen* is important; therefore things must appear right or normal. What cannot be seen, what is behind the scenes, is nobody's business but your own.

The Mexican conscience is also described as external, not internal. When Mexicans do something that is "wrong," it is invariably blamed on some outside force. Even in minor incidents, such as dropping and breaking a glass, the blame is shifted—*se rompió* literally translates as "it broke itself."

Much of the violence that has marked Mexican history, from sexual abuse of women to shootouts in *pulquerias*, can be linked to the shame culture. The common use of cruel torture by police and the gratuitous savagery of criminal gangs are symptoms of the absence of deeply ingrained guilt feelings.

Arrogance, bragging or any show of pride is taboo in a shame culture. Nothing upsets Mexicans more than exhibitions of these qualities, and as luck would have it a great deal of the normal behavior of North Americans comes across to Mexicans as arrogance or prideful boasting.

It is typical of even the most talented and accomplished Mexicans to maintain a humble attitude, downplaying their abilities and accomplishments; again, behavior that is just the opposite of what is common in the United States and elsewhere.

Foreign businesspeople aiming to do business with Mexico should keep in mind that expressions of humility will take them much further than bragging, which Mexicans regard as shameful behavior.

Being thought of as *sin vergüenza* or "without shame" is about as low as you can get in Mexico. To be shamed is about the worst thing that can happen to a Mexican.

The Mexican custom of apologizing for what often seems like anything and everything, which foreigners typically take as indicative of inability, lack of confidence or some other kind of weakness, is their way of avoiding any appearance of bragging or pride.

(There is a well-known saying in Mexico to the effect that it is not a shame to kill; but to kill and get caught is a shame—*Robar no es vergüenza. Robar y que lo agarran es vergüenza.*)

Curanderas
(Coo-rahn-DAY-rahs)

"Modern Medicine Women"

Like their North American and Canadian counterparts, Mexico's Indian tribes and nations traditionally had their medicine men and medicine women—specialists who were trained from childhood to treat both the physical and psychological ills of their people.

Interestingly, most healers in Mexico have traditionally been *curanderas* (coo-rahn-DAY-rahs) or "medicine women," possibly because one of their primary activities was serving as midwives. Among the North American Indian tribes healers have always been *curanderos* or "medicine men," sometimes called shamans in English.

In addition to using a wide range of herbs, tree leaves, bark, sap and other natural substances to treat injuries, infections and other physical ailments, the *curanderas* and *curanderos* of Mexico used osteopathy, placebos and hypnotic suggestion to effect cures.

Virtually all of the herbal medicines used by Mexico's traditional healers had been well-known folk remedies for untold centuries, and since early times were often applied by the patient themselves.

Most medicine men and women, therefore, specialized primarily in getting rid of evil spirits and magic spells, ailments that abounded in the spirit- and supernatural-oriented world of the Indians. (There is a saying in Spanish that *curanderos* are "part doctor, part poet and a little crazy"—*De medico, poeta y loco, todos tenemos un poco.*)

In Spanish folklore, passed on to Mexico, mysterious winds called *los aires* (lohs EYE-rays) were believed to be the cause of many of the ailments that afflicted people. Belief in *los aires* is still strong in parts of Mexico, and many *curandera* cures involve counteracting the evil influence of "the winds."

Some of the ancient Indians rituals not directly related to curing ceremonies were designed to keep people in mental harmony with the cosmos, thereby preventing illnesses from developing in the first place, and were thus preventive therapy. Most of the industrialized world has left these rituals by the wayside.

Still, among Mexico's Indians today, shamans in particular are the caretakers and teachers of the culture, and are responsible for the mental and physical health of the people.

One of the duties of the shamans of the Huichol tribe of Indians is to lead an annual pilgrimage to Wirikuta, several hundred miles away on the desert plains of Zacatecas, in order to search for peyote for their sacred rituals. In peyote trances, the Huichol commune directly with their gods.

The services of Mexico's numerous *curanderas* are still in demand not only by Indians and Indianized mixed-bloods but also by a growing number of modernized people who recognize that true health involves the mind as well as the body, and who continue to believe in the power of the medicine women.

Along the U.S.–Mexican border the word *curandera* has long been abbreviated to *cura*, which refers to healing or curing (by priests as well as medicine women). *Cura* is used as a nickname for heroin as well. There is an *hierbera* or herbalist in virtually every Mexican community of any size.

More and more mainstream doctors in North America are accepting the evidence that most human ailments, other than physical trauma, have a psychological element, and that treating the mind is as important as treating the body. This reorientation is resulting in new interest in the beliefs and practices of Indian shamans of Arizona, especially Hopi and Navajo medicine men, as well as the *curanderas* and *curanderos* of Mexico.

A successful Mexican businessman who was educated in the United States commented: "The use of natural herbs is growing in popularity both in the U.S. and in Mexico because the treatments work and they are less expensive than modern medicine."

Another traditional figure that is still common in rural Mexico is the *bruja* (BROO-hah) or female witch, and there is a fairly close relationship between *curanderas* and *brujas*.

Brujas specialize in putting on spells and in taking them off, as well as practicing herbal healing. They deal in spells having to do with love as well as health.

People who feel their luck or health has been made to suffer from an evil eye spell generally go to *curanderas* or *brujas* for a treatment that is known as *limpias* (LEEM-pee-ahs).

A *limpia* treatment is a spiritual and psychological "cleansing" which often consists of a combination of beaten eggs and herbs being brushed on the patient's body.

Dedazo
(Day-DAH-zoh)

"Cutting off the Finger"

When Mexico's *Partido Revolucionario Institucional* (PRI) or Institutional Revolutionary Party took over the government in 1929 it guaranteed that it would stay in power by developing a one-party system in which sitting presidents appointed not only their successors but every other political candidate in the country down to city mayors—making elections nothing more than a sham.

In common parlance, the sitting president appointed his successor and other officials by "pointing his royal finger" at them. Spanish for finger (or toe) is *dedo* (DAY-doh). Thus this succession process came to be known as *Dedazo* (day-DAH-zoh) or "The Institution of the Finger."

The first PRI candidate to propose reforming "The Finger" system was Luis Donaldo Colosio, but he was assassinated during a campaign rally in March 1994.

Ernesto Zedillo, the candidate chosen to replace Colosio, astounded Mexicans in August 1994 by promising that if elected he would "cut" the Finger off, and bring truly democratic elections to Mexico for the first time in the history of the country.

Zedillo won the presidency in what was regarded by foreign observers as the most honest election ever held in Mexico. In addition to allowing opposition candidates who were elected to assume their offices, he also appointed a number of opposition leaders to his cabinet.

Mexico's transition from an oligarchy to a democracy is not expected to go smoothly, however. Colosio's assassination, reportedly ordered by PRI hardliners, was followed by a wave of political agitation and the murder of a high-placed government official who was said to have been involved in the conspiracy.

Cynics claim that it is too early to count *Dedazo* out, and that it will continue to operate behind the scenes for the foreseeable future, not only because of resistance from PRI hardliners, but also because it has been the custom for centuries for people in power to appoint their friends and supporters to important posts. The practice is not likely to disappear any time soon.

In any event, local as well as national political power in Mexico has traditionally been in the hands of a few elite families whose members have monopolized virtually all of the key offices from one generation to the next.

This pattern will not likely be broken until political and economic reforms have leveled the playing field.

Other colloquial meanings of *dedo* include "informer" and "fink."

Día de las Madres
(Dee-ah day lahs MAH-drehs)

"The Country of Mothers"

One of the most provocative comments I have ever heard a Mexican make about Mexico is "Mexico is a country of mothers. Mothers are the most important people in Mexico!"

I was momentarily surprised by this statement because it was made by a man and because I had always automatically viewed the male chauvinistic elements in Mexican society as overpowering, and Mexican mothers as especially oppressed.

I immediately reminded myself that my Mexican colleague was naturally speaking from his own cultural viewpoint, while my reaction was typically American. I also realized in the same instant that what my friend was saying went far beyond a one-dimensional perception.

He was saying that it is mothers who have been the cement of Mexican society, holding it together and giving it its flavor, materially and spiritually, despite all of the irrationalities and violence they have suffered in the past.

He was saying that the goodwill, generosity and hospitality for which ordinary Mexicans have long been famous are a result of the moral teachings and examples set by Mexico's mothers. He was also saying that if Mexico is to flourish in the future, a great deal of the credit will belong to its mothers.

The man who made the comment to me was well known for being a "real Mexican," meaning that he believes in and follows the code of *machismo* where the treatment of women, drinking and other traditional Mexican male customs are concerned.

His view of the kind of machismo that he practices is totally positive. He is not violent; he is kind, generous and protective toward women; he is a gentleman in the best sense of the word, and also a champion of woman's rights—of course, "rights" as he sees them.

Where he differs from the beliefs and behavior that are now common among men and women in the United States is that he believes absolutely that there *is* a man's world and a woman's world, and that there are differences between them that are natural and which should be held sacred. His view is that when these differences are ignored and when attempts are made to merge these two worlds, it destroys the most fundamental foundation of society.

This does not mean he believes women should concern themselves only with motherhood and housework. He says that Mexico will not be able to resolve its political, economic and social problems without the participation of women. His philosophy is that the quality of a society is based on an equilibrium between feminine and masculine contributions, and that if either of these elements are weak or missing, society cannot function smoothly.

He used Mexico's famous *Dia de las Madres* (DEE-ah day lahs MAH-drehs) or "Mother's Day" to illustrate the vital role that mothers have historically played in Mexican society, crediting mothers with being responsible for most of the positive attributes of Mexican culture, and showing the extent to which they are honored.

Dia de las Madres is certainly a celebration of all that is good about motherhood in Mexico. Throughout Mexico it is customary for young people to gather in groups on the evening of May 9, the day before Mother's Day, and beginning at midnight on May 10, to visit the homes of respective members of the group to serenade their mothers.

The mothers prepare buffets of favorite foods and provide drinks for the carolers, turning each stop into a party. If there are 10 or 12 members in a group it is often 5 or 6 A.M. in the morning before they finish.

Just as impressive as the sentiments demonstrated by celebrating a special day for mothers is the fact that virtually all Mexicans can and do sing, and that within a group of only five or six friends there is invariably one or more who plays the guitar with enviable skill.

All things considered, Mexico would almost likely be a savage and unfriendly country if it were not for the special character, tolerance and forbearance of its mothers.

The word *madre* by itself is an exalted word, a word that embodies virtually all that is both good and bad in Mexican culture; profane one moment and sacred the next.

(See **Chingar, La Iglesia, Machismo, Malas Mujeres, Mujeres**.)

Día De Los Muertos
(Dee-ah day lohs MWERE-tohs)

"The Day of the Dead"

Before the coming of the Spanish conquistadors, most Mexican Indians lived with death as a constant companion—death not only from natural causes but also from institutionalized wars, religious sacrifices and a justice system in which punishment for relatively minor infractions was execution.

In the Indian cosmos the spirits of the dead remained among the living, to be acknowledged and communed with through rituals of song, dance, food and blood sacrifices.

Today, reminders of death are still a constant in Mexican life, from bullfights and homicides to religious icons representing death in practically every form imaginable.

Death cannot be avoided, so Mexicans make the most of it in an effort to demonstrate that they do not fear it and are determined not to let it destroy the joys of living. Rather than ignore it or attempt to hide from it, Mexicans joke about it as if it were a comic ritual.

Most of the ceremonial recognition of the dead by Mexicans no doubt had its origin in the dim past, when such rituals were designed to please and placate the spirits of departed family members, ancestors and even enemies.

Now, like Christmas and other ancient rituals that have been modernized to the point that they are more secular than religious, Mexico's *Dia de los Muertos* (Dee-ah day day lohs MWERE-tohs) or "Day of the Dead" often appears to be more of a commercial celebration than a spiritual ritual.

Dia de los Muertos is held each year on November 2, and is a major national holiday. For several weeks prior to the event, bakeries throughout the country are busy creating breads and sweets in the shape of skulls, skeletons and other symbols of death. Toy makers and others turn out tiny coffins and papier mâché skeletons* by the millions.

Some people construct altars in their homes, offices, work places and cemeteries—decorating them with marigold-like flowers—to hold offerings of food, fruit, photos of religious figures, dead relatives and so on.

The days of the great Aztec empire are recalled by outdoor markets literally overflowing with marigolds, which the Aztecs considered sacred to the dead. They are still called *flores de los muertos* or "flowers of the dead."

Beginning on the eve of November 2, Mexican families adorn their altars or kitchen tables with the favorite foods of dead family members. Many also take food to the cemeteries where deceased family members are buried. Spirits of the dead are believed to return on this day to visit the homes of those still living, and while there they absorb the spirit of the food that has been prepared for them.

After returning from the cemetery and praying before the altars, people eat "the material substance" of the food in a party-like atmosphere.

Drinking alcoholic beverages is a regular part of this ritual, adding to the festive, and sometimes wild, nature of the celebration. (All Mexicans fiestas, says Mexican writer-poet Octavio Paz, are a time for getting drunk, sharing confidences, crying, laughing and killing.)

While the central theme is the same, Day of the Dead celebrations differ widely in various parts of Mexico.

Las calaveras (lahs cah-lah-BAY-rahs) or "skeletons" have traditionally been used in cartoons and skits to ridicule politicians, artists and famous people in general.

Dignidad
(Deeg-nee-DAHD)

"The Importance of Dignity"

When authoritarian governments and religions deny human beings the opportunity and right to develop their own personal attitudes and behavior, people always compensate by going to the extreme in any number of directions. Because this denial results in internalized frustration and anger, these extremes in behavior invariably include a great capacity for emotional outbursts which can range from poetic to violent.

Mexico's Indian nations, particularly the Aztecs, were as noted for their poetry, music and singing as they were for their religious savagery. The Spaniards who colonized Mexico and created a new hybrid Spanish–Indian race and culture were equally ambivalent—highly religious on one hand and unspeakably cruel on the other.

Such ambivalent cultures invariably breed an extraordinary sense of personal *dignidad* (deeg-nee-DAHD) or "dignity," and an unbounded need for this dignity to be respected, regardless of the cost to the individual, family members, friends or strangers.

Another feature that is common to authoritarian societies that deny individual rights to their members is a highly refined system of etiquette based on hierarchical ranking and an exaggerated degree of respect. Thus Mexicans have traditionally been culturally programmed to demonstrate a high order of respect to their superiors and to be hypersensitive about their own dignity and the exaggerated consideration they expect in return.

The concern of Mexican men with their *dignidad* is a key element in their behavior, dress and manners, and especially in their living up to the masculine ideal incorporated in *machismo*, the so-called "cult of masculinity."

Mexicans must exercise extraordinary care not to damage the dignity of others; something that can be done very easily by such things as failing to address a person properly, making a remark that can be taken as a criticism, acting in some way that can be taken as a slight, not listening respectfully, interrupting someone when they are speaking, failing to praise a person's efforts, treating someone as if they were ignorant, and so on.

It often seems that the poorer and more desperate the situation of Mexicans, the more important their *dignidad* is to them, a factor that plays an especially important role in the behavior of peons as well as professional criminals.

Mexican society is hierarchical. Therefore, who one owes respect to and the kind of respect that is due is based on the relative positions of the individuals involved. In order to know what level and degree of respect to pay, and thereby to avoid damaging the other person's dignity, it is necessary to know the social status of the other person. This is not always easy to do and it is one of the reasons why Mexicans tend to be especially polite and respectful to strangers. Once the proper hierarchical rank has been established between people, they normally assume their appropriate place as equals or as inferiors and superiors.

One of the key aspects of becoming fluent in the Spanish language and in communicating nonverbally with Mexicans is knowing what the appropriate vocabulary and behavior is for all the different categories or levels of people one meets.

As it happens, behavior that is perfectly acceptable to many non-Mexicans—from speaking frankly and directly to acting in an aggressive manner—is often construed by Mexicans as being insensitive and arrogant and therefore an insult to their *dignidad*.

This is not to suggest that Americans and others are so adversely programmed that they cannot communicate and commune effectively with Mexicans. Mexicans appreciate it when foreigners are well versed enough in their language and culture to interact with them on their own wavelength. However, they don't demand it.

In fact, it is not always advisable to "behave like a Mexican" when doing business in Mexico. Naturally enough, when Mexicans encounter someone who talks and acts like a Mexican they are likely to presume that the person accepts their values and that they can treat him or her like they treat other Mexicans.

Generally speaking, about the only rules that foreigners really should follow when dealing with Mexicans is to be polite in the normal sense of the word, refrain from bragging and overstating things, avoid irritating people with criticism that won't do any good and take a positive rather then a negative approach to all the problems they encounter.

_____ 43 _____

Don / Doña
Dohn / DOH-nyah)

"Master and Mistress"

Much of the style and charm of Mexican culture derives from a highly refined etiquette which originated in the Spanish court during the Middle Ages. A significant part of this etiquette sprang from the influence of the Catholic Church, whose appeal to the elite as well as to the masses was based as much on its formalized rituals as on its theology.

Of course, the primary purpose of this stylized etiquette was to distinguish between social classes, demonstrate respect to superiors and elders and provide a basis for all interpersonal behavior.

At first this etiquette was followed only by nobles, called *hidalgo* (ee-DAHL-go) and by other members of the court. It gradually spread downward to include provincial gentry and their families, titled knights and, finally, professional soldiers of rank.

When the Spanish conquistadors and Catholic bishops came to Mexico in the early 1500s they brought this traditional etiquette with them. In the next 300 years it became an integral part of the new Spanish–Indian culture of Mexico.

Thus one of the most conspicuous and important cultural attributes that Mexicans inherited from their Spanish forbearers was an inordinate attachment to formalities and a refined form of behavior that was often more important than what was said or done.

Part of the church and court etiquette transplanted to Mexico was the use of titles to categorize people, as well as to distinguish and honor them. In those centuries, if you did not have a title of some kind you were nobody. This resulted in a proliferation of grand-sounding *títulos* (TEE-too-lohs) or titles which even ordinary people might attach to their names.

The Spanish soldiers and fortune hunters who destroyed the Aztec empire and became the masters of Mexico were called *conquistadors*, a grandiose title that means "conquerors" (despite the fact that the people they conquered were mostly primitive tribesmen and hardly worthy opponents for the Spaniards).

In the social and political systems created in Mexico by the Spanish overlords, titles denoted professional position and rank as well as race, racial mixture and place of birth.

Among the most interesting and important of the titles brought from Spain to Mexico was *don* (dohn) and *doña* (DOH-nyah), used with the first names of selected men and women—as in Don Miguel and Doña Maria.

Don, in its original Latin form (dominus) means "master," "master of the house" or "lord." *Doña* is derived from the Latin word domina, which means "mistress of the house." During the medieval period in Spain these titles were used only in reference to members of the ruling nobility.

In the early generations of the Spanish regime in Mexico, *don* and *doña* were used in conjunction with men (and their wives) of Spanish blood who were ranking members of the colonial government. Over the centuries, their use gradually seeped downward to include men and women of any race or mixture who were leaders or prominent in virtually any level of society.

Today *don* and *doña* are honorific titles used when addressing older men and women as a sign of respect for their age, and for the wisdom and character that comes with a lifetime of experiences.

The terms may be used in addressing anyone, including ordinary store-keepers, supervisors and so on, but they are especially used when referring to or addressing a person who has achieved some prominence, at least in their community.

The titles may be preceded by either *señor* or *señora* (Señor Don Miguel or Señora Doña Maria), but they are never used in conjunction with last names.

Among other things, this custom contributes to older Mexicans continuing to feel like they are valued members of their families and society, and helps them age with dignity.

Generally speaking, it is necessary to know someone before addressing them as *don* or *doña* simply because it is a very personal thing that is culturally correct only when it is meant to show respect to someone you know well.

Close friends often use the titles in a jocular manner when addressing each other. In such cases flattery as well as respect may be mixed in, but such use is not taken as insincere or insidious if it is done in good humor.

The Mexican penchant for *títulos* has diminished somewhat in Mexico since the days of the colonial administrators and the dictator-generals who followed them, but it is still the prevailing etiquette, and is an important factor in operating effectively within the culture.

To some, the use of *don* and *doña* may appear old fashioned and pretentious, but it is a warm, intimate way of acknowledging other people that adds a great deal to the fullness and charm of Mexican life.

(In *pachuco*, the jargon that developed among Mexican-American youths in the American Southwest, *doña* has a number of additional meanings, including a woman who is especially formal and snooty in her behavior, the female genitals and the slang term "pussy.")

44

Educación
(Eh-doo-cah-cee-OWN)

"The Magic Word"

Throughout the last 220 years of the Spanish period in Mexico formal education, controlled by the Catholic Church, was officially denied to practically all Indians and most of the mixed-blood population as a means of political and social control and as a way of guaranteeing a source of workers who could be more easily kept in virtual bondage. It was the official attitude of the Catholic Church that education would result in the Indians and *mestizos* losing their faith and committing blasphemy.

While the revolution of 1810–1821 ended Mexico's colonial status under Spain, it was followed by another 100 years of mostly dictatorial rule by political and religious administrations, which paid practically no attention to public education.

It was not until well after Mexico's civil war (1910–1921), which pitted the poor and uneducated against the government and the church, that serious attention was given to providing basic education to the majority of Mexicans, including Indians who lived in less remote areas.

Today, *educación* (eh-doo-cah-cee-OWN), or "education," is a magic word in Mexico, but it is a different kind of education than what is common in the United States and Canada. In some ways Mexico's educational system closely resembles that of Japan.

School curriculum is controlled by the national government. Everybody who is at the same level studies the same thing at the same time. Discipline is strict in elementary schools and high schools, but lax in colleges and universities.

At the elementary and high school levels, the educational process is designed primarily for rote learning, and emphasizes passing examinations. Students are taught conformity and obedience to authority rather than how to act independently and solve problems. They are conditioned to remain passive and wait for instructions from their teachers.

This bureaucratized approach to education has led to some of the same kind of abuses in higher education in Mexico that are prevalent in Japan. Many students and professors at colleges and universities do not bother to attend class, and in Mexico there is widespread cheating on examinations, using *acordeones* or "hidden notes" (which, however, is extremely rare in Japan).

The authoritarian atmosphere in Mexico's elementary and high schools stifles the development of individualism, resulting in young people having a weak sense of personal responsibility. Generally speaking, Mexicans are conditioned from early childhood, both at home and in school, that form and style generally take precedence over substance. In other words, they are taught that how they do things is more important than what they do—exactly the opposite of North American convention.

Educational authorities contrast American and Mexican education by noting that in Mexico education emphasizes socialization, behavior and culture, while the American system emphasizes the accumulation of factual knowledge and raising the I.Q.

The Mexican educational emphasis on understanding and dealing with human relations naturally has a profound effect on all aspects of Mexican life, and it is particularly important for foreigners dealing with Mexico to understand this factor and learn how to cope with it in a diplomatic and effective manner.

One facet of this educational process that is especially subtle in some cases and very conspicuous in others is the way Mexicans regard equality. Mexicans focus on the social dimensions of equality, while Americans focus on its individual dimensions, a culture factor that also applies to Japan. (Also as in Japan, personal connections and political influence are routinely used by Mexican students to obtain the best jobs after graduation.)

Because Americans in general are virtually obsessed with the concepts of personal equality, the preference for social equality in Mexico often makes it difficult for Americans to understand and appreciate Mexican attitudes and behavior in business as well as in private affairs.

My Mexican friends make a special point of distinguishing one of the key differences between the Mexican and the North American concept of *educación,* a difference that emphasizes how easily cross-cultural misunderstandings can occur.

When Mexicans say "he (or she) doesn't have any education," (*no tiene educación*) they do not mean the person has not been schooled in math and so on. They mean he or she has not been taught or has not naturally absorbed the finer points of Mexican culture—good manners, respect for parents and other seniors, religious piety, loyalty to one's family, courage in the face of adversity, self-respect and a highly honed sense of dignity.

Fundamental changes in Mexico's educational system, for better or worse, are not likely to occur outside the cultural context, meaning that they will occur gradually over a period of decades or generations as the culture evolves.

Meanwhile, the current political, economic and social reforms that are taking place in Mexico are primarily the products of Mexicans who were educated abroad, along with other who were educated in Mexico but were greatly influenced by American and Anglo concepts.

45

Ejidos
(Eh-HE-dohs)

"Communal Farm Villages"

Millions of Mexicans have traditionally lived in small villages in rural areas and depended on farming for their livelihood. These villages were surrounded by tiny plots of land that were cultivated as cooperatives by the residents. These settlements, the villages as well as the land, were officially known as *ejidos* (eh-HE-dohs), which can be translated as "communal farm land." Along with the huge *haciendas*, *ejidos* were the classic farming pattern in Mexico from the days of the Spanish conquistadors.

Ejido is an ancient word that goes back to medieval times in Spain, when communal lands outside of castles, towns and villages were assigned to groups of farmers and stock raisers to provide food for the residents.

One of the most important economic reforms instituted following the end of Mexico's civil war (1910–1921) was to give thousands of peasants title to 20-hectare plots of land (*ejidos*).

In the 1930s Mexican socialists tried to combine the *ejidos* into large communist-style collectives, with the usual disastrous results.

When the collective system began breaking up in the 1940s and 1950s, wealthy entrepreneurs (often with financial backing from U.S. interests) swallowed up many of the *ejidos*, pulling them together as large, mechanized farms after the pattern that had developed in southern California, Arizona and Texas. They then began growing lettuce, tomatoes and other crops which were mostly exported to the United States, a system that continues today.

Most of the Mexican farm laborers who enter the United States, both legally and illegally, come from these *ejido* villages, as do many of the immigrants who end up as workers in factories, restaurants and other service industries.

In 1992 the Mexican government passed a new agrarian law making it possible for *ejidatarios* (members of *ejidos*) to own, lease and sell the land that represents their share of the total commune. The law also allowed them to use the land to raise capital for joint ventures.

While the purpose of the law was to unleash the energy and ambition that invariably accompanies newfound freedom after generations of oppression, some fear that it will more likely contribute to destitute farmers selling off their land to large export-oriented farm operations. This, the critics add, will not only result in a growing number of landless peasants reduced to working as *peones*, but also in the buildup of more of the huge *hacienda*-type land holdings that have long plagued Mexico.

46

El Barzón

(Ehl Bahr-ZOHN)

"The Farmers' Yoke"

In November 1994 in the Mexican state of Michoacan 200 angry men carried a coffin containing the body of a farmer into the local branch of one of the country's largest banks and left it in the bank lobby for two hours. The farmers said that a threat by the local branch of Serfin Bank to foreclose on the farmer's land had caused him to suffer a fatal heart attack.

This extraordinary gesture was part of a rapidly escalating confrontation between Mexico's farmers and the nation's banks, which had raised their annual interest rates on loans to as high as 100 percent or more as a result of a dramatic drop in the value of the peso.

One month later Mexico's economy crashed. The peso was devalued by 35 percent. Prices doubled, sales plummeted and businesses laid off workers or closed down entirely. The peso went into free fall.

In the following months Mexican farmers picketed more than 800 banks, resulting in the closing of some 200 of them, in an attempt to force banks to renegotiate their loans.

This was the first time in the history of Mexico that middle-class Mexican farmers and small businesspeople had united and successfully used the power of the picket and boycott to fight back against abuses by the country's archaic banking system.

The unifying force in this new type of people's revolution was an organization called *El Barzón* (ehl bahr-ZOHN), which literally means "The Ring," referring to the metal ring on a yoke (a crossbar with two U-shaped pieces of wood that encircle the necks of a pair of oxen). It may also mean the cutting edge of a plow.

El Barzón was founded to help prevent banks from foreclosing on farmers and small business owners who had taken out loans and who could not afford to pay the skyrocketing interest rates. By 1995 the national debtor's organization had more than half a million members, and it had begun to employ aggressive tactics in its battle against banks.

In addition to picketing banks and depositing dead bodies in their lobbies, *El Barzón* encouraged its members to default on their loans, bringing further pressure against the disintegrating banking system.

El Barzón activists provided members with legal advice and attorneys. Then, if a bank attempted to foreclose on the property of a member, the organization took direct action to prevent the bank from seizing the property.

Observers of the Mexican scene described the *El Barzón* phenomenon as a "middle-class guerrilla movement" which was more disruptive than armed uprisings by Zapatista rebels, because *El Barzón* members were educated, had resources, knew how to use the legal and financial system, had professional organizational skills and could operate openly.

Fueled by the continuation of the "Peso Shock" that struck Mexico in 1994–1995, membership in the *El Barzón* spiraled upward and it began to take on the appearance of a militant political party, with goals that went well beyond reducing high interest rates.

While viewed by old-guard elements in the ruling party as a serious threat that could lead to violence, *El Barzón* was supported by most Mexicans who saw it as a positive influence in forcing political and economic reforms on a hidebound, recalcitrant government.

The influence of *El Barzón* has continued to grow and has helped bring a measure of democracy to Mexico that was simply inconceivable in the past. To the country's embattled farmers and small business class, *El Barzón* has become something of a magic word.

47

El Error
(Ehl Eh-RROHR)

"Avoiding Errors"

Probably the biggest error that foreign companies make in planning to do business in Mexico is failing to properly train home-office executives and expatriate managers who are going to be in charge of the business.

Veteran foreign businesspeople in Mexico, as well as bilingual, bicultural Mexican consultants who work with foreign companies, say that the vast majority of foreigners who have been assigned to Mexico by their companies show up without having had any language or cultural training whatsoever.

The handicaps and hardships that this oversight causes also applies to the families of expatriate businesspeople. Most families of businesspeople assigned to Mexico are delighted with the idea, and see it as an adventure that they will enjoy, which often results in a culture shock that turns the experience into one long struggle to cope.

There is virtually no end to where these cultural curve balls can come from. The foreign executive who leaves it up to Mexican managers to innovate and take action on their own when problems arise is typically disappointed and frustrated, and the problems become worse because the managers, unless totally reoriented, will unusually not make decisions on their own.

Generally speaking, neither Mexican workers nor managers will come forward with their own ideas on how to improve a work or manufacturing process unless they have been reconditioned to think and act in rational, pragmatic and individualistic ways.

Another mistake that foreigners in Mexico make regularly is assuming that Mexican workers and managers who speak and understand English will think and behave like Americans or other foreigners.

While this may be true when the Mexicans concerned are taking to and interacting with foreigners, it generally is not true when they are interacting with other Mexicans. Even when they are capable of thinking like foreigners they must behave like Mexicans when they are interacting with them. Mexicans who are brash enough to think and act like foreigners when they are interacting with other Mexicans invariably find themselves ostracized and powerless.

One key cultural factor that plagues foreign businesspeople in Mexico is the reluctance of Mexicans to point out errors or mistakes. In Mexican culture, pointing out an *error* (eh-RROHR) can be a dangerous thing to do.

In the Mexican context of human and work relations, a warm, positive attitude takes precedence over virtually everything else. Telling a coworker that he or she made a mistake is likely to be taken personally and as an offense, thus disrupting the sensitive balance in human relations that is so important to Mexicans.

One way around this cultural problem is to place all workers in small, clearly identified teams, and make the teams rather than individuals responsible for catching and avoiding errors. With responsibility depersonalized in this manner, individuals are much less likely to feel threatened or offended when errors are noted.

Another advantage of the team approach at the workplace is that the traditional reluctance of Mexicans to compete with each other on an individual basis can generally be surmounted by putting competition on an intergroup level.

A number of foreign companies in Mexico also report that they have been able to get teams to accept decision-making responsibility, greatly improving the overall efficiency of their operations.

48

Embutes
(Ehm-BOO-tehs)

"Paying for Good News"

Mexican society traditionally functioned on the basis of personal relationships which were determined by race, rank and a variety of other factors that had little or nothing to with universal principles and guidelines.

Virtually all power and authority in the country was vested in government officials, municipal bureaucrats, the military and the clergy, all of whom generally used whatever power they had to benefit themselves and their friends in a personal way whenever and however possible. The concept of public service among government employees and officials was weak if it existed at all. Generally, elected or appointed officials, as well as career bureaucrats, could abuse their power without fear of being reprimanded by their superiors because such abuse was characteristic of the whole government system.

When people who were not members of these elite groups broke custom or law or needed and requested something from the system that it actually was supposed to provide, or even if they simply displeased someone in power, they were more or less at the mercy of individuals within the system. Getting things done in this environment, especially things requiring governmental approval, licenses or some other kind of official action, often depended on having the right *contactos* or "contacts" and/or paying off the right people.

This custom had so permeated Mexican culture by the end of the Spanish era in 1821 and the beginning of industrialization in the country in the late 1800s that it naturally carried over into the business world.

It was not until the 1990s that this situation began to change, and it was as a result of reforms first introduced by the Carlos Salinas administration (1988–1994) and then added to by the following Ernesto Zedillo administration.

Some Mexican businesspeople say they can now go directly to different government agencies and bureaus and get relatively fast responses from officials—most of the time. They add, however, that contacts are still of vital importance in Mexico, and that businesspeople must spend an inordinate amount of their time making and nurturing contacts in key places.

Another factor in both politics and business in Mexico is the traditional practice of paying *embutes* (ehm-BOO-tehs) or "bribes" to journalists and news media to suppress negative news and to ensure that only good or positive news is published (a custom that is also traditional in Korea and Japan).

Of course, the practice of businesspeople and politicians winning favor with journalists by showering them with favors, food, drinks, and often sex as well, is common throughout the world. However, in Mexico some reporters for larger, more influential publications have traditionally been paid *embute* retainers on a monthly basis, particularly during election periods when having the "right" reporters assigned to candidates could change the outcome of elections.

Mexican journalists who write popular columns have generally commanded the highest *embutes* (also known as *sobres* or "things under the table" and *igualas* or "retainers"). Another form of *embutes* is pocket money to spend during political jaunts.

The *embute* practice was particularly rampant during the early decades of the Institutionial Revolutionary Party (PRI), which was founded in 1929 and was still in power in the late 1990s.

Newspaper and magazine articles that are paid for by businesspeople and politicians to ensure that they get favorable publicity are known as *gacetillas* (gah-say TEE-yahs) and are published as if they were legitimate news reports. Reporters sometimes take the lead in suggesting topics for such articles.

Critics of this system say that the overall influence of Mexican newspapers is greatly reduced by the practice of the government "subsidizing friendly journalists" and controlling the placement of official advertising.

All Mexican presidents elected since 1988 have made commitments to end *embute*-type abuses, but like so many other facets of Mexican culture, the *embute* custom is so deeply entrenched that it is not likely to disappear any time soon.

The most powerful force now acting against corporations paying for favorable publicity is the refusal of some larger companies, particularly those with international joint ventures, to continue the practice.

Politicians will probably be the last to give up the custom.

49

Empresario
(Ehm-pray-SAH-ree-oh)

"The Showmen of Mexico"

One of the special attractions of Mexico is the showmanship that is typically displayed by virtually everyone in work and in play—showmanship that is at its highest form in the bullring and in the theater.

Anyone who has ever witnessed a bullfight or a dance exhibition in Mexico has seen the studied, dramatic actions of the matador and the flamenco dancer. The matador poses, preens and struts like the king of all cocks. The flamenco dancer is equally dramatic and imperial in every gesture, every step, radiating enormous emotional and artistic power.

Speaking in a very broad sense, all Mexican men have traditionally envisioned themselves as great matadors, and all Mexican women have seen themselves as great flamenco dancers—both able to inflame the deepest passions.

These images have traditionally played vital roles in the behavior of Mexicans, influencing them in subtle as well as conspicuous ways. Mexican pride, their flare for style, their courage, their bearing, are all different aspects of these images.

The word *empresario* (ehm-pray-SAH-ree-oh) translates as "manager," but in its Mexican context it means much more than just someone who tells other people what to do. It also connotes a degree of showmanship—as well as responsibility—that goes well beyond what is common in the United States and elsewhere.

The man who stages bullfights in Mexico is called an *empresario*, and the best *empresarios* are as much showmen as the most flamboyant matadors they hire for their rings. They are producers, directors, ringmasters and financiers all in one.

Successful Mexican *empresarios*, regardless of the kind of business they are in, are expected to act like good-hearted godfathers (in the Italian sense) to their families, friends and employees, watching over them, helping them solve their problems and getting them out of any trouble that they might get into.

Foreign business managers newly arrived in Mexico are often tripped up by the personal responsibilities their employees expect them to shoulder. They unknowingly create problems that can become disastrous if they are not recognized and remedied.

One of the areas of friction that foreign managers, particularly Americans, are likely to overlook is their behavior toward the lowest employees in their hire. Higher level American executives, like ranking military officers, tend to distance themselves from the troops, paying no attention to them except on special occasions.

In Mexico that kind of behavior is considered unfriendly, arrogant and abusive. The best Mexican managers make a point of greeting and speaking to everyone in their employ, treating them with the same flamboyant courtesy and respect they extend to people on their own level. The culturally ideal Mexican enterprise, like its counterpart in Japan, functions very much like an extended family, with managers in the role of caring parents as well as employers.

Both company loyalty and productivity in a Mexican enterprise are, therefore, primarily determined by the personal relationships that exist between the manager and the employees.

To succeed on a long-term basis in Mexico the foreign manager must become an *empresario*, with all of its godfather implications. Interestingly, those who have become *empresarios* find that they get much more satisfaction out of their own job and the time they spend in Mexico, and the performance of the employees is higher.

Español
(Ehs-pah-NYOHL)

"The Many Splendored Tongue"

Español (ehs-pah-NYOHL) or Spanish ranks as one of the world's most beautiful and expressive languages. Native Spanish speakers are proud of it, and most of those who are educated learn to speak it with wonderful fluency.

In earlier times most Americans who studied Spanish as a second language were usually taught "Castilian" Spanish, which is the standard form of the language as it is spoken in Spain. (Castile, a region in Spain that begins at the Bay of Biscay and extends south to Andalusia, was formerly a kingdom and is the birthplace of Castilian Spanish.)

International travel and a growing volume of communication between Spanish-speaking countries is tending to universalize the language, but there are still significant differences in pronunciation, slang and usage in the various countries. Newcomers to Mexico who speak Spanish learned elsewhere must go through a second learning process in order to be culturally correct and to communicate fully in Mexican Spanish.

Just like North American English, Mexican Spanish is replete with colloquialisms and slang which are indigenous to the country and which make up a significant proportion of ordinary conversations, particularly informal conversations.

Becoming fluent in Mexican Spanish, therefore, requires that one also become "fluent" in the culture; in how the language is used in all of its cultural nuances. Mexican humor, for example, is in a class by itself. Learning to understand and use it correctly is a vital part of communicating in Mexico.

While Mexican Spanish abounds with invectives and lends itself to brazen confrontations, cultural restraints demand that it be used in an indirect and often extravagant manner in many daily situations. What you hear is often not what you get.

The subtleties of Mexican Spanish are especially important when conducting business, and particularly so in dealing with Mexican bureaucracy, which has its own culture.

Foreign businesspeople should also keep in mind that just because a person speaks Spanish does mean he or she can be used as an interpreter. A native Spanish speaker with a Ph.D. in the language can be a total failure as an interpreter. Interpreting on a professional level requires special skills that can usually be obtained only with professional training. Untrained interpreters invariably inject their own interpretation into the dialogue, shade meanings and do other things that influence the outcome of negotiations and conversations.

Therefore, it is especially important for businesspeople—and politicians—dealing with Mexico to provide their own interpreters and to brief them thoroughly before meetings. The more specialized and technical the subject, the more important it is to use interpreters who are already familiar with the necessary technical vocabulary.

Probably the biggest mistake that North Americans make when using interpreters is to pepper their dialogue or presentations with their own colloquialisms and slang, which makes it difficult—or impossible—for interpreters to translate appropriately.

Humor, in particular, does not cross cultural borders well because it is often based on experiences that are unique to individual cultures, a point that North Americans should especially take to heart, because as much as half or more of their off-the-cuff comments are meant to be funny.

It is also important to keep in mind that Mexicans tend to be more formal in their speech than North Americans. Keeping one's own speech on a similar level, particularly in the early stages of any relationship, will help move the relationship along in the right direction.

While Mexicans are proud of their language they are not ethnocentrically hung up to the point that they look down on people who do not speak it well. In fact, their reaction is just the opposite. They are patient and helpful, and take pleasure in the experience.

This factor alone eliminates a great deal of the culture shock that most monolingual businesspeople experience during their first weeks and months in Mexico.

Whether or not foreigners in Mexico speak Spanish, they should be especially sensitive to the use of the language in making class and hierarchical distinctions between people.

Gender, age and personal relationships are also key factors in determining the vocabulary that is appropriate for various occasions. Titles and sexually charged language are especially important aspects of interpersonal communications in Mexico.

Another key point: Mexican Americans may be fluent in conversational Spanish, but unless they have had special training, their knowledge of contemporary Mexican business vocabulary, popular slang and current usage of older terms generally ranges from weak to totally lacking. Mainstream Mexican Spanish differs significantly from Mexican-American Spanish, not only in subtle shadings, but often in both meaning and terminology. This can be the source of serious problems when high-level negotiations are concerned.

51

Esposas

(Ehs-POH-sahs)

"The Saints of Mexico"

In Mexican culture the concepts of love and sex in marriage have traditionally been separate. Young men and women are often passionately in love with each other when they marry, and the love may last for a lifetime. Yet this does not preclude the man from having sexual relations with other women.

In some marriages, love between husbands and wives was a vitally important bond; in others it either did not exist at all or played only a minor role in the husband–wife relationship. The important thing was children and the integrity and continuity of the family.

In both the Indian and Spanish customs, sex was divided into two distinct categories. There was the sex that men had with their wives for procreation, and there was the sex that men had with women who were not their wives that was for pleasure and to demonstrate their masculinity and power.

Mexican *esposas* (ehs-POH-sahs) or "wives" have traditionally looked upon their husbands as providers and protectors, not as lovers or even as good friends. The relationship with their husband was secondary to their relationship with their children.

Esposas were not permitted to demand sexual fidelity from their husbands. Both sanctified custom and the law recognized that husbands had the right to engage in sex with other women as long as they treated their wives with respect.

In contrast, wives were expected to be totally faithful to their husbands, and once married, to not even look at other men, much less have male friends.

At the same time that wives were expected to be absolutely faithful to their husbands, they were nevertheless regarded as legitimate sexual game by other men, husbands as well as bachelors, who, especially when the wives were young and still attractive, made it a custom of pursuing them relentlessly.

This contradiction naturally created an enormous amount of sexual tension in male–female relations in Mexican society, and while it made life exciting it also made it dangerous, because the culture of *machismo* also demanded that husbands take revenge against unfaithful wives and their lovers if they were found out.

With only a few exceptions, the lower one went on the social ladder in Mexico, particularly in urban areas, the more unequal the rights of wives and the husband–wife relationship were apt to be. Generally though, the husband–wife relationship in Mexico has always been more cultural than economic.

Despite dramatic social changes that have occurred in Mexico in recent decades, the core culture remains intact. The only dramatic changes in the status of wives is among couples where the husband has been "de-Mexicanized" by being educated outside of Mexico or otherwise fundamentally influenced by Anglo culture.

Mexican men like to dally with foreign women, but when it comes to marriage they generally prefer Mexican women as wives, because of the cultural conditioning that makes them more subservient to men and more willing to sacrifice themselves for their husbands and children.

Anglo women who marry traditional-minded Mexican men generally discover, much to their chagrin, that there is a world of difference between being a *novia* or "girlfriend" and being an *esposa*.

As a girlfriend they may be courted in the most romantic and passionate way, but once the marriage ceremony is over, their world may be telescoped down to a minuscule proportions and filled with taboos.

All too often, newly married wives of old-fashioned Mexican men are no longer free to come and go as they please. In addition to being expected to avoid even the most casual relationships with other men, they are sometimes forced to give up going out with girlfriends as well.

Not surprisingly, marriages between Anglo women and Mexican men who were educated abroad or who have had extensive international experience are the most likely to run smoothly.

Slang terms for wife, which are seldom if ever used by middle- and upper-class people, include *jefa* (boss), *ruca* (worn out or stale) and *vieja* (old woman).

Another meaning of *esposa* is "handcuffs."

52

Esposos
(Es-POH-sohs)

"Macho Husbands"

The sense of pride, the dignity and the courtly manners that have traditionally been characteristic of upper-class Mexican men have always reminded me of the samurai warriors of feudal Japan.

Generally speaking, Mexican and Japanese men have also had similar attitudes toward women, and treat them very much alike. Because of this cultural similarity, Mexican and other Latin men who have had occasion to live for extended periods in Japan have found it to be a kind of sexual paradise. Not only were the Japanese women unusually susceptible to their aggressive sexuality, the huge social infrastructure in Japan designed to support copious male–female relations outside of marriage was far more refined and sophisticated than anything they had experienced in Mexico.

Mexican men in Tokyo were especially appreciative of the philosophy epitomized by a saying that became popular during the middle centuries of Japan's last great shogunate dynasty (1603-1868). The saying expressed the belief that the greatest thing that anyone could hope for was to be born a man in Edo—or present-day Tokyo—be a regular patron of the great courtesan districts, and eat a special fish delicacy on New Years.

At that time, Edo was one of the world's largest cities, and filled with all of the pleasures that men might dream about—elaborate red-light districts, public bathhouses that catered to all of the sensual pleasures, thousands of inns that served as houses of assignation and over a dozen large geisha districts.

There were also dozens of drinking and dining districts, the latter specializing in the wide variety of food that had been traditional in the country for centuries, and kabuki and noh theaters, dozens of festivals every year and more.

Mexican men, like their Japanese counterparts, traditionally regarded authoritarianism and sexism as a normal part of their male birthright, and the attitude has not changed that much in modern times. (The number of Spanish and Indian words whose original meanings refer to the penis and testicles is indicative of the sexual orientation of Mexican men.)

Marriage in Mexico has never been a union of equal partners based on democratic principles. In the Mexican context, males were inherently superior to females, and had rights that did not apply to women. Husbands on all social and economic levels saw themselves as the masters of the house, and used sex as an expression of their authority and power. They believed that their primary obligation was to provide for their families and protect their wives and daughters from other men.

Mexican husbands traditionally doted on their children when they were young, but became increasingly authoritarian and strict as the children grew up. In poorer families, fathers and sons often became alienated from each other by the time the sons reached their teens, because the sons objected to the way their fathers treated their mothers and older sisters.

Recent sociological studies among poor Mexicans indicate that with few exceptions Mexican husbands on this social level have not changed their authoritarian or sexist stripes to any significant degree.

Mexican husbands who have broken with past customs and traditions are invariably those who have been intimately exposed to other forms of behavior though education or extended contact with non-Mexicans, and there are different levels of this cultural conversion, depending on how intimate and extensive the contact with more democratic cultures has been. Naturally, the most conspicuous changes are seen in affluent families that have become international in their outlook and behavior, and in families that live close to the U.S.–Mexican border and are exposed to heavier doses of American culture.

Foreign women contemplating taking Mexican *esposos* (es-POH-sohs) would be wise to keep in mind that the concept of "husband and wife" is apt to have a very different meaning in its Mexican context, and that if they are not comfortable with those differences, the shock and the strain can be unbearable.

It is still socially acceptable and common for Mexican husbands of means to have mistresses, and to have children with them. Children born to mistresses are recognized as having been born "out of wedlock," but they are normally recognized by their fathers and not considered "bastards" in the Anglo context of the word.

Some of the more common slang terms for husband include *viejo* (old man), *jefe* (boss or chief) and *ruco* (something that is old and/or worthless).

(See **Casa Chicas, Esposas, Machismo, Mujeres, Pelados**.)

53

Familia
(Fah-ME-lee-ah)

"Heart of Mexican Society"

American families typically teach their children, both overtly and covertly, to be independent, to take the initiative and to compete with others on a one-against-everybody else basis, a process that results in "active coping" with the challenges and problems of life.

Mexican parents, on the other hand, stress parental authority, respect for elders and superiors, obedience to authority, emotional dependence on the family and others and self-discipline, an approach that leads to "passive coping" with outside events and forces.

Generally speaking, American children grow up to be inner directed, and to take an individualist approach to everything, while Mexicans grow up with a group orientation and are primarily family and group directed.

Americans prize a highly competitive spirit and do everything they can to encourage their children to be competitive in school, sports and work, while Mexicans favor a group spirit that contributes to overall harmony within the group by eliminating friction, or at least keeping it to a minimum.

Americans regard and generally treat each other as individuals who have the inalienable right to think and behave as they please as long as they do not infringe on the rights of others. This generally includes doing what they think is best for themselves regardless of what other family members think.

Mexicans focus on the relational roles that are deemed to be appropriate for fathers, mothers, sons and daughters in order to contribute the most to the survival, success and happiness of the family as a whole. A daughter studies medicine because the family wants a doctor in the family. A son studies law because his family is keenly aware of the advantage of having a lawyer in the family.

In Mexico material success is generally more of a family affair than it is in the United States. Members of families who succeed in business and the professions are much more likely to share their good fortune.

Relationships in American families are generally based on the democratic concept that all members of the family are equal and have the same voting rights. Children can oppose their parents and opt out of situations that displease them, often with the encouragement of their parents.

Most American families are bound together only by the fragile bonds of love (or infatuation) between husbands and wives. Mutual dependency plays a role but it is often not enough to hold families together. When infatuation or love goes, the marriage is destroyed and families break up over what are often minor disagreements.

Mexican families, especially those in lower social classes, do not function on the basis of democratic principles. Ties are vertical, with the father at the top as the authoritarian figure. It is common for fathers in lower social classes to abandon their families if they are disobeyed or displeased. In middle- and upper-class Mexican families the love bonds and feelings of mutual obligation are very strong. Families normally remain close and supportive throughout each generation.

U.S. families (except for highly concentrated ethnic groups) typically look upon themselves as separate from their neighbors and community—as small individual groups against the rest of the world. This, in fact, is a classic theme in dramas presenting mainstream American life.

Mexican families, on the other hand, have more of a sense of being members of their community, and are much less likely to regard themselves as being alone. The "Lone Ranger family" syndrome is rare in Mexico.

One of the facets of Mexican society that binds the people into cohesive units is that family members, relatives and "blood-brother" type friends can automatically presume on the help and hospitality of all the other members. This communal character of Mexican families is another legacy of the past, when family members, relatives and friends had to support each other in order to survive in a hostile political environment which was made even more onerous by the selfish, predatory nature of the Catholic Church.

Differences between Mexicans and people from other cultures may not be very obvious—or very important—in casual, informal relationships, when normal courtesy on both sides is generally enough to avoid friction and make it possible to enjoy the others' company. But in political, business and more personal matters, these differences are always important, and sometimes insurmountable, despite the goodwill and efforts by both sides.

One of the situations that invariably brings these cultural differences to the fore, often with disastrous results, is marriage between female Anglos, particularly North Americans, and Mexican men. North Americans who have married into Mexican families usually find that they have established an intimate relationship with more than just their new husbands or wives. In many ways they have "married" their spouses' families as well. This can be very upsetting to those who are not comfortable with such intimate relations and obligations.

Cultural differences are the most critical when Anglo women marry Mexican men who are still traditional in their attitudes and behavior, and treat them the way they would Mexican wives.

Generally, there are far fewer problems when Mexican women marry foreign men, because the women move from an authoritarian, restrictive society into one that is basically democratic and free.

(See **Esposa, Esposo, La Iglesia, Machismo, Mujeres**.)

Feminidad
(Fay-me-nee-DAD)

"Femininity Mexican Style"

The hypermasculinity that has long been associated with Mexican men has also traditionally been matched by the *feminidad* (fay-me-nee-DAD) or "femininity" of Mexican women. In fact, it seems to be a given that the more masculine men are in any society, the more feminine the women tend to be, and vice-versa; the more masculine the women the more feminine the men.

There are, of course, cultural differences in the definitions of masculinity and femininity and these definitions are subject to change from one generation to the next, but in Western cultures at least the Mexican definitions are more or less the classic ones. Likewise, there are fundamental differences in whether one defines the *feminidad* of Mexican women in terms of the expectations on Mexican men or Mexican women, or in purely objective terms.

Mexican femininity has "survived" in its classic sense for religious as well as political reasons. The religions of pre-Columbian Indians and the Spanish conquistadors who conquered them taught that women were inferior to men and that they were ordained to be passive and to fulfill the needs and pleasures of men. The political philosophies of both the Indians and Spaniards were outgrowths of their religious beliefs, and were often indistinguishable. Thus the political regime that the conquering Spaniards established in Mexico followed the precepts of Catholicism. Women were denied the right to be educated or to engage in any other activity that the church considered the special preserve of men.

This regime lasted for almost exactly 300 years. During most of the time Mexicans were virtually isolated from other religious and political influences, ensuring that these Catholic precepts would permeate their culture.

It was not until the 1920s that Mexican political reformers were able to separate the Catholic Church from state government, but Catholicism, and its contradictory influence on Mexican men and women, was to remain more or less the state religion of the country down to the present time.

The macho element in Mexican culture, obviously endorsed by both the male-dominated government and the church, had an influence on Mexican women that the church surely did not anticipate. It psychologically programmed them to emphasize their feminine sexuality through their apparel, their makeup and their actions.

From a young age, Mexican girls were conditioned to exhibit their femininity and to learn how to use it as a lure to attract men—something that most cultures do, of course, but in the case of Mexico this conditioning went well beyond what was necessary to propagate the race. It became a contest between males and females.

Unlike the passive femininity of women in Japan and other Asian nations, the *feminidad* of Mexican women was positive and aggressive. They learned how to use their eyes as "sex rays" which could make men wild with passion. They learned how to walk and dance in such a way that it made men burn.

To Mexican women, *coqueto* or "flirting" was a skill that they turned into an art.

Some of the flamboyant flirting has gone out of Mexican women since they began going to school, working in public and doing things that were once reserved for men, but enough of the traditional *feminidad* remains to set them apart and make them extraordinarily attractive to males from other cultures.

Both Mexican men and Mexican women seem consciously determined to avoid what they consider the demasculinization of American men and the defemininization of American women—a phenomenon that began in the United States in the mid-1900s, and has since been promoted as a political agenda by feminists.

Said a Mexican friend: "It is amazing to us how the masculinity of American men is constantly being put down by cartoons, comics, television programs and movies, while American women are depicted as wearing the pants!"

55

Fiestas
(Fee-Es-tahs)

"Communing with the Past"

One cannot know or appreciate Mexico without extensive knowledge of its *fiestas* (fee-ES-tahs) or "festivals." *Fiestas* are the Mexicans' link with their past, their historical umbilical cord.

Fiesta season in Mexico never ends. Somewhere there is always some kind of festival going on. Every town and city in the country has a patron saint which symbolically rules over its spiritual life and which is honored each year with a fiesta. (Mexican authorities say that over 5,000 fiestas are celebrated in the country each year.)

Residents of some villages and towns describe themselves as "unlucky" enough to have two patron saints, because they have to stage two festivals a year—a reference to the cost and work that traditionally goes into such festivities.

Many of Mexico's *fiesta* celebrations are lustily pagan. Others are meant to be Christian, although Mexico has a law banning outdoor religious celebrations. (In an extreme measure designed to reduce the overwhelming control of the Catholic Church over the lives of people, the *Constitution of 1917* included an article prohibiting outdoor religious events. Thus the many religiously oriented festivals held in Mexico today are officially regarded as "theatrical performances," although people generally are not aware of this classification.)

Most of Mexico's festivals are accompanied by a great deal of uninhibited drinking, and usually end in explosions of fireworks that often last for hours.

It has been said, with much authority, that *fiestas* have been a major factor in keeping rural Mexico poor. It is undeniable that they were traditionally an important reason for the continuing poverty in many rural areas; villagers went all out for holidays, and saved for months to buy fireworks and other paraphernalia.

However, over the centuries Mexican might not have been able to endure the incredible suffering imposed on them by the church and the state if it had not been for their festivals. In the view of Mexican sociologists and others, Mexico's numerous festivals have never been representations of true religious piety or for amusement as such, but for temporary relief from reality.

During festivals, otherwise sacred customs are violated one after the other. Law and order often break down completely. Mexican sociologists say that what outsiders often mistake for unrestrained gaiety during festivals are manifestations of naked fury. They explain that the country's many *fiestas* function not to satisfy a pleasure-loving spirit but as a means of letting off repressed violence. Drunken brawls and other types of violence, they add, go hand-in-hand with festivals.

Like their remote Aztecan ancestors, who could drink only during festivals and so used the occasions for binges that did not end until they were totally drunk, lower-class Mexican men still typically engage in ritualistic drinking to absolute drunkenness during festivals. They drink to get drunk, not to enjoy themselves.

The number and character of festivals differ with the area. *Dia de Santa Cruz* or "Day of the Holy Cross" is celebrated throughout the country from May 3 to about May 5. In Tehuantepec it is celebrated with both pagan and Catholic rites—with an interesting twist. It is believed that anyone killed during the period of the festival belongs to the gods, and that the killer is safe from punishment. As a result, crimes of passion and revenge are common during the festival. Mexican scholars say this custom is a holdover from the practice of sacrificing humans to appease the gods of fertility.

In addition to the Day of the Holy Cross, Tehuanos celebrate 27 other festivals each year, some of which last for several days.

In Paracho, between Mexico City and Gaudalahara, on August 8 each year, there is a "charming" festival featuring a group of pretty girls in native costumes who lead a bull to its ceremonial slaughter. In olden days, the victim was a young man.

Mexico's famous Day of the Dead festival is a "celebration" of death; a macabre recognition of the country's pre-Columbian and colonial history during which most people died early from violence or disease.

The main annual festival in Veracruz, which is usually referred to as a carnival, is popularly regarded as Mexico's annual homosexual convention. The city's large collection of transvestites dress up in female attire, attend special food stalls and put on dance exhibitions.

Says Mexican writer Frank Gutz: "In Mexico 'active' homosexuals are not regarded as deviants and are not persecuted. Passive homosexuals are regarded as male prostitutes instead of perverts—although they do the paying."

Outsiders who are seriously interested in the deeper and more important facets of Mexico's culture must look beyond the color and pomp of the country's many festivals and study what lies beneath the pageantry.

Mexicans throw themselves into festivals and the pleasures of life—sex, eating, drinking, singing, supporting a favorite matador— with a gusto and energy that disconcerts and sometimes shocks Americans. The reason for this national syndrome, Mexicans say, is that by losing themselves in such pleasures they can forget the hardships and frustrations that are the usual order of the day.

(See **Dia de los Muertos**.)

Forajeros / Extranjeros
(Foh-rah-HAY-rohs / X-trahn-HAY-rohs)

"Foreigners and Strangers"

Most Mexicans have a built-in victim mentality which is a product of more than four centuries of physical, emotional, intellectual and spiritual abuse.

Until the early decades of the 20th Century, Mexicans who were mixtures of Spanish, Indian and other racial genes, and Mexican Indians, were generally treated by the government and a small elite ruling class, made up mostly of whites, as outcasts in their own country.

These virtual untouchables were conditioned to have a deep-seated sense of personal inferiority, to accept their social, economic and political status without complaint, and especially to feel inferior to those in power and to whites in general.

This ongoing abuse and degradation filled the outcast Mexicans with an unbounded rage against their oppressors, and primed them to be both violent and savage on the occasions that they rebelled and broke the bonds of their passivity.

Mexico's Spanish–Indian outcasts had become the overwhelming majority by 1810, when the revolution against Spain started. But it was the early 1900s before they began to take pride in their mixed race, and to feel spiritually superior to whites.

Prior to Mexico's civil war (1910–1921), regional pride had been a major political and cultural factor in the country. But there was very little national pride in being Mexican because the country was seen as distant from the people at home, and as dominated by the United States in its international affairs.

Victory in the civil war, which pitted the poor of Mexico against the dictatorial government and the church, gave rise to hopes that for the first time in the history of the country democracy and justice would prevail. This ignited strong feelings of pride in being Mexican.

Regionalism remains especially strong in Mexico today, and Mexicans refer to people from other parts of the country as *forajeros* (foh-rah-HAY-rohs) or "foreigners," with virtually all of the connotations of exclusivity—often mixed with dislike, distrust and feelings of superiority—generally associated with foreign nationals.

Foreign nationals are called *extranjeros* (x-trahn-HAY-rohs), which literally means "people from the outside." While usually translated as "foreigners" the term also sometimes used to mean "strangers," referring to Mexicans from other regions.

Dramatic political reforms that began in the 1980s and have since been continued by succeeding presidential administrations have contributed enormously to the growth of national pride in middle- and upper-class Mexicans. The better educated and the more internationally minded Mexicans are, the more likely they are to be strongly nationalistic, to have great pride in Mexican culture and to regard themselves as spiritually and morally superior to Americans and other Anglos.

Present-day Mexicans are no longer concerned about new military invasions by the United States. They are, however, very sensitive about economic excursions and are concerned that the economy of the country might once again be dominated by foreign interests.

Mexicans who are living along the U.S. border are especially sensitive to both *forajeros* and *extranjeros*. They are confronted daily with issues concerning Mexicans from interior regions who have flocked to the border looking for work in *maquiladora* factories, or seeking to cross illegally into the United States in search of work.

Their lives are also effected culturally and economically by the presence of large numbers of foreign-owned factories in special duty-free zones on their side of the border, by a daily influx of foreign tourists and shoppers, by American television and by the conspicuous disparity between their economic status and the lifestyle of Americans on the other side of a wire fence.

Foreigners who become involved with Mexicans in any way must take their newfound pride and age-old sensitivity into account in order to develop a positive and cooperative relationship.

57

Formalidad
(Fohr-mah-lee-DAD)

"Behaving with Style"

Despite its "New World" history of some 500 years, Mexico has retained many cultural elements that continue to be associated with old countries of Asia and Europe, particularly in regard to personal behavior.

In addition to the use of respect language and titles that are more reminiscent of Spain and England than Canada or the United States, Mexicans have retained "Old World" attitudes toward wearing apparel, eating and spending idle time outdoors on the sidewalks.

Another Old World cultural element that distinguishes Mexicans, including those who are very poor and often uneducated as well, is their attachment to *formalidad* (fohr-mah-lee-DAD) or "formality" in their everyday behavior.

Unlike the traditional formality of the Japanese and some other nationalities, which eventually became so stylized and mechanical that it took on an inhuman element, the formality that became a key factor in Mexican society during the long Spanish colonial period (1521–1821) remained personal and intimate and has continued to add to the quality of life rather than detract from it.

The essence of Mexican *formalidad* is respect—showing respect not only to parents, seniors and elders, but to friends and people in general, and to oneself. This respect for oneself includes dress as well as behavior. Where others are concerned it primarily relates to manner and speech.

Mexican-style *formalidad* is thus a public manifestation of both the etiquette and morality of Mexico and is one of the key ingredients in the color and flavor of Mexican life.

Just as Americans pride themselves on their informality, and are comfortable only in a casual atmosphere, Mexicans are proud of their more formal behavior and regard it is one of the most important aspects of their culture. They repeatedly point out that a degree of ritualistic formality is essential in instilling good manners and respect in children, and express concern that growing American influence in Mexico will eventually destroy this age-old custom.

Said one Mexican businessman: "American eating and working habits are especially detrimental to the traditional Mexican way of life. Until recent decades, Mexican children learned about human relations and proper behavior at the dining table during the main meal of the day. Now, many families never eat together. They are all too busy!"

However, Mexican culture is not so fragile or arbitrary that it is going to disappear or even be dramatically changed in the immediate future. Mexican children may not be so thoroughly conditioned in all of the traditional cultural formalities as they were in the past, but as they grow older and enter the adult world they must conduct themselves according to adult standards. And it is not as if that were a hardship. Most young Mexicans do not resent the traditional standards of formality and there is no conscious effort to avoid them. They are just a natural part of adulthood.

Therefore, it will continue to be important for foreign visitors, and particularly foreign businesspeople, to adjust their own behavior to complement the more formal aspects of Mexican culture.

Those who do so sincerely generally find that it is not so difficult to live with as they originally imagined, and that they, in fact, gain a great deal of emotional satisfaction and contentment from Mexican *formalidades*.

58

Frontera
(Frohn-TAY-rah)

"The Wild North"

North American colonists had their frontier, a seemingly endless expanse of mostly uninhabited land that stretched westward beyond their imagination. This circumstance played a seminal role in the development of the American colonies and their independence from England, and has continued to impact in the most fundamental way on the history of the United States.

Mexico also had its *frontera* (frohn-TAY-rah) or "frontier," and if anything, it played, and continues to play, an even more important role in Mexican history. But the territorial similarity between the Mexican frontier and the American frontier is about the only thing they had in common.

Unlike the American colonists, the first Spaniards to come to Mexico did not come as refugees or immigrants looking for new lands to settle. They did not bring their wives and children with them. They were heavily armed raiders, seeking gold and other pillage.

The subsequent conquest of the Aztec empire in 1519-1521 by these Spaniards was not a fight over land but the act of pirates, aimed at capturing booty and slaves. Their exploration trips to the far north over the next century were not in search of new lands to settle. They were treasure hunts.

If it had not been for the discovery of huge deposits of silver in central Mexico in the mid-1500s, the history of Mexico would have been totally different. Several million Indians who died of European diseases might have lived. There probably would not have been enough Spanish men in the country to create a new race of Spanish-Indian mixtures.

As it happened, the Spanish administrators, their military garrisons and the Catholic Church turned Mexico into a private oligarchy and kept its borders closed for some 300 years.

It was not until the growing number of mixed-bloods, ostracized by the Spanish and Indians alike, began moving into the northern territories in the 17th and 18th centuries as cowboys, ranchers, vagabonds and bandits that the country's northern frontier began to play a role in Mexican history.

These men and their families were escapees from adversity and hardship which were far more severe than anything encountered by the European immigrants who were flocking to the American colonies and spreading westward.

Mexico's first frontiersmen, further toughened by the environment of the northern territories as well as ongoing social, economic and political discrimination by the government and Spanish colonials, gradually developed an independent spirit and mindset that distinguished them from all other Mexicans.

It was these tough *norteños* (nor-TAY-nhohs) or "northerners" who took the lead in the fight for independence from Spain in 1810-1821. They were equally prominent in the rebellion against French rule in the 1860s, and again played a leading role in the civil war of 1910-1921, which finally rid the country of domination by military and religious dictators.

Still today, leaders of change in the political, economic and social spheres in Mexico are primarily from the northern frontier states, particularly Chihuahua and Sonora.

Mexicans who live in the northern states bordering the United States are still commonly referred to as *fronterizos* or "frontiersmen," because their spirit, attitudes and manners clearly distinguish them from other Mexicans.

Fronterizos is also sometimes translated as "borderlanders" when it is used in reference to people who live close to the U.S.-Mexican border.

Because of their proximity to the United States and the fact that hundreds of thousands of them cross the border regularly—some of them daily for work, shopping and other purposes—*fronterizos* are more directly and deeply influenced by American attitudes and behavior than other Mexicans, including those who live only a few miles farther south.

Mexico's northern frontier therefore offers something of a microcosm of what much of the rest of northern and central Mexico will be like in the future, as more and more American technology and culture flows southward.

The frontier spirit of Sonora is both dramatized and promoted by one of the state's leading newspapers, *Diario de la Frontera* or *"Frontier Diary,"* published in Nogales.

A derogatory slang term for people who live close to the U.S. border and affect some of the mannerisms of Americans is *pocho* (POH-choh), which literally means something that is discolored or mixed up. The whole area along the Mexican side of the border is sometimes referred to as *pocholandia* or *gringolandia*.

59

Gachupines
(Gah-choo-PEE-nays)

"Those Who Wear Spurs"

Spaniards brought the first modern-day horses into the Americas shortly after Columbus stumbled onto the "New World," and horses played a vital role in the conquest of Mexico by Hernán Cortés and his small army of soldiers.

When Mexico's Indians were first confronted by mounted soldiers in armor they thought they were seeing half-human half-animal monsters, an image that the Spaniards promoted with enthusiastic zeal.

Horses and Spaniards were thereafter closely associated, and it wasn't long before all Spaniards in Mexico were known as *gachupines* (gah-choo-PEE-nays) or "Wearers of Spurs." [Throughout the 300-year reign of the Spaniards (1521–1821), Mexican Indians were prohibited from owning and riding horses.] *Gachupín* was later refined to specifically mean European-born Spaniards, and eventually became a derogatory reference to the Spanish overlords.

Shortly after Mexico City fell to Cortés and his Indian allies, hundreds of other Spaniards began arriving from Cuba and other parts of the Caribbean, including the worst kind of riffraff, all seeking gold, slaves and women.

In a move to end the greed-fed treachery, killing and debauchery by the surviving conquistadors and the later arrivals, the Spanish Crown decided in 1530 to appoint viceroys from Spain to act as governors of the new territory. But it was to be 1535 before the first appointee arrived.

Thereafter, *gachupines* occupied the top of the hierarchal pyramid in Mexico. All government and primary commercial positions were reserved exclusively for them. As the Spanish regime expanded its political and economic activities in the colony, it required more and more administrators from Spain. Eventually the total number reached approximately 80,000.

The policy of the Spanish Crown of allowing only European-born Spaniards to occupy positions of authority in Mexico was to have an extraordinary social, political and economic impact of "New Spain." As conquerors who ruled with absolute authority and practiced racial and caste discrimination with extreme fanaticism, the *gachupines* were a despised minority, generally hated by every other group in the country.

Spanish administrators were assigned to Mexico for anywhere from a few to several years. Following the completion of their assignments, some of them chose to make Mexico their permanent home because life in Mexico was far better than it was back in Spain.

Gachupines (and Mexican-born Spaniards) had lifetime indentured servants and workers whom they did not have to pay. They lived in villas and *haciendas* that in Spain only the wealthy could afford. Because they were so far away from their superiors in Spain, the administrators took advantage of opportunities to indulge themselves in whatever way they chose.

Horses continued to play a significant role in the lives of the Spanish administrators of Mexico, not only as transportation but also for recreation. Horse racing and horse shows became popular sports.

It was the hated *gachupines* who created many of the traditions of the *caballeros* and *charros*, who afterward gave Mexican culture a great deal of its image and style, from its rodeos and bullfights to the bandits and *federales* of prerevolutionary days.

The most important contribution that the *gachupines* were to make to Mexico was biological. The Spanish-born colonial administrators brought their wives with them to Mexico, and the younger families naturally continued having children. Some of the Mexican-born Spanish offspring eventually returned to Spain. But as the generations went by, more and more of them remained in Mexico, forming a distinctive class of their own.

The overriding factor in the lives of this new class of Spanish Mexicans was that they were barred by Spanish law from achieving any of the higher administrative offices in the country. There were no restrictions on them accumulating property, however, and some of them went on to become fabulously wealthy as operators of gold and silver mines and agricultural estates.

Interestingly, Mexicans who are the most vociferous in their criticism of the justice, legal and economic systems in Mexico say that the country is still mostly run by *gachupines*—meaning by people who behave more like foreigners than Mexicans, putting their own personal interests above those of ordinary Mexicans and the country at large.

One of them said with great vehemence: "Hernán Cortés is still in charge of Mexico!"

(See **Criollos, Haciendas, Mestizos**.)

Gringos
(GREEN-gohs)

"'Greasers' of the North"

Lukeville, Arizona is a small settlement on the U.S.-Mexican border in southwestern Arizona that serves as international gateway to the Mexican resort city of Puerto Penasco—better known in the United States as Rocky Point.

In the early 1960s an enterprising American businessman who owned most of the property surrounding the immigration and customs facilities astride the border began calling the area "Gringo Pass" in his promotional literature and advertisements. The businessmen knew that the nickname would be easy for everyone to remember, and would attract attention to his store, service station, motel and other facilities at the gateway. As far as he was concerned, the image of "Gringo Pass" was totally positive.

In earlier times, however, the use of the word *gringo* (GREEN-goh) in any reference was likely to be derogatory. There are two interesting stories about the origin of the word *gringo*. One, reported as gospel, goes like this:

During the Mexican–American War of 1846–1848 U.S. soldiers marching through the dry deserts of northern Mexico often sang the old ballad, "Green Grow the Rushes, Oh!"

Mexicans began identifying the song with Americans, and soon shortened "Green Grow" to *gringo*, in reference to any American or English-speaking Caucasian.

A more likely explanation is that *gringo*, an old word meaning "gibberish," was originally used to describe anyone who could not speak Spanish well.

At any rate, the word quickly became a part of the Mexican national conscience after the invasion of Mexico by the United States in 1847 and the influx of foreigners into the country in the following decades.

For more than a century after *gringo* came into common use it had a strongly derogatory connotation, and was more or less the equivalent of the English term "greaser," a name created by Americans living along the Mexican border as a disparaging reference to Mexican men (and apparently derived from the fact that they commonly used a heavy, aromatic pomade in their hair). By the 1970s most Americans living along the Mexican border, as well as those visiting Mexico from other parts of the country, had begun using *gringo* in referring to themselves, in a neutral and often humorous sense.

Today, *gringuita* (green-GHEE-tah), the diminutive female form of *gringo*, is also often used by Mexicans as an affectionate term for foreign girls.

Another commonly used Spanish term for foreign women who are blonde is *huerita* (whey-REE-tah). Like most darker people who have been made to feel inferior because of their color, Mexicans tend to equate whiteness and blondness with beauty.

Some observers add that Mexican men equate blond hair with highly charged sexuality. As a result a growing number of Mexican women, particularly those in the sex and entertainment trades, have bleached their hair blonde.

Mario ("Mike") De La Fuente of Nogales, Mexico, played a significant role in helping to defuse the term *gringo*. He wrote an autobiographical book titled *I Like You, Gringo—But!* which was a bestseller on both sides of the border in the 1970s.

Mike, whose father was prominent in Mexican politics in the early 1900s and was marked for execution by some of the rebel groups involved in the 1910 civil war, escaped with his family to Texas and lived there until he was in his early 20s. During that period he became the first foreigner ever to play professional baseball in the United States.

After returning to Mexico, De La Fuente became a highly successful bullfight impresario, and built a business empire in real estate, publishing, banking and cable television in Nogales, Sonora. He also served for several decades as an unofficial "Ambassador of Goodwill" between Sonora and Arizona.

The acceptance of the word *gringo* by foreigners, combined with the weakening of Mexican antagonism toward Americans, has taken virtually all of the virulence out of the term, and today it is generally used in casual reference to English-speaking non-Mexicans.

Gringo is still a slang term, however, and should not be used by businesspeople or others in formal situations, even in casual conversation with people with whom they are not on intimate terms. Mexicans are especially sensitive to language, regardless of the circumstances, and take a high level of decorum seriously.

In Chicano communities in the southwestern United States one may hear the term *agringado* or *agringada* in reference to Mexican-Americans who have lost most or all of their native cultural heritage and merged into the white middle-class culture of the United States.

Other old slang terms for Anglo-Saxon foreigners include *bolillo* (boh-LEE-yoh), a kind of French bread, and *gabacho* (gah-BAH-cho), which was originally French for "bad act," then came to mean "Frenchified," and, finally, any Anglo foreigner.

Another explanation of the use of *gabacho* to mean a foreigner is that it is an adaptation from the word *gabacha,* which means "apron." When Mexican men noted that foreign men often helped their wives in the kitchen, something a Mexican male wouldn't dream of doing, they began calling such men *gabachos* or "aprons."

61

Haciendas

(Hah-see-EN-dahs)

"Fiefs, Serfs and Gunslingers"

Most North Americans equate the term *hacienda* (hah-see-EN-dah) with a large Mexican-style adobe house which has an inner courtyard and lots of flowers and vines, a romantic image created by a popular song and many Hollywood movies.

Historically, the term *hacienda* has meant something altogether different to Mexicans. In the early decades of the Spanish regime in Mexico, which began in 1521, Hernán Cortés, the conqueror of the Aztec empire, all of his surviving Spanish soldiers and eventually other Spaniards of some rank were rewarded for their services by receiving land grants or estates, which included the Indians living on the tracts of land involved.

These estates came to be known as *haciendas* (also as *latifundios*), and were the equivalent of the feudal landed estates of the English and other European nobles during the Middle Ages (A.D. 476–1453), where both agriculture and stock-raising was pursued. The manor home on a *hacienda* was called *casa grande*.

When the Indians who lived within the borders of the land grant were required to pay tribute in kind or cash to the owners, the grants were officially recorded as *encomiendas* (en-come-ee-EN-dahs), a term for a custom that had existed in Spain since Roman days.

Just like their European counterparts, the larger and better administered *haciendas* of Mexico were virtually self-sustaining. Their peons (serfs) produced almost everything that was needed for them to function as independent fiefs and make a profit for their owners.

Also like their European counterparts, the Mexican owners of *haciendas* were a law unto themselves, running their fiefs according to their own rules and regulations, and lording it over their peons as both judge and executioner. All of the estate masters maintained armed guards and enforcers, and in later centuries, professional gunmen.

Throughout the long centuries of the Spanish regime in Mexico (1521–1821), the *mestizo* and Indian peons attached to the *haciendas* were treated more or less like slaves by most owners and their overseers.

Conditions on the *haciendas* became even worse between 1821 and 1921, a period when Mexico was ravaged by wars (with the United States and France and its own civil war) and primarily ruled by bandit-generals and generals who behaved like bandits.

According to historians and travelers, the worst years for the *hacienda* peons throughout this era was during the reign of General Porfirio Díaz, from 1876 to 1880 and again from 1884 to 1911, and the bloody and destructive civil war years from 1910 to 1921.

In addition to living in hovels and being forced to eat a diet that barely kept them alive (average longevity was around 30 years), many *hacienda* workers were paid in coupons that could only be exchanged for food and other items in "company" stores operated by the *haciendas*, a system that helped make many of the owners fabulously wealthy and contributed to a destructive cycle of alcoholism and drug use among the peons.

During the Diaz regime, a large percentage of all the agricultural land in Mexico was divided up into *haciendas* which were owned by some 25 Mexican families and a number of foreign family groups, such as the Guggenheims.

It was not until 1924 that incoming "revolutionary" presidents of Mexico began breaking down the traditional *hacienda* system and dividing the land among the peasants who worked it—a program that continued into the 1950s.

However, later socialistic governments began experimenting with collectivizing the small plots of farmland in an effort to gain from the economies of scale. But, as usual, such communizing efforts failed and made many of the peasants worse off than they had been.

As the decades passed, more and more of the small farms were bought out by large enterprises that joined them together, in effect returning to the *hacienda* system under another name.

Today, millions of Mexican farmers and farm workers still live in shacks and adobe houses that are little better than huts, without running water or sewerage facilities. And large numbers of them cross the border into the United States each year to find work at better paying jobs.

Another historical note: several of the largest and most famous of the early land grants incorporated huge areas in what is now Texas, New Mexico and Arizona. The Peralta Grant included Arizona's Superstition Mountains east of Phoenix and Scottsdale, reputedly the site of the legendary Lost Dutchman Gold Mine.

(See **Braceros, Campesinos, Coyotes, Los Pollos**.)

62

Humildad
(Oo-meel-DAD)

"Dealing with Humility"

Most foreigners who spend more than a few months in Mexico eventually become captivated by the people and their lifestyle. They find themselves literally addicted to life in Mexico, and often prefer it to anything they have experienced before. The attraction that Mexico has for foreigners ranges from things that are so subtle they are well below the conscious level, to attitudes and customs that are so conspicuous they virtually shout for attention.

In the subtle category are such things as the uncritical way Mexicans accept outsiders in their midst, their natural goodwill and friendliness, and their quiet courtesy.

The more conspicuous attractions of life in Mexico include such things as the formal courtesy of Mexicans, their way of dining, their music, their festivals and a relaxed atmosphere that permeates the culture.

Another of the cultural characteristics of the vast majority of Mexicans that adds a special flavor to life among them is their innate *humildad* (oo-meel-DAD) or "humility." The poor of Mexico are especially humble in their attitudes and behavior.

Humility is, of course, one of those refined traits that makes it possible for humans to live together peacefully in communities. In some people it seems to appear spontaneously. Others learn it through a gradual process which is often painful. And some, of course, want nothing at all to do with it.

Most Mexicans came by their *humildad* the hard way. For nearly five centuries they were brainwashed in humility by the Catholic Church and by a ruling class that made it necessary for survival.

The Church taught that independent thinking and behavior was immoral; that people should sacrifice their own personal desires for their families and communities. The church limited education to the sons of well-to-do families, making it inevitable that the majority of all Mexicans would remain in poverty.

Government laws, especially during the Spanish colonial regime from 1521 to 1821, also severely limited the options that were open to Indians and mixed-races. They literally had no political rights. Because they were not able to develop their individuality and were forced to sublimate their personal desires, the emergence of strong feelings of *humildad* was inevitable.

Times have changed in Mexico, but the historical legacy of humility as a national trait lives on in most Mexicans, and it continues to be both an asset and a liability. On one hand, the humility of the poor and disadvantaged has become a psychological barrier that helps bind them to their poverty and makes them unable—and unwilling—to help themselves. Many continue to behave as if their humble lifestyle was preordained and there is nothing they can or should do about it. This attitude is one of the reasons why people in rundown homes and neighborhoods do not join together to improve their situation.

On the plus side, the innate *humildad* of most Mexicans—especially the young and women—makes them warm and thoughtful and therefore easy to get along with and pleasant to be around. They are generally unpretentious by nature, are filled with goodwill and have sunny dispositions.

Where foreign businesspeople are concerned, the inherent humility of the majority of Mexicans—men as well as women—often causes problems because foreigners tend to underestimate them. Mexicans are reticent about promoting themselves the way Americans and other nationalities do.

Mexican businesspeople expect their foreign counterparts to take the initiative in finding out who they are and what their qualifications are. Furthermore, they give as much credence to character and family background as they do to business experience and technical skills.

In situations where Mexican businesspeople feel they are being treated as country bumpkins—something that happens frequently—their natural humility quickly gives way to resentment.

63

Igualdad
(Ee-gwhahl-DAHD)

"The Vertical Society"

The concept of *igualdad* (ee-gwhahl-DAHD) or "equality" as it is known in Anglo and Western European cultures has never been a part of the Mexican experience. The original Indian cultures of Mexico were vertically oriented, class-structured societies under the authoritarian rule of chiefs, priests and kings. Class was generally hereditary and was maintained by the strictest sanctions.

When Mexico fell to Spanish conquistadors in 1521 the Spanish replaced the Indian system with their own autocratic, class and caste system which was the antithesis of equality in any sense, political, social or economic. European-born Spaniards ruled Mexico directly from 1521 until 1821, and for most of the next 100 years the country was in the hands of Mexican-born Spaniards who continued the authoritarian, class- and caste-steeped rule of their racial and ethnic forbearers.

From the early 1600s until the 1920s the Catholic Church was the co-ruler of Mexico, generally exercising far more influence over the lives and fortunes of the people than the civil government. The church, which became richer and more powerful than the Spanish administrators, played a significant role in sustaining and nurturing *in*equality among the castes and classes of Mexicans.

For more than 300 years the people of Mexico lived under church policies that were specifically designed to keep the Indians and poor mixed-blood *mestizos* uneducated and totally subservient; as virtual spiritual, economic and social slaves to the church.

It was not until the latter half of the 20th century that Mexico's political and religious institutions had evolved enough to begin implementing political, social and economic reforms based on such principles as fairness, equality and justice.

Today the institutions of Mexico are still primarily authoritarian and weighted in favor of the elite. Equality, in all of its various nuances, exists only as an ideal. Life in Mexico in the 1990s is filled with inequalities based on gender, skin color, family background, education, degree of affluence, occupation, language, regional customs—even on the distance from Mexico City. Yet outsiders looking through the windows of Mexico should keep in mind that some of the things they perceive as inequalities may be regarded as both natural and preferable by Mexicans.

One area where the values and perceptions of North Americans and Mexicans may differ significantly is in attitudes and behavior involving male and female relations.

The prevailing view of Mexicans is that there is a man's world and a woman's world, and while the twain meet and mate, they do not and should not merge.

Mexican women as well as Mexican men maintain that there are fundamental differences between males and females which make it impossible for them to be treated the same in every instance—and the height of stupidity to try.

The concept of unisex strikes Mexicans as not only missing the whole point of nature's wisdom, but as ignoring one of the greatest pleasures of life.

Of course, this does not excuse the fact that Mexican men have been culturally conditioned to regard women as inferior to men and to take malicious and harmful advantage of them.

In fact, a strong case could be made on the proposition that until Mexican women achieve political, social and economic equality with men, *igualdad* per se in Mexico will remain an unreachable ideal.

In the meantime, foreign companies in Mexico that have hired significant numbers of Mexican women are playing an important role in helping women achieve a degree of economic and social parity with men.

Television, which in Mexico as in the United States is devoted mostly to fluff and sleaze, is, however, having a dramatic influence on the image and role of women in Mexico. In addition to presenting women as symbols of sexuality, Mexican television also demonstrates that women can be strong, talented individuals who can make big money and survive without men watching over and controlling them.

64

Imagen
(Ee-MAH-hen)

"In the Eye of the Beholder"

The American Revolution in the 1770s was a great inspiration to ordinary Mexicans of that time. They saw Americans fighting for their independence from Great Britain as analogous to their own relationship with Spain, and in 1810 they too rose up in a rebellion against their distant overlords.

But this positive *imagen* (ee-MAH-hen) of the new United States was to be destroyed only a few decades later, beginning in the 1830s when Americans colonized the Texas portion of northern Mexico, and culminating in the 1840s when the United States invaded Mexico and seized the northern two thirds of the country.

For the next century and more the United States was regarded by Mexicans as an immoral, hegemonic giant primarily interested in exploiting their natural resources and labor—a fear that was borne out time and again by the behavior of American politicians and industrialists.

Harsh discrimination against Mexicans who became American citizens by virtue of their homeland being annexed by the United States, and against later generations of Mexican Americans born in what previously had been Mexico, added to the unsavory reputation of Americans.

Discrimination by Anglo-Americans against Mexican Americans did not begin to subside until the American cultural revolution of the 1960s—carried live on television. This revolution forced Americans to recognize the extent of racial and ethnic discrimination in their own country and resulted in the majority of them undergoing a seminal change in their social attitudes and behavior.

Overt discrimination by Anglo-Americans is no longer a major concern of Mexicans but what does have educated Mexicans deeply disturbed is that the influence of American culture is gradually eroding all of the social values and customs they hold dear.

Although Mexicans do not blame individual Americans for their cultural invasion, they, like almost everyone else, tend to see Americans in stereotypical images that are made of bits and pieces built up over the generations.

It is therefore necessary for every American newly arrived in Mexico as a visitor or on business to virtually start from scratch in creating a positive *imagen* that Mexicans can relate to in a positive way.

This means that Americans in Mexico must be aware of and follow the more common forms of etiquette and avoid breaking the more obvious taboos in both behavior and dress.

American and other foreign businesspeople, in particular, should dress well when in Mexico. They should stay in reputable hotels and frequent upscale restaurants and lounges. And by all means they should be conservative in their behavior, preserving their own dignity as well as that of their Mexican counterparts.

Generally speaking, Mexicans do not have a positive *imagen* of Americans as cultural human beings, and this is the first obstacle that an American must overcome in order to establish good, strong relationships with Mexicans. This means that not only the personal appearance and manners of Americans must be acceptable, they must also demonstrate high levels of goodwill, generosity, honesty, sincerity and loyalty to friends.

Another important factor in developing cooperative relationships with Mexicans is being knowledgeable about the country itself; in particular, its political and cultural history. Few things turn Mexicans off more rapidly than discovering that a newly arrived businessperson has made no effort whatsoever to learn anything about the country.

65

Indigenismo
(Een-dee-heh-NEES-moh)

"Indianism Si; Indians No"

By the early 1900s Mexico's Spanish–Indian mixed-bloods, historically called *mestizos*, had become the overwhelming majority in the population and had begun to realize that they were the typical Mexican.

Encouraged by a number of writers and educators, these people began looking upon earlier *mestizos*—the revolutionary soldiers, the bandit-generals, the painters and the writers—as the source of their political and intellectual consciousness and as the true heroes of the country. Their Indian ancestry became the source of the spiritual and artistic side of their being.

This outlook and the process it inspired came to be called *indigenismo* (Een-dee-heh-NEES-moh), or the "indigenation" of Mexican culture and history. Over the next half century, virtually all educated Mexicans became dedicated *indigenistas*.

In another remarkable turnaround from attitudes and practices that had existed for more than 400 years, the *indigenistas* began to regard the Indian-based spiritual side of their cultural heritage as superior to the Spanish side.

However, this recognition of the spiritual contribution of Mexico's Indians did not result in any elevation of the economic or social status of the Indians themselves. As a group, they still remain at the bottom of Mexico's social and economic order.

But *indigenismo* has become a potent force in Mexican culture and is now playing a significant role in the politics of Mexico. Indian protests and demands can no longer be ignored on the basis of Indians being "nonpeople." Mexican intellectuals can no longer live with the dichotomy of accepting their Indian relatives on one hand and denying them on the other, without suffering from the contradiction.

A rebellion by large numbers of Mayan Indians in the state of Chiapas in 1994 brought the *indigenismo* concept into the forefront of Mexican politics, presenting the elite of the country with a direct challenge to live up to their new philosophy.

Like other historical legacies that continue to plague Mexico, nearly five centuries of discrimination against its Indians will not be resolved quickly. But the intellectual conversion of most Mexicans to *indigenismo* is finally speeding up the process.

66

Indios

(EEN-dee-ohss)

"The First Mexicans"

When Hernán Cortés and his band of fortune hunters arrived on the Gulf coast of Mexico in 1519 central Mexico alone was inhabited by somewhere between 21 and 26 million Indians, making up some 149 tribal nations. (Historians disagree on the population figure.)

Despite the cruel custom of human sacrifices and slavery practiced by some of the tribes, the standard of living of most of Mexico's Indians at that time was well above the subsistence level, and the majority lived safe and fulfilling lives.

Contemporary historians have noted that when Cortés arrived in Mexico in 1519, Indians living in what is now northern Mexico and the southwestern United States had no rich, no poor, no criminal class, no prisons, no institutionalized orphans, no widows who wanted to remarry and no red light districts—all of which followed upon the arrival of European culture into these areas.

The Spaniards, in their racial, religious and cultural arrogance, looked upon the Indians as savages who had no personal or civil rights of their own, and as worthy only of being subjugated and used—the same attitude that marked most Europeans who flocked to the New World in the 16th and 17th centuries.

During the first generation after the conquest of Mexico, most of the Spanish priests assigned to the new colony were enthusiastic about educating the Indian population. Thousands of their young students quickly became fluent in Spanish and were as learned as their Spanish counterparts. But during the first generations of Spain's rule in Mexico educated Indians were denied the right to become priests, and were barred from all skilled trades and professions.

All Indians who came under the administrative control of the Spanish regime and church authorities were required to give one tenth of everything they produced or earned to the Church. They could not own land, carry arms or ride horses.

In addition to the mass slaughter of Indians that occurred during the conquering of Mexico, millions more died from diseases the Spaniards carried over from Europe. Spaniards turned most of the surviving Indians into slave laborers, working them from 12 to 16 hours a day.

The hundreds of thousands of both urban and rural Indian men that were forced to labor in mines for 12 hours a day were the worst off. They were required to make 12 daily round trips into shafts as much as a third of a mile deep, each time carrying out 200 pounds of ore.

During their sleeping periods, Indian mine workers were kept chained or in locked and guarded pens. Any infraction or sign of malingering was met with flogging. A common punishment was 200 lashes, which was often fatal.

Besides breaking up Indian families by conscripting the men for forced labor, the Spaniards also made a practice of interbreeding with the wives and daughters of the Indians, further disrupting their lives and reducing the pure Indian population.

In addition, as a result of these restrictions and other factors, a large percentage of the demoralized Indian men became alcoholics, and in fits of rage would kill each other rather than attack their powerful and ruthless oppressors.

Within the first 100 years of the Spanish reign in Mexico, the diseases the Spaniards brought in from Europe, combined with their harsh rule, destroyed more than 80 percent of the Indian population. Colonial population records reveal this explosive decline in the number of Indians in Mexico from 1519 to 1810, when Mexicans revolted against Spanish rule:

1519—25.2 million

1532—16.8 million

1548—6.3 million

1568—2.6 million

1590—1.9 million

1595—1.3 million

1605—1.075 million

1625—1.0 million

1793—2.5 million

1810—3.6 million

When it became obvious that the system imposed upon the Indians of Mexico was rapidly destroying them, some of the more influential Catholic missionaries in the country finally prevailed upon their superiors in Spain to intercede with the king and convinced him to declare the slave system unlawful. But the relationship between the former slave owners and the Indians remained virtually the same.

Eventually, there were a small number of so-called *indios naborias* or "free Indians," who were half-slave, half-free. They were required to farm small plots of land and/or produce handicrafts, and pay tribute to the Spaniards.

Because the Indians of Mexico were dying in huge numbers—literally like flies—the Spanish administrators started importing African slaves to take their place in the mines and fields. Between 1521 and 1650 an estimated 130,000 blacks were sold to the Spanish colonists. Eventually another 80,000 was added to this number. (In 1746, 79 percent of the population of Veracruz was black slaves.)

Because the blacks brought into Mexico were physically and spiritually stronger than the demoralized Indians (they were physically larger than the Indians, and they had not suffered the debilitating effects of seeing their homelands conquered and the whole way of life of their people destroyed), the Spanish were especially careful to prevent them from gaining enough strength to rebel against their masters. Punishment for those who showed any independence included flogging, castration and execution.

About the only Indian tribes that survived the Spanish conquest of Mexico more or less intact were those that lived in remote, inhospitable areas of the country in the far north and far south, and in central mountainous areas that did not have the lure of gold and silver. (Some of the smaller Indian nations in the area of present-day Guadalajara were ruled by female elders, which no doubt helped fuel the early belief among Spanish conquistadors that there were Amazons somewhere in Mexico.)

During the 18th century, the Spanish overlords in Mexico City sent numerous military expeditions against the holdout Indian tribes of the northern deserts and mountains. The war against the Tarahumuras, Yaquis and others was usually one of extermination. On a number of occasions when large Indian groups surrendered, they were sold as slaves to plantation owners in Yucatan, completely displacing them.

Despite a number of successful campaigns against the northern Indians, the Spanish army was generally no match for the guerilla tactics of these Indians—they could "disappear" into vast mountain ranges. In desperation, army units tried poisoning beef and other food and leaving it in areas where it would be found by the Indians.

The Spanish administrators in Mexico City also began paying bounties for the scalps and heads of Indians, bringing a large number of bandits and other unsavory types into the campaign to eliminate the Indians.

When Mexico's war of rebellion began in 1810 there were hundreds of thousands of Indians who had been completely dispossessed and displaced. They literally had no homes, no jobs and no income, and roamed the cities and rural areas as vagabonds, eating whatever they could find, reduced to live as hunter-gatherers—much as their primitive ancestors lived hundreds of thousands of years ago.

Despite the vast cultural differences between the Spaniards and Indians of Mexico in the 16th century there were a number of similarities that were to play key roles in the future of Mexico.

The cult of masculinity that the Spaniards brought to Mexico was not a totally new thing to most of the Indian population. Indian Mexico was mostly a man's world, and the only taboos the Indians had against sex were social, not religious.

It is not necessary to refer to historical records for descriptions of the courting and sexual customs of many of Mexico's Indian groups. The customs have not changed to any significant degree in several centuries and can be observed in contemporary Indians. Some of the more interesting of them are mentioned below.

Chamula Indians still practice trial marriages—at either the boy's home or the girl's home. If the boy is satisfied with the way the girl cooks and keeps house, and if she is satisfied that he is a good worker and will support her, the marriage is sexually consummated. If either of them decides that they want out, the final step is not taken and the trial is over.

Totonacas near Papantla are still polygamous, the men keeping as many as four or five wives.

Unmarried members of the Tehuantepec tribe in southern Mexico have traditionally practiced "free love," engaging in casual affairs that are known as "behind the door marriages." Because of this custom, Tehuantepec men do not like to marry virgins. They consider it too much trouble to "break them in." They also prefer to marry women who already have one or two children, considering the children a kind of dowry.

Mexican Indian tribes that survived into modern times and continue to follow many of their traditional ways include the Chamulas, Lacandones, Mayas, Mixtecas, Nahuas, Otomís, Totonacas, Tehuantepecas, Zapotecas and Zinacatecos.

Indians make up about 30 percent of Mexico's population. Altogether, there are some 54 distinct Indian tribes in present-day Mexico, each with its own language and with some of its traditional customs intact. (In 1995 government authorities estimated the Indian population of the country as somewhere around 24 million—approximately the same number that inhabited the country when Cortés and his band of plunderers arrived in 1519.)

There are about 90 identifiable Indian languages and dialects spoken in Mexico today, including Apache, Chontal, Huave, Huasteca, Huichol, Maya, Mixtec, Nahuatl, Otomí, Purapecha, Seri, Yuma, Zaptopec and Zoque.

(Linguists have recorded over 50 Indian languages and over 500 Indian dialects in Mexico.)

Yet virtually all of Mexico's Indians remain outside the mainstream of Mexican society, scrabbling for a living as tiny-plot farmers or makers of handicrafts. Local bosses and the church continue to control most of their lives.

The overt brutality with which the Indians were systematically treated for generations has generally disappeared. Now, they are more likely to be ignored as an embarrassing reminder of the country's history. Both their persons and their efforts are devalued by mainstream society. The tradition of regarding them as *sin razon*, or "without reason," first popularized by the Catholic Church in the 16th century, continues.

Indians who suffered most from the conquest of their homeland by Spaniards were those whose native languages were destroyed and replaced by Spanish. The substitution of Spanish for their own native tongue set them adrift in a new cultural sea where there were no beacons, no stars to steer by.

Even when they were able to retain their languages, the descendants of the once-great Olmecas, Toltecas, Mayas, Aztecas and other Indians of Mexico existed in another dimension, reduced to shadows of their former selves.

With opportunities for education and economic progress virtually nil, the Indians also lived in the shadows, almost invisible, making it convenient for the elite to ignore them altogether or to assume that they were satisfied with their lot.

Over the generations the traditional passivity and shyness of the Indians was shattered only when their lives became utterly unbearable and they resorted to violence in an effort to change things. These uprisings were rare, however, making it possible for those in power to continue rationalizing the plight of the Indians by blaming their fatalistic attitude and generally passive behavior.

Finally, the past caught up with the present in the early 1990s, when Indians in the southern state of Chiapas mounted an armed rebellion that attracted the international press and embarrassed the Mexican government. This resulted in the plight of the Indians becoming the topic of a national debate and the government making promises to initiate programs to aid them.

One of the main arguments of some of those who advocate increased aid for Mexican Indians is that it is unconscionable for the upper class of Mexico to exalt the Indian aspects of their spiritual heritage while continuing to discriminate against Indians and denying them the full fruits of citizenship.

Most non-Indian Mexicans resent being racially or socially associated with Indians in any way. In border slang the word *indio* (EEN-dee-oh) is commonly used in reference to people who are dark-complexioned, uneducated, of low socioeconomic class and without financial prospects.

Mexican Indians prefer to be called *Mexicanos* or by their tribal name. Polite contemporary terms for Indians used by upper-class people are *gente indigena* or "indigenous people," and *indigenas* or "natives."

(See **Indigenismo**.)

Juniors
(Who-nee-ORRS)

"The Playboys of Mexico"

Among the more conspicuous of the present-day elite in Mexico are the sons and daughters of rich politicians and businessmen—the so-called *juniors* (who-nee-ORRS), many of whom are famous as the country's leading playboys and playgirls.

The press, which often chronicles the pastimes and peccadilloes of the young and rich, divides them into "business juniors" and "political juniors." Female *juniors* are sometimes called *Las Niñas Bien* or "The Well-to-do-Girls."

Some *juniors* are serious, hard-working and ambitious to succeed on their own. Others are more interested in taking advantage of their family wealth to have fun. Large numbers of this latter group regularly congregate in Acapulco, Cancun, Puerto Vallarta and other exclusive resorts. They are known for driving expensive cars, disobeying all traffic rules, wearing expensive imported fashions and throwing money around to get whatever service or indulgence they want.

Juniors represent a large percentage of the young Mexican men who make something of a profession of pursuing and courting the more attractive female tourists—who usually travel in pairs or small groups—and the annual crop of foreign coeds who flock to Mexican universities. (The main hunting season for Mexican playboys runs from June through September.) Playboys who concentrate most of their efforts on American coeds going to school in Mexico are less successful than those who devote themselves to tourists, according to stories they tell.

Said one: "When the coeds first arrive they are anxious to make friends and a good impression, so they go all out to be cooperative and compliant. But their naivete and goodwill is soon scraped off and they become more realistic in their attitudes toward the mass of young men who rush them."

Many of the *juniors* and other Mexican bachelors who court visiting American coeds have attended schools in the United States and are bilingual—and most have a common complaint. Virtually all of the girls use them as language tutors, and many of the coeds expect their relationships to remain platonic.

"Some of the girls are so naive they will move into a bachelor's apartment and live with him but refuse to have sex with him and trust him not to force them!" exclaimed one *junior*. To Mexicans, both male and female, such behavior defies explanation.

Mexican *juniors* also accuse American girls of being cold and mechanical in their lovemaking. Said one: "They have been overly stimulated by movies and magazines and are free to do whatever they want, but they don't know how to express their emotions. Their reactions follow the right form, but they are not really passionate."

Added another: "Mexican women have to be dominated before they feel secure, but American girls resist domination. The Mexican girl is more conscientious as a wife and mother. She is always there. She is a slave without being a slave. When I marry I will marry a Mexican girl because she will sacrifice for her family."

Sophisticated *juniors* have mixed attitudes toward Mexican girls. They feel sorry for them and sympathize with them because of the disadvantages they have in relating to men. At the same time they are slightly contemptuous of them for not being more aggressive and asserting their rights as individuals.

Juniors are contemptuous of the old chaperon system which still lingers on in some families—even in the capital—and are especially incensed when girls use the church as a prop, a weapon and a refuge in their dealings with men.

Young Mexican men in general know the weaknesses of Mexican women and take cynical advantage of them. They know Mexican women cannot stand being ignored, that having been conditioned to the flattering and domineering attention of men, they become unsettled without it.

"We know that if we behave indifferently toward women for a short period and then abruptly become domineering, we can have our way with them," explained one.

In their role of gallant ladies' men, Mexican men have developed flattery to a diabolical art. They become so clever at catering to the ego of women that those who are not used to this type and amount of passionate attention are apt to be overwhelmed by it. Said one: "Older foreign women, especially, tend to become giddy and can be led around like puppets on a string."

Juniors are favored clientele in the exclusive and expensive whorehouses in Mexico because they frequent them often and spend money freely. They generally prefer houses that are staffed by foreign as well as Mexican women.

The most notorious of the *juniors* are the younger ones, in their late teens, who spend money lavishly to get whatever they want—usually cars, women and drinking sprees in exclusive nightclubs.

On the business side, older *juniors*, especially those educated in the United States and Europe, have become a major influence in the economic development of Mexico and in the slow but inexorable move toward a truly democratic government. These sons of affluent Mexican families are using their bilingual, bicultural abilities to help advance the political and economic transformation of Mexico that began in 1910, when the country exploded in a revolution against the abuses of its colonial and dictatorial past.

As more of these *juniors* move into responsible business and political positions, the future of Mexico will be more assured.

68

Juntos
(HOON-tohs)

"Mexican Togetherness"

It is a well-established fact that most people who experience things together, regardless of the nature of the experiences, develop special bonds. It also appears to be true that when such experiences are difficult and a great deal of suffering is involved, the bonds are tighter and longer lasting.

Historically, there are few people who have suffered more than Mexico's *mestizos*, or Spanish–Indian mixed-bloods, who now make up some 60 percent of the country's population. From the beginning of their history in the 16th century to the early years of the 20th century, mixed-bloods were made to suffer virtually every pain and indignity known to man.

However, this crucible of suffering did not create strong feelings of *juntos* (HOON-tohs) or "togetherness" among the *mestizos* as a national group;

apparently because the racial, social and economic discrimination against them from the beginning of their history was so severe they had no opportunity to develop a sense of self-worth and identify with each other in a positive way.

As "half-breeds" not accepted by the Spanish or the Indians, the *mestizos* had no legitimate place in the world. This, Mexican social scientists now say, resulted in *mestizo* men in particular growing up hating everyone, including themselves and everyone like them.

The feelings of worthlessness, hopelessness and isolation that infected and enraged *mestizo* men fed a plague of violence and savage cruelty that was to afflict Mexico until recent times.

The same feelings also contributed to especially tight bonds within *mestizo* families and to the obsessive lavishing of emotions on personal relationships. But these bonds and emotions were so intense that they too regularly erupted in violence, exacerbating the lives of the people.

It was not until the beginning of the 20th century, when the mixed-bloods of Mexico outnumbered and managed to outfight their oppressors, that they began to recognize themselves as a "new race" and start the long and difficult struggle to create an acceptable identity for themselves.

There is surely no more eloquent testimony to the violence and cruelty of this struggle than that recounted by Mexican-American writer Victor Villaseñor in his remarkable book *Rain of Gold* (Dell Publishing, 1992), in which he tells the life stories of his *mestizo* grandparents, parents and relatives from the late 1880s to the end of the 1920s. There is also no greater testimony to the passions, fierce love, tenacity and resourcefulness of Mexican women, without whom there would have been no story to tell.

Villaseñor's tale of gold, murder, rape, revolution, starvation and anguish, mixed with moments of extreme happiness resulting from tiny triumphs, melds the reader into the heart and soul of *mestizo* Mexicans, revealing their innermost fears, frustrations and joys.

Time and again it also reveals that it was blind hatred that drove *mestizo* men to extremes of macho behavior and prevented them from making use of the power of *juntos* to better themselves.

Until the political and economic reforms that began in the late 1980s there were so many negative factors in the lives of most Mexicans that it was impossible for them think or behave in terms of national togetherness. Their much-praised *juntos* was still more of a personal and family thing than a feeling of group or national unity.

Although there is still a wide and conspicuous social and economic gap between the *mestizos* and Mexicans of European descent, they now share a common feeling of Mexicanness, and are beginning to share feelings of *juntos* as well.

If the reforms that began with the Salinas administration in 1988 continue there is every reason to believe that the *juntos* of Mexico may become a major national asset which will incorporate many other cultural assets, providing Mexico with advantages that are similar to those that helped to make Japan an economic superpower.

La Gerencia
(Lah Heh-REHN-see-ah)

"Management in Mexico"

Business management in Mexico is, of course, a natural reflection of the culture, which means that it differs significantly from management in the United States and Canada. In fact, the style of *la gerencia* (lah heh-REHN-see-ah) or "management" that has come to be associated with North American business practices contradicts almost everything in the Mexican way.

Mexican society has traditionally been hierarchical and authoritarian. Both position and status came from holding and exercising power, not sharing it. In families, the father ruled absolutely. In schools children were taught to be dependent on and feel inferior to those in power. In companies and government offices the head man exercised dictatorial powers and expected absolute submission from employees.

Status has traditionally been everything in the eyes of middle- and upper-class Mexicans, and it was generally measured in terms of family background (indicated by both paternal and maternal surnames), academic degrees and professional position rather than actual knowledge, experience or achievement.

In traditional Mexican organizations it was virtually unheard of for those in power to delegate any of their authority. Questioning authority was a serious offense, generally met with swift punishment. Disagreeing with a superior was just not done.

Direct confrontations have traditionally been dangerous in Mexico, not only because of the authoritarian nature of the culture but also because of the extreme sensitivity of the people to any perceived slights to their face and dignity, and their propensity to resort to violence to wipe out the dishonor.

Under these circumstances, middle managers and workers in Mexico have traditionally required specific instructions and ongoing guidance and approval from their superiors because they were afraid to do anything on their own. This also meant that they did not take responsibility for what they did.

Virtually all of the problems that Mexicans encounter today in initiating and following through on business projects of whatever kind are a result of specific cultural factors that North Americans regard as irrational. Difficulty in delegating authority, the reluctance of employees to take responsibility on their own, failure of management to continue checking every detail of a project out of a sense of dignity or fear of insulting workers, and reluctance to create and work in a highly structured system, all have a detrimental impact on both control and follow-through in Mexico.

Studies of Mexican business practices have revealed that Mexican executives are great at theorizing, planning and making presentations, but are weak in documentation and implementation. Grand-sounding plans and projects in Mexico often do not get off the ground floor, or are stopped before they are completed because of unforeseen difficulties and problems that develop along the way and are not solved.

When projects fail to deliver on their promises, the planners typically blame others, creating frustration and ill will on all levels. Many Mexicans complain that government regulations as well as the personal factors involved in dealing with officials and bureaucrats make it impossible to do business in a rational, businesslike way. They add that traditionally the Mexican government was anti-business unless the "right" officials were profiting directly.

Among other things, Mexicans do not like to receive bad news or be messengers of bad news. Courtesy and social conventions often take precedence over virtually everything else. What is said is generally more important than what is done. These factors frequently result in mistakes being made and problems being ignored.

When there are problems in-house that cannot be resolved, it is common for Mexican executives to call in influential friends from the outside to act as mediators or render decisions that take both sides into consideration.

The Mexican way is to use diplomacy and reach a consensus which is often ambiguous enough that it can be interpreted in more than one way so no one's feelings are hurt.

Traditionally, only family and close personal connections could be trusted in Mexican society, and this belief is still an important factor in politics, business and personal affairs. In their hiring practices, Mexican businesspeople typically put such factors as family relations and personal connections above technical knowledge and experience, with the result that companies may have a highly congenial and loyal work force, but one that is lacking in many crucial skills.

By the same token, any lackluster performance of failure of foreign firms in Mexico is typically blamed on the failure of foreign managers to give sufficient emphasis to human relations in their management style.

Business consultants in Mexico repeatedly point out that Mexicans expect the workplace to have a home-like atmosphere where they are treated more like family members than hired hands, including a conspicuous form of stylized respect that extends down to the lowest ranking employee.

For the most part, the degree of loyalty and effort extended by Mexicans on every level of employment is based on whether or not they perceive their superiors as good and decent people who have employees' personal interests at heart and who are not just using them to make money.

Unlike like most North Americans who regard idleness as sinful and work as a religious activity through which one achieves virtue, Mexicans tend to look at work as a necessary evil, and idle time, or recreation, as essential to fulfilling life. However, many Mexicans have learned to combine the North American commitment to work with their own equally powerful impulse to enjoy themselves.

My favorite response to this dual challenge was made by Mario ("Mike") De La Fuente, a very successful Nogales businessman, who said: "I work like a *gringo* and play like a Mexican!"

(See **Buena Gente, Cortesia, Negocios**.)

70

La Iglesia
(Lah Ee-GLAY-see-ah)

"Devils in Priests' Clothing"

The first Catholic priests arrived in Mexico less than two years after Hernán Cortés had destroyed the Aztec empire (1519–1521), and well before a number of the outlying Indian nations were subdued. A larger group of Franciscans arrived in 1524. Dominicans arrived in 1525, Augustinians in

1533 and Jesuits in 1571. (The Jesuits later became so independent minded and so concerned with the economic welfare of the Indians and *mestizos*, rather than their spiritual exploitation, that their enemies in the other orders prevailed upon the king of Spain to have them arrested and expelled from Mexico.)

In 1531 a religious event occurred—or is said to have occurred—that was to have an extraordinary influence on the rest of Mexican history. According to a story told by the clergy, on December 12 of that year the Virgin Mary appeared three times to a Christianized Indian named Juan Diego at Tepeyac Hill outside of Mexico City, a site that had long been considered a spiritual center by Mexican Indians.

In one vision the mother of Jesus Christ is said to have instructed Diego to build a church on the site. In another vision she told him to pick some roses that were growing miraculously on the hill, put them in his cloak and take them to the bishop of the local diocese.

The story goes on to say that when Diego opened his cloak in front of the bishop they discovered an image of a dark-haired, brown-skinned woman imprinted on the inside of the garment. The site where the roses were picked was renamed Guadalupe, and the miraculous image on the cloak came to be known as *Nuestra Señora de Guadalupe*, or "Our Lady of Guadalupe."

From that period on the Catholic Church promoted Our Lady of Guadalupe as the patron saint of all Indians, and used the imagery to help it achieve virtually absolute spiritual, intellectual and economic control over the Indians of Mexico.

Present-day Mexican critics of the Catholic Church say the church deliberately created the Indianized mother of God as a ploy to seduce Indians into submitting to the church and doing its bidding without question.

In any event, most of the first Catholic priests assigned to Mexico from Spain following the conquest were as fair-minded and as idealistic as a Catholic priest of that time could be. But they were deadly serious about their goal of converting Mexico's 24 million people to their brand of Catholicism and in increasing the power and wealth of the Catholic Church.

Immediately upon their arrival in Mexico the priests ordered and supervised the wholesale destruction of Indian temples and religious artifacts, including books and anything else that appeared to have religious importance to the Indians. They prohibited the Indians that were under their direct control from conducting any of their traditional religious services, and punished them severely if they broke the taboo.

When Mexico fell to the Spanish, Cholula, a leading Indian spiritual center with a population of around 100,000, had 365 temples—one for each day of the year. The newly arrived Spanish priests supervised the destruction of all of the temples, and vowed that they would build a church on each temple site. (Only 11 churches were eventually built in the city.)

In the early decades of the colonization, priests in Mexico City founded a college to teach the surviving Aztec nobles Spanish, Latin and theology. Other priests established schools throughout the country for the education of ordinary Indians.

The priests used conscripted Indians as laborers to build the schools as well churches, the latter in every city and in virtually every town and village in the country. By 1810 there were over 12,000 Catholic churches in the country.

The Maya, in Yucatan, were among the last of the Indian nations of Mexico to be crushed by the Spaniards and to come under the control of Spanish priests. In 1562 a priest named Landa took part in burning the astronomy, history and religious books of the Maya, noting afterward that the burning caused them a great deal of pain and suffering.

Church leaders eventually divided Mexico into three separate parishes, but kept Mexico City under the joint rule of the various religious orders.

By the end of the 16th century, the more benign and supportive behavior of the Spanish priests had changed dramatically.

In just 89 years, from 1521 to 1610, Mexico's Indian population dropped from around 24 million to only 1.5 million as a result of diseases brought in by the Spaniards, overwork, starvation, mistreatment by their Spanish overlords, and the breakup of Indian families.

As conditions in Europe evolved, the Spanish Court demanded more and more gold, silver and other produce from Mexico. This resulted in the Spanish rulers in "New Spain" redoubling their demands on the surviving native population.

Newly arrived colonial administrators, as well as priests, obsessed with making their mark in the New World and increasing the power and wealth of Spain and the Catholic Church, began to treat the Indians more as slaves than indentured workers.

Indians were forced to work in mines and then were routinely locked up during their sleep periods. They were worked seven days a week for 12 or more hours each day, and were never allowed to leave the mining compounds. Indians working on *haciendas* and ranches were similarly guarded to make sure they did not escape.

Decades after the conquest, one of the priests newly assigned to Mexico was so shocked to see that the surviving Indians were being used as beasts of burden that he had a small band of burros brought in, which he gave to the Indians in his parish. This tiny herd was the origin of the burro as the national beast of burden in Mexico for the next 300 years.

From around 1610 on, church leaders, in close collaboration with the government and military, began to oppose all attempts to make education available to the Indians and mixed-bloods. It was the church's position that education would "spoil" the people—meaning that the church would lose control over them if they became educated. The college for the descendants of Indian nobles was closed. The other Indian schools were either closed or converted over to white Spanish students only.

By the end of the first century of the colonization of Mexico the church had become wealthy by charging for its various religious rituals and licenses, and from gifts received from rich estate and silver mine owners. Fines and penalties collected from "sinners" in 1649 alone amounted to three million pesos. Much of this growing hoard of wealth was used to buy up real estate of all kinds.

Religious orders also lent money at five percent interest, using the income to buy more land and city property. As early as 1683 one third of all the property in Mexico was owned by the Catholic Church.

However, not all of the wealth accumulated by the church was used solely to increase its own power. Among the good works of the church were the operation of schools and hospitals for the upper classes. Some convents provided food for the desperately poor who could no longer feed themselves. (But some of the convents have been described as "palaces," in which each nun had her own personal Indian or *mestizo* servant.)

Historians say that by 1630 most of the large number of lower ranking priests in Mexico were arrogant, ignorant, obsessed with sex and totally corrupt, spending much of their time drinking, gambling and fornicating with Indian and *mestizo* women. In the words of one historian, they had no faith, no morals and no limits.

In 1697 church leaders even prevailed upon the viceroy to allow the church to take over and administer all of Baja California as its own personal fief. This mandate was maintained until 1847—a period of 150 years.

In the 1700s Mexico was divided into eight dioceses, with each of the eight bishops drawing annual salaries that ranged from 90,000 to 130,000 pesos—the latter, by today's purchasing standards, is the equivalent of about $2 million. The annual income of a skilled craftsman in Mexico at that time was around 160 pesos.

In 1810, when the first organized rebellion broke out against Spanish rule in Mexico, there were only 10 small schools for Indians in the entire country.

In 1823, two years after Mexico had won its independence from Spain, Mexican authorities estimated that the Catholic Church owned one half of Mexico, and held mortgages on most of the rest of the country.

Records of that time show that the church owned 47 percent of all the land making up Mexico City, and that the Dominican order alone owned 25 percent of the land in the state of Oaxaca.

Spain's notorious religious Inquisition was brought to Mexico by the first bishops, who arrived shortly after Hernán Cortés conquered the Aztec nation in 1521. (All bishops automatically had Inquisitorial powers by virtue of their office.) The first officially appointed Inquisitor, a Dominican, arrived in 1528.

In 1570 Spain's feared Holy Office of Inquisition established a full branch in Mexico, charging it with the responsibility of rooting out and reconverting repentant heretics, and burning those who did not satisfy the Inquisition judges.

Over the next 250 years (until 1820) the Holy Office in Mexico—continuously run by Dominicans—actually burned fewer than 300 victims, but it tortured and imprisoned tens of thousands.

With so few non-Catholics to keep its priest-judges busy, Mexico's Inquisition Office took upon itself the additional responsibility of censoring all printed materials allowed into the colony. In later centuries its members assumed the role of political commissars as well, deciding on what was politically correct and incorrect. Two of the items that were banned from Mexico were the American *Declaration of Independence* and the *U.S. Constitution*.

The few advantages upper-class people enjoyed—because the church ran so much of their lives—were 85 religious holidays every year, plus a variety of other events that large numbers of people participated in (one of which was viewing inquests held by the Holy Office of Inquisition).

Prior to 1857 the church was the sole source of birth and death certificates, marriage licenses, adoptions and burial permissions, all of which required the payment of fees. All sacraments also required fees. For a peasant a baptism or last rites cost the equivalent of five months of income. At the same time, the annual income of the church was more than five times that of the colonial government.

The church also controlled all education, basically limiting it to some five percent of school-age children in the country.

The *Constitution of 1857* was Mexico's first attempt to separate the church from the government and to establish a bill of rights for ordinary citizens. *La Ley de las Iglesias*, or "The Law of the Church," decreed that churches could no longer charge poor people for sacramental blessings, and that people who could afford to pay would be charged modest fees.

After the *Constitution of 1857* was passed, the clergy refused to absolve, marry or bury anyone who supported it. This resulted in a three-year civil war between conservative church advocates and the reformers which cost the lives of thousands. In 1861 the reformers won.

President Benito Juárez (a Zatopec Indian) nationalized all church properties, closed many monasteries and convents and made the government responsible for issuing marriage licenses and burial permits.

The church retaliated by persuading France to invade Mexico and establish a monarchy, with Archduke Maximilian of Austria as the emperor. By 1862 a large French army had defeated the poorly equipped Mexican forces and occupied the country. To escape execution President Juárez went into exile in the United States (where he worked for a while in New Orleans rolling cigars).

It was 1864 before Maximilian and his empress arrived in Mexico City, and he turned out to be so liberal—approving of a number of the reforms instituted by Juárez—that the church and his royalist supporters soon abandoned him.

Once again the Mexicans, under the leadership of the exiled president and with material help from the United States, rose in rebellion. They defeated the French in 1867 and executed Maximilian. Juárez returned to Mexico City and the office of the president.

When Juárez died in office in 1872, many of the reforms his administration had instituted soon disappeared. The church reclaimed many of its former properties and prerogatives.

Some 40 years later one of the primary goals of the Mexican civil war of 1910–1920 was to eliminate the stranglehold that the church still had on Mexico.

After deposing the Porfirio Díaz dictatorship in 1910 and then fighting loyalists for six more years, the successful revolutionary leaders promulgated a new constitution that once again nationalized church property, prohibited the church from owning any property other than the land churches were on, banned church involvement in education, decreed that only Mexican nationals could become priests, outlawed religious processions, made it unlawful for priests to appear in public in their priestly garb and prohibited them from discussing politics and voting.

An article in the *Constitution of 1917* declared in part that "the clergy is the most baneful and perverse enemy in our country. (It has) tremendous hate for democratic institutions, the deepest hate for the principles of equity, equality and fraternity. (It) transmits only the most corrupting and terrible morality."

But the new government did not have the power to enforce these constitutional provisions and things went on exactly as they had before, with the church continuing to undermine the efforts of the government to reform the country's educational and economic systems. Fighting between competing generals and local warlords also continued, with over one million people losing their lives between 1910 and 1920.

When Plutarco Elias Calles was elected president of Mexico in 1924, he quickly moved to wrest control of the country away from church. This ignited a new rebellion. The bishops obtained permission from the Pope in Rome to take the entire Catholic Church of Mexico out on strike. The clergy was ordered to close all churches, to stop performing any religious services whatsoever and to began stirring up the peasants against the government.

The poor people of Mexico, conditioned for centuries to be submissive and dependent upon the church, were devastated. Following the instructions of the parish bishops, priests throughout the country began whipping their parishioners into a frenzy, calling on them to defy the government and force it to back down.

Under the banner of *Viva Cristo Rey!* ("Long Live Christ the King!") peasants in the western states of Mexico launched a guerilla war against government forces and public facilities, embroiling the country in a three-year orgy of sabotage, burning, rape and killing.

However, the rage of the peasants had very little to do with the immediate concerns of the church. For them it was an excuse to vent frustrations and hatreds that had been building for centuries. They began attacking anyone who had a business or property, killing the men, raping their wives and daughters, then stealing whatever money they could find.

American ambassador to Mexico Dwight Morrow acted as an intermediary in helping to arrange a truce between the government and the church, and in 1929 the churches reopened for business.

For more than 300 years Mexico had had two governments, the civil one and the church. It was to be some 40 more years before the tentacles of the church could be torn away from the throats of the people of Mexico, in a slow and painful process that has not yet been fully realized.

Today many educated Mexicans openly blame the Catholic Church for the general poverty of the country. They say that the church policy of forbidding birth control and encouraging married women as well as young single girls to have unlimited children is both irresponsible and inhuman, and prevents a large segment of the population from being able to help itself.

Government records show that in the 1920s, 70 percent of all births in Mexico City were "natural" births, meaning they were not within wedlock, a phenomenon sociologists blamed on the church, saying they condoned a system that allowed upper-class men to have unrestricted sex with lower-class girls and women.

Just as in past centuries, in villages and towns throughout Mexico it is common to see young women who have never been married but who have several children, often by different men.

Surely one of the greatest sins of the Catholic Church of Mexico was that for century after century it taught that it was the God-ordained fate of the poor and uneducated to suffer and that the only acceptable response was to be pious and passive and to endure.

The church also endorsed and practiced the custom of treating men and women differently. Generally, the attitudes and behavior of men contradicted the most fundamental tenets of the church, while women were held to the highest possible standards of Christian morality.

Again generally speaking, Mexican men went to church only on New Year's Day and during Holy Week, and totally ignored its teachings at all times. Said one long-time male friend: "The church is for women and children."

It was not until the latter half of the 20th century, by which time the Catholic Church of Mexico had lost most of its oppressive economic and political power, that new generations of bishops and priests gradually became advocates of the people and began to assume roles that were positive rather than negative. (Mexico did not renew "diplomatic" relations with the Vatican until 1993.) But the legacy of negativism built up by the Catholic Church over more than 400 years will no doubt continue to plague Mexico for several generations.

71

La Ley
(Lah Lay)

"Land of the Lawless"

A Mexican woman who was in the United States illegally told an interviewer that the reason she preferred to live in the United States was because Americans obeyed laws, while Mexicans did not. Her response was indicative of the pathetic history of law and order in Mexico.

During the Spanish era in Mexico, which began in 1521 and lasted until 1821, Mexico was ruled jointly by the court of Spain and the papacy of Rome, both of which were absolute dictatorships. Indians and mixed-bloods were treated more like property then human beings. They had no right to participate in government in any way, and were kept in a state of virtual bondage. To make matters worse, the overwhelming majority of the Spanish administrators and Catholic bishops who were assigned to Mexico were corrupt, and routinely ignored the court and papal laws they were supposed to enforce.

Following Mexico's revolutionary war against Spain in 1810-1821, the newly independent country adopted the *Code Napoleon*—the French civil laws prepared under the direction of Napoleon Bonaparte between 1804 and 1807—as the basis for its legal system.

The primary purpose of *Code Napoleon* was to preserve the government and ensure a peaceful and tractable population by limiting the rights of people and mandating swift, severe punishment if they contravened any of the codes.

Under this system people could be arrested without due cause and held for virtually any length of time before being charged or brought to trial, and were considered guilty until they could prove themselves innocent.

People who were arrested did not have the right to retain legal counsel to represent them prior to the beginning of a trial. Most of the people who were arrested could not afford representation during trial, or had never heard of the concept. Sentences were passed by judges acting entirely on their own.

One of the laws passed during the reign of the dictator Porfirio Díaz (1876-1910) was *La Ley de Fuga*, or "Law of Escape." Under this law prisoners who tried to escape could legally be shot and killed. In reality, the law was used on virtually every level of the government, from local policemen to the president, to eliminate political prisoners and others who had been arrested and were in the way. All authorities had to do to justify such killings was claim the prisoners had tried to escape.

In this environment law enforcement agencies in Mexico used their powers to take advantage of people. Individual police, military personnel, customs officials, immigration officers and security agents used their powers to enrich themselves. "Justice" was based on one's ability and willingness to pay bribes or "fees."

When assaulted, robbed or wronged in any way, ordinary citizens almost never went to the police because they feared them and because they knew they would have to pay for any "service."

Thus ordinary Mexicans did not regard the police, the court system or judges as upholders of the law or guardians of justice, but as agents of the government who utilized their power to victimize the people. In that milieu there was no incentive for people to obey laws.

One of the ways affluent Mexicans managed to tolerate this system in more recent decades was by making use of the *amparo* (ahm-PAR-oh) or "injunction." By getting a court to issue an *amparo* (by paying a fee) they were able to stop all legal proceedings against them, giving them time to develop a defense and/or prove their innocence, or simply to keep the proceedings bottled up.

It was not until the 1990s that the government of Mexico began a genuine effort to eliminate the more blatant abuses of laws by those charged with the responsibility of upholding them, a process that will no doubt take one or more generations.

Visitors in Mexico are therefore advised to be very careful about running afoul of the legal system. Among other things, there is no plea bargaining or trial by jury.

There is one factor in the legal and penal system of Mexico, however, that is regarded by many as far more enlightened and humane than the United States' system. Prison inmates are allowed conjugal visits from wives, girlfriends or prostitutes every two weeks.

Another custom that distinguishes Mexico's penal system from the United States' is that prisoners who have the money are allowed to buy virtually anything they want. Affluent prisoners can live more or less like they are in a hotel, including having their meals brought in from the outside.

72

La Leyenda Negra
(Lah Lay-YEN dah NAY-grah)

"The Black Legend"

From the beginning of the great period of world exploration by the English, Spanish, Portuguese and other Europeans, the race to discover and colonize new lands was a competition between political and economic ideologies but also a competition, more important in many ways, between religions—Catholicism and Protestantism.

This competition between Catholic and Protestant nations was fueled by different religious views as well as by starkly different work ethics. These differences immensely affected the way explorers and later colonials looked upon and treated the native peoples they discovered.

Protestants accused the Catholics of being blinded by their lust for gold, being cruel beyond belief in their treatment of native Indian populations, destroying native cities and cultures, and subjecting natives to the harsh hand of the Catholic Church.

Both Spaniard and Portuguese colonials were painted by Protestants as being so arrogant that they would not stoop to do any kind of work with their hands, turning the New World Indians they conquered into slave laborers for that. They were also described as being so obsessed with sex that they turned female Indians into sex slaves.

These accusations, endlessly repeated over many generations, grew into *La Leyenda Negra* (lah lay-YEH-dah NAY-grah), or "The Black Legend," which depicted Spanish colonials as the epitome of evil.

On the other hand, the English and other non-Catholic colonizers did not attempt to enslave the natives of the lands they conquered and use them as laborers, or to use them as sexual partners. Their general policy was to exterminate them, or to drive them off of their ancestral lands and isolate them from colonial society.

Some historians credit Bartolomé de las Casas with sowing the seeds of the Black Legend. A Dominican priest who came to the New World as chaplain to the "conqueror" Panfilo de Narvaez (who was sent from Cuba to Mexico to arrest Hernán Cortés), Las Casas thereafter spent his long life trying to protect Indians and to expose the cruelty of the Spanish conquistadors.

Las Casas, who was privately and publicly referred to as *El Protector de los Indios*, or "The Protector of the Indians," escorted a group of Indians to Spain to prove to the queen that they were "human" and not beasts, as was commonly believed. Las Casas made his point by showing the queen that the Indians were capable of laughing—something beasts did not do.

In defending themselves against *La Leyenda Negra*, contemporary Mexicans have pointed to the fact that their Spanish forbearers not only merged racially with the Indians they conquered, they also extended to them the spiritual and intellectual benefits of the Catholic Church.

This claim sounds hollow in light of the fact that the Spanish conquistadors who conquered Mexico, and the Catholic priests who followed them, systematically destroyed the temples of the Indians, killed their leaders and banned the practice of their religions, leaving them, in Octavio Paz's words, "in a solitude so complete it is difficult for a modern man to imagine it."

In any event, the privilege of becoming Catholic could hardly be said to have made up for all of the hardships and suffering inflicted upon the Indians of Mexico, or the mixed-bloods produced by the Spanish policy of miscegenation.

With their gods banished and their lifestyles rendered asunder, Mexico's Indians were totally demoralized. Within less than 100 years their numbers dropped from some 25 million to 1.5 million. Millions succumbed to European diseases, others to the harsh treatment meted out by their new masters.

At the same time, the mixed-bloods sired by Spaniards with Indian women became a puzzle of minutely defined castes who were not accepted by either the Spaniards or Indians. It was to be nearly 400 years before the mixed-bloods of Mexico were to be fully recognized not only as a *new* race but as the predominant race in Mexico—ultimate proof, as far as many were concerned, that the anti-Spaniard "Black Legend" was a false charge.

Today, generally speaking, discrimination in Mexico is more cultural and economic than racial. Pure-blooded Indians who speak Spanish, are educated and dress and behave like mainstream Mexicans generally do not encounter overt racial discrimination in day-to-day living. In politics, business and the professions, however, there is ongoing bias in favor of European blood. The more European blood people have the more the system favors them. Discrimination on this level is generally not openly expressed, but shows up in a variety of subtle ways.

Even the most casual survey of the top positions in Mexico, in whatever field, reveals a preponderance of people whose racial background is more European than Indian.

La Raza of Mexico—and other Latin American countries—is still trying to find its place in the sun.

73

La Moda
(Lah MOH-dah)

"Looking Good"

During Mexico's long colonial period under Spain racial extraction and social status were primary factors in the creation of the culture that was eventually to become known as Mexican.

Both European-born and Mexican-born Spanish residents of New Spain, as the colony was called, were distinguished not only by the color of their skin, their attitudes and their behavior, but also by the clothing they wore.

As an elite ruling class that did not have to engage in manual work to sustain itself, the Spanish-blood residents spent a great deal of time and money on their appearance. Men and women alike wore highly stylized apparel that was in stark contrast to the clothing worn by Mexican Indians and, within two generations, the rapidly growing number of Spanish–Indian mixed-bloods. The more Mexican society became splintered into racial groups and stratified by social classes, the more important apparel became as a symbol of status.

After Mexico won its independence from Spain in the 1810–1821 revolution, people were free to dress in whatever style they chose. But continuing poverty and the weight of 300 years of history kept most Mexicans locked in to the same habits and costumes that had traditionally marked them.

Members of Mexico's upper class continued to emphasize *la moda* (la MOH-dah) or "fashion" as a key part of their social plumage. Following the short French period in the 1860s, French fashion became the in thing for most well-to-do Mexicans.

It was not until the appearance of a small middle class in the mid-1990s that a significant number of ordinary Mexicans could afford to "dress up" in style in order to demonstrate their new social status.

Apparel is still an important part of one's social and economic image in Mexico. Businesspeople and other professionals generally follow a strict dress code that calls for suits and ties for men and conservative dress for women.

When anyone in a high position in Mexico flaunts this dress code, it is news. The only people who routinely break the code are those who are self-made, having risen from the lower or middle class through their own efforts. There is more fashion leeway for artists, writers and other individualists who are not locked into the establishment for their livelihood.

Foreign businesspeople in Mexico are well advised to follow the custom of formal attire when they are at work. To Mexicans it is still a social statement, but it goes beyond that in that it also symbolizes the attainment of a certain level of education and cultural standing.

Where foreign women are concerned, the situation is especially sensitive. Older Mexican men are still more likely to judge foreign women on the basis of what they wear than on any professional skills they may have. In their minds, any kind of revealing apparel suggests that the women are advertising their availability—not to mention the fact that many Mexican men do not believe that women are capable of performing as well as men.

Mores concerning both *la moda* and the role of women are changing among the younger generations, however. Young men do not always demand, or expect, women to dress conservatively or behave in a conspicuously demure manner.

But whatever the situation, the foreign visitor or resident should be aware that Mexicans pay an inordinate amount of attention to *la moda*, and it continues to be important to them.

(See **Glossary, Buena Presentación**.)

La Policia
(Lah Poh-lee-SEE-ah)

"The Police Versus the Public"

Mexican history abounds with horror stories about the brutality, criminal activities and greed of both its military and municipal police. Instead of having organized gangs like the mafia of Italy and the United States, and the yakuza of Japan, Mexico had its *policia* (poh-lee-SEE-ah), who behaved more like gangsters than citizen-orientated law enforcement agents.

The role and character of Mexican police was set during the Spanish colonial period from 1521 to 1821, when laws were designed to protect and preserve local and federal governments rather than the people, and authorities and officials on all levels used their positions to enrich themselves at the expense of the people.

Law enforcement was a cruel reflection of the racial and cultural discrimination the Spanish administration practiced against Mexico's Indians and mixed-bloods, combined with the predatory and pecuniary nature of the Catholic Church. Ordinary people were treated as objects to be preyed upon, and were punished viciously if they resisted in any way.

Early in the history of Spanish rule in Mexico the clergy and the military conspired to legally exempt themselves from civil laws, meaning that they could virtually do as they pleased and neither the municipal police nor civilian courts could touch them.

Mexico's municipal police were not included under this special exemption law, but the police throughout the country generally assumed the same special privilege that the clergy and military reserved for themselves.

This exemption law was repealed by *The Constitution of 1857*, but it was not enforced. For all practical purposes, the military, clergy and police remained above civilian law until the last decades of the 20th century. Thus common citizens lived for generation after generation in a society in which they were victimized rather than protected by the military and police forces of the country, a situation that did not begin to change significantly until well after the civil war of 1910–1921.

Today, despite cultural changes in the attitudes and behavior of Mexican police in general, as well as attempts by the government to ensure much higher standards of morality among police and other security agencies, the news media and individuals say that the use of intimidation, torture and other forms of force by police is still common throughout the country.

Mexico has several categories of police and security forces, including some that are private, without any judicial oversight. Regular "beat" police in Mexico are called *preventivos*. They wear uniforms and are charged with preventing run-of-the-mill crimes. Cops in charge of controlling automobile traffic in towns and cities are called *transitos*. Mexico's uniformed highway patrol cops are called *policiá del caminos*. Then there are the *judicial federales*, who wear plain clothes, and the *judicial*, who are described as "general purpose" police.

In rural areas *ejidos*, or farm cooperatives, maintain their own private security militia, whose members are called *comisionados*. They do not have the authority to arrest or incarcerate people.

Granaderos are an elite police force in Mexico City which specialize in quelling riots and breaking up public demonstrations against the government. According to press reports, the *granaderos* have built up a reputation for brutality.

Finally, there is the *Servicio Secreto* or Secret Service, whose members are concerned with matters of national and international security.

Among the more feared "police" in Mexico are the *guaruras*, or "bodyguards," hired by rich landowners, politicians and businesspeople. These tough-looking and tough-acting men are often referred to as *nacos* (thugs) by the people at large.

People who get involved with the police, particularly traffic cops, generally attempt to settle the matter on the spot by paying a *multa* (MOOL-tah) or "fine" directly to the cop to avoid being arrested and taken to jail, which is almost always an expensive ordeal. Among the slang terms for jail: *jaula* (cage) and *bote* (can).

Visitors who do not speak Spanish or speak it poorly and are not familiar with the "going rates" for this kind of bribe or *mordida* (literally it means "bite") are at a serious disadvantage when it comes to arriving at an acceptable amount to offer, and making the offer diplomatically enough that the cop will not take offense.

About the only practical advice for situations of this kind is to remain very calm, apologize, make up some plausible excuse if you were at fault, plead poverty and try to appeal to the officer's sympathy.

Virtually every "authority" on Mexican police and the justice system says that if you are driving in a rural area and hit an animal, drive away as quickly as you can if your car will still move. Thousands of miles of roads and highways are not fenced and animals wander across them day and night. On winter nights cows habitually lie on the pavement because it holds heat for several hours after sundown.

There is a special word for government officials and policemen who make a practice of extracting especially large bribes or payoffs from their victims. They are called *mordelones*, which might be loosely translated as "the big biters."

(See **La Ley, Moralidad, Mordida**.)

75

La Raza
(Lah RAH-zah)

"The Cosmic Race"

Mexico is the only major country in the world in which the bulk of the population consists of the racial merger of the indigenous people with European whites and African blacks—a merger that produced a new breed of people. One writer christened this mix "the Cosmic Race" as a way of glorifying both the new race and its unique culture.

In the early years of the 19th century it became vogue among Mexican intellectuals to refer to the mixed-bloods of Mexico (and Latin America) as *La Raza* (lah RAH-zah), "The Race" or "The People."

The term *La Raza* was apparently first used in 1908 by Mexico's education minister Jose Vasconcelos, who created the motto, "Through My Race the Spirit Will Speak," for the newly established National University. It was also Vasconcelos who was the first to formally and publicly recognize that the mixed-bloods of Mexico had become the predominant race in the country.

In the minds of Mexicans and other Latin Americans where mixed-bloods are prominent, *La Raza* is a superior race in a humanistic, philo-sophical, spiritual and artistic sense, made up of people who are a product of the best of Europe and the best of the New World.

Transcending their mixed-blood heritage, Mexicans of this new race have taken the position, "*Yo soy puro Mexicano*," meaning, "I am pure Mexican."

The merging of the white and Indian races began in Mexico within a matter of hours after Hernán Cortés and his band of 500 plus soldiers landed in the vicinity of present-day Veracruz—a city he founded— in 1519.

A nearby tribe of Indians presented the "god-looking" foreigners with 20 female slaves as servants and sex partners. These women went to the captains in the group. Following a pattern already set in Cuba and on other Caribbean islands appropriated by Spaniards, the remaining soldiers quickly availed them-selves of other Indian women, having different partners as often as possible.

Virtually all Spanish men who arrived in Mexico before and after the con-quest, including most of the Catholic priests, made a regular practice of hav-ing sex with multiple Indian partners.

Following Mexico's independence from Spain in 1821 the infusion of pure European blood into the racial genes of Mexico was considerably reduced. But the Mexican-born Spaniards who remained in the country after the revolution continued the custom of using Indian servants and field work-ers as casual sex partners, often on a prodigious scale.

After the end of the Porfirio Díaz reign in 1911 and the beginning of the 10-year civil war, there was another slow-down in infusion of pure European blood into the Mexican race.

The next major infusion of pure white blood into Mexico was in the 1930s, when the royalists of Spain were defeated in that country's civil war. Mexico allowed 50,000 of the losing royalists, mostly men, to come into the country as political refugees. Some of these men married into *mestizo* families.

Despite the emergence of a *mestizo*-ized race as the primary "color" in Mexico, racial discrimination on the basis of color is still rampant, although official spokespeople vociferously deny it.

The ancient Spanish and Indian belief that white-skinned people are superior remains deep-seated in the consciousness of Mexicans of all shades.

Spoken or unspoken, blonde women are regarded as the epitome of feminine beauty. Light-skinned and light-haired men and women are promi-nent in the movie and television industries. The lighter the skin and hair of commercial models, the better their chances of success. The upper class of Mexico is predominantly pure white or mostly white.

There is a saying in Mexico that clearly reveals one aspect of the traditional attitude toward racial color which goes, "*Gringos no, gringas si,*" which figuratively means, "White men no, white women yes." This advocates "whitening" of the Mexican race by Mexican men having sexual relations with white women at the same time prohibiting white men from having sex with Mexican women.

Despite this failing, the concept that Mexicans (and the mixed-races in other Latin American countries) constitute a new *raza* is a vital factor and will have an increasingly important influence on the interests and welfare of the rest of the world.

Dia de la Raza, or "Race Day," is celebrated on October 12 in Mexico. However, more and more people now prefer to call it *Dia de la Hispanidad*, "The Day of the Hispanics."

76

Las Posadas
(Las Poh-SAH-dahs)

"Getting Ready for Christmas"

In the American Southwest most people would interpret the word *posada* (poh-SAH-dah) as "inn" or "lodging," and that is its original meaning in Mexico as well.

But in Mexico *las posadas* does not mean "the inns," as in several inns. Instead, it refers to a traditional nine-day-long ceremony that marks the journey of Joseph and Mary from Nazareth to Bethlehem and their search for lodgings when they arrived in that city. *Las Posadas* is a modernized version of that journey, which is more like a month-long party.

Although now purely Christian, the traditional *las posadas* (the lodgings) ritual is said to have been adapted from an Aztec practice, which involved parties held in nine private homes prior to a major festival.

In the contemporary Mexican ceremony a host family makes arrangements with eight other families to sponsor the first eight preliminary *posada* parties at their homes. The organizing family hosts the ninth and last *posada*.

All of the members of the nine families, along with their relatives and friends, are divided into two groups. The first group becomes pilgrims accompanying Mary and Joseph in a candle-lit procession to the first inn (the home of the first host).

The second group, which is the smaller of the two groups, joins the host family and prepares for the coming of the pilgrims. The first *posada* is held on the night of December 16.

When the pilgrims arrive in front of the host home they sing a song asking for shelter. The man playing the role of Joseph carries on a conversation in verse with the host or the "innkeeper."

At first the innkeeper refuses to provide lodging for the pilgrims and threatens to drive them away. But he gradually comes to understand that he and his "inn" are about to become part of a momentous event, and invites the pilgrims into his home.

After the pilgrims enter the home, the second group waiting inside welcomes them with a song. Then food and drinks are served. The final event of the celebration is the breaking of a large *piñata*.

As with all *piñata* parties, anticipation and excitement is built up by blindfolding those who are trying to break the *piñata*, and moving it back and forth so the first several people strike out.

The house hosting the *posada* is decorated with a landscape made to look like Bethlehem, with the nativity scene (*nacimiento*) as its centerpiece. The following day the decorations are moved to the next house scheduled to host the celebration.

On December 24, the ninth and final night of the festivities, the setting in the home of the chief host is a manger, representing the place where the baby Jesus was born.

One of the highlights of this night is "rocking the statue of the baby Jesus to sleep," and then appointing godparents for him. One week later, on January 6, the godparents sponsor a 10th *posada* that depicts the visit of the Three Wise Men to the manger to pay homage to the newborn Christ. This party ends with the sponsors passing out gifts to all of the "pilgrims."

The traditional version of *las posadas* is now generally staged only in smaller cities and towns. In large metropolitan areas the custom has become little more than an excuse to have a party every night during the Christmas season.

Beginning as early as December 12 and lasting until January 5, groups of people go from house to house in the evenings to eat, drink, sing and otherwise have a good time.

For many people during this period, partying takes precedence over work and virtually everything else.

77

LatinoNet

(Lah-TEE-no-net)

"The Hispanic Connection"

Despite their racial and cultural links, Mexicans and other Hispanics in Central America, the Caribbean, South America, the United States and Canada had very little significant contact with each other for centuries because of their mutual poverty and various political, economic and geographic barriers.

That began to change dramatically in the latter half of the 1900s with the introduction of democratic and free-market principles in most of the Latinized countries. Another event occurred in November 1994 in San Francisco which is having equally dramatic consequences.

That was the date *LatinoNet* (la-TEE-no-net), the first on-line, nonprofit minority computer network was launched, a network that put Hispanic nonprofit organizations, legislators, professionals, academics and students in the United States, Mexico, Cuba and Puerto Rico on the information superhighway.

In addition to facilitating communication among these groups, *LatinoNet* provides a wide range of useful information to subscribers, including a master calendar of Hispanic events, a directory of nonprofit Hispanic organizations, Hispanic population and demographic data, and information about job training, employment opportunities, scholarships for students and grant opportunities for nonprofit organizations.

According to the March 1995 edition of *Hispanic* magazine, published in Austin, Texas, *LatinoNet* was founded by Dr. Armando Valdez, a communications research specialist who earned his doctorate at Stanford, taught at several California universities, then established his own consulting firm.

Hispanic contributing editor Federico Cura reported that the Hispanic-oriented network was initially funded by donations from the Telecommunications Education Trust of the California Public Utility Commission, the Hispanic Communications Foundation of the Bay Area, Pacific Bell, Apple Computer, Pacific Gas & Electric and NYNEX.

An additional grant of $450,000 was received from the National Infrastructure Administration of the U.S. Department of Commerce to fund the creation of 10 regional training centers throughout the United States and Puerto Rico to provide technical support and customer service.

Recognizing that most Hispanics live in or near poverty and cannot afford computers or user fees, *LatinoNet*, supported by such companies as Pacific Bell and GTE, partners with nonprofit Latin groups that are active in their communities, and provides them with the equipment and training they need to make use of the network.

Mexicans and other Hispanics see the *LatinoNet* as both an information highway and a unifying force that will help bring them together to focus their energy on issues ranging from education to immigration, and greatly enhance their political and economic options.

Non-Hispanics who want to join *LatinoNet* are welcome; and it is both the growing economic clout and political power of the combined Hispanic communities and countries that is attracting the attention of businesspeople and politicians alike.

La Verdad
(Lah Bahr-DAD)

"The Many Shades of Truth"

When people who have been weaned on empirical thinking and behavior encounter life in Mexico, one of the things that disturbs them most is the perception that Mexicans often do not think or behave in a purely logical manner. These visitors complain that Mexicans are not only illogical in much of their behavior, but that they also play fast and loose with *la verdad* (lah bahr-DAD), or "the truth," telling lies even when there is absolutely nothing to be gained, when the truth would not hurt or put them in any kind of jeopardy.

This fundamental difference in attitudes and behavior derives from the fact that Mexicans operate on a different value system. What may be illogical and untruthful to outsiders, often makes perfect sense to Mexicans.

To begin with, *la verdad* in Mexico has never been based on absolute, objective facts or principles, but on circumstances, a purely Oriental concept that still prevails throughout much of Asia, including such countries as Japan, Korea and China.

The basis for this Mexican–Oriental concept of truth is "personal reality," as opposed to "objective reality." What is truth for one person may not be truth for another; what is true at one time may not be true at another time.

One of the basic "principles" of personal truth is to answer listeners or questioners in a way that will not upset or disappoint them, thereby avoiding any negative repercussions. The rationale for personal truth is simple— maintain harmony and a sense of rightness or correctness, stay out of trouble and please the other person.

In his book on Mexican character titled *The Labyrinth of Solitude*, Octavio Paz wrote that the lies Mexicans habitually tell reflect both what they lack and what they desire, and that many of the lies are told with such artistry that they become superior to reality.

The Spanish word for a lie, *mentira* (men-TEE-rah), does not have the same connotation in Mexican culture that a lie or lying has in Anglo-Saxon societies. Telling a *mentira* is not seen as a sin against God, or as a deeply unethical or immoral thing. It has more of the connotation of a harmless fib, or even a joke.

Said one long-time expatriate: "Mexicans have difficulty saying 'no' to anything. They typically agree to appointments, dates and other commitments knowing that they can't keep them, in order to keep everyone happy for the moment."

Generally speaking, Mexicans consider it rude not to give a positive answer to any question. If they don't know the answer they often make one up.

People who are habitually late or don't keep appointments at all are often referred to as *muy informal*, "very informal." Mexicans tend to be very tolerant of such behavior, as this mild description indicates.

In authoritarian, hierarchical societies such as Mexico the last thing ordinary people want to do is come under suspicion or criticism from higher-ups and risk incurring their wrath. A way of avoiding that is to intuitively divine what their superior wants to hear at the moment, and make sure that is what they get. To people who have no authority, no power, no way of protecting themselves, reality is what will allow them to survive and cause them the least amount of harm at that particular moment.

This approach to truth can be very upsetting to North Americans and others who are conditioned to believe that "genuine truth" is also "honest truth"—that the speaker believes or knows what he or she is saying is true.

The Mexican interpretation of personal reality does not always encompass the concept of honesty. Mexicans typically say things they know are not true simply because they would like for them to be true, a kind of virtual reality which they make up. There is no malicious intent in this presentation.

It is a spiritual, amorphous world that may be in another dimension as far as reality-conscious people are concerned, but it is real to Mexicans.

Mexicans do not feel compelled to identify, qualify or quantify things in absolute terms or according to absolute rules. That, they say, would take the variety and joy out of life because it does not allow for adapting to circumstances.

This amorphous view of the world conflicts directly with the philosophy and psychology of North Americans and others who have been culturally conditioned to see things in solid, unchanging mathematical terms, and to regard any other view as both inefficient and irrational.

To further complicate political and business as well as personal affairs in Mexico, there is more than one kind of "Mexican truth." The truth in Mexico City is not necessarily the truth in other regions of the country. What is accepted as perfectly proper behavior in one region of Mexico is often quite different in another region.

Of course, North Americans and others tell "white lies" by the tons and regularly leave the truth out in order to avoid problems, as well as to deliberately mislead people. But deliberately telling "black lies" is not only frowned on socially, it is also often against the law.

Being able to discern the real truth from personal truth remains a major challenge in dealing properly and effectively with Mexicans. The "real" truth is sometimes referred to as *la mera neta*, or the "clean, genuine, net truth."

Another cultural factor that impacts directly on "the truth" in Mexico— just as it does in Asia—is the obsession with "saving face." Lower-class Mexican men in particular typically go to extreme lengths to avoid loss of face, including concealing the truth, misrepresenting facts and taking revenge against people who damage their sense of honor and dignity.

As in many other areas of traditional Mexican behavior, there are noticeable changes toward a more principle-based view and use of truth taking place among those who have been educated abroad and those who have had extensive experience in international business.

(See **Caballeros, Cortesía, Mañana**.)

79

Libertad

(Lee-bayer-TAD)

"The Limits of Liberty"

A prominent Mexican businessman said to me: "Mexico is an Oriental country. Our way of thinking and behaving has traditionally been different from the Western way. Today, just because we drink Coca Cola and eat McDonald's hamburgers does not mean that we can or will think and act like Americans."

He was reflective for a few seconds, and then added: "But looking at the political, economic and cultural trends in the United States and Mexico today reveals a shocking phenomenon.

"A great many Mexicans are, in fact, trying to turn themselves into a traditional image of Americans—people who are positive in their outlook, fair-minded, ambitious, hard-working and very much concerned about their country. While great numbers of Americans seem hell-bent on turning themselves into the worst kind of Mexicans—people who are negative, unambitious, irresponsible and prone to violence.

"Furthermore," he continued, "we are in danger of being inundated by the most destructive aspects of American culture—drug use, violence, broken families, teen pregnancies and turning our lives into rat races to accumulate and consume more and more—all in the name of political reform and economic progress."

The businessman went on to say that many of the negative things that Mexicans are absorbing from the United States derive from the American concept of *libertad* (lee-bayer-TAD), "liberty" or "freedom," particularly as it is interpreted by individuals.

"Americans are culturally conditioned to think of themselves as individuals first and often last as well," he said. "Their relationships with their families, coworkers, communities, society at large and the United States itself are way down the line in their priorities—and often are not considered at all.

"The egocentric concept of personal freedom is seductive on the surface but it is like a virus that eats away at the soul and stability of a society. It has always been a given that there must be limits to individual freedom for any society to function properly."

A growing number of Mexico's political, economic and social leaders who have risen above the constraints and weaknesses of their traditional culture now agree that if the country is ever going to escape from its past, individuals must have the freedom to be ambitious, innovative and entrepreneurial, and they have designated *libertad* as one of the primary factors that is absolutely essential for the reinventing of Mexico.

But they are determined to redefine the meaning of *libertad*, to make it both compatible with and supportive of a rational, practical and progressive society that puts the needs of the many before the gross appetites of the few.

The Mexicanized version of *libertad* is quite different from the commonly accepted American version. It does not grant carte blanche to behave independently or individually, to think only of oneself or one's personal interests, or to behave irresponsibly under any circumstances.

Libertad in this new Mexican sense means freedom to work together in a positive, cooperative and responsible way to solve problems, and to create and implement plans for building an affluent and genuinely humane society.

Added my businessman confidant: "This concept of *libertad* is primarily based on respect—respect for oneself, for families, for neighbors, and for society in general. It means that social relationships and mutual responsibility take precedence over the individual."

As these new advocates of Mexican-style *libertad* see it, Mexico's biggest challenge for the next two or three generations will be to achieve economic growth and social progress without sacrificing the family values that have sustained the country in the worst of times.

They add that what they must strive for is achieving a cultural balance between what is best about Mexico and what remains positive and good about the United States.

Foreigners who take up residence in Mexico and engage in business there must give up some of the freedoms they may have taken for granted in their own countries. But they will find that enthusiastically and publicly adopting Mexico's new philosophy of *libertad* will more than make up for any disadvantages that might result.

(See **Amistad, Amor, Motivación, Respeto, Reto, Solidaridad**.)

80

Los Pollos
(Lohs POH-yohs)

"Border-Crossing Chickens"

Before 1921 there were no guards or immigration officials along most of the U.S.–Mexican border. The border was there but it was marked at only a few of the more popular crossing points. People went back and forth across the line as casually as one crosses a street.

Over the next several decades the U.S. policy regarding Mexicans crossing the border to work ranged from virtually total exclusion to major campaigns to attract more workers into the country, depending on the economic and political situations in the United States.

By the 1980s the number of Mexicans entering the United States to work, both legally and illegally, had become a flood and was a vital factor in the economies of all of Mexico's northern states and some of the central states as well. Hundreds of villages in these areas existed almost entirely on money sent back to families, usually wives and children, by men who had "gone north." There is probably not a single village in central and northern Mexico that has not seen many of its men make the often long and always dangerous trek northward to cross the border and work in the United States.

Many villages have been left virtually empty of young and middle-aged men during harvesting seasons in the United States and practically all of the villages have had men who never returned; some were killed or died on the way, others abandoned their families and stayed in the United States.

In common parlance, Mexicans who cross the border into the United States illegally are called *pollos* (POH-yohs) or "chickens," a label that was probably derived from the macabre sense of humor Mexicans, who equate the border-crossers with chickens, because chickens generally end up being plucked and devoured.

An earlier name for those crossing the border illegally was *alambristas* (ah-lahm-BREES-tahs), from the word *alambre* or "wire," referring to the metal wire the U.S. immigration authorities used to fence off the international border. This was sometimes shortened to *alambres* (ah-LAHM-brays).

Men who specialize in smuggling *pollos* into the United States are known as *coyotes*, or along some border areas, as *polleros*, which can be translated as "chicken wranglers." (*Pollero* is also a slang term referring to a man who is sexually attracted to young girls.)

In *pachuco* jargon, crossing the border without the help of *coyotes* is sometimes referred to as *a la brava*, which means something like "doing it on courage alone," or "on impulse," without caution.

In more recent decades, it has not been just men who became *pollos*, but women as well; some follow husbands and sons, others set out on their own to escape poverty or the stifling control of their fathers and mothers, often a combination of both.

Anthropologists Marilyn P. Davis quotes one Mexican woman who had been in the United States for years as saying that one of the reasons why she liked it was because people in the United States obey laws while people in Mexico do not, and that in the United States if anyone ignored your rights you could sue them, while in Mexico you have no legal recourse. The woman added: "I don't understand Mexicans!"

Over the years it has been common for Mexican men who came to the United States illegally and ended up staying for several years—or permanently—to begin living with other women and have second families. More often than not, these men eventually stop sending money home to their first families, leaving them on their own.

During the 1990s *los pollos* were said to be the fourth largest producers of income along the border, after tourism, commerce and foreign-owned *maquiladora* assembly plants.

In the mid-1990s the American Immigration Service instituted a variety of new strategies for stanching the flow of illegal Mexicans into the United States. One of these programs, initiated by the Border Patrol in El Paso, Texas, succeeded in reducing the daily influx from around 10,000 to approximately 1,000.

This new effort involved stationing Border Patrol officers within sight of each other along a 20-mile stretch of the border, an approach that impressed American immigration officials along the rest of the border.

Since making the border impregnable to illegal entry is virtually impossible without building a Great Wall from the Pacific to the Gulf of Mexico, the flow of Mexican workers into the United States will probably continue until there are enough well-paying jobs in Mexico to make it a less attractive choice.

(See **Braceros, Coyotes.**)

81

Machismo
(Mah-CHEES-moh)

"The Cult of Masculinity"

According to some Mexican sociologists, historians and others, *El Machismo* (ehl mah-CHEES-moh), often translated as "The Cult of Masculinity," has been one of the most important factors in Mexican society for well over 300 years.

Machismo is an elaboration on the word *macho* (MAH-choh), which is usually translated into English as "manly." But in the full Mexican context *macho* means a great deal more than manliness.

Spanish-style machismo was introduced into Mexico by the Spaniards who conquered the country in 1519–1521 and ruled it as a virtual slave kingdom for the next 300 years. The particular brand of machismo brought by the Spaniards had existed in Spain for more than half a millennium, primarily absorbed from the Saracen Moors, a mixed Berber–Arab race who invaded and settled in Spain in the eighth century. While Spanish machismo was based on male superiority, it was not absolute and it contained a significant degree of chivalry that gave it a romantic aura.

When this relatively mild cult was combined with the Spanish lust for the conquest of foreign lands, gold and converts to Catholicism, plus their contempt for non-European natives, it became a powerful weapon for subduing and destroying native populations around the world.

In Mexico *machismo* became a virulent scourge that brought immeasurable suffering to a whole nation, and violent death to hundreds of thousands.

The Spanish conquerors of Mexico planted the seeds for this new virulent form of machismo by adopting a policy of interbreeding with the Indians to produce a non-Indian population, but then treating the resulting mixed-blood offspring as untouchable outcasts. To make the situation of these mixtures worse, they were also disowned and denied by the Indians as well.

As their number swelled over the generations, the mixed-bloods began trying to create an identity and a role for themselves by imitating the attitudes and behavior of the ruling Spaniards, particularly the Mexican-born Spaniards who had developed their own culture based on an exaggerated form of machismo. Mexico's new race of mixed-blood men, in their terrible need to justify their existence, took the masculinity cult of the Spaniards to its most extreme. To them machismo meant the repudiation of all "feminine" virtues such as unselfishness, kindness, frankness and truthfulness. It meant being willing to lie without compunction, to be suspicious, envious, jealous, malicious, vindictive, brutal, and finally, to be willing to fight and kill without hesitation to protect one's manly image.

Machismo meant that a man could not let anything detract from his image of himself as a man's man, regardless of the suffering it brought on himself and the women around him. In this respect, says Mexican writer Octavio Paz, machismo is a defensive posture, not an aggressive one, and is designed to make men invulnerable to their enemies and capable of withstanding any adversity.

The proof of every man's manliness was his ability to completely dominate his wife and children, to have sexual relations with any woman he wanted, to never let anyone question, deprecate or attempt to thwart his manhood, and never to reveal his true feelings to anyone lest they somehow take advantage of him.

By the time the 300-year-long Spanish enslavement of Mexico ended in 1821, this Mexicanized masculinity cult had spread downward to include the Indianized mixtures, and had firmly established itself as a way of life.

Among the most prized characteristics of the macho man was an extraordinary indifference to danger and to suffering, and the ability to suffer in silence for long periods of time without any sign of impatience, pain or frustration.

Over the next 100 years machismo was to become even stronger and more pervasive. Men were afflicted with a lust for violence and killing. All who could afford it went about armed. Shootings of almost sublime senselessness became daily occurrences.

This insane orgy of blood-letting by mixed-blood Mexican men reached its climax in the late 1800s, and did not begin to wane until the 1920s, after the last great revolution finally ended the absolute power of Mexican-born Spaniards and the church.

The cult of masculinity no longer rules absolutely in Mexico, but it is still a major element in all aspects of Mexican society, giving the society much of its character, style and tone.

Any Mexican male who does not demonstrate a certain degree of masculinity is automatically assumed to be a wimp, impotent, a homosexual or bewitched. Among the poor, lower classes, failure to behave in a masculine manner or loss of masculinity is often attributed to witchcraft. If a previously masculine man becomes mild-mannered or stops using his wife or sweetheart, it is almost always presumed that some other woman has bewitched him, and that he cannot help himself.

Bragging and refusing to take no for an answer continue to be symptomatic of the macho behavior of lower-class Mexican men, especially when they are drinking. Refusing to accept a drink or stopping after one or two drinks must often be done with the utmost diplomacy to avoid getting involved in a conflict.

One of the more irrational results of Mexican *machismo* is the institutionalized practice of debasing women on one hand while glorifying them on the other. Generally speaking, Mexican men feel they must take whatever sexual advantage they can of women because it is expected of them.

Mexican men look at every attractive foreign woman as a special challenge to their masculinity. Writer Carl Franz notes in his insightful book, *The People's Guide to Mexico*, that Mexican men will "go to almost any length to lay a *gringa*."

Mexican law favors men. Under Article 77 of the *Mexican Civil Code* a man can divorce his wife if she commits adultery. But a wife can divorce an adulterous husband only if the act took place in their home, if there is a public scandal, or if he insults her.

Mexican men who maintain mistresses or consort with other women are within their legal rights as long as they are discreet about their affairs and are polite to their wives.

Wife-beating is a legal offense in Mexico, but it is still common. Not only is this "practice" the result of lingering Spanish–Moorish influence on Mexican men, it is also based on "religious" beliefs derived from both Indian and Spanish cultures.

Spanish men traditionally beat women because they were thought to be tainted by original sin and deserved punishment, and because they believed that the only way they could prevent women from exercising their full sexuality was to regularly beat them into submission.

(It has also been said that Spanish men suffered from a deep-seated fear of latent homosexuality as a result of the influence of the Catholic Church, and to combat the fear they were cruel and sadistic toward women.)

Among a number of the Indian tribes of Mexico the men believed that if they did not beat their wives regularly their wives would be punished even more severely after death. Thus a husband who beat his wife was saving her from a later hell by beating it out of her in advance.

Despite significant changes in Mexican culture in recent decades, *machismo* is alive and well, not only in Mexico but also among first and second generations of lower-class Mexican Americans—the so-called *Chicanos*.

Some Mexican Americans who are often in Mexico on business say that generally speaking the most macho men in the country today are the border cops, who have to be especially tough to compete with the gangs and other unsavory characters that the border attracts.

Said one: "Except for the uniforms, border cops can be the worst of the lot, using their power to extort money and sex from both Mexicans and Anglos."

Many violent acts of so-called machismo occur when men are drunk. A case in point is recounted by Luis Alberto Urrea, a former undercover Mexican-American cop in Tijuana, in his shocking book *Across the Wire—Life and Hard Times on the Mexican Border*. Half a dozen men who lived in the neighborhood of a grandmother and her 13-year old granddaughter got drunk one night and tried to break into the grandmother's home to take the girl by force.

It is characteristic of macho men to resent being accused of acting in a macho manner when the accusation involves excessive drinking or their harsh and unfair treatment of women. If the situation involves drinking they are likely to become irrational and violent. If it involves women they may take revenge some other way.

As in other authoritarian, chauvinistic societies where drinking is a special macho ritual, Mexican men regularly bring pressure against each other and casual acquaintances to overdrink.

Outsiders can usually disentangle themselves from this situation by announcing firmly, "*No, gracias. Me hace dano!*" "No, thank you. Its not good for me!"—meaning that if you drink any more you will get very sick, and while you appreciate the offer, you prefer not to make yourself sick. Mexicans who do not want to drink for whatever reason sometimes say, "*Estoy tomando antibioticos*" ("I am taking antibiotics").

In some cases these drinking rituals are carried to the extreme. Called *barracheras* (bah-rah-CHAY-rahs), they require that the participants go wild—going from one drinking place to another, eating copiously, visiting a whorehouse, and ending up totally drunk and exhausted.

Despite the masculine violence that is usually associated with *machismo*, it is not just a stud complex. There is also a strong element of romance that is expressed in music, singing, poetry and male–female interdependence.

Men who represent themselves as the epitome of machismo are not above crying, and frequently become sentimental over things that are decidedly feminine.

The female equivalent of *machismo* is *marianismo*, but one doesn't hear very much about this obvious female aberration in Mexico.

Some of my male Mexican friends who read the manuscript of this book objected to my basically negative description of *machismo*. They pointed out that the higher one goes socially in Mexico the more positive the influence of machismo.

They equated *machismo* with masculine values and behavior that are the epitome of idealized manhood. They see the truly macho man as one who supports and protects his family in the face of all odds, who disciplines his children to be upright, honest and hardworking.

Upper-class Mexican men, they continued, see this positive side of *machismo* as one of the most admirable facets of Mexican culture. In their view, Mexican-style *machismo* is a key factor in the molding and sustaining of the family and personal relationships; as the source of the discipline that instills courtesy and high moral standards in their children.

(See **Chicanos, Criollos, Gachupines, Mestizos, Pelados**.)

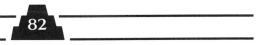

Madres

(MAH-drays)

"Mexico's Secret Weapon"

The Virgin of Guadalupe, the Mexican version of Mary, the mother of Jesus Christ, is the symbolic mother of all Mexicans. Everything that is good and bad in Mexico is ritualistically laid on her head.

The relationship between *madre* (MAH-dray) or "mother" and all that is good and evil in Mexico is so strong in Mexican culture that the word has become one of the most used, most honored, most sensitive and most dangerous words in the language.

Madre is used in good as well as bad references to motherhood, in prayers and in the most serious kind of insults. In fact, Mexicans are so sensitive to the word that some "cultural experts" recommend that foreigners simply not use it at all because it is so easy to misuse.

These experts say that a casual and seemingly innocuous comment about the health or circumstance of someone's mother can be taken the wrong way. (One of my Mexican friends said: "If foreigners want to refer to someone's mother in Mexico it is safer to say *'Mama'*.")

When used in positive references to motherhood, the word *madre* instantly conjures up an image of mothers who are a cross between angels and saints—mothers who are still virginal, who are kind, tender, loving, loyal, and self-sacrificing. In other words, the mother of Jesus Christ incarnate.

This glorification of motherhood in Mexico is described in the term *Marianismo*, which translates more or less as "Virgin Maryism." The colloquial term for the same concept is *Mamaismo*.

Mexican mothers may have been considerably less than angelic over the centuries, but because they have traditionally been oppressed by machismo-driven husbands and conditioned to remain passive and suffering by the church, they have more than qualified as saints.

In typical Mexican families mothers were a cross between slaves and queen bees. They sacrificed themselves to their children and husbands, but life within the household revolved around them, not the fathers.

Historically, Mexican men on all levels of society have regarded child raising as women's work, and have been part-time fathers at best, generally spending holidays and some of their weekends with them.

Another vital factor of motherhood in Mexico has been the extraordinarily high number of children born out of wedlock to poor teenage girls, and, among the poor, the number of fathers who abandon their families altogether, leaving their survival up to the mothers.

Thus the mothers of Mexico have historically been burdened by two sets of morality and ethics—one for men and one for women—in which women were expected to be paragons of virtue, while men lived by a totally different set of rules.

That this sexist-oriented culture developed and persisted for so many centuries can again be laid on the altar of the Catholic Church, which treated women as inferior and demanded that they live by the highest possible standards while sanctifying, or ignoring, immoral behavior by men.

A businessman–social critic commented that the only Mexican mothers who were successful in bringing up truly moral and ethical children were those in Mexico's small middle and upper-middle classes, where families were stable, the relationship between husbands and wives was closer and the role model presented by the fathers was more positive.

The prevailing historical situation of mothers did not begin to change significantly until the 1980s, by which time the negative influence of the church had weakened considerably and the rising standard of living had begun to bring more people into the middle and upper-middle classes.

Obviously, Mexico will not be able to achieve an ethical, moral society until the traditional male attitude toward women and child-raising changes on the upper as well as the lower levels of society, so that the moral teachings and examples of the mothers of Mexico will not be for nothing.

One of my Mexican colleagues adds that contemporary Mexico is already "a society of mothers," and that Mexican society in general is becoming more and more matriarchal as the economy improves.

Malas Mujeres
(MAH-lahs moo-HEHR-ehs)

"Bad Women of Mexico"

Mexican men have traditionally looked upon women, particularly Mexican women, more as abstract symbols of womanhood than flesh and blood human beings who have feelings and needs, a phenomenon no doubt derived from the religious image of women as passive creatures who can be—and should be—brought to life only by joining with a man.

Mexican men have also believed that women should be secretive, that they should hide their feelings and suppress their passions behind a mask; that they literally should have no will of their own. An ordinary woman (not a prostitute) who did anything overtly to attract a man was likely to be regarded as a whore, or at least as having the soul of a whore and the potential of becoming one.

In the ideal male Mexican context, women were allowed to attract men only by the magnetic force of their hidden sexuality, like a cosmic black hole that pulls light into itself.

The morality constructed for women by men, in concert with both Indian beliefs and Catholicism, was based on the assumption that female sexuality was naturally passive, designed to be penetrated from the outside, and therefore naturally vulnerable to aggressive male sexuality. This put women in the role of frail goddesses who were to be worshipped but controlled and used by men, and punished if they failed to live up to this image.

By putting women on a pedestal and denying them any will or rights of their own, Mexican men were able to keep women in a subservient position, subject to their will and the will of the church, while at the same time honoring them and crediting them with bringing tenderness, piety and order to the human race.

Women who did not fit this manmade image, who showed signs of independence and aggressiveness, were subject to being labeled as *mujeres de mala conducta* or "women of bad conduct," and put down by a variety of derogatory slang terms on the order of "pussy" and "piece of ass."

Interestingly, in the traditional cosmos of the Mexican male, *mala mujer* (MAH-lah moo-HEHR) was not necessarily synonymous with a prostitute. A prostitute was a women who sold sex as a commercial product, and therefore engaged in business. Many married women engaged in prostitution on a part-time or full-time basis, sometimes with the consent and cooperation of their husbands. But this did not automatically make them "bad women."

A *maja mujer* was more likely to be a women who acted like a man, a woman who looked upon the church with contempt, came and went as she pleased, had male friends and had sexual relations with men of her own choosing.

The concept of the *mala mujer* has been weakened considerably in present-day Mexico, but it still colors the attitudes of Mexican men, especially toward Anglo–American women. The independence and aggressiveness of single American women in particular strikes the typical Mexican male as immoral.

Mexican women are often contradictory in their views of American women. While they will admit that they envy the independence and freedom of American women, they generally regard the morality of their own Mexican attitudes and lifestyles as superior.

Much of the negative impression that both Mexican men and women have traditionally had of North American women derives from the behavior of the large number of female tourists who flock to the seaside resorts of Puerto Vallarta, Acapulco and elsewhere. Unaccompanied by males, many proceed to engage in affairs with local men.

The fact that Mexican females are equally susceptible to affairs, particularly with aggressive males, does not appear contradictory to Mexican women because they are able to blame the behavior on the men.

The concept of *mala mujer* continues to haunt Mexican women by adding to the psychological barriers that restricts them to a segregated world. But sexual emancipation is definitely on its way and television is probably the most powerful force. Mexican-style "soap operas" in particular are changing the image as well as the behavior of Mexican women. In scenes that verge on the pornographic, very "proper" young women are regularly depicted as "like water for chocolate"—sexually "hot" and ready to bed attractive men at the first opportunity.

84

Mal Del Turista

(Mahl dehl too-REES-tah)

"Montezuma's Revenge"

In the 1960s a task force of health officials, acting on behalf of Mexico's tourism industry, inspected the food served in several thousand restaurants that catered to visitors.

The report filed by the inspectors was a shock to travel agents and potential travelers alike, but not to the hundreds of thousands of people who had visited Mexico in the previous decade. The report stated that over 65 percent of the restaurants were serving food unfit for human consumption.

A significant percentage of the people who had visited Mexico prior to the publication of this report were aware that something was wrong, because more than half of them invariably came down with some degree of diarrhea while they were in Mexico. But they had no inkling of the extent of the problem.

All of the members of my own family who visited the interior of Mexico during the 1960s and the 1970s, without exception, came down with severe cases of diarrhea—one of them so serious that she required hospitalization for several days and outpatient treatment following an emergency return from her vacation trip.

Over the centuries, Mexicans themselves had developed some resistance to the bacteria that causes diarrhea, but they were not totally immune, and frequently suffered as much as visitors. In fact, the prevalence of the affliction was one of the reasons why so many Mexicans traditionally behaved in the listless manner that was so common it seemed to be a Mexican characteristic.

Someone, it is unclear whether Mexican or foreign, being very much aware that the affliction struck the majority of foreigners who visited the country, nicknamed the sickness "Montezuma's Revenge." Later, because tourists were the most susceptible to the ailment, Mexican wags also began calling in *mal del turista* (mahl dehl too-REES-tah).

The problem was—and is still—caused by poor sanitation in the preparation of food and in the water supply, but it is no longer the national scourge it once was. It is, however, still serious enough that precautions should be taken before or soon after eating in unregulated restaurants and food stalls.

It is not a good idea for businesspeople, diplomats and others visiting Mexico in any official capacity to refer to the affliction as "Montezuma's

Revenge," or *mal del turista* for that matter. Mexicans are sensitive about the problem and are apt to take such comments as out of place. It is much more diplomatic for visitors in these categories to say they have an upset stomach (*un mal del estomago*) and need to take a rest.

From the beginning of the travel boom to Mexico in the 1950s, some people have attempted to gloss over the seriousness of *mal del turista* by saying that it wasn't caused by unsanitary conditions, but by bacteria that were different from the bacteria in the United States and elsewhere. Others, especially members of the travel industry, often claimed that it was caused by changes in altitude or busy schedules, and their advice was for visitors to keep their schedules light, and rest more. Of course, none of these claims were true and the advice to take it easy was both meaningless and misleading.

While sanitary conditions in much of Mexico have improved dramatically in recent years, the standards in many areas remain well below those existing in most industrialized countries. Visitors in Mexico should not underestimate the potential seriousness of *mal del turista*. As in earlier decades, in the worst cases it can be totally incapacitating and require hospitalization and long-term treatment.

More responsible travel writers advise that when visitors are in doubt they should drink only bottled liquids and avoid raw foods (except for fruits and vegetables that have to be peeled).

Another good idea is to stock up on *Lomotil* or *Vibramicin* (available over the counter in Mexico) and take low doses of one or the other of these preparations regularly if you are going to out-of-the-way places for short periods of time. Some travelers take daily doses of Pepto-Bismal.

Interestingly, in all of the years that I have visited the border towns of Tijuana, Nogales, Ciudad Juárez or any of the cities in the northern states bordering the United States, I have never come down with *mal del turista*.

85

Mañana
(Mah-NYAH-nah)

"Qué Sera Sera!"

It has been said that North Americans live for the future without much thought of the past, while Mexicans live for the present and their past is always with them.

Mexicans have never been obsessed with planning for the future. Historically, theirs was a world in which getting through each day was enough of a challenge. There were no guarantees on what was going to happen the following day—or even that they would be alive.

For most Mexicans, there were few if any changes they could make in their lives. The seasons changed. People and things aged and died, or perished in some kind of violence. Each day and each season was practically the same, so there were few reasons for anticipating that things were going to be better.

Much of this attitude was a legacy of Mexico's Indian past. The early Indians of Mexico were master astronomers and created calendars for keeping track of the seasons. But they did not segment time into hours, minutes or seconds, or look upon it as something that was continuously moving at great speed. They didn't have the contemporary outlook that time would pass them by if they didn't move fast enough to keep up with it.

The Spaniards who invaded and occupied Mexico in 1519–1521 also came from a society whose lifestyle was based on the slow passage of time and a variety of rituals that required a sedate pace. The mechanization that followed the industrial revolution in Europe was barred from Mexico until the 19th century, so Mexicans were not forced to learn how to keep up with machines.

Most of Mexico was still not mechanized and not "on European time" in the latter decades of the 20th century; thus the cultural view of time in Mexico has remained quite different from what it is in North America, Europe and many other countries.

North Americans think of time as moving in a straight line at a constant speed which is literally measured in seconds ticking off inexorably. They plan their work, play and other activities to happen in sequence, and are concerned about filling every bit of time to prevent it from being wasted.

Mexicans do not look upon "idle" time as time wasted, but as something to be enjoyed; it has its own place in life and is its own reward. In other words, doing nothing is doing something. It nurtures the spirit and the soul.

Traditionally, Mexicans have never attempted to keep activities or events separate, in their own precise time slots. Exact schedules were not part of their lifestyle. There were time frames, but they were flexible.

Because time was not measured in tiny increments and the length of time it took to do things was not qualified, there was no sense of being late or of time being wasted.

Some of the areas where *la hora Mexicana*, or "Mexican time," most often clashes conspicuously with precise time-keepers are business appointments and invitations to social events.

While there are exceptions among businesspeople who have been conditioned to keep North American time or *la hora Americana*, "on time" is about half an hour after the set time, with up to one hour being acceptable, unless *la hora Americana* is agreed upon in advance.

It is not uncommon for Mexican businesspeople to schedule more than one appointment at the same time (because it is common for people not to show up), and to make appointments for times they know they are not going to be in their offices.

Where social events are concerned, particularly at private homes, being on time generally means arriving at least one hour and often up to two hours after the set time, unless a *la gringa* time has been specifically agreed upon.

Given this loose view and use of time, it is not surprising that Mexicans spend a great deal of time standing in lines, particularly at government offices. Bureaucrats are notorious not only for keeping "Mexican time," but for adding an additional dimension that takes the slow, leisurely use of time to new heights.

Saying that things are going to be done—are going to happen—by a specific time or date is more of a polite reply than a commitment, which brings us to *mañana* (mah-NYAH-nah).

Spanish language dictionaries say that *mañana* means "tomorrow," and that is the meaning taught to foreign students of the language. But "tomorrow" is a literal translation, not the true cultural meaning of the word.

In its normal cultural context *mañana* means "sometime in the near future, maybe." Behind the term are such unspoken things as "If I feel like it," "If I have the time," or "If nothing unexpected happens."

About the only way around inconveniences caused by unadorned *mañana* responses is to diplomatically qualify how the word is being used; to specify, with a smile, *tiempo Americano* or "American time."

Anthropologists add that the Mexican way of using time derives, at least in part, from the fact that they have traditionally had so little control over their lives. Disregarding that normal expectations where time was concerned was one of the few things they could do that gave them a sense of power.

Forcing people to wait for appointments is one of the ways that Mexicans demonstrate their power and gain "face." By the same token, being forced to wait for an extended period of time results in loss of face, and how long people are forced to wait is a measure of their status as far as the other party is concerned.

Interestingly enough, Mexicans themselves prefer that things that impact on them be done in a timely fashion. And, as the psychology of Mexicans changes from viewing time as an unending circle and doing things "when they want to be done," to using time and getting the most out of it, more and more people are adopting the American sense of time.

When requesting appointments it is important to keep the long midafternoon *siesta* custom in mind. The best hours for appointments are usually between 10 A.M. and noon, and between 4 and 6 P.M.

86

Maquiladoras
(Mah-kee-lah-DOH-rahs)

"Working for the Gringos"

In 1964 Mexican businessmen along the U.S.–Mexican border came up with a Border Industrialization Program (BIP) which was designed to relieve mass employment caused by the ending of the American *bracero* (Mexican farm worker) program, under which several hundred thousand Mexican field hands had been allowed to do seasonal work in the United States.

With the consent of the Mexican and American governments, the BIP group offered special customs exemptions and other advantages to any foreign company that established a factory in one of the *maquila* or "work" areas. (The original meaning of the word *maquiladora* goes back to colonial Mexico when millers ground someone else's grain and kept a portion of the finished product for their services. The finished product was called *maquila*. The place where the milling was done became known as the *maquiladora*, of "finished product place.")

Under the terms of the agreement, *maquiladoras* (mah-kee-lah-DOH-rahs) could be 100 percent foreign owned. With proper approval they could be established anywhere in Mexico. Foreign technicians and managers needed to operate the facilities could reside and work in Mexico. Customs procedures and other government formalities were eased, and the Mexican government agreed to promote industrial parks for the *maquiladoras*, first along the Mexican–U.S. border, and then in the interior.

Attracted by the promise of cheap Mexican labor, a number of American and foreign-owned companies accepted the invitation of the BIP organization, and in 1965 established the first "in-bond" factories in these special zones.

In the mid-1970s the number of *maquiladora* factories began spiraling upward. By the mid-1990s there were over 2,200 *maquiladoras*, mostly in Tijuana and Mexicali in the state of Baja California Norte, in Acuña and Piedras Negras in Coahuila state, in Ciudad Juárez and the city of Chihuahua in Chihuahua state, in Nogales and Agua Prieta in Sonora state, and in Matamoros, Nuevo Laredo, Reynosa and Rio Bravo in the state of Tamaulipas.

The largest concentrations of the in-bond plants were in Tijuana across from San Diego, and in Ciudad Juárez, across from El Paso. Altogether, the companies employed more than half a million people.

From the beginning the BIP-sponsored *maquiladoras* were politically, economically and socially controversial. North American critics complained that they exported U.S. jobs to Mexico, and made it possible for U.S. manufactures to produce goods cheaper in Mexico, then import them into the United States and sell them at prices lower than what other American companies cold afford, thereby undercutting American industry.

One of the reasons for the cheaper labor in Mexico was that the majority of the workers in the offshore plants were girls and women—some as young as 13.

Environmentalists accused a significant percentage of the Mexican-based companies of polluting the air and soil in their vicinity as well as dumping harmful chemicals into stream that flowed across the border into the United States. Both the Santa Cruz River flowing into Arizona from Nogales, Mexico, and the Rio Grande River separating Ciudad Juárez from El Paso, were described as "open sewers."

Job opportunities offered by these new factories resulted in a massive influx of people along the U.S.–Mexican border, particularly into Tijuana and Juárez. Most of these newcomers moved into *colonias* or "shanty towns" which appeared almost overnight on the outskirts of the cities, creating horrendous infrastructure and social problems.

By the mid-1990s health authorities had begun to report an alarming incidence of birth defects among children born to women working in some of the factories and living in the *colonias*. These defects included unde-scended testicles in young boys, and girls who were well past the age of puberty but did not menstruate.

In addition to these serious health problems, and an upsurge in vio-lence and crime caused by the concentration of large numbers of people in the *maquiladora* districts, there were regular complaints by female employ-ees of sexual harassment that went beyond the kind that had been traditional in Mexico for centuries. Factory managers in charge of hiring, as well as com-pany doctors performing physical examinations and supervisors in charge of workers, were accused of using their positions to demand sexual favors from female job applicants and employees. Social workers say the female employ-ees of the *maquiladoras* were especially susceptible to such pressure because they had already been conditioned to a "slave mentality" when con-fronted by superiors, and were in such a desperate need of work that they would do almost anything to get and keep a job.

Not surprisingly, many Mexicans were highly critical of the first *maquiladoras* because of the low wages they paid, and referred to the jobs they offered as "slave labor."

Said one Mexican businessman who was involved in leasing land for *maquiladora* sites: "When foreign companies first began setting up plants here their primary purpose to was take advantage of the cheap labor—to make as much money as they could as quickly as they could.

"They were not concerned about the lives of their employees. As time went by, they began to discover the cost of absenteeism—by employees who were ill and had serious personal problems—and a high employee turnover rate, and gradually began improving their working conditions.

"But it was competition from newer, incoming plants that finally forced the *maquiladoras* to change their entire approach. The newer plants began hiring the more experienced and better employees away from the older firms by offering them higher wages and more benefits.

"This forced the established companies to raise their own pay scales, and then to add day care centers for working mothers, transportation allowances and one or two meals a day. Now, more and more of the companies are offering employee housing as well."

One of the cultural factors that bedeviled some of the earliest *maquilado-ras* was extraordinary absenteeism on Mondays. In some factories, as many as 30 percent of the employees would not show up on Mondays because of *San Lunes* or "Saint Monday"—traditionally taken off as a religious holiday.

The management of one of these factories solved this problem by giving all employees who showed up for work on Mondays tickets that allowed them to attend a party held by the company every Saturday.

In addition to U.S.- and Mexican-owned *maquiladora* firms, companies headquartered in Canada, France, Hong Kong, South Korea, Sweden and Taiwan also have factories in the in-bond zones.

American corporations with *maquiladora* operations include American Hospital Supply, Black and Decker, General Electric, Hughes Aircraft, IBM and Rockwell International. Japanese companies with in-bond plants in Mexico include Canon, Casio, Kyocera, Matsushita, Pioneer and Toshiba. Lucky-Goldstar (also known as the L.G. Group) and Samsung are among the South Korean companies in the special zones.

Mariachis
(Mah-ree-AH-chees)

"The Soul Singers"

Mexico is rightly famous for its minstrels—men who dress in cowboy-like suits, wear huge, wide-brimmed hats, and provide a very distinctive kind of music for many public functions as well as leisure-time entertainment. These are the famed *mariachis* (mah-ree-AH-chees), a term that dates back to the time of the French invasion of Mexico and the short lived reign by Emperor Ferdinand Maximilian (1864–1867), the Austrian archduke who wanted to remake Mexico in the image of his own country.

Maximilian introduced the custom of having musicians play at receptions following marriages, and the musicians came to be known as *mariachi*, a corruption of the French term for "marriage."

Historians say that the institution of *mariachi* music began in the state of Jalisco (as did the famed Mexican Hat Dance and the equally famous tequila), and one of the main squares in Guadalajara is appropriately named *Mariachi Plaza*.

Guadalajara, the capital of Jalisco and one of the garden cities of the world, still claims to be the *mariachi* capital of the world as well.

Every night *mariachi* bands gather in the plaza, waiting to be hired for the evening. The bands often play while waiting—to attract attention to themselves, and as a special treat for the crowds that throng the plaza. Songs that listeners invariably hear are the soulful *Peregrina* and the old standby, *Viva El Amor*.

Many North Americans are familiar with the special kind of music played by *mariachis*, not only because of visits to Mexico but also because of the number of Mexican restaurants in the United States that feature *mariachi* bands. Most of these people appreciate the songs and sounds of the *mariachi* bands as being "authentic Mexican," and frequently comment on the romantic nature of many of the most popular *mariachi* tunes.

But I believe there is a powerful element in *mariachi* music that is too subliminal for most short-time visitors to pick up on, one that is decidedly sexual in nature. In fact, I think *mariachi* music is aphrodisia in sound—music to seduce by.

Mexican men, consciously or not, have long been aware of the effect that *mariachi* music has on women—and on themselves—and have used it accordingly. Not surprisingly, the effect of *mariachi* music is generally much stronger on Mexicans than it is on non-Mexicans because the latter are unable to completely abandon themselves to it. Nevertheless, it acts as a powerful stimulant to most non-Mexicans as well, and certainly gets them in the mood for romance.

Mexican men have traditionally used *mariachi* bands as accomplices in their courting and seductions, and the connection between *mariachi* and romance continues to play an important role in Mexico.

Some people say that if carried beyond a certain point by the more sensually inclined, *mariachi* music can be a temporary substitute for sex itself. (Maybe for an outsider, but not for a Mexican!)

Mariachis are so common in Mexico that it is difficult for the visitor to avoid them. For those who would like to test my theory of *mariachi* music being an aphrodisiac, the bands can, of course, be hired for any occasion in private as well as public settings.

In Mexico City bands that are not already booked customarily gather in the early evening at Plaza Garibaldi. Generally, the fancier the *charro* (urban cowboy) costumes worn by the members of a *mariachi* band, the higher the band's fees.

In addition to a number of romantic songs, *mariachis* also perform *rancheras*, or Mexican-style country and western songs, and *corridos*, which are old ballads that were very popular throughout the country before the advent of newspapers and radios, and are now only occasionally heard.

Mexico's early balladeers were the equivalent of Europe's wandering minstrels, bringing both news and entertainment to people in outlying towns and villages.

Regardless of the musical genre, there are few things in Mexico that compare with sitting in an open-air restaurant with friends or a sweetheart on a balmy night, eating good food, getting a little tipsy on beer, tequila or wine, and listening to the sad–happy songs of the *mariachis*.

Visitors should keep in mind that if roving *mariachis* approach their bar stool or restaurant table and ask them to play, or indicate that they are going to play, the guests are expected to pay a fee if the *mariachis* are allowed to proceed. *No, gracias* is usually enough to get them to move on.

At restaurants and at nightclubs where *mariachis* are provided as entertainment, there is no extra charge for a table-side serenade. But if you are with a date and the music contributes to the mood, you can get extra mileage out of a tip.

In recent times, some *mariachi* bands with especially skilled musicians have been playing classical music with great success in Mexico and abroad.

88

Masoquismo
(Mah-soh-KEES-moh)

"Built-in Masochism"

The dictionary defines masochism as an abnormal condition in which sexual excitement and satisfaction depend largely on being subjected to abuse or physical pain, whether by oneself or by another, and deriving pleasure from being offended, dominated or mistreated in some way. Another facet of masochism is that the masochist tends to turn any sort of destructive force inward or upon himself or herself.

Virtually all literature on Mexico notes that Mexican culture has traditionally been characterized by a deep, wide streak of *masoquismo* (mah-soh-KEES-moh) or "masochism," which colors practically every aspect of Mexican life. The *masoquismo* element derives primarily from medieval Catholicism and to a lessor extent from some of the religious beliefs of the Aztecs and other Mexican Indians.

The Catholic Church impregnated the people with the concept that their physical, sensual bodies were evil, and that they were condemned to an eternity of suffering in Hell if they did not believe in and obey God and his ministers.

In its warped religious zeal the church aimed to control all thought, and taught that just as Jesus Christ had suffered for his beliefs, all mankind was doomed to suffer as well. Suffering came to be equated with piety. The more one suffered, the closer he or she came to God.

Women, tainted by original sin and a sexuality that no man could match, were chosen by the church to suffer the most. The biggest burdens women were forced to bear were the inadequacies, ignorance, prejudices and fears of men.

Men in some of Mexico's Indian tribes also believed that women should be dominated by men and kept in their place by force.

The church concept that only Catholics were fully human in the eyes of God led the Spanish conquistadors, priests and colonials to treat the Indians and later Spanish-Indian mixtures with cruel contempt. Thus for centuries both Mexican men and Mexican women were brainwashed into believing that suffering was natural and that it was ordained for them to be dominated and abused.

In this cultural context, people were conditioned to take a perverse pleasure in their suffering and in the suffering of others. Those who were in positions of power—the military, the police, government officials and the clergy—deliberately used their power to make people suffer. Tortures of the most heinous kinds were routinely carried out by the military, the police, and priests assigned to the Office of the Inquisition.

As a result of systematic oppression and abuse by the religious, political and economic systems of the country, masochism, including a strong tendency for self-destructive behavior, was the only release for most Mexicans.

Today *masoquismo* is still a conspicuous element in *machismo*, in bullfights and gang fights, in festivals that involve excessive drinking and flagellation, and in many other areas of Mexican life.

89

Mercados
(Mayr-CAH-dohs)

"The Importance of Bargains"

Typical North American visitors in Mexico are frequently upset by attitudes and behavior in Mexico that to them appear to be impolite, improper, immoral, irrational—even criminal—and cannot understand how Mexicans put up with such an system. From the Mexican viewpoint, these visitors suffer from having been overly conditioned to expect everything to be structured and fixed in one unchanging form, and to be as fast, practical and convenient as is humanly possible.

One of the many differences in Mexican and North American values that is frequently singled out as a good example is the Mexican custom of price-bargaining or *regateo* (rag-gah-TAH-oh) in the country's *mercados* (mayr-CAH-dohs) or open-air markets, many of which are operated by Indians. (In Mexico City and other major cities open-air markets are also called *tianguis* (tee-AHN-gwis).

Many foreign visitors in Mexico regard bargaining for the price they are going to pay for something as bothersome, embarrassing, irritating and dumb. A typical attitude is "Why don't they just charge a fair price and be done with it?"

Most visitors who are inexperienced in price-bargaining are inclined to feel that they have been cheated even when they succeed in getting the seller to come down by as much as 50 percent. They see the whole system as evidence that Mexicans are too unstructured, too impractical to be successful on an impressive scale.

Mexicans, on the other hand, see the *mercados* and the custom of bargaining as one of the most fundamental and enjoyable facets of their culture, as an opportunity to put the otherwise mundane action of buying something on a very personal level by to interacting with the seller as a human being, demonstrating their knowledge and bargaining ability and enjoying the interplay—with both sides pleased by the results.

Mexican shopkeepers and street vendors expect their customers to bargain with them. When uniformed visitors do not bargain, and accept the first price offered, the sellers regard them as foolish; as dumb people just throwing their money away.

In many ways, bargaining in the *mercados* of Mexico is a microcosm of the business world at large. It reflects the Mexican custom of personalizing all relationships, of investing time and their lives in humanizing all transactions, business as well as everything else.

Obviously, one of the things that the Mexican custom of bargaining ostensibly does is distance the value of an object from the material it is made of and the time it took to make it, concepts that are deeply ingrained in the thinking of North Americans and others.

And, of course, the foreign businessperson will say that you cannot run a manufacturing company with employees on such a philosophy, and that the culture of Mexico will have to change dramatically before it can become a major industrial power. That is no doubt true.

But to Mexicans such changes have their negative side because they destroy part of the traditional essence of Mexican life, human aspects of the culture that make it so spiritually satisfying.

In the meantime, North Americans and people in the industrially advanced countries have discovered the highly mechanized, efficiency-oriented societies do, in fact, take something vital away from the human spirit. In contrast, these countries are now struggling to overcome problems they have created for themselves.

Violence in the North American workplace is just one of the symptoms of a society that has dehumanized to the point that it is on the verge of destroying itself. And interestingly, many of the antidotes being prescribed for the workplace violence read as if they came directly from the rule book of the Mexican way of doing things. Some of these anti-workplace violence guidelines follow: use humane management, nurture respect and individual dignity, acknowledge employees' lives outside of work, help all employees feel valued and involved and provide employees with ways to safely discuss problems and deal with stress.

For Mexicans the *mercados* are something like community centers where people interact on a personal level, get to know each other as human beings, develop skills in dealing with each other and enjoy themselves.

90

Mestizos
(Mehs-TEE-zohs)

"White on Dark"

Well before Hernán Cortés and his band of soldiers conquered the Aztec empire of Mexico they had begum a systematic program of breeding with Indian women, both captives and female slaves given to them as "gifts," not only to satisfy their hypersexual desires, but also as an official policy which was designed to dilute the Indian population and create a new breed of people.

This was not a new policy created by Cortés and his men. It was a program backed by the Spanish government and the Catholic Church of Spain as a way of spreading both political and religious influence over the inhabitants of the so-called "New World."

Spanish men of this era, heavily influenced by the culture of the Moors (a Moslem people of mixed Berber and Arab descent who invaded and conquered Spain in the eighth century), needed no government or church urging to interbreed with the Indians of Mexico. They prided themselves on their virility, and the pursuit of women was one of their primary activities.

After the conquest of Mexico and the enslavement of the Indian population, large numbers of Indian women voluntarily became the sexual partners of Spanish men in the hope that their children would not be classified as Indian slaves.

The half-Indian half-Spanish offspring of these perfunctory unions came to be called *mestizos* (mehs-TEE-zohs), which is a Yucatecan word referring to a traditional costume featuring two main garments, one white and one dark.

Many of the first generation of *mestizos*, born to the conquering conquistadors themselves, were accepted into white society because of the elite positions of their fathers. These upper-class *mestizos* merged into the ranks of the *criollos*, and whenever possible, married Europeans.

For the mixed blood offspring of other Spaniards, particularly those who were illegitimate, it was another world. By the third generation of mixed-bloods, the term *mestizo* had all of the repugnancy of the English word "half-breed," and was a stigma that was to afflict mixed-blooded Mexicans like some loathsome disease for more than 400 years.

"The *mestizos* were treated like non-people," said a present-day Mexican businessman.

In imposing their regime on the hapless Indians of Mexico the Spaniards took full advantage of their natural obsession with sex and their positions as lords and masters. By 1600, or 81 years after Cortéz's landing on the Gulf coast of Mexico, the results of the sexual productivity of the Spanish was much in evidence. The *mestizaje* (people of Spanish–Indian ancestry) population numbered in the tens of thousands.

In addition to maintaining Indian girls as concubines, the Spanish over-lords claimed and took sexual rights to any girl or woman who caught their eye. It is recorded that the Spanish owners of *haciendas* reserved the right to have sexual intercourse with the daughters of their workers on the eve of the girls' weddings. The famous Mexican song *La Borrachita* is the lament of a young girl who must leave the side of her groom-to-be and go to the hacienda to fulfill her sexual obligations to the master.

Most of the Spanish clergy in Mexico also participated in the program to raise non-Indian colonists. It is recorded that after 1600 most lower-ranking priests kept mistresses and sired large numbers of children. Many priests used their special position solely to satisfy prodigious carnal appetites. It is noted in Mexican history that one particular priest in Rio Blanco raped 56 women a total of 126 times in the year 1721.

This particular priest was finally "brought to justice" only after he banished a woman and her family from his parish because she successfully resisted his sexual advances. He was relieved of his duties for two years and restricted to his home.

By the end of the 1500s the *gachupín* and *criollo* Spaniards were following a strict apartheid policy which prevented the *mestizos* from being absorbed into the Spanish community. As a result, the majority of them grew up more Indian than Spanish.

Some *mestizos* remained wholly Indian in their beliefs and way of living. Others found themselves isolated in between. They were outcasts that were not accepted by either side. As more decades passed and the mixed-blood population spiraled upward, the *mestizos* gradually formed a third "race" that was neither Spanish nor Indian.

By 1650, there was over 160,000 *mestizos*, with more than 30,000 of them in Mexico City, where they made up a large class of untouchables known as *leperos* or "social lepers." (They were also commonly referred to as *leparos* or "beggars.") Barred from becoming craftsmen, shopkeepers or professionals, the *mestizos* lived in ghettos. Most of them survived by begging and stealing. Despised and feared by the ruling whites, the *leperos* were routinely subject to unspeakable abuse, and many suffered immensely.

However, unlike the Indians who were literally benumbed by the sudden collapse of their world, the *mixtures* aspired toward improving their condition. and being outcasts from the bottom as well as the top of society in New Spain, the *mestizos* learned early how to use their wits.

Driven by an overwhelming desire to identify with their Spanish relatives, particularly the growing number of egotistical, pleasure-loving *criollos*, rather than their Indian side, the *mestizos* emulated the Spaniards as often and in as many ways as they could.

While the *mestizos* were young the primary influence on them was Indian. As they grew older they looked to the Spaniards as models. As a result, typical *mestizos* were not only mixed racially, they were also a blend of Spanish and Indian cultures.

Mestizos were most influenced by the characteristics that were the strongest in the Spaniards and Indians. This meant they got a liberal dose of mysticism, superstition and belief in magic from their Indian relatives. From the Spaniards they got an absolute belief in male superiority over women, along with all of the attendant attitudes and behavior that goes with this complex.

Then began a development which was to mold the character and personality of male *mestizos* into something that went far beyond the arrogant, sex-minded Spaniard, and the sensual, mystic-minded Indian. In their terrible, frustrating obsession to have identity of their own, *mestizo* men turned the already strong male superiority complex of the Spaniards into a fanatical cult of masculinity.

As a substitute for their poverty, their inalterable status as social lepers and a sense of utter inferiority—racially, socially and economically—*mestizo* men built up an imaginary world for themselves in which the only goal was total masculinity, fueled by an intense hatred of their Spanish overlords.

As the Indian workers died by the millions—mostly from European diseases—they were replaced in the mines and the plantations by African slaves and mixed-bloods. (Later, some Arab and Chinese blood would be fused into the mixed-blood gene pool.) For generation after generation, the only occupations open to *mestizos* were those at the bottom of the economy.

The hard lives of the *mestizos* made them incredibly tough and resilient. Their numbers increased against all odds. Over the decades, they began to be more numerous than the whites.

Between 1700 and 1800 the situation of a few mixed-bloods improved. Spanish administrators offered small land grants in the far northern Bajio frontier area to some *mestizo* families, both to get the them out of Mexico City, and to encourage settlement in the northern territory.

Large numbers of *mestizos* also became bandits, hiding out in the mountains, waylaying travelers and raiding villages and towns.

But it was not until after Mexican independence from Spain in 1821 that *mestizo* men were allowed to become craftsmen and foremen, and to work as lower-echelon clerks and maintenance crews in local and national government offices.

Mestizos were not to have their revenge against the Spanish overlords until well into the 20th century—400 years after Cortés and his men began their program of miscegenation—when they rebelled against the church and government.

The civil war of 1910–1921 provided an opportunity for lower-class *mestizos* to demonstrate their independence and manhood openly for the first time, and not surprisingly, many of these demonstrations went to the extreme and were often violent. (Among the various ways lower-class Mexican men have characteristically demonstrated their fearlessness in modern times has been to drive vehicles recklessly and ignore traffic lights when crossing streets.)

Despite the common characteristics of present-day *mestizos* throughout Mexico, there are striking and sometimes profound regional differences in their character and manners. Men from the state of New Leon are said to be generally humorless and stingy. Veracruzanos from the gulf state of Veracruz have the reputation of loving food, music , poetry and dancing. They delight in the ritualistic use of foul language, to the point that in some districts the use of such language is a cult within itself. Men from Veracruz are also known for their "hot blood" and for the especially high percentage who maintain mistresses. Yucatecans are characterized as being naive, warm and ingratiating. Men from Jalisco are noted for their love of *mariachi* music and their flamboyant manners.

Mexico's Indians and Indianized mixtures, however, are invariably described as mostly silent and solitary except during festivals and drinking bouts. Then, says writer-poet Octavio Paz, they often become possessed by violence and frenzy and "their souls explode."

Not all of Mexico's famous 19th and 20th century *mestizos* were bandits or politicians. The great suffering of the Mexican people also produced a pantheon of *mestizo* artists, poets and writers who have chronicled the history of their country in masterpieces of art and prose.

Among the more famous *mestizos* in just the arts alone (in addition to Octavio Paz, whom I have quoted several times): Carlos Fuentes, Diego Rivera, David Alfaro Siqueiros, Rufino Tamayo, Cantinflas, Lucha Reyes, Frida Kahlo, Efrain Huerta, and Anthony Quinn.

There is, perhaps, no greater testimony to the tenacity of the human spirit than the Mexicans' love of music. In 1843 Madame Calderon de la Barca, one of the most perceptive chroniclers of life in Mexico during the first half of the 19th century, wrote that music in Mexico was a "sixth sense," an integral part of the *mestizo* spirit.

In his provocative book, *The Mexicans*, journalist Patrick Oster provides a summary portrait of the Mexican character that is both fascinating and haunting.

Oster says Mexicans are more interested in magic than in logic; they prefer fantasy to truth; they joke about death and often have little regard for life; they revel in black humor; they are fatalistic and seemingly satisfied with their lot no matter how mean; they are often heroic; they drive do-gooders wild and they are resilient beyond all understanding.

Despite the efforts of mainstream Mexicans to ignore the Indian part of their history, it is so inextricably bound in their way of life that they cannot do so. The national culture is a graft of Spanish and Indian cultures. Mexican superstitions, their attachment to festivals, their views of death and sex, the roles of mothers and fathers, village life, even the common etiquette of Mexico, all have roots in the country's Indian past.

But generally speaking, modern-day *mestizo* Mexicans, who make up some 60 percent of the population, do not think of themselves as mixed-bloods or as descendents of Spaniards and Indians unless something calls attention to their racial heritage. They are just Mexicans.

In matters of schooling, housing and employment in ordinary jobs, skin color now plays only a minor role, if any. In marriage and higher status jobs and professions, however, skin color and ethnic background are still important factors.

Mexico
(MEH-he-coh)

"A New Self-Image"

Mexico's famous Aztec Indians called themselves *Mexica*, which historians say is probably the name of the place, somewhere in the northern part of present-day Mexico or the southwestern United States, where the tribe first originated.

The great valley where the *Mexica* established themselves and built their capital, Tenochtitlán, eventually came to be known as the Valley of Mexico.

After Hernán Cortés and his band of conquistadors conquered the Aztec empire in 1521, they destroyed Tenochtitlán, built a new Spanish-style city on the site and christened it *La Ciudad de Mexico*, or "Mexico City." Shortly afterwards the whole region was renamed "New Spain," or *Nuevo España*, and following the discovery of huge silver deposits in the mid-1500s it quickly became the jewel in Spain's colonial empire.

For the balance of the 300-year Spanish regime in Mexico the country was officially known as *Nuevo España*. But as the generations passed and the number of Spaniards born in Mexico eventually outnumbered those dispatched from Spain as colonial administrators, Mexican-born Spaniards began referring to themselves as *Mexicanos* or "Mexicans" and the country as Mexico (MEH-he-coh).

The "country of Mexico" was officially born on September 27, 1821, when the victorious rebel general Augustín de Iturbide (who earlier been a rabid royalist) decreed the end of "New Spain" and the birth of *La Rupublica de Mexico*, or "The Republic of Mexico."

However, independence from Spain did not change the lives of most Mexicans outside of Mexico City and the other large urban areas, and there was no sudden emergence of a national Mexican identity. To the large mass of poor mixed-blood farmers, "Mexico" remained a remote city that had little to do with their lives.

This situation was to remain very much the same until the civil war of 1910–1921 swept away the ruling clique of generals and bishops, and brought dramatic reforms that encouraged the development of a national consciousness. But even these changes did not affect the majority of Mexico's Indians, and today they still generally think of themselves as members of their tribes rather then as Mexicans.

One of the things that newcomers learn early is that when Mexicans use the word "Mexico" in ordinary conversation there is a good chance that they are referring to *La Ciudad de Mexico*, or Mexico City, not the whole country. It is also common for Mexicans to refer to Mexico City as *Distrito Federal* or "Federal District," a political designation similar to "metropolitan area." The abbreviation of Federal District, *el DF*, pronounced "ell deh EFF-ay," is also commonly used in regular conversation and writing.

In some instances it is necessary to use the term *La Republica* (the Republic) to be perfectly clear in referring to the country of Mexico.

Another thing to keep in mind is that many educated Mexicans resent citizens of the United States referring to themselves as "Americans." They point out that as residents of the North American continent since the 1500s, they have equal claim to the title. Although this resentment is greatly diminished from what it was in the past, some present-day Mexicans continue to be especially sensitive to this perceived American arrogance.

As early as the fight for independence from Spain in 1810–1821, some Mexicans of Spanish descent referred to themselves as "Americans" in order to distance themselves from the ruling Spaniards and from Spain itself.

In ordinary speech, most Mexicans refer to the United States as *El Norte* (El NOR-tay), or "The North." The more formal designation for the United States is *Los Estados Unidos* (lohs ess-TAH-dohs-OO-NEE-dohs). Americans are commonly called *Norte Americanos* (NOR-tay ah-may-ree-CAH-nohs) or "North Americans."

Out of politeness Americans in Mexico might refer to themselves as *Norte Americanos* instead of *Americanos*, and reap the benefits that accrue from this sensitive respect for Mexican feelings. Political and economic reforms instituted in Mexico in the 1980s and 1990s have done a great deal to instill new pride and strengthen in Mexico the sense of national identity among all mainstream Mexicans. Given Mexico's turbulent past, however, there is some danger that continued progress in these areas will eventually result in Mexican nationalism becoming virulent.

92

Moctezuma
(Moke-tay-ZOO-mah)

"The Unlucky Monarch"

Spanish conquistadors conquered the island of Cuba shortly after the beginning of the 16th century. By 1517 they had colonized the island and were sending out expeditions to explore other potential areas to add to their growing empire.

Yucatan was discovered by an expedition from Cuba in 1517, but the exploring party was repulsed by Mayan warriors. In 1518 another Cuban expedition explored the Gulf coast and heard from its Indians that a great and fabulously rich city existed in the distant highlands.

Upon hearing this, Diego de Velasquez, the governor of Cuba, announced his intention of putting together a larger expedition to find the great city, and was persuaded by his private secretary (assistant), a 33-year-old man named Hernán Cortés, to bring him into the enterprise as a junior partner and to make him the leader of the expedition.

Cortés was a successful planter who was notorious for his seductions of women (one of whom he was forced to marry). He was also well educated, a rarity in those days, as well as courageous and ambitious. He was to prove himself a master at political maneuvering and one of the most farsighted of the Spanish conquistadors of that era.

Velasquez put up two thirds of the money for the expedition, and Cortés put up the other third. While preparations for the expedition were underway, Cortés's many enemies reported to Velasquez that he could not be trusted, that he was just waiting for a chance to leave the island and strike out on his own, and that he would never come back whether or not he discovered gold or other Indians to conquer.

Velasquez immediately rescinded the commission he had issued to Cortés, but he was too late. Cortés learned of the move, immediately took command of the ships that had been assembled and sailed out of Havana Harbor. For the next 90 days, he cruised around the island, gathering more ships, men and supplies on his own, then headed for the Gulf Coast of Mexico.

Landing near what is now Veracruz, Cortés was lucky again. He learned that there were two Spanish survivors of a shipwreck living with the local Mayan Indians. One of them, a priest named Jeronimo de Aguilar who had learned how to speak Mayan, joined Cortés's band as his interpreter and advisor.

Cortés then marched up the coast toward a Tabasco Indian city. The Indians, who thought he was a god, immediately showered him with gifts, including 20 Indian slave girls.

One of the female slaves, Malinche, was the daughter of a Nahua Indian lord, and spoke Nahuatl, the largest and most important of the Indian languages, as well as Mayan. Malinche was first given to a member of Cortés's band, but when Cortés learned about her background he took her for himself, baptized her and gave her the name "Marina."*

Cortés also had all of the other slave women baptized because he had established a rule that his men could not fornicate with non-Catholics.

Despite his buccaneer instincts, Cortés was a stickler for protocol. He proclaimed himself Captain-General of the expedition and founded the city of Veracruz as a permanent camp. Then he sent a ship to Spain to inform the

---

*In later generations, Spanish writers gradually upgraded Malinche's contribution to the conquest of Mexico, and began honoring her by referring to her as *La Malinche* and *Doña Malinche*. However, today the word is synonymous with "traitor."

king, promising the crown one fifth of any wealth (gold and Indians) that he might discover. He then burned the remaining ships to keep the already complaining men in the expedition from giving up and going back to Cuba.

Immediately afterward, like any good general about to attack an enemy, Cortés began to gather intelligence from the local Indian tribes, using both the priest Aguilar and his new mistress, Malinche, as interpreters.

When the fugitive Cortés and his 11 ships, 550 soldiers, 16 horses, several huge "attack" dogs (greyhounds and mastiffs weighing up to 200 pounds) and portable cannons arrived on the Gulf coast of Mexico in 1519, the supreme ruler of the Aztec empire was Moctezuma II, a superstitious man who respected and feared the gods of the past.

Moctezuma lived in a luxurious palace with two wives and a large harem. His huge staff included artists, craftsmen, jewelers, dancers, musicians and jugglers. Cortés later wrote that Moctezuma changed clothes up to four times a day, and never wore the same costume twice, always giving them to his staff after he wore them once.

The cards were stacked against Moctezuma from the beginning. In addition to his more cautious nature (his predecessors had all been fiercely aggressive warriors), a number of the larger Indian nations within and on the edges of the Aztec empire were waiting for an opportunity to free themselves from the Aztec yoke.

It didn't take Cortés long to discover the political situation in Mexico and take advantage of it. Before marching on Tenochtitlán, the Aztec capital in the Valley of Mexico, he arranged military alliances with a number of these nations. But Cortés and his men had something else going for them that went beyond their armor, cannons, horses, steel swords and Indian allies.

Moctezuma thought that Cortés was the legendary Toltec king Quetzalcoatl coming back as a god to reclaim his throne, a promise Quetzalcoatl had made centuries earlier. The Toltec king was said to have opposed slavery and human sacrifices and was forced to give up his throne and flee, vowing to return. He and his small band were said to have sailed away into the Caribbean.

The prophecies foretold that Quetzalcoatl would return as a god to reclaim his throne in 1519, the very year that Cortés arrived. (The neighboring Zapotec Indians had a myth that a race of "god-men" would descend from the sky, build great palaces and bring them unparalleled prosperity.) According to the myth, Quetzalcoatl had very light skin, light-colored hair and wore a full beard, a description that fit Cortés perfectly.

Moctezuma and some of his priestly advisors were profoundly influenced by the Quetzalcoatl myth when they first heard about Cortés's arrival. Runners brought Moctezuma drawings of the Spanish ships, Cortés, his men and their horses, which appeared to be proof that Cortés might very well be the legendary god returned in human form.

In any event, Moctezuma made one mistake after another in dealing with the Spaniards. His first move was to order the Spaniards be treated as honored guests. He sent them gifts of gold and precious gems. One can imagine the effect this had on the gold- and sex-obsessed Spaniards.

When Cortés and his army arrived at Tenochtitlán, located on an island in a large lake (Lake Texcoco) on November 8, 1519, they were met on one of the causeways connecting the island to the mainland by Moctezuma and his entourage of nobles, ministers and aids, all of whom were decked out in their finest clothing and jewelry.

Moctezuma greeted Cortés as his humble subject, saying that he had been holding the throne of the empire in trust for him and that he (Moctezuma) was happily returning it to him. History does not reveal how much of this was clearly translated for Cortés, but in any event, he behaved with the authority and arrogance of a god.

Much of Tenochtitlán, which covered five square miles in area and had a population of 300,000 (larger than any city in Europe at that time), turned out to see Cortés and his horses and fighting dogs. But not all of them welcomed the strange-looking foreigners. Several of Moctezuma's leading ministers openly showed their disapproval of the Spaniards.

Despite repeated warnings from some of his advisors that the Spaniards should not be trusted, Moctezuma delayed making any decision about them. He continued to treat them royally. They stayed—together—in their own private quarters in a palace in the heart of the city.

Within no time, Cortés took Moctezuma captive and confined him in a locked and guarded room within the Spanish quarter, totally isolating him from his family and court. Some of the disapproving ministers were also taken captive and imprisoned in the Spanish quarters.

Telling Moctezuma's remaining ministers and aides that the king was ill and being treated, Cortés began issuing one order after the other in the name of the king.

At the urging of his men, Cortés had a huge hoard of gold, silver and precious gems brought to the Spaniards' quarters from all over the empire. He also had a Christian statue erected in the great hall of the main Aztec temple.

After putting up with this situation for six months and becoming increasingly suspicious, leading Aztec nobles and priests began openly agitating for the expulsion of the Spaniards.

In the meantime, the governor of Cuba had assembled another expedition of 1,000 men, under the command of explorer Panfilo Narvaez, and ordered it to Mexico with instructions to arrest Cortés and return him to Cuba in chains.

Indians brought the word to Cortés in Mexico City that Narvaez and his fleet had been spotted. Cortés took most of his men and made a high-speed march to Veracruz to intercept Narvaez, ostensibly to negotiate with him. He left one of his chief lieutenants, Pedro de Alvarado, and 80 men in the palace to guard Moctezuma and their other noble prisoners.

Instead of talking to Narvaez, Cortés attacked his camp under the cover of darkness and a pouring rain, and captured him. Cortés convinced Narvaez's men to switch sides by promising them gold, women and titles. He than sank Narvaez's ships by having holes drilled in their hulls.

By this time smallpox, brought into Tenochtitlán by one of Cortés's men, was spreading among the Aztec population in the capital city; it quickly became an epidemic that killed thousands.

While Cortés was gone, Pedro de Alvarado, in charge of the troops that were left in Tenochtitlán, gave the Aztec priests and nobles permission to celebrate a fiesta in the Sacred Precinct, and then closed the gates and attacked them.

In the next three hours, according to historical records, the Spanish soldiers slaughtered some 600 unarmed chiefs and nobles, wiping out the majority of the Aztec leadership.

Hearing the news, Cortés rushed back to Tenochtitlán with a large army of Tlaxcalan allies as well as soldiers from the Narvaez expedition, and was allowed by the still-disorganized Aztecs to rejoin his troop in the city.

But soon afterward the Spanish quarter was put under siege by the aroused population. Cortés forced Moctezuma to go out on the roof of the palace and order the siege ended. In the subsequent melee, Moctezuma was killed—some historians say that Cortés and his men, others that his own people stoned him to death.

With Moctezuma dead, the throne went to his brother, Cuitlahuac, a much more decisive man who was determined to destroy the Spaniards. He assembled an army of warriors to attack the Spanish quarters, but wave after wave of them were cut down by rifle and cannon fire. Still they persisted.

On the night of June 30, 1520, the Spaniards loaded themselves down with the treasure they had accumulated and tried to escape under cover of darkness.

Aztec sentinels discovered them and sounded the alarm. Then the portable wooden bridge the Spaniards were crossing over broke under the weight of their horses and the hoard of gold they were carrying. In the battle that ensued, over half of the Spaniards and some 4,000 of their Tlaxcalan allies were killed. A number of the Spaniards drowned because of the weight of the gold they were carrying in their pockets and strapped to their bodies.

Cortés himself was captured during the fighting, at which point the Aztecs broke off the attack, as was their custom when an enemy leader was taken. This allowed a squad of Cortés's men to rescue him.

Cortés made his way to the capital of Tlaxcala, where he assembled a new army of Spaniards and Tlaxcalans and over the next year conquered or formed alliances with all of the Indian tribes surrounding the Aztec capital.

In lining up allies to attack the Aztecs, Cortés suspected the Cholulans of holding back and being against him. He ordered his much enlarged army to attack the Cholulans, killing an estimated 3,000 before they surrendered.

In the spring of 1521 Cortés laid siege to Tenochtitlán with 1,000 Spanish troops and 50,000 Indian warriors, attacking via the causeways and 13 fighting boats that had been built in Tlaxcala and carried to the lake surrounding the Aztec capital.

In the meantime, Chiutlahauc (and tens of thousands of other Aztecs) had died of smallpox. The new ruler, Chauhtemoc, continued the battle.

But starvation and disease finally defeated the new king and his men, and the mighty Aztec empire of Moctezuma was no more. Tenochtitlán was reduced to ashes and rubble. The canals were filled with stones and debris from the leveled city and converted into broad thoroughfares.

Convinced that the Aztecs had a great hoard of gold stashed somewhere, the Spaniards tried to force Cuauhtemoc and other surviving Indian nobles to reveal its location by oiling their feet and roasting them over open fires. There was no storehouse of treasures. (Cortés later hanged the crippled Cuauhtemoc during an ill-fated expedition to the south.)

After the conquest, Cortés wrote five letters to the king of Spain, and as he expected, was pardoned for his crime of stealing the Cuban governor's expedition, and generously rewarded for his feat of conquering the Aztec empire.

Eighty years later, only 8,000 Indians and 7,000 Spaniards lived on the site that had once been one of the six largest cities in the world.

Moctezuma is remembered in the United States today in the Marine ballad, "The Halls of Montezuma," and in "Montezuma's Revenge," a reference to diarrhea. Mexicans regard him as a great hero.

93

Moralidad
(Moh-rah-lee-DAD)

"Reality Versus Religion"

It has been noted that one of the fundamental differences between the Mexican and North American cultures is that American culture is rooted in Christian ethics, while Mexican culture, despite the influence of Catholicism, is based more on hierarchical social relationships and rituals.

Most people with Western European backgrounds have been conditioned to think of ethics and morality in absolute, universal terms which automatically apply to everyone everywhere, regardless of their color, creed or social class. The essence of this ethical system is generally derived from the morality that is reflected in the teachings of Christianity, with emphasis on honesty, fairness, kindness and justice for all.

The contrast between Mexican and North American morality begins with religion and God. In North American, God is viewed more as a distant, abstract spirit that created all, inhabits all, knows all and will eventually take revenge against those who do not believe in him and obey his word.

Despite this North American view of God as a distant, abstract spirit, Americans nevertheless view religion as a philosophy from which they can gain an absolute sense of right and wrong and which applies to all people, in all situations at all times. It is this sense that is the basis for American morality.

Of course, Americans do not always live up to the standard of behavior prescribed by this morality, but it nevertheless provides a solid foundation for them to judge their own behavior and that of others.

In Mexico, on the other hand, *Dios* is seen in much more human terms, as a genuine, concrete father figure who is present at all times and is intimately involved in watching over and protecting people. (And because the God of Mexicans is on the spot and is responsible for all things, he is subject to being mocked and criticized when things go wrong.)

In its Mexican context, religion has traditionally encompassed myths and superstitions that influenced the behavior of people on every level at all times. But it went well beyond that and became inseparable from the culture itself, from a specific, detailed way of life that was close, personal and human-oriented. One could not *be* Mexican—could not think like or act like a Mexican—without adhering to the various rituals of daily life.

Mexican *moralidad* (moh-rah-lee-DAD) has traditionally been based more on obligations to oneself and one's social obligations to others than on abstract religious principles. It was made up of shared values, a common behavior, and a deep interest in protecting and sustaining the family and the community. It incorporated trust, respect and responsibility. But it did not include "goodness" or "fairness" or "justice" in the abstract Christian sense.

The traditional Mexican interpretation of *moralidad* is far more flexible than the North American concept because it is based on the situation at hand rather than abstract principles. For one thing, it is fundamentally different where male–female relations are concerned. There have, in fact, traditionally been two moralities in Mexico, one for men and another one for women, children and the poor (a phenomenon that is not, of course, unique to Mexico).

Mexican morality does not prohibit premarital or extramarital sex for men, and sanctions a two-faced attitude toward the sexual behavior of women. Most Mexican prostitutes, for example, are deeply religious and see no contradiction in their occupation, keeping religious icons in their rooms, and praying for protection from diseases and other dangers.

Mexican men have traditionally been paranoid about their wives committing adultery with other men, but have traditionally spent a great deal of time and energy seducing other men's wives. In middle- and upper-class families, young men are expected to have ample sexual experience before they marry, but they expect their brides to be virgins.

Moralidad in business and politics in Mexico has traditionally been based on doing whatever was necessary to accumulate as much power and wealth as possible, rather than on principles of fairness, equality or justice. Laws that were founded on unchanging principles were ignored or subverted to achieve personal goals. Corruption was the way of life.

Mexico's traditional *moralidad*, in all of its social, political and economic nuances, was therefore fundamentally different in both subtle and conspicuous ways from North American morality, and for generations was a source of a great deal of the misunderstanding and friction that occurred between the two societies.

Mexican morality in both business and politics began to shift dramatically in the 1970s and 1980s, becoming more rational and humanistic. But this change suffered a setback during the Salinas administration (1988–1994), when the educational system became dominated by leftist thinking, and teachers virtually stopped teaching such values as honesty, veracity and goodwill toward others.

When Ernesto Zedillo, himself an ex-teacher and a strong supporter of Mexico's traditional family values, took over as president in December 1994, new textbooks were published and distributed. Teachers were ordered to actually teach the classes assigned to them. The leftist influence that had dominated the teaching profession has since mostly disappeared.

Equally important is the fact that more and more Mexican businessmen and politicians are gradually adopting moral principles that bring their values and standards into line with international laws and customs.

As Mexico's involvement with the international community grows, the morality of all of its social institutions will no doubt be influenced for the better.

Mordida
(Mohr-DEE-dah)

"The Great Over-Bite"

For more than four centuries the government in Mexico was rife with bribery and an undisguised form of extortion on every level. Officials and civil employees routinely used the power of their positions to augment their incomes. Higher officials generally managed to become rich within a few years.

The process was simple. There was a price for any type of documentation, approval, cooperation or help from any local, provincial or federal government official, bureaucrat, clerk or street cop. It was also customary for bureaucratic appointees to kick-back half of their first year's salary.

There was no official recourse of any kind because the police and the courts were among the most corrupt—and the most feared because they routinely used both threats and real force and imprisonment in their dealings with the public.

After the 1910-1921 revolution in Mexico, various reform policies were announced by succeeding presidents and their ministers. But the system of corruption was so deeply ingrained in every level of government that nothing changed.

In the 1960s, when tourism began to assume national importance in the Mexican economy, new efforts were made to reduce the *mordida* (mohr-DEE-dah)—literally a "bite"—put on foreign travelers by immigration officials and police.

Over the next decade or so there were periodic announcements that the age-old system of *mordida* had been eliminated from Mexico, but these pronouncements were nothing more than diplomatic smoke.

During the 1970s and 1980s some progress was made in controlling *la mordida* at Mexico's international airports, where it was far more difficult for immigration officials to openly—or surreptitiously—demand bribes from incoming visitors. But the practice remained rampant at ground border-crossings, where travelers could easily be separated from others and delayed for any length of time, and among law enforcement agencies, particularly cops, whose power to arrest and imprison was virtually limitless.

Still today if one encounters official resistance in any form, or runs afoul of the law in a relatively minor way, including occasions when those concerned are perfectly innocent, both Mexicans and experienced foreigners say it is best to forget principle, find out as quickly and as subtly as possible how much money will do the job, fork it over and be on your way.

Farmers and fruit growers who transport perishable products across state borders and through any state or federal government checkpoints are especially susceptible to graft on a grand scale, because any delay could cost them the whole shipment. The word is that many of these "inspectors" become millionaires.

Automobile accidents and traffic violations cause visitors in Mexico more trouble than anything else. Visitors must keep in mind that (1) in Mexico *it is against the law* to have an accident of any kind; (2) when two or more cars are involved in a collision, all of the drivers are considered guilty; and (3) it is a crime to pick up and/or otherwise help persons injured in traffic accidents before the police arrive.

There are occasions when foreigners have stopped to give aid to people hurt in highway accidents and the police were fair enough to let them go. There have also been cases where the good Samaritans themselves were arrested, jailed, made to suffer for days and forced to buy their way out.

Says a Mexican friend: "In Mexico you will find that only officials have rights. In minor incidents involving the law, only an idiot bucks the system."

Foreigners with extensive experience in Mexico advise anyone involved in an automobile accident in which there are no serious injuries to leave the scene immediately, and disappear if their vehicle will still move.

Mordida is not to be confused with *propinas* or "tips." A *propina* is a relatively small sum of money that is paid for favors or services rendered, and is therefore the same as a gratuity in any other country.

A *mordida*, is a payment for some service that should be free. These are paid to get some action taken in a timely fashion and, probably the most important of all, to avoid or get out of trouble with the police and other law enforcement agencies.

Probably the most common of all situations in which the payment of *mordida* is an institution is in encounters with the police. One of the ploys most commonly used by "victims" is to apologize to the police officer, say you don't have time to go to the police station to pay a fine, and ask him to do you the great favor of paying it for you. You may have to haggle over the amount of the "fine," but even paying double what you think is "fair" is better than the alternative. And don't expect a receipt.

About the only way a person can sometimes avoid having to pay a "fine," is to have some personal connection with a highly placed government or police official and tell the police officer that he will take care of the matter by contacting the appropriate authorities. Police officers don't want problems with powerful politicians or their superiors.

In some cases, the custom of *mordida* is so ingrained that it is represented as a special service. For instance, there are often multiple windows in immigration offices: a "free" window where obtaining a document can take up to two hours or more; a window where payment of several dollars results in service in 30 minutes or less; and a third window where payment of a substantial amount of money results in service within two or three minutes.

Mordelones, or "biters," are police officers who specialize in extracting larger bribes than usual. At border crossings there is still a common conspiracy among the police and immigration officials to cooperate with selected "civilians" to extract money from people driving across the border. One of the ploys used by these consortiums is to wave cars over to where boys or men wipe off their windshields and expect to be paid, all under the watchful eyes and with the aid of uniformed police, who make it look very official.

Another term commonly used in reference to "official" *mordida* is *el pequeño poder* (el pay-CANE-yoh poh-DAYR), which literally means "the little power." This refers to bureaucrats who extort money (usually small sums) out of people for services that are supposed to be free. One of the most common techniques of exercising *el pequeño poder* is simply to delay taking action on a request until the person comes through with a "fee."

95

Motivación
(Moh-tee-vah-cee-OWN)

"Motivating Mexico"

For more than 200 years of the Spanish reign in Mexico it was the policy of the colonial government and the church to keep the mass of people illiterate and ignorant, and to prohibit them from engaging in enterprises or professions that would have bettered their economic and social status.

By example as well as edict, the Spanish overlords of Mexico taught racial and social discrimination, the inferiority of women, dishonesty, cruelty and virtually all the other qualities typically demonstrated by the arrogant, the avaricious and the corrupt.

These draconian customs and laws, strictly and cruelly enforced for generation after generation, stifled ambition in the people and conditioned them to accept their lot without complaint.

When Mexico finally broke away from Spain in the revolution of 1810–1821, little improved in the lives of the Indian and mixed-blood population. In fact, both their economic and political situations became worse in many ways.

Finally , in 1910 the poor of the country rose up in a bloody civil war in a desperate effort to remove the double yokes of the church and the elite dictatorships which had kept them in bondage since the revolutionary war.

This time, progress was made. Education was taken out of the hands of the church, many peasants were given title to the lands they farmed and industry was encouraged. But politically the people remained in bondage.

Having been conditioned for centuries to passively accept their poverty and powerlessness, the bulk of the population remained politically mute. They existed at a subsistence level and did not enter into the economic activity of the country.

It was not until the third quarter of the 20th century that an entirely new breed of Mexican leaders, most of them educated abroad, came to the fore and began changing things. At the same time, technology, particularly in communications and television, along with new economic opportunities, began to alter the traditional mindset and behavior of more and more Mexicans.

In the late 1980s and early 1990s a genuine cultural revolution began in Mexico, a revolution that is still underway and which is having both a positive and a negative effect on the country.

One aspect of this cultural revolution that is especially conspicuous—and positive—is summed up in the word *motivación* (moh-tee-vah-cee-OWN) or "motivation." Prior to this era, most Mexicans simply did not have the motivation—the drive—to bring about fundamental changes in their lifestyles.

The overall passivity and the sense of helplessness so deeply ingrained in the Mexican psyche over a period of nearly 500 years is far from gone, but it is going, and in the segments of society that are regularly exposed to international influences it is disappearing rapidly.

In a list of the seven most important words in Mexico today, given to me by businessman Lorenzo De La Fuente Manriquez, *motivación* was the second word on the list (*solidaridad* was first, and the others were *amistad, reto, amor, respeto* and *libertad*.)

Said De La Fuente: "Without motivation nothing can be achieved. No matter how many opportunities are presented to people who are economically and politically deprived, they will not take advantage of the opportunities if they are not motivated—and breaking the chains of passivity and ennui that have afflicted Mexicans for so many generations must be the first step.

"To motivate people we must show them things can be done—that the abuses of our justice and economic systems can be and are being eliminated."

De La Fuente went on to say that the day of self-proclaimed political demigods in Mexico was over. "Those who take on kingly airs and make excathedra pronouncements are no longer believed. Finally, after so many centuries, the people just laugh at them."

Still today, and for at least one or two more generations, every foreign businessperson who sets up shop in Mexico must learn how to successfully motivate employees to take a personal interest in their work, to be personally responsible for what they do and how they do it and to do their best.

96

Mucha Mujer
(MOO-chah Moo-HEHR)

"Women Who Are Too Much"

Mexican women received the right to vote in all elections in 1953, but that was hardly social emancipation. Traditionally kept ignorant and virtual prisoners of men, Mexican women suffered for centuries under a double standard for men and women, as well as political discrimination.

Sudden political freedom in itself could not change this deeply ingrained way of life. It was not until industrialization began on a national scale in the 1960s and 1970s, when Mexican women left their homes to work in offices and factories, that they began to enjoy some personal choice in their lives.

Gradually at first and now at an ever increasing pace, industrialization is breaking down the old patterns of thought and behavior that stifled the spirits and the intellect of Mexican women for nearly half a millennia.

Women by the hundreds of thousands have been freed from the prisons of their homes and from the feudalistic domination of their fathers and husbands. Others are joining them daily in a steady, irresistible stream.

Although it will take at least another generation and probably more before this process fully emancipates the majority of Mexican women, its results have already altered the appearance and character of the country.

Said an admiring Mexican male: "Not only is industrialization freeing Mexican girls for the first time in our history, it is also making them better looking. Generally mothers no longer swaddle their babies—not realizing the far-reaching effects this has on their children."

In and near larger towns and cities, children are worked less and educated more. Much of the secretiveness and furtiveness that traditionally characterized relationships between young men and women have disappeared. The chaperoning that still goes on in the upper classes is strictly sham.

More and more marriages are now growing out of true affection and feelings of mutual trust and responsibility. Young newlyweds think it is only natural for them to want an apartment or house of their own, instead of living with relatives.

But one characteristic that remains common to Mexican girls and women is romanticism. Young or old, high class or low, they are romantic to a fault—something that makes them especially susceptible to unscrupulous men.

Mexican women who are especially sensual and have strong sexual drives, both of which are traditionally taboo for women after they marry, are often referred to as *mucha mujer* (MOO-chah moo-HEHR), which literally means "much woman" or "very womanly." It is the female equivalent of *muy macho* (very manly).

The term has two uses. In one instance it refers to a woman who is the epitome of womanhood—sexy looking, very feminine and one to whom a man is a must. The other use, slightly on the negative side, refers to a woman who is too sexual for a particular man, meaning the man is not masculine enough to satisfy her. In this case, it is a criticism of the man, not the woman.

The *pachuco* jargon that developed in Mexican-American communities along the U.S.-Mexican border between 1920 and 1940 was filled with references to women that reflected traditionally sexist attitudes. A woman who was especially sensuous was often referred to as a *bestia*, meaning animal, beast or nonhuman. Another *pachuco* term used in reference to sexually attractive women, and meant to be complimentary, was *muy buenota*, which figuratively means "well stacked."

As Mexican women grow older, most of them gradually work their way out from under the ongoing tyranny of their husbands and lovers. Some turn the tables completely and begin controlling their men, particularly if the men have overindulged and lost some of their potency.

Some wives and widows have traditionally referred to their husbands as *ceros a la izquierda* or "zeros to the left," meaning they are worthless or "nothing." Others say that macho men are men who eat beans and belch chicken.

Once Mexican women have experienced freedom from male domination they are understandably reluctant to return to it. Many widows, in fact, prefer to live with a man in *unión libre* or "free union," because this status allows them to keep some of their freedoms and still have the conjugal services of a man.

Summing up, on the lower rungs of society Mexican women are generally more mature and stable then Mexican men (which, of course, is true of virtually all women in all societies). And women are a leading influence in the social and economic revolution now going on in the country.

Because both the bodies and minds of Mexican women were oppressed for so many centuries, as they gain more freedom they can be expected to play an increasingly active role in the affairs of the country.

In the meantime, the legacy of the masculinity cult of Mexico continues to hang over them.

97

Mujeres
(Moo-HAYR-ehs)

"The Feminine Mystique"

From the beginning of the Spanish reign in Mexico in 1521 until the early 1900s Mexican women, including those in the elite ruling-class families, were deliberately kept ignorant of the world at large. It was scandalous for a woman to learn how to read, write or speak her own mind.

The now-famous female poet-playwright Sor Juana Inez de la Cruz (1651–1695), who managed to educate herself and was so brilliant that she astounded the men of her time, wrote that virtually all of the complaints that men had about women were caused by the men themselves.

In its idealized Mexican context, womanhood is equated with love, goodness, understanding, sincerity, caring and obedience to men and the church. Once a women is married, her femininity is to be expressed only in these terms. Over the centuries, the only solace the women of Mexico had from the sexism and irresponsibility of machismo-dominated men was the Catholic Church—not as a refuge, but as a place where they could hope to win religious merit by passively accepting the punishments inflicted upon them.

Many Mexican women also traditionally looked to the church for spiritual support because they believed that the priests had the only masculine shoulders they could lean on without getting into trouble—something that in the past was far from true, in both a physical and spiritual sense.

Young Mexican women were conditioned to have a strongly sensual image of themselves and to behave in a sexually provocative manner. But the church denied them the right to actually express their sexuality even after marriage. At the same time the church upheld the macho behavior of single as well as married men.

Says Mexican writer Frank Gutz: "In the past Mexican women were taught to believe coitus was an ignoble but unavoidable requirement of marriage, and that they should seek no pleasure from it—although it was accepted that men should. It was usually not possible to make an average Mexican girl admit that sex by itself, even after marriage, was desirable or wholesome. She could not or simply refused to enjoy the sex act for fear of being shamed. So her husband sought his pleasure elsewhere."

Insiders say that the demands and fears of Mexican husbands would not allow wives to be romantic or passionate in their relationships, and that women were forced to reserve their "soft love" for their children, whom they practically smothered.

Both Mexican men and women were conditioned for centuries to believe that the sexual attraction between men and women was so strong that when they were alone together, by design or by coincidence, they could not resist the compulsion to engage in sex.

This belief led to the tradition of the *duenna* (DWAYN-nyah) or chaperon accompanying dating couples, and to the custom of having third parties present when men and women met in private settings for reasons other than sex.

Despite the church taboos against women expressing their sexuality and the social barriers to intimacy before marriage, there was a great deal of premarital sex in Mexico. If a single middle-class Mexican girl really wanted a particular man her passion could be fierce. And since mistresses had only their charms and passion to hold men, they made a point of keeping their patrons worn down to a nub.

Once a Mexican man had sex with a woman he tended to become very possessive and jealous and consider the woman his private property. Some went so far as to forbid girlfriends or mistresses from having outside friends of either gender, or going out by themselves.

Isolating newly married women from their friends and society in general was yet another way in which men exercised power over women. By denying women either the will or the ability to control their own behavior, men were able to presume that it was necessary for them to protect women from themselves.

Although this cultural factor has been weakened considerably among the middle and upper classes in Mexico's urban areas, it remains strong enough that it still must be taken into consideration to avoid the appearance of impropriety and unpleasant repercussions.

Today, Mexican women do not think of themselves as being the equals of men or as the same as men with only minor physical differences. There is a man's world and a woman's world, and the North American idea of downplaying the differences between men and women and advocating that they be treated alike remains alien to both men and women.

The concept of American-style women's rights and women's liberation is something that the majority of Mexican women simply do not think about. If it is brought to their attention they are most apt to say that they do not want to behave like American women because such behavior is immoral.

Yet there have always been dichotomies in Mexico's double standard for men and women. Middle- and lower-class women traditionally worked in the fields alongside of men and endured the worst kind of hardships to survive and raise families. During Mexico's civil war (1910–1921) hundreds of thousands of women traveled with soldiers, carrying ammunition, feeding them and caring for them when they were wounded.

Until recent times Mexican women did not expect men to be sensitive to their rights or needs because there were few historical precedents for such behavior. The fact that men regarded themselves as the protectors of women while the culture permitted them to misuse and abuse women to an extraordinary degree was a special irony for women.

Mexican women who have had one or more marriages, a number of children, been widowed or become grandmothers, generally have more freedom than other women. Many of them treat men with varying degrees of contempt, and do exactly as they please.

Mexican women who become aggressive and domineering (and there are plenty of them) are sometimes referred to as *muy mandonas*, which is more or less the Spanish equivalent of "battle axes."

The biggest problem facing most poor women in Mexico continues to be having too many children too early. Many have two or three children by the time they are 20, often out of wedlock. Until 1970 the government of Mexico urged women to have as many children as possible, giving medals to the most prolific women in the country.

Nowadays, a growing number of Mexican women are having themselves sterilized to avoid pregnancy. They justify the procedure by saying it is a one-time sin, while taking birth-control pills is a sin every time a pill is taken.

Because of the aggressiveness of Mexican men, Mexican women have traditionally had three choices in their behavior. They had to appear either as aloof and untouchable, be flirts who advertised their availability or make themselves as invisible as possible by avoiding eye contact and blending into the background. More and more middle- and upper-class Mexican women are overcoming this historical handicap, and are now able to behave in a more natural, balanced manner when in the presence of men. But it will no doubt be generations before all Mexican women can achieve that goal.

Despite these negative factors, dramatic changes are taking place in the lives of better-educated and foreign-influenced Mexican women. It is no longer culturally taboo for married women to work in factories and offices.

Little by little, women are also beginning to participate in the political life of the country. Thousands became involved in the election campaigns of the 1980s and 1990s as fund-raisers, and proved that they could be especially effective. There were women on the presidential election committees of Ernesto Zedillo in 1994. A growing number also have become candidates for office. In December 1994 a woman became the head of the long-ruling Institutional Revolutionary Party (PRI), which had been an exclusive male bastion since its founding in 1929. Today, there are women in government on both the state and national levels—something that would have been unthinkable just a short while ago.

Said a politically active businessman: "*El machismo* still exists in Mexico, but it is evolving. The challenge now is how to get women in general involved in politics and business without destroying the unique role that they play in family life and in the overall culture of the country—so that both men and women benefit socially as well as economically."

98

Negativismo
(Nay-gah-tee-VEES-moh)

"Recharging the Mexican Character"

Many Mexicans, particularly those who have become bilingual and bicultural and are therefore able to see their own culture more clearly, say that most of Mexico's ongoing economic, social and political problems can be laid on the altar of the Catholic Church, on the policies of the Spanish administrators during the country's long colonial period and on the dictators who followed them.

They say that despite the centuries that have passed since the Mexican revolution against Spain and their civil war against the church and the dictatorship that succeeded the Spanish, these problems have still not been resolved because the people of Mexico were so deeply conditioned in *negativismo* (nay-gah-tee-VEES-moh), or "negativism," that they became incapable of helping themselves.

Said one: "For six days a week for more than 400 years the political and economic systems of Mexico oppressed and abused the people. On the seventh day the people went to church. There the priests continued the oppression and the abuse—brainwashing them into believing that they were evil and destined to go to Hell.

"During this long period virtually every influence brought to bear on all Mexicans outside of the small, elite ruling class was negative. To put it in vulgar terms, they were forced to eat shit every day for so long that it eventually got to the point where it became normal and was all that they could expect.

217

"Given the environment created by the church and the government and perpetuated for generation after generation there was simply no way the people could develop a positive image of themselves or Mexico, and this legacy continues to cloud the minds and hearts of a significant proportion of the population."

These critics say that the biggest challenge facing Mexicans today is to purge themselves of this *negativismo* and to develop a new, positive "can do" spirit combined with a sense of self-respect, individual and mutual responsibility, solidarity and cooperativeness.

This remolding of the national character and spirit of Mexico took a great leap forward after the election of Carlos Salinas to the presidency in 1988, and then with his successor Ernesto Zedillo in 1994. Zedillo rode into the office of the presidency on a wave of nationwide enthusiasm by committing his administration to a complete break with the past.

One of the most potent symbols of this was Zedillo's inaugural parade through the streets of Mexico City in an open car on December 1, 1994. To the surprise and pleasure of most Mexicans, he made the nationally televised ride accompanied only by his wife. Prior to this, all of Mexico's incoming presidents were accompanied on this traditional ride by their predecessors sitting next to them in the back seat and conspicuously uniformed generals occupying the front seat.

During his campaign for the presidency, Zedillo sent teams of men and women to cities and towns throughout the country to hold forums and get input from local business and educational leaders in a program called "100 Questions 100 Answers."

After his election (but before his inauguration) he followed up by inviting some 500 Mexican businesspeople to a meeting in Mexico City and letting them do the talking, which set a new tone and revolutionary approach to government.

In every Mexican city that I have traveled to in recent years, the leaders in instilling a new "it can be done" and "I can do it" spirit into young Mexicans are entrepreneurs, both men and women, who founded their own companies, or they are the sons and daughters of founders who had emancipated themselves from the rigor mortis of negativism.

Said one of these successful sons: "We are no longer guided by so-called Mexican *or* American thinking for that matter. We are being guided more and more by universal principles that are applicable anywhere, at all times, in everything that we do."

Yet most of my Mexican friends, including those who themselves are well over the age of 60, say that despite the dramatic breaks with the past initiated by Zedillo and others, *negativismo* will continue to plague Mexico for one or more generations simply because it has been an integral part of the character of Mexicans for centuries and cannot be removed like an old coat.

99

Negocios
(Nay-GO-cee-ohs)

"Business Mexican Style"

Most North American businesspeople dealing with Mexico for the first time, like their counterparts going into China, Japan, Korea and other parts of Asia, usually go through several frustrating and costly years of learning that culture counts, and that it generally comes first.

Mexican culture differs significantly from North American culture—philosophically, spiritually, emotionally and intellectually. Values, expectations, manners, morality, ethics—all are different to varying degrees, and all impact on the conduct of *negocios* (nay-GO-cee-ohs) or business.

Mexican author Octavio Paz recites a long list of differences between Mexicans and Americans: Mexicans love myths and legends; Americans love fairy tales and detective stories. Mexicans are fascinated by horror; Americans are repelled by it. Mexicans delight in fantasy and fantasizing while Americans prefer hard reality. Americans are automatically trusting; Mexicans are automatically suspicious. Mexicans are pessimists; Americans are optimists. Americans delight in telling light-hearted jokes; Mexicans are masters at heavy sarcasm. Americans are put off by foreign things; regarding them as some kind of contamination; Mexicans revel in intimate contact and have little sense of contamination of the body or the soul.

Americans are critical of themselves and others, and welcome change; Mexicans eschew criticism and are afraid of change. Americans look forward to a golden age in the future; Mexicans have traditionally tried to hold onto or return to a golden age of the past—an orientation that virtually prevented change during the entire span of the 300-year colonial era.

One difference between Mexicans and Americans that has special significance in both business and private affairs is the tendency of Americans to be completely open and frank; to tell all and trust other people to do the same.

Mexicans, on the other hand, have been conditioned to distrust everyone; to hold back, to be reserved and maintain invulnerability by never revealing their true thoughts of feelings.

Perhaps the most basic difference between North Americans and Mexicans is that people raised in the Anglo-American tradition are conditioned to emphasize strength, power, doing and achieving, while Mexicans emphasize being and existence, and give more credence to thought and human relations.

One of the key cultural factors in the Mexican way of doing business is the role and importance of personal relationships.

Unlike in the United States and Canada, for example, an impersonal, blanket approach to personnel management generally does not work in Mexico. It is crucial that foreign managers know their Mexican employees individually and be flexible in dealing with each one.

Consideration must be given to a variety of specific problems that regularly confront individuals, including such things as weddings, illness, deaths in the family, transportation problems and housing.

Failure to show personal interest in individuals and their problems invariably results in low morale and less-than-enthusiastic approach to getting things done. The personalized nature of human relationships in Mexico makes people suspicious of cooperative group efforts that are not founded in personal relationships.

It is especially vital that foreign executives establish close personal relationships with their top Mexican managers from the very beginning. This means getting acquainted with them from day one, including finding out about their families and background; treating them with formal courtesy on the job; having informal, intimate talks with them away from the office, over drinks and meals; and going out of the way to keep them in the circle of communication.

Generally speaking, being culturally correct is the only way to succeed in Mexico. For outsiders, this often means turning what might otherwise be negative factors into very positive forces that make the difference between success and failure.

At the same time, there are some cultural factors in Mexico that are negative in nature and cannot be made positive by "culturally correct" behavior by anyone. The only way they can be changed for the better is for Mexicans themselves to change.

One of these cultural handicaps, which Mexican businesspeople themselves deplore, is the casual attitude that Mexicans have toward maintenance once a project has been completed, an attitude that has been a conspicuous part of the overall culture for generations.

Roads, buildings and most other kinds of infrastructure are typically allowed to deteriorate, even when funds for their maintenance are available.

Another cultural factor that foreign businesspeople must learn to live with, which Mexicans don't regard as negative, is the Mexican concept of time.

A rule of thumb that might be used to estimate the amount of time a project is going to take in Mexico is to multiply the time it would take in the

United States by two or three, depending on its complexity. The more people and government offices that are involved, the longer it usually takes to do things in Mexico.

Other business rules to live by:

1. Don't belittle Mexico or Mexicans, individually or collectively. It won't help and will probably hurt.

2. Don't complain publicly about the "weakness" or "failings" of Mexicans or government offices. It won't change things and will probably make them worse. Maintain a positive, problem-solving stance that incorporates culturally acceptable methods.

3. Don't criticize or discipline employees publicly no matter how much you think they deserve it. Such actions shame them, and may make them your enemy for life. Do it privately and diplomatically.

4. Don't "underdress" or behave in an excessively casual manner (like putting your feet on your desk during "informal" meetings). Keep in mind that Mexican behavior in general, including attire, tends toward the formal.

Until recent times, wearing apparel and social class in Mexico were closely related. For the most part, class determined what one wore, making upper-class people extremely sensitive about their dress and what other people were wearing.

The Catholic Church also played a significant role in setting conservative standards of dress.

Still today, the higher the social and economic class of someone the more concerned they are with how they look. Well-to-do men and women spend an inordinate amount of attention on clothing and grooming, and regard anything less as low class.

While cultural behavior in Mexico can be a barrier to business that is difficult to cross, there are other differences that go beyond culture. One is the institution of the public notary.

In the United States a notary is little more than someone authorized to validate signatures. American notaries have nothing at all to do with drawing up documents, so getting a document notarized is a simple procedure that is inexpensive, or free.

In Mexico, on the other hand, only attorneys can act as *notarios publicos* or

221

"public notaries," and their fees are based on their status as lawyers plus notaries. Setting up a corporation and engaging in other types of business in Mexico can therefore be substantially more expensive than it is in the United States.

Foreign companies setting up operations in Mexico often find that the cost of doing business is considerably higher than what they expected. The base pay that Mexican factory employees receive is substantially lower than what their American and Canadian counterparts get, but there are many more costs involved.

Mexican law stipulates that workers are entitled to a variety of benefits that are over and above what most workers receive in other countries. Mexican workers may also receive other benefits which are not required by law, but which are fairly common among larger corporations. These benefits include:

Aguinaldo (ah-ghee-NAHL-doh)—This a mandatory Christmas bonus equivalent to one month's salary.

Bonos (BOH-nohs)—These are coupons (not required by law) that are redeemable at food and general stores, and in some cases are a portion of the employee's salary. Employers are allowed to pay up to 21 percent of the individual's base pay in coupons, depending on the minimum wage paid in the area. (There are three minimum-wage regions in Mexico: Guadalajara and Monterrey, Mexico City and the rest of the country.) Some companies make use of *bonos* not only because they are tax deductible but also because the coupons represent income for employees that is not taxable, and is therefore an advantage to them as well.

Fondo ahorro (FOHN-doh ah-OH-rroh)—This is a savings plan, via payroll deductions, that some employers offer to their workers. If the plan is offered, all employees must participate in the program. The employer matches the amount deducted from the workers' salaries.

Instituto Mexicano del Seguro Social (IMSS) (ins-tee-TOO-toh meh-he-CAH-no dehl seh-GOO-roh soh-cee-AHL)—The Mexican Social Security Institute oversees a national health care and financial assistance program operated by the government for workers. The program covers illness, permanent disability, maternity and sick leave, retirement, burial costs, childcare and unemployment compensation when an employee is dismissed from work.

Instituto Fondo Vivienda Nacional de los Trajabadores (Infonavit)—The National Workers' Housing Fund Institute operates a government savings program designed to help workers buy government-built housing. Workers who participate in the program and do not end up buying a government-built home get their money back plus interest.

Overtime—The official work week in Mexico is six days (48 hours), but salaries paid to employees are based on a seven-day work week. Employees are supposed to receive double pay for the first nine hours of overtime, and triple pay for all hours thereafter, as well as for hours worked on national holidays.

Paid vacations—After being employed by the same company for one year, Mexican workers are legally entitled to a one-week vacation, during which they are paid one quarter of their daily base salary.

Profit Sharing—After the first year of operation, Mexican law states that companies must pay 10 percent of their profits to their employees.

Sistema de Ahorros para el Retiro (SAR) (sees-TAY-mah day ah-OH-rrohs pah-rah ehl ray-TEE-roh)—All Mexican companies are required to pay two percent of the base pay of each employee into SAR (the retirement savings system), a government-operated retirement program, similar to the Social Security system in the United States.

In actuality, only the small percentage of Mexico's labor force that works for large, nationally known companies regularly receives some or all of these benefits. Other Mexican employers, particularly of small companies, simply ignore them, and generally pay off whatever government officials are concerned if they are called on the carpet for it.

Foreign companies setting up operations in Mexico are expected to abide by all of the laws and customs of the country.

100

Ni Modo
(Nee MOH-doh)

"It Can't Be Helped!"

In societies with oppressive, harsh political and religious regimes that continue for several generations, the common people, those on the bottom of the hierarchy, develop a variety of cultural traits which have helped them cope with their powerlessness. These include extreme reluctance to attract the attention of the authorities, or anyone in a powerful position, never acting on their own or standing out from the crowd in any way, extraordinary politeness to people in positions of power, an unwillingness to accept responsibility, and dependence upon those in charge to make all decisions and initiate all actions.

Interestingly enough, such societies also develop a detailed, highly stylized personal etiquette which controls all interpersonal relationships, particularly those between inferiors and superiors.

Traditional Mexican society is a classic example of these religious and political forces. From the beginning of the Spanish colonial period in 1521 until the last decades of the 20th century, common Mexicans were subjected to extreme religious and political oppression.

One of the key figures of speech relating to the culturally conditioned attitudes and behavior of ordinary Mexicans is *ni modo* (nee MOH-doh), a colloquialism that meant "there is nothing that can be done," or "it can't be helped."

In Mexico, because there were so many things that ordinary people could not change or do anything about, particularly things having to do with government offices and officials in general, *ni modo* became a commonly used phrase.

This term subsumes a great deal of the passive behavior that has been traditionally associated with poor and underprivileged Mexicans. When things did not go according to plan, or as expected, the typical response was *ni modo*. The people involved were simply incapable of getting uptight about it.

Much of this passive response was religious in nature. For generations, the Catholic Church taught the poor of Mexico that there was virtue in poverty, that they should not be envious of those who had more, and should content themselves with being willing servants of God.

The church also taught that when things went wrong it was the will of God, and should be accepted as part of the hardship people had to endure to remain faithful to the teachings of the church. Man, the church said, could not influence or control nature (God), and should not try.

The passive nature of disenfranchised Mexicans was further complicated by the attitude that "living" took precedence over work, that work was not a virtue within itself and that one should work only hard enough, fast enough and long enough to "make a living."

The deeply entrenched American concept of working hard today for the sake of the future was not part of the Mexican psyche. To them, the future was unknown and unpredictable, and their primary obligation was to get through the day, and, if possible, enjoy themselves in the process.

In Mexico today the average person on every level of society does not regard work itself as moral and not working as immoral. And people have not yet been conditioned to believe that it is a waste of time not to do things as quickly as possible.

The "work ethic" is growing in Mexico, but it will probably be two or three generations before it reaches the level that exists in most non-Latin countries.

In the meantime, Mexican and foreign businesspeople must continue to deal with the *ni modo* syndrome on a case-by case basis, creating their own employee incentive programs within the context of what their employees will accept.

No Hay
(No Eye)

"There Isn't Any!"

During the 1970s and 1980s Mexico's highest paid movie and television star was a comedian named Hector Suárez, who not only achieved fame and wealth as an entertainer, but who was also a significant influence in bringing about political reforms in the country.

Suárez was something like the Red Skelton of Mexico. He specialized in creating oddball characters whom he used in humorous skits to make social and political statements. One of the most memorable characters was named Ciriaco, whose signature line was *no hay* (no eye).

No hay literally means "There is none," or "I/we don't have any"—one of the most commonly heard phrases in the Mexican vocabulary.

Ciriaco, dressed in overalls and wearing a huge mustache (to represent all common Mexicans) went around saying *No hay!* in all kinds of humorous situations in a symbolic reference to the perennial shortage of almost everything in Mexico for generations.

Suárez's primary themes were barbed jokes about the avarice, cruelty, irresponsibility, lying, machismo and vanity that had been typical of the Mexican character since the Spanish era, and ridiculing the many abuses of the government.

It is said that Suárez's barbs were directly responsible for a number of reforms in government practices, and that he was a major influence in encouraging other people to speak up about government abuses and their problems.

No hay is still heard in many parts of Mexico, but much less often than before.

Omerta
(Oh-MAYR-tah)

"The Great Code of Silence"

The Spanish *conquistadores* who stumbled upon Mexico in the early 1500s were raiders seeking gold. The colonial administrators who followed them were charged with extracting as much wealth as possible from the land and its Indian inhabitants.

The Catholic Church, in an unholy alliance with the Spanish government, also seized upon Mexico as a source of wealth as well as souls. For both the church and the government of Spain, Mexico was a cash cow.

Thus from the beginning of Mexico's Spanish colonial period in 1521 politics and plundering on a grand scale were indistinguishable. Political office was traditionally the surest way to wealth in this environment.

For the 300 years of the Spanish regime this philosophy and practice prevailed. Government officials, church leaders and military officers used their power to enrich themselves, their families and their friends. It was government by a few for the few.

Mexico's successful revolution against Spain in 1810–1821 did nothing but change the country's masters. The grand orgy of theft by politicians and government officials went on. History notes that between 1821 and 1910 there was only one president—Benito Juárez, a Zatopec Indian—who did not use the office as a license to steal.

The Mexican civil war in 1910–1921, a bloody struggle between the powerless poor and the political-military-church triumvirate, again failed to change the morality and behavior of the establishment. With but few exceptions, government officials, from the lowest cops on the streets to presidents, continued the institutionalized custom of enriching themselves.

The higher the political office, the greater the opportunities to convert power and privileges to cash and property. There were simply no limits to the venality of people in the system because that *was* the system.

Rather than adhering to a moral philosophy based on principles of right and wrong, Mexican politicians and government bureaucrats followed a deeply entrenched practice that Mexican historian Lorenzo Meyer called *omerta* (oh-MER-ta), an Italian word referring to the "code of silence" oath taken by Mafia gang members.

The *omerta* code guaranteed that newly installed presidents and other officials would not investigate the abuses of previous administrations, thereby protecting them and ensuring their own immunity after they left office.

After the so-called Institutional Revolutionary Party (PRI) took over the country in 1929 it further sanctified the code of *omerta*. From the mid-1930s on Mexican presidents behaved like Mafia dons, amassing great wealth during their single six-year terms, then adhering to a strict code of silence no matter what they were accused of afterward.

The code of *omerta* suffered its first serious setback in 1995 when President Ernesto Zedillo's attorney general arrested Raul Salinas, the older brother of his predecessor and mentor, Carlos Salinas, on suspicion of having ordered and financed the assassination of reform-minded José Francisco Ruiz Massieu, the number two man in the ruling Institutional Revolutionary Party.

Ex-President Carlos Salinas, himself an ardent reformer who had already broken many of the taboos established by his own PRI party, broke the *omerta* code himself when he went on television to proclaim his brother's innocence and refute the claim by the Zedillo administration that he was responsible for the economic crisis that struck the country at the beginning of the year.

The arrest of Raul Salinas and the television response by his brother, the former president, prompted historian Meyer to declare that Zedillo, whom he had described as a weak president, had destroyed the Mexican custom of *omerta* and that it was a very important historical event.

Meyer will probably turn out to be correct in his prediction of the demise of *omerta* as it applies to ex-presidents and other high government officials. Mexican leaders can no longer hide from the scrutiny of the news media or their political opponents.

However, these isolated incidents, plus the newly vigilant news media and a growing opposition, are not enough to quickly eliminate venality from Mexico's ruling establishment or to wipe out the code of silence and collusion that has been the hallmark of Mexican politics since day one. *Omerta* will no doubt continue to exist like a virus in Mexican society until the culture itself undergoes a fundamental change, and morality is no longer an arbitrary thing that changes with the circumstances.

Orgullo
(Ohr-GOOH-yoh)

"The Comfort of Cultural Pride"

From 1521 to 1910 the vast majority of Mexicans—meaning those of mixed blood and the native Indians—lived in a society that was reigned over by a small political, military and ecclesiastical elite that treated the average Mexican with a combination of contempt, physical and mental abuse and cruel indifference. In addition to relegating the mixed-bloods and Indians to second- or third-class status, the ruling elite made it virtually impossible for the majority of them to improve their situation. Both the government and the church followed policies of denigrating the worth of the mixed-bloods and Indians, literally brainwashing them into having low opinions of themselves and accepting their condition as ordained by God.

In this environment it was impossible for the mixed-bloods and Indians to develop normal racial and cultural *orgullo* (ohr-GOOH-yoh) or "pride." There was no way they could take pride in what they were because there was no foundation for any such pride—no personal accomplishments, no great heroes who had succeeded in improving their lot, no grand dreams.

The only pride that they were capable of developing and expressing was personal. For men, this pride was centered on their masculinity and on upholding the male image they had of themselves. The pride of women was centered on motherhood and religious piety.

It was not until the time of Mexico's civil war, which began in 1910 and ended in 1921, that mixed-bloods, who had actually made up the majority of the population since the 1700s, began to visualize themselves as a distinctive race and nationality. Then they began to develop racial and national pride.

Over the next half century Mexicans went overboard on national *orgullo*. Reacting to the centuries of oppression and unfair treatment by their own institutions as well as foreigners, they became oversensitive and irrationally proud, especially in situations involving foreigners.

In contrast, most Mexican Americans attempted to distance themselves from their racial and cultural heritage and merge into mainstream America, but they met with only limited success. For the majority, the cultural vacuum left in their lives put them in a kind of interdimensional limbo.

By the 1980s both Mexicans and Mexican Americans had begun to come to terms with their racial and cultural identities. The sharper edges of Mexican pride were rounding off, and they were becoming more comfortable with who and what they were.

Mexican Americans had also realized that trying to give up their cultural legacy and remake themselves in the image of Anglo Americans was not only unnecessary but also unwise, because they lost more than they gained.

Three of the most important Mexican-American movements that strived for a reconcilation with their Mexican heritage were the appearance of Hispanic student organizations on high school and college campuses, the emergence of Hispanic writers on the American literary scene and the widespread acceptance of Hispanic music and singers.

Remarkably, these new Hispanic writers included a number of female novelists and poets who for the first time began revealing the world as it truly was for Hispanic women in the United States. Among the most notable of this new breed of Latina writers (and their latest books) are Julia Alvarez (*In the Time of Butterflies*, Algonquin Books); Denise Chavez (*Face of an Angel*, Farrar, Straus and Giroux); Sandra Cisneros (*Loose Women*, Alfred A. Knopf) and Ana Castillo (*Massacre of the Dreamers*, University of New Mexico Press).

All of these movements indicate a new comfort level that Mexicans and Mexican Americans have with the positive attributes of their culture, which in turn is contributing to a more balanced pride in their heritage.

Pachucos
(Pah-CHOO-cohs)

"Rebels in Disguise"

Minority groups that do not fit into a larger society because of cultural
and racial differences often go to extremes to create an identity and world of
their own. In the process they frequently exacerbate their tenuous and dangerous position by making themselves more different from the mainstream
than they were to begin with.

In the 1920s and 1930s thousands of young Mexican and Mexican-
American youths migrated from West Texas to the Los Angeles area in
Southern California by hopping on freight trains. They sought jobs in factories
and other businesses that were springing up in the area.

This mass movement was not all volunteer. The El Paso Police Department
arrested large numbers of youths, sentenced them to prison and then told them
the sentences would be suspended if they left town and never returned.

When these youths were asked by Mexican Americans in Los Angeles
where they were from, the newcomers replied that they came from El Paso.
The locals soon began calling them *pasucos*, a term concocted from El Paso
that roughly meant "someone from El Paso." This word gradually evolved
into *pachucos* (pah-CHOO-cohs), which was easier to pronounce.

As time went by these new arrivals began referring to themselves as
pachucos in a conscious effort to distinguish themselves from everyone else,
including other Mexican Americans.

Over the next two decades the *pachucos* reacted to growing racial and
cultural discrimination by creating a language and dress style of their own.
They also assumed an air of impassive indifference mixed with contempt,
and developed a propensity to lash out in sadistic violence against anyone
who crossed them.

Literature on the origin and behavior of these youths attributes their
self-styled character to the fact that they were born into a hostile society.
Also, they ultimately lost most of their traditional culture—their language,
their religion, and virtually all the ties and rituals that made up the Mexican
way of life.

Not being allowed to become Americans, and not wanting to be
Mexicans, these alienated youths chose to make themselves conspicuously

different from both groups in appearance and behavior, both as a disguise and as a challenge to those oppressing and victimizing them.

It was the *pachucos* of Los Angeles, along with some blacks and Filipinos, who gave birth to the exaggerated apparel designs known as "zoot suits," which were marked by long coats, "pancake hats," pants with balloon legs and narrow cuffs and thick-soled shoes.

Zoot-suiters also wore their hair long, slicked back and ending in a so-called "duck's tail." Another part of the zoot-suit costume was heavy watch chains made of gold.

The zoot suit was quickly adopted by American blacks and it was they who made it nationally famous because of their high profile in Harlem and other black communities, and in movies and music. Mainstream America and the media treated the zoot suit as the height of hip fashion where black Americans were concerned, but when Mexican Americans were involved, it was associated with gangs and criminal behavior.

By the 1940s the special jargon created by the *pachucos*, combined with slang from the Juárez–El Paso underworld, had become a virtual dialect, a "code" that made it possible for their members to almost totally separate themselves from both Mexican-American and Anglo societies. The *pachuco* subculture also spread across the American Southwest to all of the border cities connected to Los Angeles by railroad.

During the 1940s there were frequent battles between the *pachucos* and U.S. soldiers stationed nearby who came into the Mexican-American areas of Los Angeles to pick up *pachuca* girls. Similar conflicts also occurred in San Diego, Tucson, El Paso and other border cities.

The Mexican-American areas of Los Angeles were eventually declared off limits to U.S. soldiers after strong protests from the Mexican government. But after the end of World War II in 1945, street battles erupted again, this time between *pachucos* and roving bands of white high school youths who resented the fact that some white girls were attracted to the *pachucos*.

Because of the arrogant and sometimes violent behavior of the *pachucos*, coupled with their outlandish apparel, the news media began referring to *pachucos* as gang members, a label that quickly stuck, creating more tension between this subgroup of Mexican Americans and society at large.

By the end of the 1940s the world of the *pachucos* had become glamorized to an extraordinary degree, both by younger Mexican-American youths who were attracted by the flamboyant lifestyles affected by the *pachucos*, and particularly because of a number of songs that were written about them that quickly became bestsellers—despite that fact that the songs were originally intended to put the *pachucos* down.

Mexican poet and writer Octavio Paz, who spent a number of years in Los Angeles in the diplomatic service of Mexico, described the *pachucos* as enigmatic, "sinister clowns" whose purpose was to terrorize rather than entertain. He went on to suggest that the phenomenon of the *pachucos* represented irreconcilable differences between the cultures of Mexico and North America, and that all people whose mother culture was pulled out by the roots faced a similar fate. One of the most dangerous results was a tendency for the *pachucos* to swing from enervating depression to fits of destructive frenzy—a syndrome that has, in fact, plagued Indian and *mestizo* Mexicans since the beginning of the Spanish colonial area in 1521.

Mexican Americans no longer face the same degree of social ostracism that existed during most of the 1900s, and the more destructive tendencies of the *pachuco* syndrome have significantly diminished. But young Chicanos—the contemporary term for Mexican Americans—still continue to feel different.

The *pachuco* culture was short lived, yet its influence is so powerful that it continues today to be discernable in the attitudes, behavior and speech of less educated Mexican Americans, particularly those who reside in the American states bordering Mexico. A disproportionate amount of the domestic and street violence that presently occurs in towns and cities along the U.S.–Mexican border in still perpetrated by *pachuco*-like young Chicanos who have not yet made the transformation to a new culture.

However, in concert with a substantial decrease in the degree and variety of discrimination faced by present-day Chicanos in the United States, there has been a corollary reemergence among Chicanos of pride in their native cultural roots. This dramatic change is made even more impressive and important by the fact that a growing number of Anglo and other Americans now regard the bilingualism and biculturalism of Mexican Americans as an enviable asset, a syndrome that will no doubt increase with passing time.

(See **Chicanos, Ranflas, Violencia**.)

Palancas
(Pah-LAHN-cahs)

"Leveraging Your Way to Success"

Creating an ideal scenario for business success in Mexico is not difficult. The first step is to identify and bring in a man who already has an interest in Mexico and has demonstrated this interest by preparing himself for a career in the country. (I say "man" because foreign businesswomen face special problems in Mexico and may be seriously handicapped in winning the respect and cooperation that is necessary to build a business from the ground up.)

The man selected should be at least fairly fluent in contemporary Mexican Spanish and be determined to master the language fully in the shortest possible time. He should also be culturally sensitive to Mexican feelings and have great respect for them as a people. But at the same time he should be old enough and well-enough grounded in his own culture to maintain his values and integrity, and to react diplomatically regardless of the provocations.

The second step is to send the man to Mexico for anywhere from weeks to months to do nothing but get himself (and his family if there is one) settled in the city of choice, and then spend the rest of his allotted time identifying key government officials and individuals in his area of business, and establishing close, personal relationships with them.

The reason for establishing this network of contacts in advance is that virtually all business in Mexico is based on the use of *palancas* (pah LAHN-cahs) or "levers"—meaning government officials who have the power to get things done by virtue of their official authority, and private individuals who are able to exercise similar clout through their own authority and connections.

Every successful businessperson in Mexico has a network of *palancas* made up of family members, relatives, former classmates, friends and business associates who they depend on for information, advice, contacts, recommendations, etc.

Of course, individuals who make use of their *palancas* incur reciprocal obligations, so that the networks cross-pollinate.

Naturally, the higher the level of the government official or corporate executive the more clout they have and the more people seek to network with them, adding exponentially to their ability to achieve their own goals. It is, in fact, this *palanca* factor in business in Mexico that made it possible for a few families to own and control more than half of the total assets of the country.

Establishing a network of *palancas* in Mexico can be fast and easy, or it can take years and be very difficult, depending on the character, personality and skill of the individuals involved, and what tangible advantages they—and their companies—have to offer.

But there is no choice in the matter. Every new business in Mexico, regardless of its level, must establish a network of connections and thereafter be able to call on their *palanca* power.

It is also a given that virtually every business transaction in Mexico must be accompanied by some form of "special consideration" given to one or more people who were directly or indirectly involved in the transaction.

Where government offices are concerned, whatever forms, licenses or permissions that are required are simply held up until the matter of "special consideration" is settled.

This consideration may be in the form of a favor, some kind of gift or other benefit, or a sum of money, depending on the parties and circumstances.

Outsiders may regard such "payments" as *mordida* (the bite) and therefore unethical. But generally speaking, when such transactions take place as a result of their leverage, Mexicans regard them as legitimate recompense.

Foreign businesses in Mexico must learn how to cope with this additional cost element. Some end up simply putting a trusted Mexican employee in charge of negotiating and handling such "social" obligations.

Paseos
(Pah-SAY-ohs)

"Making Passes at Girls"

One of the areas of human behavior that most "civilized" societies have never been able to cope with in a humane way is sex. And since most so-called civilized societies in recent history have been dominated by men, it has been women who got the short end of the stick.

Traditionally most such societies in both the East and the West simply denied the sexuality of women, forcing them to ignore and sublimate their sexual desires and needs, or suffer the consequences.

Of course, this problem exists because the sexual instincts of human males is the same as that of stallions, buck kangaroos and a variety of other male animals—have sex with as many females as possible and prevent them from having sex with other males.

The problem is further complicated by the fact that in male-dominated societies the stronger the sex drive of males, the stronger and more elaborate the taboos and rules they have to fashion to control the sexual behavior of females.

In Mexico the cult of masculinity—introduced into the country by the Spaniards after they conquered the country in 1521 and thereafter greatly intensified by their mixed-blood Spanish-Indian offspring—took the male–female problem to new dimensions.

Rather than force the women of Mexico to totally deny their sexuality and behave in an absolutely passive manner toward males, Mexican men created a system that constantly and perversely stoked the sexuality of females from a young age, but prevented the majority of them from exercising it except under extremely controlled conditions.

While young men were culturally conditioned to spend a great deal of their time and energy in attempting to have sex with as many women as possible, they were also conditioned to be obsessed with the idea that the women they married had to be virgins.

One carefully controlled occasion when young Mexican girls who were candidates for "good" marriages could publicly show themselves off was at ritualistic *paseos* (pay-SAY-ohs), which literally means "parades" or "trips" but in this case means something like "courting parades."

Paseos were originally popularized by the young sons and daughters of *gachupines* and *criollos* who would often ride around the town, city square or park on horseback or in horse-drawn carriages, the latter complete with black slave attendants in colorful uniforms.

Girls responded to boys they found attractive by smiling at them or handing them flowers, and the courtship began. Bands were often on hand to play soulfully romantic tunes during the parading. And parents watched from the sidelines.

The tradition of the *paseo* developed into an everyday part of life in Mexico. Teenagers and single men and women in their 20s gathered at the main square in villages and towns, usually on Sunday evenings. Then, under the watchful eyes of older people—most of whom were just onlookers—the boys walked around the square in one direction, and the girls, in pairs or groups or three or four, walked in the opposite direction so they passed each other one by one.

Much of the stylized refinement that was characteristic of the *paseos* in earlier times is gone now, the victim of far more vulgar times. Some of the boys and young men delight in making risque, even insulting, comments to individual girls as they pass them.

In earlier times, *paseo* participants who had decided on whom they would like to court would then try to attract each other's attention by staring and otherwise indicating their interest with their eyes and facial expressions. Nowadays they are more likely to speak to each other.

The boy is almost always the most aggressive in trying to attract the attention of the girl he wants. If the girl responds, they leave the circle together or make arrangements to meet somewhere.

Smaller villages and towns traditionally had only one *paseo* a week, usually on a Saturday or Sunday evening. Larger cities often had two, one on Saturday and the other in the middle of the week.

In some cities the Saturday night ceremony was sometimes referred to as the *Tight-Dress Paseo*. Older girls in dresses as tight as suntans paraded around the square like walking tubes of nitroglycerin. Bold-eyed men, their eyes smoldering with desire, sometimes in cars, kept pace with the girls as they circled around and around. The air was sexually charged, filled with suppressed excitement.

For generations there were three weekly *paseos* in Monterrey—on Thursday, Saturday and Sunday. The ceremonies began at 9 P.M. and lasted for approximately an hour and a half. The strollers were mostly in their mid to late teens.

Guanajuato also traditionally had three *paseos* a week—on Tuesdays, Thursdays and Sundays, in the famous *Jardin de la Union*, beginning at 8:30 P.M. After the *paseo* the young people of Guanajuato would congregate on nearby Morelos Street where they winked, whistled and otherwise flirted with each other until late in the evening.

In addition to the *paseo* the city of Puebla had another formalized occasion for boys and girls to establish personal relationships, the famous *Combat of Flowers*, usually held on May 5. On this occasion, boys threw or handed flowers to the girls of their choice. If a girl responded by picking up or accepting the flowers, it meant she was willing to accept the boy as a suitor.

Like so many other traditional customs of Mexico, the *paseo* is falling victim to the much faster and mechanical way of life fostered by industrialization. It survives today only in smaller cities and towns.

Said a Mexican friend: "In Mexico [City] and other larger cities, the disco has replaced the *paseo*. Young people go to the discos to meet, display themselves, dance and have a good time."

The *paseo* is a marvelous social custom that should be adopted worldwide.

When expressed as *un paseo*, the meaning is quite different. This refers to an actual trip that one makes for pleasure, not business. In bullfight terminology, *paseo* refers to the parade of the matadors and their entourages around the ring prior to the beginning of the exhibition.

Patrones
(Pah-TRON-ehs)

"The Ultimate Bosses"

Throughout the history of Mexico, men in positions of authority such as farm owners, business owners, heads of labor gangs, or bosses of political groups made up a special class of people with powers and responsibilities that went well beyond what is common in North America. Such a man was generally addressed as *patron* (pah-TRON), a word that means "boss" or "chief," and during Mexico's long colonial period under Spain was primarily associated with landowners.

In earlier centuries, *patrones* were local Indian bosses who acted more or less like chiefs, controlling the activities and lives of the people under them. Indian *patrones* also acted as go-betweens with Spanish authorities in their areas.

In addition to having virtually absolute power over the people under them, *patrones* also—in theory at least—had responsibility for them as well, an arrangement that goes with authoritarian, paternalistic societies.

One of the primary criteria for underlings was total loyalty to these men in powerful positions, a kind and degree of loyalty that transcended all other relationships and obligations, including law. This ensured the continued goodwill and support of the *patron* who in turn protected the underling.

These days, bosses and overseers in general, including bosses of criminal gangs, are called *patrones*. Political leaders and criminal bosses, and particularly in more recent times drug lords, have traditionally represented the epitome of these men of power.

In the historical context of the *patron* system, bosses were obligated to provide for and protect their employees in exchange for their loyalty and support. But in reality, the relationship between bosses and underlings in Mexico has always been heavily in favor of the *patrones* because of their superior social status.

When this paternalistic *patron* mentality involves government agencies and business enterprises, it becomes a major handicap to an efficient operation, because subordinates are typically not allowed to make decisions on their own. Everything has to be decided by the *patron* and orders must be given by him personally before anything new or different can be done.

Top business executives in Mexico invariably inherit some of the *patron* syndrome. It is still unusual for them to delegate both responsibility and authority. Employees, including middle-level managers, still generally wait for orders to come down from the top before they move on anything.

Because of the *patron* system. Mexican employees tend to relate more to their bosses than to their companies. Thus the common practice of North American firms of regularly rotating the executives they assign to Mexico means that employees have to start over again with each new boss, and develop the rapport and relationships that are essential to their morale and optimum performance.

Foreign companies that follow this rotation policy are especially handicapped if they do not have competent Mexican managers to carry on effectively regardless of who is in the executive's chair.

Businesspeople who have had previous experience in Japan will find that many of the insights and skills they developed there can be applied to Mexico. Japan's *oyabun*, for example, are the cultural equivalent to Mexico's *patrones*.

The attitudes and behavior of *oyabun* and *patrones* are even more closely matched if one thinks in terms of Japan's *oyabun*, who are members of the *yakuza*, the professional criminal brotherhood of Japan. Both demand the same kind and degree of loyalty and sacrifice.

This does not mean that all *patrones* (or all *oyabun*) are cold-hearted abusers of their power. Many are genuinely concerned about the welfare of their workers, and are generous in the benefits they provide to their employees and their families.

But all *patrones* are sensitive about their image and the respect they receive, and few things can be more unproductive and unwise than getting on the bad side of a *patron*, especially one who has real political power.

Not surprisingly, one of the facets of political and business success in Mexico is establishing and continuously nurturing good relations with *patrones* in all pertinent areas of the economy and government.

(See **Compadres, Juntos, La Gerencia, Moralidad, Negocios**.)

Pelados
(Pay-LAH-dohs)

"The Plucked Ones"

Unrefined passion is the *elan vital* in Mexican life. No matter what the subject or occasion, the intellect of the average Mexican soon gives away to passion, which is not only blind but one of the most stubborn of all emotions. (After passion, Mexicans of all classes have traditionally concerned themselves with etiquette, elegance and art.)

Mexican men have traditionally made an art of using sexually charged language and flirting with women at every opportunity. In earlier times Mexican men were also easily irritated and always on the lookout for slights or insults to their honor or that of Mexico; this often led to violence. Men did not feel at ease unless they were demonstrating their maleness.

It is said that the essence of Mexican manhood can be found in its purest form among the slum residents of Mexico City—the famous *pelados* (pay-LAH-dohs) or "plucked ones," a sardonic reference to the fact that chickens are plucked of all their feathers before being chopped up, cooked and devoured.

Totally impotent as far as the rest of the world was concerned, the *pelados* sought justification for their existence in their virility and their ability to command obedience and respect from their families, and respect from others. They rejected all morality except their own.

Pelados demanded total loyalty and obedience from their wives, and total obedience and love from their children. About the only thing they felt obligated to do in return was protect the women in their families from the outside world, particularly from predatory males such as themselves.

When a *pelado* wanted to remind himself and others of his courage, superiority and rights as a man, he was apt to shout out that he had "balls." He attributed any success he may have had to that fact. (Some of the many slang terms used to refer to testicles are *bolas, canicas, huevos, pelotas, ramo, talegas* and *tanetas*.)

The historical image of the *pelados* has been graphically described in Mexican literature. According to Mexican anthropologists, the *pelados* equated masculinity with power. When they were overcome with joy, anger or enthusiasm for themselves or their countrymen, they liked to shout, "*Viva Mexico, hijos de la chingada!*"—"Long Live Mexico, you sons of raped mothers!"

Such men often admonished their sons and daughters by saying to them, "I am your father!" When used in this manner the expression was meant to humiliate, to emphasize the father's absolute responsibility for the existence of the offspring. It was something like saying, "You are nothing but an accident resulting from my having laid the woman who is your mother!"

The preoccupation of the *pelados* with playing the role demanded by the cult of masculinity led them to believe that manners, dignity and "face" were more important than anything else. But being cynical and suspicious, their personal relations tended to be shallow and to suffer from constant strain. Virtually everything the *pelados* did was in defense of their image of themselves.

The profuse courtesy, hearty sincerity and flowery language that were characteristic of the *pelados* were all walls behind which they buttressed themselves; a pose that they generally dropped only when they were sick, drinking or so distracted by violence or passion that they forgot to "act."

Drinking did strange things to the *pelados* and to other poor, less educated Mexicans. They were apt to shout, weep, sing or become sadistic and homicidal. They were also prone to go completely berserk and try to destroy everything they felt inferior to, whether this was a stranger, a passing bus or a brick wall.

Pelados tended to equate love with lies and betrayal, and to exaggerate their feelings toward women they wanted; first, to give the impression that their love was so strong they were helpless (and thereby win the woman's sympathy), and second, to avoid having their own feelings hurt when the romance ended.

Love tended to be a constant battle for both *pelado* men and women. To men, victory was succeeding in having a woman sexually. Once they accomplished that, their ardor very often disappeared instantly.

Pelados were also prone to look upon sex as a sardonic joke. They usually treated women brutally only after they had had sex with them, apparently in a subconscious effort to take revenge against the women for having caused them to demonstrate characteristics that they regarded as unmasculine—tenderness and unselfishness—during the courting stage.

The most passionate *pelado* wanted immediate recognition of his masculinity. If he didn't get it he became furious and would typically strike out blindly. For example, a man would trick a woman into a private place and begin preparing to have sex with her. If she resisted he would become violently angry and shout that she was insulting him by denying his manhood. He was therefore justified in beating her and taking her by force.

The quintessence of *pelado*-type *machismo* was to kill for passion or take revenge against an adulterous wife and her lover. More often than not there was no quixotic chivalry in the vengeance. The wronged man did not like to challenge an enemy openly in even combat. He preferred to take no chances and strike when the odds were in his favor.

The *pelado* syndrome was taken to its extremes by the slum dwellers of Mexico City and other large urban areas of Mexico, but it was—and still is—discernable throughout Mexican society. In 1979 Mexican sociologists estimated that over half of the population should still be classified as *pelados*. Mexican social authorities have since observed: "Scratch any Mexican and you will find a *pelado* underneath."

Octavio Paz, the famous Mexican poet-writer, described *pelados* as masochists and instinctive nihilists, and said that it was senseless to argue with them. He added that having to maintain and prove their manliness at all times made the *pelados* into habitual liars. "They lie for the pleasure of it, and also to conceal their true thoughts and emotions from the outsiders," he said.

This last refers to poor Mexicans who, when sober, tend to hide their feelings behind a many-sided mask. Their conversations are indirect and veiled. Everything is disguised behind a facade of indifference and remoteness. They will ostensibly attach great importance to trivial things, and moments later will treat something very serious as if it were of no consequence at all.

Most Mexican men still today reflect many of the characteristics of the *pelados*. Middle-class educated males in particular have many of the same attitudes about women, sex and masculinity as the traditional *pelados*, but under ordinary circumstances their behavior is far more subtle. (Wealthy men who want to get rid of rivals usually hire professional killers to do the dirty work for them.)

The *pelado* syndrome is also visible in the behavior of many Mexican immigrants living in the United States—legally or illegally—including uneducated Chicanos, a factor that contributes a great deal to the extraordinary amount of violence by Chicano gang members.

(See **Machismo, Pachucos, Ranflas.**)

109

Personalismo
(Pehr-so-nah-LEES-moh)

"Dignity First, Law Last"

The first thing that foreigners in Mexico—whether businesspeople or tourists—should know about Mexicans is that their behavior, both private and official, is generally controlled by the code of *personalismo* (pehr-so-nah-LEES-moh), not law, logic, fairness, equality or any other objective principle.

Personalismo embodies the Mexican belief that personal dignity takes precedence over all other considerations, including the ethical and the moral—and woe to anyone who slights or attacks the dignity of a Mexican.

In colonial Mexico the principle of *personalismo* eventually came to override virtually everything else in Mexican life, because individuals who were not members of the Spanish ruling class were not protected by any concept of human rights or by any laws designed to guarantee such rights.

Another thing that foreigners in Mexico should understand is that Mexican law is based on the Napoleonic Code, not English jurisprudence, which means, in effect, that people apprehended by the law for any reason, justified or not, are presumed to be guilty until proven innocent, and are generally treated as such.

Or, as is often the case in Mexico, they are held until they buy their way out of the clutches of the police, whether they are innocent or guilty. There is no such thing as legal plea bargaining or trial by jury in Mexico. The judge decides all.

Fair play and justice have long been recognized principles in Mexico, but until recent years they were seldom practiced. Few Mexicans, especially those in official positions, were able to break the traditional *personalismo* code and conduct themselves according to absolute notions of right and wrong.

It also meant that government officials and minions on every level have traditionally interpreted the laws according to the circumstances, primarily in ways that would directly benefit themselves, their families and their friends.

This situation has improved considerably in the last few decades, but arbitrary arrest, illegal detention and systematic torture are still routine occurrences.

There are thousands of daily incidents pointing up the arbitrary, illegal actions of the various police forces in Mexico City alone. The majority of the victims remain silent because they fear revenge by the police.

The sorry state of the law in Mexico goes back to the days of the *gachupines* and *criollos*. Because they were so far away from Spain (official contact was often only once a year) and because they were primarily dealing with Indians and *mestizos* who were generally not recognized as franchised citizens under the law, Spanish landlords and officials basically conducted themselves as police, jury and judge, and answered only to themselves.

Indians were treated as indentured slaves and the mixed-races as despised and distrusted outcasts. Both Indians and *mestizos* learned the worst from their Spanish overlords—to lie, cheat, steal without conscience; to oppress women and to treat people below them with contempt.

Because the code of *personalismo* was traditionally the primary philosophy of politicians and bureaucrats as well as the military and the police, it set the standards for Mexican society.

Over the centuries the personalized nature of politics, business and professional relationships in Mexico meant that it was perfectly natural for presidents, generals, business tycoons and all other individuals in positions of power to surround themselves with their kin, friends and close followers, and thereafter to use their power to enrich themselves at the expense of the public.

The injustices and savage cruelties spawned by this warped system read like some impossible horror story. The very worst aspects of Mexican culture were traditionally revealed in the behavior of the police and the military.

About the only people in Mexico who did not succumb to this antisocial philosophy were the Indians who lived in remote areas of Mexico and had very little, if anything, to do with the mainstream of society, and the poorest of the mixed-races who were mostly farmers. These groups lived by the traditional rules and customs of their villages and communities, and, except when pushed beyond endurance, were peaceful, hospitable and kind.

Despite some progress in recent decades and numerous pronouncements of "reforms" in government, from ministers down to traffic cops and border guards, the code of *personalismo* remains paramount in official Mexico.

One thing that really upsets uninitiated foreigners in Mexico who become the victims of crimes is that the police often demand a cash payment, in advance, before they will undertake any kind of investigation. Unless one has connections with senior government officials or bureaucrats who have influence over the police, the only recourse is to pay up or shut up.

110

Peyote
(Pay-YOH-tay)

"Entering Other Dimensions"

Like most early peoples around the world the Indians of Mexico have traditionally been animists who believe that all things in nature have a spirit which is part of the immaterial force that animates the universe. These beliefs were the foundations of their cultures, permeating their lifestyles and religious practices, and providing the creative forces behind their arts, crafts and places of worship.

Pre-Columbian Mexican Indians were as concerned with the spirit world as they were with the material world, and spent a substantial amount of their time and energy attempting to communicate with, and placate, a variety of spirits and gods.

The size and architectural sophistication of many of the temples built in Mexico, ages before Columbus and Cortés, rivaled the most magnificent edifices constructed in Egypt and elsewhere in ancient times, attesting to the mathematical and astronomical accomplishments of the Indians of Mexico as well as to the power of their religious beliefs.

In many ways, the religions of Mexican Indians and other old peoples around the world were vastly superior to Christianity, Islam and other more recent religions because they were holistic and ecologically oriented.

Also, like other ancient people, many of the Indians of Mexico tried to literally enter the spirit world in order to communicate directly with the spirits and to attain knowledge that could not be learned in the material dimension.

One of the ways a number of Mexico's tribes attempted to cross the boundaries between the spirit world and the world of the senses was through taking a hallucinogenic drug called *peyote* (pay-YOH-tay), which was extracted from the peyote cactus. Trances induced by *peyote* could last for two or three days.

Among a number of the Indian nations of Mexico, particularly the Huicholes and the Tarahumaras, *peyote* was considered sacred, and was the core of a number of cults observed by annual festivals.

There are numerous records of the visions seen by Indian medicine men and others while in *peyote*-induced trances. Some of the descriptions include traveling great distances, reliving the past and seeing the future.

For some people the *peyote*-induced trance experience was so powerful that it had a permanent effect of their character and personality, much like the state of enlightenment sought after by Oriental mystics and others.

In addition to using *peyote* for its extraordinary trance-producing and libido-arousing effects, some Mexican Indians believed one could get rid of enemies by touching then with the "hair" of a peyote plant, or by tossing the "hair" over one's shoulder in the direction the enemy was walking.

Another form of the word *peyote* is *empeyotado* (em-pay-yoh-TAH-doh), which figuratively means something like "made love-crazy by peyote." It also is used to mean a person who has been made to fall in love by the magic of *peyote—peyote* buds that are put into drinks designed to be love potions.

Mexico's Aztec Indians used a milder hallucinogen called *teonanacatl* as a religious as will as recreational aid. A natural growing fungus, *teonanacatl* was regularly served to guests at the beginning of special banquets. In addition to inducing mild visions, it also made the guests inclined toward lechery. *Teonanacatl* was also eaten with honey just before sunrise in a kind of semi-religious ceremony.

Peyote is still commonly used by some Mexican Indian tribes, and in the 1960s American Indians in the state of Nevada won the legal right to continue using the hallucinogen in their religious ceremonies. The same right was extended to other North American Indian tribes in 1994.

It is reported that adventurous visitors to Mexico can still arrange to be taken to isolated areas where, for a fee, they can experiment with *peyote*. Some who have done so said it made them sick. Others said that they entered a strange world discovered by Indians ages ago which is still a mystery to even the most learned men.

111

Piropos
(Pee-ROH-pohs)

"Tossing Gallantries at Girls"

Life in Mexico is filled with a variety of picturesque and socially important customs that are provocative not only because of the color and pageantry involved but also because of what they tell about the culture; stories that often do not have happy endings.

To an outsider, much of the behavior of young Mexican men toward girls may seem to be the epitome of romanticism. They shower them with flowers and sweets, and send them passionate love letters that are filled with the most extravagant declarations of love and devotion.

But there is often a dark side to the courting of lower class, less educated young men. If a girl hesitates, or spurns the young man courting her so passionately, the would-be lover is just as ready to threaten suicide or some other form of violence. He typically begs, cajoles, threatens and makes fantastic promises in order to have his way.

If the girl finally consents to meet her suitor the young man wastes no time in trying to sleep with her, insisting that it is the only way they can prove their love. If the girl resists his physical advances, the man may cry, plead and again threaten violence.

But once the girl gives in, the attitude of the young man generally changes completely. In many cases, he will simply drop the girl and begin the same routine on other women.

If the girl, now minus her virginity and possibly even pregnant, persists in trying to continue the relationship, the man often accuses her of taking advantage of his passion, of being no better than a whore; he may even beat her.

If it happens that the girl is pregnant and her parents try to force the man to marry her, or at least pay child-birth expenses, the man typically will vilify the woman and do all he can to avoid any responsibility.

In addition to participating in *paseos* in an effort to meet girls, it has long been a tradition for middle- and lower-class teenage Mexican boys and young men in their 20s to gather at street corners in the evenings, and wait for girls—who, of course, are very much aware of what is going on—to pass by.

Bolder young men make outright sexual proposals to girls passing by, but most follow the traditional, ritualized custom of calling out *piropos* (pee-ROH-pohs) or "gallantries" (amorous or flirtatious comments) to girls who appear sufficiently attractive to them, a custom said to have originated among Spain's Gypsies in medieval times.

Among the more common of the *piropos: Qué bonita!* (Kay boh-NEE-tah), "How beautiful!"; *Qué guapa!* (Kay WHAH-pah!), "What a body!"; *Qué chula!* (Kay CHUU-lah!), "What a doll!" or "How cute!"; *Qué mona!* (Kay MOH-nah!), "What a cutie!"; *Que linda!* (Kay LEEN-dah!), "How beautiful!"; and *Qué monumento!* (Kay moan-yuu-MEN-toh!), "What a monument!"

This latter *piropo* might be followed by something like: "If I were the mayor I would build a monument to you!"

Other more imaginative *piropos* include such declarations as: *Dios mío! Tanta curva y yo sin frenos!* (DEE-ohs ME-oh! TAHN-tah Coo-vah ee yoh sccn FRAY-nohs!) "MY God! So many curves and me without brakes!"; and *Bendita sea la madre que te pario!* (Ben-DEE-tah say-ah lah MAH-dray kay tay pah-ree-OH!) "Bless the mother who gave birth to you!"

Men who cruise red light districts in Mexico, where the girls stand in the doorways or in front of the houses, also commonly yell out *piropos* to the prostitutes displaying themselves. In this case, a popular *piropo* is *Qué pechos!* (Kay PAY-chohs) or "What tits!"

Many *piropos* take the form of haiku-like poetry. Others are only slightly veiled sarcasms that demonstrate the typical Latin attitude toward women.

Young men who regularly gather on street corners to ogle women and engage in the ritual of *piropos* know that they are not likely to succeed in getting dates with any of the girls on the spot, and the practice is more ceremonial than anything else. Some of the older "street flirters" patronize prostitutes after an evening of stoking their sexual desires.

Meeting and getting acquainted with a girl on a street corner is known by the interesting phrase of "cornering" her. But it is rare for single young girls from upper-class families to be met in this manner because they are usually not out on the streets alone at night, preferring instead to frequent exclusive restaurants and clubs.

Despite growing affluence in the urban areas of Mexico, particularly the incrcasc in automobiles and telephones, along with far more freedom for teenage boys and girls to meet and date, the practice of tossing complimentary and flirtatious comments at girls and women, wherever they might be, remains a popular male custom.

Older Mexican men as well have traditionally been noted for using very complimentary language to attractive women they encounter when the women are not in the company of other men.

And naturally enough, the custom of the *piropo* is not a one-sided ritual. Girls and women knowingly and willingly participate in the custom by dressing to attract men, behaving in a provocative manner and appearing in places where they know they will be seen and admired by men.

112

Pobreza
(Poh-BRAY-zah)

"Mexico's Poverty Syndrome"

Individualistic and independent-minded people tend to blame poor people for being poor, maintaining that they could help themselves if they really wanted to escape from poverty. This, of course, presumes that they have both the ability and the opportunity to improve their economic situation.

In Mexico *pobreza* (poh-BRAY-zah) or "poverty" was traditionally a condition enforced onto the bulk of the population by the church and the civil government. For more than 300 years the Catholic Church of Mexico, which was in charge of education and many other facets of life for most of this period, was vehemently opposed to education for the masses and to any effort to create economic opportunities for the poor.

During this same period, the civil government was dominated first by colonial administrators from Spain and later by a small elite class of people who also believed that their best interests were served by keeping the masses illiterate and poor. In this environment it was virtually impossible for the poor to help themselves.

Because this officially promoted situation existed for nearly half a millennium, those in power looked upon poverty as the natural state for the poor class, while the poor looked upon themselves as victims of social injustices; but they were so intellectually and emotionally oppressed that for generation after generation they accepted their fate stoically.

One of the key ways the church influenced the mass of poor Mexicans to accept and endure poverty was by conditioning them to believe that *envidia* (en-bee-DEE-ah), envy, was one of the greatest of all sins and to go to extreme lengths to avoid being envious of others.

This culturally conditioned trait is one of the reasons why Indians and other poor Mexicans have generally been passive and have accepted so much abuse from the church, the government, landlords, bosses and others.

It was not until 1910, nearly 400 years after the conquest of Mexico by Spanish fortune hunters, that the poor of Mexico finally rose up in a rebellion against their oppressors. This now famous revolution against the church and the elite of Mexico did not end institutionalized poverty, but it was the beginning of a painfully slow process that continues today.

The big difference now is that the poor of Mexico are becoming more and more aware of the causes of their poverty. They are no longer content with it or passive about it. The government is making an honest effort to reform itself and create an environment in which the poor *can* help themselves; and the church no longer attempts to thwart these efforts.

But the masses of Mexico, particularly the Indians, have existed in a state of poverty, officially maintained by the establishment, for so many generations that it will take at least one, and maybe two, generations before the poverty syndrome can be erased from their spirit and mentality.

Said a foreign-educated Mexican businessman: "The poor must first be instilled with a positive sense of self-worth, ambition and solidarity before the cycle of poverty can be broken. To casual observers that process may appear to be well underway, but they are seeing only the surface of things.

"After so many generations of institutionalized poverty, it became so much a part of the character of most Mexicans that they lost the will to help themselves. The dilapidated condition of so many homes, buildings, streets and other structures in Mexico is one of the symptoms of this age-old conditioning.

"Just the application of some gringo-style 'elbow grease' could make all the difference in the world in the quality of life of most poor Mexicans. But that too would require a fundamental shift in the character of Mexicans which is not going to happen on a large scale any time soon.

"We face an enormous challenge that involves the whole of Mexican culture—how to reeducate the people to become self-reliant, self-starting, and to work together for their mutual benefit."

A key part of this re-education is, in fact, the growing feelings of envy among poor Mexicans as the influence of the church weakens and mass exposure to television creates demand for a better, richer lifestyle.

113

Pochas / Pochos / Pochismos
(POH-chahs / POH-chohs / Poh-CHEES-mohs)

"The Discolored Ones"

In the past Mexicans have often referred to the United States as "The Colossus of the North" because of the extraordinary influence—much of it negative—that it has had and continues to have on Mexico.

Asked to comment on this subject, Mexicans invariably say that virtually all of the social influence that the United States has on Mexico today is negative; that American cultural influence is a major factor in the growing problem of juvenile delinquency and the breakdown of the family system.

They add that this negative factor is only partially mitigated by the positive influence of American technology and business knowhow flowing into the country. Said one: "We want to be affluent, but we don't want to be American!"

Mexicans react to American influence in different ways, depending on a variety of circumstances. For those who live along the Mexican–U.S. border, American influence of one kind or another is something they live with—and react to—every day.

Certain words, such as *pocho* (POH-choh), have taken on special meanings. *Pocho* originally meant something that was discolored; that had been soiled or spoiled by the discoloration. It is now used by Mexicans as a derogatory slang term in reference to Mexican boys (*pochos*) and girls (*pochas*) who live along the border and try to act more like Anglos than Mexicans. It is also used in reference to young Mexican Americans, both males and females, especially when the individuals concerned do not speak fluent or standard Mexican Spanish and behave in a manner that Mexicans consider arrogant.

But much like the word *gringo*, which has gone from being totally derogatory to only slightly derogatory, and on some occasions neutral or even laudatory, *pocho* is also gradually undergoing a change.

Older Mexican men now sometimes refer to young Mexican-American girls who are attractive as *pochas* without any negative connotations.

Pochismos (poh-CHEES-mohs), or "border slang," is made up of combinations of English and Spanish words. Some *pochismo* words are so contrived that non-*pochos* cannot understand them, making them a virtual dialect.

This *pocho* language was created by, and is still mostly used by, hustlers, pimps and youth gangs along the U.S.–Mexican border.

Some of the more obvious examples are alscrin/ice cream; bracelete/bracelet; carro/automobile; champu/shampoo; esmart/smart; ganga/gang; poka/ poker; postofe/post office; swera/sweater; troca/truck; troquero/truck driver.

Although it is necessary to know these words to fully understand the psychology and behavior of Mexican Americans and Mexicans who live near the border, it is not advisable for Anglo-Americans or others to use them because there are too many possibilities for such use to be taken the wrong way.

Politicos
(Poh-LEE-tee-cohs)

"The Lowest of the Low"

During the 1994 presidential campaign in Mexico, candidate Luis Donaldo Colosio made the statement, "*La politica es fria, cruel y despiadada, Veo una Mexico con hambre y sed de justicia!*—Politics is cold, cruel and despicable. I see a Mexico that is hungry and thirsty for justice!"

Mexicans could not have agreed more with Señor Colosio, who shortly after making this statement was assassinated, reportedly on the orders of high-placed politicians who did not want to see him become president and implement the kind of reforms he was talking about.

Despite a quantum change for the better in the behavior of presidents, ministers, governors and other government officials in Mexico since the 1920s, "politics" and "politician" are still dirty words to most Mexicans.

During the Spanish colonial period in Mexico, which lasted for 300 years (1521-1821), Mexico was run by a cabal of European-born Spanish administrators and Catholic bishops whose primary purpose was to extract as much wealth as possible from the people and the land.

Politics and politicians in their current sense were strictly prohibited by the Spanish court. Rules and regulations came down from the colonial viceroy, and from the church, as fiats. The people had no voice in government.

Mexico won its independence from Spain in 1821 and became a republic in name in the following years, but the coldness and cruelty of which Colosio spoke so eloquently continued from one generation to the next.

With but few exceptions, governmental offices on every level were controlled by a few men who used their positions to enrich themselves and their friends, while inflicting cruel and unusual punishments on the people at large.

Until recent decades, the fundamental moral code in Mexico in both private and public life was a broad-based patrimony. Mexican politicians automatically assumed a patrimonial attitude toward their constituents and jurisdictions, acting as if they were owners and masters rather than representatives. Tax funds that came with the offices were spent as the officeholder pleased, which meant that they were primarily used to enrich themselves and their families and friends. It was this moral code that kept the wealth of Mexico in the hands of a few families.

Mexicans have traditionally been devoted to personalities rather than principles, thus the appeal and power of revolutionary leaders, caudillos and presidents. Caudillos brought stability because of their charisma and willingness to use naked power.

In addition to exploiting the economy and masses to enrich themselves, government and church leaders made it virtually impossible for ordinary citizens to better themselves. They ignored the need for mass education, in fact they restricted it, and enforced a variety of restraints that stifled ambition and prevented independent enterprise, except by a favored few.

Mexico began holding elections every six years in 1924, but until 1994 all presidents and other ranking politicians were handpicked by the incumbent president and his closest political allies. The people voted but the voting was meaningless; fraud was commonplace.

It was not until 1994 that a nearly fraud-free election was held in Mexico, and for the first time in the history of the country the people began to feel like their votes counted and that the government really represented their interests.

By this watershed year a whole new postrevolutionary generation of businesspeople, bureaucrats and politicians, with a totally different set of cultural experiences, had come to the fore. Unlike their predecessors who had been weaned on authoritarianism, personalism and violence, these men were pragmatic realists, if not champions of democracy. They brought with them an honest desire to reform the political and economic systems of the country.

Some Mexican businessmen have reported that changes in the attitudes and behavior of government officials was nothing less than revolutionary.

Said one: "Before, when someone got elected to or was chosen for a political office their so-called constituents never heard from them again. They literally disappeared, and it was virtually impossible to get in to see them if you did not have powerful political pull and did not buy your way in. Now, politicians have not only become more accessible, some of them are actually coming to us, asking what they can do to help us."

Another point of extraordinary importance in the evolution of politics in Mexico is that with the election of Ernesto Zedillo as president in 1994, the people of Mexico can safely criticize government officials for the first time in the history of the country.

"Also for the very first time," said a politician turned businessman, "people became able to do things—often just little things—that Mexicans had been wanting to do and waiting to do for centuries."

Other areas where dramatic improvements have already been made and are continuing to improve include the behavior of immigration and customs officials along the U.S.–Mexican border and the conduct of bank officials.

But full-blown democracy, justice, human rights and equal protection before the law are not going to come soon or easy in Mexico. The attitudes and customs that make up Mexican style *politicos* (poh-LEE-tee-cohs) are such an integral part of the cultural legacy, so deeply embedded in the institutions and psyche of the power structure, that they cannot be readily eliminated.

When Indian peasants squatted on some 100,000 acres (40,000 hectares) of land following the Zapatista rebellion in Chiapas state in 1994, local landowners threatened to revive the dreaded *guardias blancas*, or death squads (inactive since the early 1980s) to eliminate them.

Fortunately, this did not happen, in part because of the presence of the foreign news media, and also because of growing internal pressure for genuine reforms in government policies regarding the Indians.

Foreign governments and businesses can speed up political and economic reform in Mexico by continuing to bring pressure on their Mexican counterparts to make step-by-step changes in the most conspicuous and damaging problem areas.

Foreign governments should also keep in mind that politics in Mexico is still a man's world, and be wary of putting women in roles that are considered the exclusive preserves of men, particularly on a presidential level.

For example, if an American president sent his wife to Mexico to represent him and the United States, Americans would typically regard it as a wonderful demonstration of the status of women in the United States and the enlightened liberalism of the president.

Mexican men would be more likely to regard such an event as indicative of the failure of Americans to distinguish between the proper roles for men and women, and as an insult to their own president.

Proyectismo
(pro-yeck-TEES-moh)

"The Projectitis Syndrome"

Mexican behavior regularly confuses outsiders because it often varies considerably from one moment and one occasion to the next, depending on the cultural context. Contradictions in behavior are the rule rather than the exception.

The religious piety of Mexicans, particularly women, is a hallmark of their character, and impacts directly on virtually every aspect of their lives. At the same time, both Mexican men and women can be outrageously irreligious from the Anglo viewpoint.

Superstitions and belief in magic still abound in Mexico, and they have a significant impact on the lives of most poor Mexicans. Even well-educated people with a pronounced international outlook are respectful of the spirit world and are careful to follow customs designed to keep the spirits friendly.

Historically, Mexican *patrones* (bosses), generals, *caudillos* (dictator/warlords), governors, presidents and others in power have imposed their will on others by brute force and the force of their personalities. However, once in power, these leaders have traditionally preferred to paint a flowery picture and depend on strong appeals to the emotions to influence and persuade others, rather than using logic and the "cold, hard facts" preferred by Americans and other Anglos.

The tendency of Mexicans to mix cultural factors from their Spanish and Indian backgrounds into all of their present-day affairs—social, business and political—results in attitudes and behavior that foreigners often find frustrating.

One of the results of this cross-cultural fusion is that Mexican politicians and businesspeople have traditionally "suffered" from a syndrome called *proyectismo* (pro-yeck-TEES-moh) or "projectism." That is, they habitually dreamed up exciting projects without subjecting them to critical analysis to determine whether or not they were feasible, and then ordered their subordinates to carry them out.

Proyectismo is still alive and well in Mexico, and is a factor that foreign politicians and business interests should keep in mind when in dialogue with their Mexican counterparts.

Mexicans can present their proposed projects with a great deal of emotion and drama, but tend to base their expectations on faith rather than facts.

The reverse side of the *proyectismo* syndrome is that Mexican officials and businesspeople tend to be overly pessimistic when responding to the presentations of others, and will insist that any relationship be structured in such a way that there is virtually no risk to them.

Another cultural factor that impacts on projects in Mexico, regardless of which side proposes them, is the different perception of time. While the foreigner may want a project to be on line within a year and to make a profit within two years, the Mexican side may be inclined to set very flexible deadlines, or no deadlines at all.

The only recourse foreign interests have in doing business in Mexico is to be forewarned, so that they can anticipate many of the cultural problems that are likely to occur and create a scenario for dealing with them. They should position themselves to respond in a flexible but practical way to unexpected problems.

Pulque
(POOL-kay)

"Opiate of the Masses"

Pulque (POOL-kay) a frothy brew made from the sap of the maguey plant, was the national drink of the Indians in the central and northern regions of Mexico long before Columbus set sail, and is still a staple among Mexican Indians and lower-class people.

Just about everyone who has tried *pulque* says that it has a "slimy consistency," and a fairly strong nutty flavor. (Modern-day nutritionists add that it is also chock full of vitamins and proteins and is the healthiest of all alcoholic drinks.)

Just how important *pulque* drinking was in Aztec society is dramatically demonstrated by the fact that there were 400 gods of drink and drunkenness in the Aztec pantheon.

But in pre-Columbian times, the drinking of alcoholic beverages by most of the Indians of Mexico was strictly controlled. The old and the sick could drink anytime because it was believed that the alcohol helped them by "warm-ing" their blood. However, as the masters of a far-flung empire that required a high degree of ability and efficiency to run, the Aztecs wisely had strong laws against indiscriminate drinking.

No one under the age of 50 was supposed to drink at any time except during festivals or official celebrations. If a lower class Aztec was found drunk in public twice at any other time, he was beaten or strangled to death in front of other young men as an example. Nobles were strangled in private the first time they were caught drunk during an unauthorized period. Still, it is recorded that there was a considerable amount of clandestine drinking.

As a result of the severely enforced ban on unauthorized drinking, festivals and other occasions when younger people could drink openly were very pop-ular with Aztecs. Many of the Aztec drinking bouts ended in wild sex orgies.

Aztecs measured the degree of a man's drunkenness in terms of a num-ber of rabbits. A drunkenness of 15 rabbits made one good company. A drunk-enness of 400 rabbits was complete intoxication.

During the Spanish colonial regime, which began in 1521 and lasted until 1821, as well as during the following 100 years of mostly dictatorial rule by white descendants of the Spaniards, the *gachupin* and *criollo* owners of landed estates sometimes exploited the Indian fondness for drinking by "pay-ing" their Indian peons in *pulque* instead of credit at the "company" store.

In addition to each town having a number of *pulquerias*, or *pulque* bars, there were also traveling vendors who carried jars of *pulque* on their heads and made house calls.

Modern-day Mexico still suffers from excessive drinking by men in all classes, but particularly by Indians and lower-class *mestizos*. Festivals and weddings frequently turn into mass drunks. Many urban slum-dwelling men regularly drink to excess without any special pretext, causing enormous prob-lems for their families and society in general.

In an attempt to reduce the amount of drinking, the government in the 1960s passed legislation restricting the number of hours drinking places could stay open, explaining that the move was an effort to "preserve the family."

The law noted that throughout Mexico's history men in the lower classes had habitually squandered a large proportion of their earnings on drink, and that drinking was the indirect cause of most of the countless murders and the unimaginable violence that had characterized much of Mexican life for centuries.

The new law set closing times for drinking places on the basis of their type. *Pulquerias* and *cantinas*, where it is mostly the poor who drink, were to close at 1 A.M. Bars, cabarets and lounges patronized by middle- and upper-class customers could legally remain open until 2 A.M.

In practice, however, it quickly became unwritten law that places with second-class licenses (usually *pulquerias* and *cantinas*) were allowed to stay open for an extra hour, and places with first-class licenses could stay open an additional two hours. Bars and lounges in hotels catering to tourists, visiting businesspeople and affluent Mexicans appear to set their own hours.

In the 1980s the consumption of *pulque* began to drop off as more and more Mexicans joined the middle class, leaving the beverage behind as a low-class drink.

But *pulquerias* still abound in Mexico. Patronized almost entirely by men and "ladies of the night," they remain the Mexican equivalent of the saloons of the "Wild West" period in American history.

Cantinas, which also abound, are more like the American roadside taverns. They serve all kinds of drinks and are primarily patronized by lower-class men and rough-and-ready women. *Taquerias* are small intimate bars which generally cater to a higher class of patron than the above drinking establishments.

Two types of Mexican nighttime drinking places that often confuse visitors are the so-called cabarets and nightclubs; the real difference between a Mexican cabaret and a nightclub is a matter of some dispute.

In general, any place with a first-class license that is actually considered first class, and which has a floor show, caters to couples and has few if any *fichadoras* (female hostess/taxi dancers who usually double as parttime prostitutes), is generally called a nightclub.

A place that has all of these qualifications, but which features a large selection of *fichadoras* and caters more to male clientele, will most likely be called a cabaret. Second-class places with second-class licenses whose stock in trade are their *fichadoras*, and which may or may not have entertainment, are also called cabarets.

In past years, foreign men visiting in Mexico with their wives and girlfriends were advised to never let them dance with other men, particular in lower-class drinking places, because this was taken as a sign that they were sexually available to other men. That is still good advice.

Drinking is more of a social custom in Mexico than in many other countries, and plays an especially important role in male relationships. The ability and willingness to drink is equated with masculinity, and particularly among the lower classes, often becomes a contest.

Foreigners who do not drink or want to pace themselves are best advised to claim a medical reason.

Quinceañeras
(Keen-say-ah-NYAY-rahs)

"The Big Day for Girls"

The first really big day in the lives of most Mexican girls is when they turn 15 and become *señoritas* (sen-yore-REE-tahs), an event that is celebrated by a *quinceañera* (keen-say-ah-NYAY-rah), which literally means "15th birthday." It is one of the most important rites of passage in Mexican culture.

This is the day on which Mexican girls make the all-important social transition from childhood to adulthood—from being girls to being women. It is marked by an elaborate church ceremony and private events.

Quinceañeras, also known as *quince años* or "15 years" date back to the Mayan and Toltecan period in Mexican history. They are similar to the *bar mitzvah* or "son of command" ceremonies conducted for Jewish boys at the age of 13 when they are considered to have reached adulthood and are required to assume responsibility for their moral and religious duties.

The closest thing that Anglo societies have to mark the coming of age of young girls is the debutante ball, which is limited to a tiny percentage of girls in upper-class society and consists of little more than a dance party at which the girls wear formal gowns (and dance at least once with their fathers).

In Mayan times the *quinceañera* marked the occasion when girls were divided into those who were to dedicate their lives to religious services and thereafter be attached to some temple, and those who were to be married.

In present-day Mexico *quinceañeras* are mass family and friend affairs. Parents, grandparents, uncles, aunts, cousins, godfathers and godmothers—all contribute and come together for the occasion. They reaffirm their relational ties and their religion and celebrate the formal recognition of adulthood and its responsibilities.

Girls honored by *quinceañeras* receive a variety of symbolic gifts to remind them of their new status as adults, who are responsible for their own social and spiritual behavior. These gifts include such things as rosaries, Bibles, crowns, religious medals and flowers.

The flowers symbolize a young woman's responsibility to her community, emphasizing the beauty of the relationship, as well as how fragile it is and how carefully it must be nurtured in order for it to survive and grow.

In earlier times young girls especially looked forward to their *quinceañeras* because they were announcements to their communities that the new young ladies were eligible for courting and marriage; they would also thereafter be treated differently by their parents, families and friends.

While participation in *paseos* or "courting parades" and dating were allowed after the *quinceañera*, young couples were chaperoned and not allowed to be alone together in order to prevent sexual intimacy before marriage.

Today, the custom of chaperoning dating couples has virtually disappeared from the upper and middle classes in Mexico but it continues to be an integral part of the lives of young people in towns and villages where the old traditions have survived.

Older Mexicans, who are seeing many of their traditions fade into the mist of history, describe the *quinceañera* as one of the most important facets of the country's traditional culture, and credit it with being one of the keys that bonds families, nurtures maturity among the young and instills in them a strong sense of responsibility.

One 85-year-old man who had participated in dozens of *quinceañeras* for his own daughters, granddaughters and the daughters of friends went so far as to say that among families who continued to practice the custom, as well as the traditions of chaperoning and godfather and godmother parenting, there was almost never any juvenile delinquency among the younger generations and they went on to achieve the highest educational levels and success in business or some profession.

From the early 1900s until recent times, many Mexican-American families did not practice the custom of the *quinceañera* as they tried to become more American and thereby avoid discrimination.

But lately less discriminatory attitudes among Anglo-Americans and the reemergence of pride among Mexican-American families in their cultural heritage has resulted in this ancient custom being reintroduced into their lives.

The custom of the *quinceañera* is indeed an admirable one which should be adopted, long with a similar one for boys, by all societies that do not formally recognize the passage from childhood to responsible adulthood. (Boys in Mexico are not recognized as adults until they reach 18.)

In North America, for example, the young generally continue to be treated as children, without serious responsibilities, until they are in their late teens and even early twenties.

This cultural failure dramatically delays the maturing process, contributes to acute frustration among the young and results in much of the youthful violence that plagues American society.

China's great sage, Confucius, taught a long time ago that human beings need such rites in order to become socialized and to live useful, contented lives.

Ramflas
(RAHM-flahs)

"The Low-Riders"

In 1935 Harry Westergard, the owner of an auto body repair shop in Sacramento, California, customized a 1935 Ford convertible by lowering the body until it was only a few inches above the ground. He then upholstered the interior with crushed velvet and decorated the body in bright multicolors.

Teenage boys in the area were fascinated by the world's first *ramfla* (RAHM-flah) or "low-rider," a Chicano term that originally meant "jalopy" or an old beat-up car (now also known as *carro bajito* (CAHR-roh bah-HEE-toh), which literally means "low car." Some of these boys began hanging around Westergard's shop. One of them, George Barris, eventually set up his own shop in Sacramento and went on to become the "King of the Kustomizers."

Barris later moved his operation to Lynwood in Los Angeles and founded Kustom City. Then he moved his shop to North Hollywood, and became a vendor to the movie industry, creating such one-of-a-kind vehicles as the "Batmobile" and "Munster Koach" for Hollywood films. But Barris' major contribution to American culture was the *ramfla*, or low-rider, which resulted in the creation of a subculture of its own among Mexican-American youths, providing one of the most colorful—and, according to some, disdained—manifestations of Chicano identity and pride in the history of the American Southwest.

By the 1940s Mexican-American low-rider enthusiasts had become known as *pachucos*, which was a made-up term that apparently originated in Los Angeles in the 1920s to describe young Mexicans and Mexican Americans who flooded into the city from El Paso, Texas. The *pachucos*, also known as *cholos* (CHOH-lohs) or "crazy guys," adopted the *ramflas* as a part of their image.

In a further effort to create a unique identify for themselves the low-riders began wearing trousers that were tight at the bottom, with balloon-style legs, and long jackets with conspicuously wide shoulder pads, a style that was to become a new addition to the world of fashion, known as *tacuche* or *tacuchi* in Spanish and "zoot suit" in English.

One American journalist disputes this origin of the zoot suit, however. He credits a black busboy names Clyde Duncan, who lived in Gainesville, Georgia, with being the first person to create and wear a zoot suit. The journalist says Duncan ordered it from Globe Tailoring Company in Chicago in the early 1940s—and paid $33.50 for it. The zoot suit style that Duncan ordered came to be known as "The Killer Diller."

In any event, blacks in Mississippi picked up on the zoot suit, followed quickly by blacks in Alabama, California and then Harlem in New York. By the mid-1940s four out of 10 American youths, black, white and mixed, including Japanese–American teens imprisoned in the so-called "Relocation Camps," were wearing zoot suits—and there was a female version of them as well.

An ambitious Mexican-American entrepreneur inaugurated a monthly magazine called *Low Rider* in January 1977, printing 5,000 copies of the first issue. Some two years later, monthly circulation was over 100,000 copies, and the magazine had become the bible of *ramflas* technology, style and use.

During the last years of the 1970s, the low-rider phenomenon received national and international coverage in such publications as *The New York Times* and *Natural History*. In more recent times, the popularity of *ramflas* has gone up and down in cycles; they are more popular in some areas than in others, apparently depending on the influx of first- and second-generation Mexican Americans, who use them to make fashion as well as cultural and political statements.

(A derogatory joke about low-riders had to do with the custom of some owners to replace the regular steering wheels in their cars with tiny diameter metal chains. The answer to the question, "Why do *pachucos* have chain steering wheels?" was, "So they will already be in handcuffs when they are arrested.")

Low-riders were no doubt the inspiration for the appearance of "high-riders" which became one of the "in" things for young Anglo-Americans cruising up and down town and city streets in the 1980s in the southwestern United States.

Another word used in reference to low-riders, as well as to any old car that has been fixed up, or to a big fancy car, is *carrucha*. It is also the equivalent of "wheels." (A *carrucho*, on the other hand, generally refers to a marijuana cigarette.)

(See **Chicanos, Pachucos.**)

Respeto
(Ray-SPAY-toh)

"Love, Hate and Fate"

Another cultural value where Mexicans, North Americans, and other non-Latins often do not see eye to eye and end up misunderstanding each other is in the matter of *respeto* (ray-SPAY-toh) or "respect."

There are significant differences between the meanings of respect and *respeto*. North Americans tend to respect people if they are talented, law-abiding, diligent, productive and successful. Such characteristics as thoughtfulness, generosity and loyalty are also usually tacked on somewhere near the end. Anglos generally base their respect for others on well-known and recognized principles such as fairness and equality, often without reference to the emotional side of life.

Mexicans, on the other hand, respect people for their age, their professional position, their power, their social status and their level of attention to personal relationships, with the latter generally taking precedence over all of the other factors.

Father–son, father–daughter, mother–son, mother–daughter, brother–sister and superior–subordinate relationships, as well as a web of relationships with relatives and godparents, impact on the importance and interrelated flow of respect in Mexico.

Because personal relationships are based on factors that change with circumstance, Mexican-style respect may seem to be arbitrary and undependable to outsiders. Developing and nurturing respect in Mexico therefore requires more of a personal, emotional investment than it normally does in principle- and logic-oriented societies.

One of the biggest mistakes that North Americans make in their business relationships with Mexicans is presuming that they can win and keep the respect of their Mexican counterparts or employees by setting an example of working hard and sacrificing their personal lives for their companies. To Mexicans that kind of behavior is more than foolish. It is highly detrimental to one's own character and personality because it prevents one from enjoying life, which Mexicans have traditionally regarded as more important than work, and it is equally destructive to family life.

The strong personal element in Mexican *respeto* encompasses sexual attitudes and relationships as well, and this is very touchy territory because it involves the so-called cult of masculinity in all of its nuances.

Traditionally, Mexican men have expected—and demanded—respect for their virility and their success in seducing women. They have also expected respect for their courage and fearlessness, especially in the face of death.

Mexican bus and taxi drivers have traditionally been notorious for courting death, driving like they were being pursued by demons. And, of course, the bullfight is the ultimate way for a Mexican to prove manliness and courage and thereby earn respect and admiration.

Today, the role and importance of respect remains a vital aspect of life in Mexico, although its character has changed somewhat. People in high positions still expect respect for their dignity and face, but if they gained their positions through family and other connections, such respect is no longer guaranteed.

The demand by Mexican men for respect for their sexual prowess is far less obsessive these days, but it is still there. Bus drivers, particularly those serving the travel industry, no longer feel compelled to act like wild men, but they expect *respeto* for their professional status.

Interestingly, Mexicans have never viewed physical toughness, fearlessness and strongly masculine behavior by men as precluding them from having an equally strong intellectual and philosophical side.

Ernest Hemingway was especially admired by Mexicans and other Latins because he was a fighter, an adventurer, a drinker, a lover of women *and* a prize-winning author of deeply humanistic works.

Like the samurai warriors of feudal Japan who prided themselves as much for their ability to write poetry and appreciate art as for their skill with the sword, the most macho of Mexican men like to think of themselves as poets, singers and philosophers.

Generally speaking, Mexicans do not judge people on the basis of their accomplishments, but on the kind of person they are—if they are loyal, generous, respectful, kind and if they have "soul" and "character." In the Mexican context personality and character are more important than any technical skill or dedication to hard work.

Mexicans have never shaped their lives around mechanical, absolute rules and limitations. Their world was—and still is to a significant degree—based on emotional needs first and material needs second. Mexicans tend to look upon the North American way of life as too robotic, too devoid of emotion and spiritualism, the very things that give life its flavor and make it worthwhile.

Respeto is regarded by Mexicans as one of the most important elements in Mexican culture and therefore one of the most important words in their language.

A growing complaint among Mexican businesspeople caught up in the increasing mad rush of economic growth is that they are becoming more and more like the Americans, Japanese and others who work so much they no longer have time for their families and the really important things of life.

Despite the gradually changing mores, however, respect in Mexico still has a class element. Affluent families with maids treat them as servants, not as their equals. They do not like to see foreign families in Mexico "spoiling" their maids by treating them like members of the family.

One of the many reasons why Benito Juárez, the Zatopec Indian who rose to become the president of Mexico in 1858, is regarded by most Mexicans as the greatest statesman the country has produced is that he adhered to the philosophy that "respect (for all people) is the foundation of peace."

(See **Amistad, Amor, Libertad, Motivación, Responsabilidad, Reto.**)

Responsabilidad
(Ray-spawn-sah-bee-lee-DAD)

"Staying Out of Trouble"

Mexico's famed writer-poet Octavio Paz once described the traditional Mexican way of life by using the phrase *el vacile* in reference to what he called the "irresponsibility, irrationality, passion, fearlessness, driving ambition and whimsicality" of Mexicans.

By itself *vacile* (bah-SEE-lay), means to vacillate, to dilly-dally, to never make up one's mind, to avoid responsibility—all characteristics that have traditionally been associated with Mexicans, but particularly poor urban residents living in slums.

Two other key words traditionally associated with the character of Mexicans are *aguantar* and *relajo*.

Aguantar (ah-gwahn-TAR) means "to endure," "to bear." The ability to endure things that are virtually unendurable was the only thing that sustained Mexican Indians and *mestizos* for more than 400 years, and it is still a vital trait in the survival of more than half of the population.

Relajo (ray-LAH-hoh) is a cultural denominator that means something like "chaos." It is a term used by some Mexican anthropologists to describe or explain typical Mexican behavior. *Relajientos*, the anthropologists say, are people who introduce a chaotic element into everything they do; people who tend to be disorganized and irresponsible and to be more interested in human relations and spiritual things than in hard work and sticking to projects they start.

Mexicans have historically been programmed to have a negative view of personal *responsibilidad* (ray-spawn-sah-bee-lee-DAD) and to avoid it whenever possible. Americans and other Anglos, on the other hand, have been programmed to regard personal responsibility as a positive attribute which is essential to a progressive smooth-working society.

This contradictory way of looking at responsibility was, of course, a direct result of generations of conditioning in different political systems—autocracy in Mexico and democracy in the Anglo world. The more personal responsibility ordinary individuals have in dictatorships, the more their lives are in danger.

American generally think in terms of personal responsibility first and social responsibility second. In Mexico, responsibility tends to be just the opposite—social first and personal second.

Mexicans have a highly honed sense of responsibility for all of the basic family and friend relationships as part of their sense of honor and social obligations. But in nonfamily and nonfriend matters, Mexicans, like the Japanese and most other Asians, characteristically attempt to diffuse or shift responsibility to outside forces or to whatever group they may belong to.

This difference in emphasis can be upsetting to Americans and others dealing with Mexicans, and must be handled in a thoughtful and diplomatic way for the dealings to proceed smoothly.

Still, not all of the *vacile* character of Mexicans is negative from a humanistic view point. The whimsicality and passion that are a part of it have contributed enormously to the Mexican passion for art, music, poetry and the other refinements of life. Despite generation after generation of political and economic abuse which would try the souls of saints, love, laughter and good fellowship have remained overriding traits in the Mexican character.

The Mexican attitude toward personal responsibility began to change in the 1980s, but most Mexicans who have escaped the cultural handicaps of their past say it will be one or two generations before the negative *vacile* patterns of behavior can be purged from the Mexican character.

121

Reto
(RAY-toh)

"Facing the Challenge"

Reto (RAY-toh) is another ordinary word that has taken on a totally new connotation since the revolutionary political and economic changes began in Mexico in the 1980s. Having picked up momentum in the 1990s, they are still transforming the country.

The original meaning of *reto* is "challenge," but in its new incarnation it represents a call for Mexicans to totally change the way they have traditionally thought and behaved.

Explains a Mexican colleague: "The original American settlers who came to the North American continent, and all of the immigrants who have followed them, came to escape religious and political prosecution by authoritarian churches and governments, racial and cultural discrimination and lack of economic opportunities. They came to build new lives for themselves and in the process they built a new country.

"The Spanish conquistadors who came to Mexico, on the other hand, came in search of gold and slaves. They came to pillage and rape rather than to build.

"From the beginning the Spaniards treated the Indian inhabitants of Mexico as nonhuman, as evil, and as worthy only of being raped and enslaved. The Indians who survived the original massacres and the diseases of the Spaniards were brainwashed in negativism, and conditioned to believe that their way of life was evil, and that they were inherently, irrevocably inferior.

"Thus from the inception of what is now Mexico, the bulk of the people—the native Indians as well as the mixed-bloods who eventually became the majority—were deliberately programmed to think and behave in a negative way.

"The political, social and economic systems that prevailed during the 300-year reign of the Spanish colonials, and for more than 100 years after we won our freedom from Spain, stifled virtually all ambition before it could be born.

"In this oppressive environment, people were basically satisfied just to survive from one day to the next. They were programmed from one generation to the next to just do enough to get by.

"Overcoming that legacy is one of the greatest challenges facing Mexico, and that is why *reto* is now such an important word."

My colleague went on to say that Luis Echeverría, president from 1970 to 1976, was the first Mexican leader to make Mexicans aware that they could have a better life; that they too could create an affluent society.

"He did this," my friend continued, "by first taking a negative approach—the only approach Mexicans understood. He hit them in the stomach with a series of proposals that economically united the country for the first time in its history."

Much of the enthusiasm surrounding the inauguration of Ernesto Zedillo as president of Mexico in December 1994 was generated by this new vision of the *reto* that Mexicans face. But the negativism that is inherent in the culture is still overpowering. Added my friend: "Virtually all Mexicans relive the conquest (by Hernán Cortés and his conquistadors) every day of their lives. The conditioning goes on. The message is: 'The only way you can make it in Mexico is to lie, steal and kill.'

"The few who have escaped this debilitating legacy are those who had especially strong parents, grandparents, and close family friends who were able to imbue them with positive, progressive attitudes, a sense of personal responsibility and the ambition to achieve something better for themselves and their families.

"Among the challenges facing Mexicans today is to counter the negative conditioning of the past by example, by basic education and by an ongoing public campaign to condition all Mexicans to look upon the various challenges of life with a positive outlook. We must look at every problem or obstacle as an opportunity to make things better. We must replace the worn-out lament that nothing can be done with the idea that we can do *anything* if we make up our minds to do it and work together."

The *reto* facing foreign politicians and businesspeople dealing with Mexico is to understand the historical origins of the Mexican character, and to develop scenarios that will help both sides take a positive approach to their differences.

122

Señoritas

(Say-nyohr-REE-tahss)

"Young Ladies of Mexico"

Señorita (say-nyohr-REE-tah), the Spanish equivalent of "Miss," is more than just a gender designation. It is a special title of courtesy for girls who are 15 and older, and for single women. Historically, the title has had a romantic image, but, in fact, it was used to hide much of the discrimination traditionally faced by the young women of Mexico.

Until modern times education was denied to Mexican women, and their lives were minutely controlled by the Catholic Church and by customs growing out of the so-called "cult of masculinity," which was the defining factor in Mexican society.

From the first decades of the Spanish era in Mexico young girls were conditioned to believe that the only thing of real value that they had to offer a man was sex and children, and they were culturally conditioned to behave in a seductive manner in order to attract men.

Yet at the same time girls were also taught that they should be ignorant of sex and fear it. Among other things this resulted in the perverse belief that if they feared sex enough, men would be gentle with them.

From about the age of eight or nine, girls were segregated from boys. As they approached puberty, they were usually watched constantly to make sure that they were never alone with males except brothers or fathers, because it was assumed that any other male would immediately seduce them.

By the time most upper-class girls were in their midteens they were motivated by one idea: get a man to marry them so they could escape the stifling atmosphere of their homes and gain a measure of freedom. Lower-class girls generally sought to marry early in the hope that they would be able to escape from the daily toil of housework and abuse commonly inflicted upon them by overprotective fathers and brothers.

Depending on their class, young women would generally use one of three techniques in attempting to achieve their goal of marriage. If they were low class they would use some degree of force and deception to "trap" men into marriage such as claiming to be pregnant or having been "ruined" by the loss of their virginity. If they were middle class they would try to suck men into their net by emphasizing their virginity and utter helplessness.

Upper-class girls specialized in playing hard to get, unmercifully teasing their suitors, who obligingly worked themselves into a passionate frenzy and married them to get revenge.

The lower the class of the Mexican *señorita* the less likely she was to latch onto a husband, and the more likely she was to end up as a single parent with several children. And life for those who succeeded in getting married was generally not what they wanted it to be. Most found that they had merely exchanged one set of restrictions and servitude for another.

It was not until the mid-1900s that middle- and upper-class Mexican parents began to recognize the need for their daughters to associate more freely with eligible young men, and began to loosen the traditional restraints. At first, a few young girls in groups of two or three could be seen in public places on their own, or escorted by one man who was often a relative.

By the end of the 1970s, hundreds of very pretty and eligible but dateless girls could be seen on Saturday nights in the most fashionable restaurants and coffee shops of Mexico City and the major provincial capitals. Some could also be seen cruising around the streets in their own cars.

Young women who went to work in the branch offices of American companies in the 1950s and 1960s, primarily in Mexico City, were to play a leading role in the movement toward social emancipation for Mexican women.

This was the period when Mexico was still infected with the "hate everything American virus," so it took considerable courage for these young women to become "traitors" to their own country by working for the hated *gringos*.

The three most important qualifications Mexican girls had to possess in order to work for American companies as secretaries were the usual mechanical skills, fluency in English and beauty. These qualifications, plus the fact that they were paid better than most Mexican men, soon made them role models for millions of other young Mexican women.

The majority of these revolutionary young women were from affluent families, and their reasons for working were social rather than economic. By working they were able to get away from their homes and enjoy a measure of personal freedom that had previously been unheard of in Mexico.

Mexican bachelors who had been educated in the United States found the girls especially attractive because they could establish relationships with them without getting involved with their families. The girls were especially prized as brides by foreign-educated bachelors who also worked for American companies, and as mistresses by well-to-do businessmen and politicians who wanted them as trophies.

In present-day Mexico male–female relations among the young vary widely, depending on the education level, social class and economic status as well as on the location. The better educated and the higher the social and economic class, the more likely it is that courtship and other customs are similar to practices in the United States, Western Europe and elsewhere.

Some middle- and upper-class parents are more strict than others in setting curfews for their daughters, but generally young people on this level come and go as they please. The old tradition of the *duenna*, or chaperon, has virtually disappeared everywhere except in some rural areas, and even there it is more of a ceremonial thing. Generally, marriages on this level are based on mutual affection and trust, and most men no longer try to keep their wives isolated.

It is among the less educated poor that the macho traditions of the past are the strongest, and where women have the longest way to go in achieving even partial equality with men. Some stories told by poor young Mexican women to anthropologist and oral historian Marilyn P. Davis (*Mexican Voices/American Dreams*) sound like horror tales from the Middle Ages of Europe.

Davis relates stories of young women whose fathers and mothers still forbid them from having friends, criticize them constantly, force them to do nothing but work and literally kick them out of the house if they show any signs of independence.

One 20-year-old girl who said she could no longer stand this kind of treatment and announced that she was going to the United States to work, told how her mother and older married sister played a recording of *Las Golondrinas* all day prior to her departure to make her sad and to try to persuade her to stay home.

A young man told how his father kicked his sister out of the house when the family learned she was pregnant, even though she had no money or place to go. When the son protested on behalf of his sister, the father abandoned the family.

Paraphrasing the comments of a middle-aged Mexican male who had spent half of his life in the United States: Life for the poor urban girl is complicated and often filled with danger. She lives in a man's world, where the men are predatory and ruthless. She is subjected to regular physical and emotional violence. Women bear the brunt of the negative side of Mexico's cult of masculinity. They are the whipping post and the blood sacrifice. Reprieve comes only with old age.

Middle-class girls in Mexico are less exposed to physical and emotional violence than in earlier years, although men still take advantage of them at every opportunity. One of the burdens of these young women is the "virginity complex" which still prevails in middle- and upper-class men. The idea of marrying a girl who is not a virgin is inconceivable to many of them.

Of course, men in these classes are very active sexually before and after marriage. They routinely engage in affairs with wives and widows, and with lower-class working girls among whom virginity is not so essential to marriage.

This double-edged situation results in middle- and upper-class Mexican girls making the most of their sex as bait when they are young. From the age of 14 or 15 they tend to flaunt their femininity. They take great delight in walking with their breasts thrust out, their stomachs pulled in and their hips rotating.

Upper-class Mexican girls and women seem to take special delight in flirting with other men when they are out with dates. To the uninitiated foreign male, this can be very disconcerting—and dangerous, if he is foolish enough to try to do anything about it.

When this kind of behavior is combined with the penchant Mexican girls have for wearing tight blouses, sweaters and skirts to accent their breasts, hips and legs, the combination can be deadly. (When a sweater or blouse is so form-fitting that it appears to be pasted on a girl's breasts it is said to be *pegado* (pay-GAH-doh), "pasted on," or *pintado* (peen-TAH-doh), "painted on.")

Young girls in the border cities and towns, strongly influenced by American ideas of liberated women, can be especially forward. By the time they are 11 or 12 years old they are already expert at using "the language of the eyes" to communicate with boys and men. Using only their eyes they can express desire, guile, sarcasm, contempt and a kind of naked, callous teasing that few men can stand.

Despite the hardships and abuse traditionally inflicted upon Mexican girls and young women by the "cult of masculinity," it also had a positive influence on them. The male-dominated, sensually oriented culture conditioned them to be romantic to the extreme and to have warm, delightful personalities. As they grew older, they developed an extraordinary spirit and strength that made it possible for them to survive in a hostile world, to have families and to hold them together in the face of unbelievable odds.

The ambition of most young Mexican women today is to get an education, to obtain a well-paying job and to marry men who will treat them as valued partners—all goals that continue to be a dream for most of them.

But the spirit, strength, goodwill and good humor of Mexico's young women constitute a treasure far greater than gold and silver, and Mexico will not begin to reach its full potential until Mexican women are free of most of the cultural and economic restraints of the past.

(See **Mujeres, Paseos, Serenatas**.)

123

Serenatas
(Say-ray-NAH-tahs)

"Romance á la Mexico"

One of the few admirable customs the Spaniards brought with them when they invaded Mexico and conquered the Aztecs and their allies in 1519–1521 was the *serenata* (say-ray-NAH-tah), or "serenade," which consisted of young men courting girls by singing love songs to them at night beneath their windows.

During the first generations of the Spanish reign, the *serenata* was strictly a Spanish custom, but it was gradually absorbed by the growing population of *mestizos*, or mixed-bloods, and eventually became an integral part of the non-Indian culture of Mexico, adding a special ambiance that helped to mitigate some of the harsher aspects of life.

In earlier times "under the window" serenades that took place at or just before dawn were often referred to as *gallos* or "roosters," because that is about the time that roosters start crowing.

Birthday serenades arranged by boyfriends or husbands, and sometimes featuring a special song written for that purpose, were traditionally staged between the hours of 2 and 4 A.M. The song *Las Mañanitas* contains romantic references about waking the lady up.

The custom of the courting *serenata* flourished in urban as well as rural Mexico until the advent of cars, high-rise apartments and other changes in lifestyle made it impractical, especially in the larger cities.

However, as late as the 1980s it was still fairly common in most villages and towns and in a few larger cities, notably Monterrey, Villahermosa, Guanajuato and Tampico.

Young men customarily enlist their buddies to join them in *serenatas* for girls they are courting or want to court. Wealthy swains may hire professionals to do the singing for them. It is also common for young men to take their girlfriends to restaurants or clubs with house bands that specialize in serenading courting couples.

Girls and women who are the targets of home *serenatas* who do not want to accept the attentions of their suitors do not acknowledge the performances in any way (such as turning on a light or opening a window). However, their fathers may come out, insult the singers and order them to go away.

If the suitors are welcome, and especially if they have advised the girls in advance, the girls may respond by appearing at a door, window or on a balcony. It has also traditionally been the custom for welcome suitors to be invited in, fed and offered drinks.

While much of the courting in Mexico today has been Americanized, the *serenata* may be one of the few traditional customs to survive because of the overall importance of music and singing to Mexicans.

Virtually every Mexican can sing well enough to put on an entertaining performance, at least for his or her friends. And in practically every group of boys there is almost always at least one who can play the guitar.

These factors have been the key to the survival of the *serenata*, and hopefully will keep the custom alive for future generations to enjoy.

While quite different in cultural merit, serenading by bands in restaurants, many of which have open-air areas, has survived in the *mariachis*, those roving minstrels whose songs tell stories that reflect the heart and soul of Mexico.

(See **Mariachis**.)

Sexo
(SEX-oh)

"Sex Versus Love"

The Anglo-European idea that sex should be preceded by and based upon love is a relatively recent cultural invention because such a social convention could not emerge except in societies that were democratic enough for individuals to have a choice in their mates.

The now popular romantic view of male–female relations was primarily a product of societies that came under the influence of Christianity, which traditionally prohibited sex outside of marriage as a means of social and political control, but which generally allowed young people to select their own mates after they had pined away in abstinence for many years.

Since both romance and love are ephemeral things that come and go like the wind, male–female relations in societies that have attempted to enforce the love–sex approach have traditionally ranged from the sublime and uplifting to barbaric and destructive, and "cheating" by both men and women has been common.

Sexual traditions in Mexico retain many of the elements that are more characteristic of non-Christian societies around the world, despite a seemingly overpowering element of Catholicism, which emphasizes chastity before marriage and monogamous fidelity afterward.

Generally speaking, love and sex are not inclusive in Mexico. Love is important and is held up as the bond that binds families—but not necessarily husbands and wives—together. Unlike in the United States, where sexual satisfaction is close to the core of both love and marriage, sexual pleasure in Mexico has traditionally been regarded as a separate issue.

For married women in Mexico, sexual satisfaction in the sense of achieving climax during intercourse and otherwise enjoying the act, was not a consideration; the important thing was to achieve pregnancy and have children. It was, in fact, practically taboo for wives to show any signs of enjoying sex with their husbands because men considered such behavior "whore-like" and as a sign that they could not trust their wives to remain faithful to them.

Mexican men, on the other hand, looked at sex with their wives as a demonstration of their masculinity and power over them; whatever pleasure they derived from the act was incidental. Whenever they wanted to engage in sex for the pleasure of it they went to lovers and prostitutes.

Prior to marriage Mexican men also felt free to engage in sex with as many women as possible, including single women who had never been married, married women, divorcees, widows and prostitutes. Such behavior had nothing at all to do with their religious beliefs or with any religious rituals they might observe, because sex was not seen as a religious matter.

Sociologists explain this difference in the way Americans and Mexicans see sex by describing Americans as "inner directed" where sex is concerned, while Mexicans are "other directed" in sexual matters. In other words, sexual behavior in the United States is a matter of individual moral choice and conscience, traditionally based on the concept that it is evil outside of marriage. Mexicans, men in particular, have been conditioned to believe that sex is a social function that has nothing to do with their inner sense of right and wrong.

Mexican men attribute their sexual behavior outside of marriage to external forces that are often beyond their control—the overwhelming need to demonstrate masculinity and power, and passion that they cannot resist.

Sociologists attribute many of the problems that have traditionally been endemic in Mexico—large numbers of young unmarried women with children, equally large numbers of wives who have been abandoned by their husbands, conflicts among men over women—to the "other directed" sexual mores. The result is that men engage in sex with many partners without taking responsibility for their behavior.

In Northern Mexico and in Mexican-American communities the use of the word *araña* (ah-RAH-nyah), or "spider," to refer to a prostitute or any woman who is sexually promiscuous is indicative of the male attitude toward women in general.

Sexual behavior in Mexico is gradually evolving away from the ancient concept that it is primarily a representation of male power, but it will be many generations before the last vestiges of this primitive legacy are eradicated from Mexican culture.

Among other things, Mexican women will have to repudiate many of the teachings of the Catholic Church, and actively work toward achieving political and economic equality with men.

But certainly not all of Mexico's sexual mores are negative or destructive. Sexuality in Mexico has both masculine and feminine attributes that are especially seductive and emotionally satisfying to both Mexicans and foreigners alike.

There is a subtle sexual character to virtually all aspects of life in Mexico that is a significant part of its cultural charm and is one of the magnets that attracts and holds people in its titillating embrace.

Siesta
(See-ES-tah)

"Letting the World Go By"

Mexicans are under increasing pressure to give up many of their traditional attitudes and behavior and replace them with what might be called "the American lifestyle," a lifestyle that most Mexicans and a growing number of Americans regard as irrational and self-destructive.

Unfortunately, the American lifestyle is difficult for Mexicans to resist. It is something like the new, aggressive religion (Catholicism) brought to Mexico in the 16th century by the Spanish conquistadors and the missionaries who followed them. When combined with all its other implications, from economics to politics, it is simply overwhelming.

Despite the hardships inflicted upon Mexico's Indians and Spanish–Indian mixtures by Spanish administrators and the Pope's "troops" during the colonial period, there was traditionally a graceful element in the lives of many urban Mexicans not dependent upon economic affluence, that included music, singing, dancing, poetry, philosophical contemplation and lively conversation.

The poorest of Mexicans—if they weren't actually starving or being abused to death—were able to live relatively dignified lives high in emotional, intellectual and spiritual satisfaction.

Foreigners who visited Mexico during colonial times, as far back as the 18th century, were deeply attracted by the personality and character of Mexicans, and commented endlessly on their attachment to cultural arts and their joyous approach to life.

Fortunately, one of the traditional customs of Mexico that has withstood the onslaught of modernity and conspicuous consumption is the age-old practice of the *siesta* (see-ES-tah), the long midafternoon break from work that apparently goes back to ancient times—possibly as far back as when people foraged for food in the early mornings and evenings and stayed out of harm's way during the day.

So far, businesses in Mexico, from banks to neighborhood retail shops, have accommodated themselves to the traditional *siesta*, which may begin as early as 1 P.M. and last until 4 P.M., by setting their hours accordingly.

Banks in Mexico are open on weekdays from 9 A.M. to 1:30 P.M. Some, particularly in major cities, reopen at 4 P.M. and stay open until 6 P.M. On Saturdays and Sundays banking hours (for those that are open) usually begin at 10 A.M. and thereafter follow the normal weekday schedule.

Normal hours for business offices and shops are 9 A.M. to 2 P.M. and 4 P.M. to 7 P.M. Government offices are generally open from 8 A.M. to 3 P.M.

Because the workday, meals and normal after-hours activities in Mexico run anywhere from two to four hours later than in the United States, some people do, in fact, go home during the weekday *siesta* period and take a short nap. Others take care of personal business.

Most Mexican businesspeople use the daily *siesta* periods for long lunch meetings with associates and clients as a key part of their ongoing business and social lives. They also use them for making and nurturing the new personal relationships that are so important to their business.

There is a tendency for foreign businesspeople visiting in Mexico to regard a daily two- to three-hour lunch break as a gross waste of time, and to chaff visibly at the experience.

Even knowing the purpose and importance of such meetings does not make it easy for some visitors to accept them, because they are so anxious to "make progress" that they cannot relax. And, of course, some of this anxiety derives from worrying about their hotel bills and what their bosses back home would say about them having two-hour lunch parties every afternoon instead of working.

The point, of course, is that these *siesta* lunches are often the most important parts of the day, for they are where friendships, which are the foundation for all business deals in Mexico, are made.

(See **Comida**.)

Simpatico
(Seem-PAH-tee-coh)

"Something to Strive For"

Historically in Mexico people who were not pure Spanish were not protected by law or by any sense of chivalry for the underdog or weaker individual, or even by ordinary courtesy. The common fate of all but the tiny upper class of the country was to be victims, one way or the other, virtually every day for their entire lives. This resulted in a deep, fundamental need for concepts and customs that would mitigate the awful feelings of vulnerability that afflicted the bulk of the population.

Part of this support was provided by the church, despite the fact that the church itself was one of the primary oppressors of the people and directly responsible for much of their misery. Both men and women, but women in particular, were expected to sacrifice their lives to men in positions of power and to the church.

Mixed-blood men could not be satisfied with just the solace of the church, however. They attempted to deal with the discrimination they encountered every day by constructing an imaginary world of overpowering masculinity that called for a strict code of conduct among themselves and in their behavior toward women—a perverse reaction that only made things worse for everyone.

But all of this suffering over the generations did not smother the humanity of the *mestizos*, and as their social and economic situation gradually improved, their natural sympathy and goodwill toward people of their own kind grew until it became a primary trait in their character.

Today, if all mainstream Mexicans were asked to list their two or three most important cultural traits, *simpatico* (seem-PAH-tee-coh) would almost always be on the list.

In its Mexican context *simpatico* refers to a person who is sympathetic, understanding, pleasing, friendly, well-behaved, trustworthy—in fact, exactly the opposite of the attitudes and behavior Mexicans were subjected to for centuries.

Some Mexican Indians believe in what they call *El Gran Simpatico*, literally, "The Great Sympathetic (Thing)," which, they say is a special "organ" near the heart that controls the flow of life force through the body. This site, they say, is also the site of the soul, and when one is dispirited it feels like a great weight on the chest. They add that when the soul is not fed properly, energy stops flowing through the body and it dies.

It cannot be said today that the behavior of most Mexican men toward women is *simpatico*, whether by Mexican or non-Mexican standards. But the extremes of chauvinistic behavior that have traditionally been typical of Mexican men, particularly those in the lower classes, are no longer as characteristic of younger Mexicans.

Middle-class Mexicans in particular, but most lower-class Mexicans as well, have overcome a great deal of the legacy of sexism and brutality of earlier years, and when they are at peace with themselves and others there are no warmer or more caring people anywhere.

The *simpatico* character of this new breed of Mexicans is especially noticeable to foreign visitors, who are not used to such demonstrations of thoughtfulness, caring and hospitality. And it is one of the reasons why so many North Americans and other nationalities become permanent residents in Mexico.

This also is one of the reasons why so many Mexicans who come to the United States to work cannot wait to get back home and wrap themselves back in the warm folds of the *simpatico* culture. There is, in fact, a movement among more affluent Mexican Americans to either move back to their ancestral homeland permanently, or at least buy property there and spend as much time there as possible.

Said one such man in El Paso: "The contrast between the pace of life in the United States and in Mexico is so dramatic that it begins the instant you cross the border.

"There are physical inconveniences in Mexico, of course, but these are more than made up for by the laid-back, relaxed atmosphere; the sense that you don't have to be busy every hour of the day; that you don't have to feel guilty if you don't produce something every day.

"There is an emotional and spiritual quality to life in Mexico that is missing in most American homes, even the homes of Mexican Americans and other groups that have maintained many of the cultural ways of their ancestors."

More and more Mexican Americans who have succeeded in business in the United States say they are going to retire in Mexico, or at least live there part of the time after they retire.

It is this human aspect of present-day Mexican culture that gives Mexicans confidence in themselves; confidence that, given the opportunity, they can create a better world for themselves.

Unlike the word "sympathy" in English, there is no element of "pity" in *simpatico*. If someone says, *Tengo mucha simpatica para* "anybody," it means they have a lot of admiration for the person concerned.

Solidaridad
(Soh-lee-dah-ree-DAHD)

"Working Together"

History could well mark the 1990s as the decade when Mexico finally began the process of becoming a nation unified by a common commitment— to eliminate the evils that had plagued the majority of its people for almost 500 years. When Ernesto Zedillo assumed the presidency of Mexico on December 1, 1994, it was on a platform dedicated to severing the political, economic and social chains that had kept the country enslaved in a time-warp of civil and ecclesiastical despotism since the beginning of the Spanish colonial period in the 1520s. The foundation of Zedillo's platform was summed up in the word *solidaridad* (soh-lee-dah-ree-DAHD), or "solidarity," which he had conceived while he was still a member of the government of his predecessor, Carlos Salinas, who served as president of Mexico from 1988 to 1994.

Zedillo and his aides developed a plan to virtually reinvent both the government and the economy, replacing the tyranny of the government with true democracy and the splintered, feudalistic economy with a capitalistic, market-oriented system. Significant progress in that direction was made during the last part of the Salinas administration, so when Zedillo took over the presidency in December 1994, the revolutionary changes he had master-minded were already off to a good start.

Today, if you ask most any Mexican to name the most important words in the Mexican language, *solidaridad* will always be at or near the top of the list.

Solidaridad had never before existed in Mexico—politically, economically or socially. Despite all of the efforts that had been made to reform the government and the economy following the civil war in 1910–1921, the whole of Mexico was divided by every possible political, economic, social and cultural division, including racial castes, social classes, political and economic fiefdoms, a small elite group of rulers at the top and a poverty-stricken mass at the bottom.

Zedillo, his team and a growing number of young reform-minded political allies realized that without a unified effort that combined all social and political elements in the country, any attempt to democratize the government and marketize the economy would fail.

Solidaridad thus became both the foundation of their program as well as a slogan that was reminiscent of the *Grito de Dolores* or "Cry of Dolores," which inspired the revolutionary war of freedom from Spain in 1810.

Mexican business leaders say that now the program has progressed to the point that, despite ups and downs, it cannot be reversed; that the expectations of the people have reached a critical point. Foreign executives who want to do business with Mexico would do well to add *solidaridad* to their vocabulary. They should become familiar with the government philosophy and programs aimed at improving social conditions and protecting the environment.

Business projects that contribute to the overall economic and social goals of the government will find that the political environment in today's Mexico is friendly and cooperative.

"Banks are one example," said a Mexican businessman, "They now act like banks. Politicians are an even better example. Instead of being impossible to see, they now come to see us, asking us what they can do to help. The spirit of *solidaridad*, of working together, is spreading into all levels of society for the first time in the history of the country."

He added: "In order for Mexico to truly achieve its potential we must all work together, hand-in-hand, men and women, without concern for economic or social advantage. *Solidaridad* points the way."

Televisión
(Tay-lay-bee-see-OWN)

"The Good and the Bad"

Televisión is rapidly replacing the Catholic Church as the single most powerful and important influence in Mexico. It is changing the way Mexicans think and behave, and is therefore impacting on every aspect of Mexican life.

The economic impact of television in Mexico is astounding. One graphic example: Commercials carried on cable television in the northern portions of the state of Sonora for Walmart, Safeway and McDonald's quickly made the sales of the Nogales, Arizona, branches of these three stores the highest or near the highest in their chains.

Some observers say that the political influence of television in Mexico is doing more for the human rights of women workers and others than all other forces combined. It is making people politically aware and informed for the first time in the history of the country.

Television has been especially important in revolutionizing the thinking and behavior of Mexican women, particularly housewives and mothers, who in the past knew almost nothing about what was going on in the country because they did not read political, business or financial publications, and did not discuss such things with men.

Now, before, after and in between "soap operas" and quiz and game shows women watch and listen to the international as well as domestic news.

Said a cable TV executive: "Television has made Mexican women aware for the first time of the social and economic problems of the country on a national basis, and it is not only helping to bring them into dialogues on these issues, it is also encouraging them to become politically active as fundraisers and candidates for office."

A great deal of the economic effect of television on Mexican women and the traditionally disenfranchised urban poor and rural Indians is that it exposes them to other lifestyles, to other choices. It also increases their level of frustration and anger and encourages them to take aggressive action to help themselves.

Television is also helping to emancipate Mexican women from the cultural restraints and bonds traditionally inflicted upon them by the "macho cult" of men. The soap operas in particular (*telenovelas*) depict women as self-aware, strong, free-spirited, ambitious, blatantly sensual and often sensually predatory as well. More than one female character has said, "When are we going to have sex? I do not like to be left like hot water for chocolate!"

The female role models on TV are involved in business and politics, and routinely get the better of men by intelligence and guile.

As in the United States and elsewhere, there is also a negative influence from television in Mexico. But it does not appear to be as negative in Mexico as it is in some other countries, particularly the United States. Surveys show that the positive content of television programming in Mexico is significantly higher than what it is in the United States.

"We have our sleaze and junk programs, but generally speaking they are not as sleazy, as junky, or as common as they are in the U.S.," said a cable network executive.

"A great deal of what passes as humor or comedy on American television is degenerate, and must make a terribly damaging—and frightening—impression on young viewers. Comedy in Mexico is generally more uplifting than negative," he added.

Mexican men who have occasion to watch both American and Mexican television also say that the content of American comedies and soap operas is invariably designed to portray men in a negative light. They say that these programs typically depict men as weak, incompetent, irresponsible, deceitful and immoral—even unnecessary in raising children—and that this is one of the primary reasons for the breakdown of law, order and morality in the United States, especially among the young.

A representative member of this group added: "We are trying to prevent *televisión* in Mexico from being used in this destructive manner."

Tertulia

(Terr-TOO-lee-ah)

"Exercising the Intellect"

It has been said for ages that adversity builds character. Few people in the world have endured more adversity than the Indians and mixed-blooded people of Mexico, who together make up some 90 percent of the total population.

From the beginning of the Spanish colonial period in Mexico in 1521 to the middle of the 20th century, generation after generation of Mexican Indians and the overwhelming majority of Spanish–Indian mixed-bloods suffered unspeakable racial and cultural discrimination, spiritual domination, physical punishment, lack of medical care and education and wretched poverty.

But even within the caldron of this pain and misfortune, most Mexicans maintained an astounding spirit of goodwill, courtesy and hospitality, along with a deep-seated appreciation for beauty, music and the arts.

Another facet of Mexican character that was forged in pain, frustration, and the constant threat of disaster was an emphasis on personalized relationships that linked families and friends together, not only for protection but also for the joy and contentment that comes from such intimate bonding.

Educated Mexicans have traditionally had an abiding devotion to poetry and other forms of literature. It impacts directly and dramatically on their lives and adds a special dimension to their philosophical outlook and their daily behavior.

Part of this extraordinary aspect of the Mexican character no doubt derives from their Indian ancestors, whose lives were bound up in spirituality and in pleasing the spirit gods through song and dance, all of which required a contemplative nature and an intellectual approach to life.

In contrast to their more barbaric practices, the Aztecs and other educated Indian nations of Mexico had a cultural tradition of poetry long before the appearance of Spanish conquistadors in 1519. This tradition has remained embedded in the psyche of their cultural and racial descendants—contemporary Mexicans.

The Spanish conquistadors also brought with them a cultural tradition of meeting with friends for intense periods of political, social and literary discourse. These meetings, often held in cafes (indoor as well as outdoor if the topics were not politically dangerous), were known as *tertulias* (terr-TOO-lee-ahs), which might be translated as "exercising the intellect" through discussions about philosophy, political concepts and literature, and sharing the creation and contemplation of poetry. (The term *tertulia* came from the name of a Roman theologian, Quintus Tertullianus, circa 150–230 A.D., and was first associated with a private area in theaters where men met to discuss theology and other weighty matters.)

The Spanish and Indian traditions of *tertulias* were combined in Mexico, and somewhere along the way the element of entertainment, particularly singing and dancing, was introduced into the *tertulia* custom.

For generations in Mexico it was common for groups of people to get together, in cafes and bars or in homes, to spend several hours discussing politics and literature, or helping each other polish poetry they had written. They gossiped, showed off their knowledge or talents and engaged in various kinds of courtship.

Famous writers and artists often were the focal points for many of the *tertulias*, with their "talk fests" attracting other celebrities and the rich and the powerful.

Mexican old timers say true *tertulias* are rapidly becoming a thing of the past because people now work too much and have neither the time nor the energy to devote to such intellectual pursuits. But the discourse goes on, and groups of people still meet regularly in the same bars, lounges, restaurants or wherever on the same day of the week or month to talk.

Mexicans in general are still more interested in philosophical contemplation than in the more mundane and practical aspects of life, a trait that North Americans and other concrete- and progressive-minded people often find irritating, and regard as economically counterproductive.

A positive response by foreigners to this aspect of the Mexican character can provide access to the inner circles of Mexican society, reduce the incidence and influence of culture shock and provide a variety of personal contacts that can be useful in business as well as private affairs.

While the term *tertulia* may not be familiar to younger Mexicans, virtually everyone in the middle and upper classes belongs to some kind of group that meets informally, where the tradition of exercising the intellect continues to flourish. Most often these days it is only long lunches.

Most foreigners who take up residence in Mexico for business or other professional purposes generally have many opportunities to become members of these casual groups and enjoy both the companionship and contacts that result from them.

(For many generations the most famous *tertulia* in Madrid has been a place called *El Jijon*; for the Spanish community in Paris it was the *Barrio Latino*. One of the numerous places traditionally popular in Mexico City is *Tepito*.)

Toloache
(Toh-loh-AH-chay)

"Witches and Love Potions"

One common cultural characteristic that gets stronger and more important as one goes down the social and economic scales in Mexico is a belief in the supernatural. The closer one gets to the Indian world, racially and ethnically, the more powerful and important is the psychic side of life.

Witchcraft is alive and well among Mexico's Indians and among the lower-class mixtures who make up the bulk of the population, and it plays a variety of roles involving the health and welfare of the people.

Until recently, witchcraft was sometimes used as a weapon against competitors in business or against enemies of one kind or another. But it was most often used in matters involving sexual relationships.

If a man seemed to have suddenly lost his sex drive, his wife or sweetheart typically assumed that he had been bewitched by some other woman, and began trying to identify the guilty party. One of the traditional ways of "bewitching" a man or woman was to seduce them into drinking a potion made from the *toloache* (toh-loh-AH-chay) plant, known to cattlemen throughout the American Southwest as "loco weed." Among other things, the *toloache* weed contains scopolamine, which is a common ingredient in sleeping pills.

While I am not aware of testimonials from non-Mexicans regarding the efficacy of *toloache* love potions, a growing number of Americans and others who have been treated by *brujas* (witches) or *brujos* for a variety of ailments that did not respond to modern medicine have testified that the treatments worked. In these treatments the witches used a variety of herbs in combination with massages and incantations.

It is unlikely that the typical foreign traveler or businessperson in Mexico will be offered a *toloache* drink or want to try one on someone else. But if either case should occur, this information might help prepare them for what they are getting into.

131

Triste
(TREES-tay)

"Sadness in Mexican Life"

The conquest of Mexico by Spanish conquistadors in 1519–1521 was a classic example—on a massive scale—of what happens to a people whose traditional way of life is suddenly and savagely altered by force and design. In addition to the European diseases that killed some 80 percent of the Indian population—estimated to have been around 24 million when the Spaniards arrived—the Spanish practice of separating Indian families through labor conscription and sexually monopolizing younger Indian women did much to destroy the cultural roots of native Mexicans.

But the final blow in breaking the spirit of the conquered Indians who were under direct Spanish control was the destruction of their religious beliefs and the enforced replacement of their languages with Spanish.

By severing the Indians from their languages and religions, the Spaniards destroyed the very foundations of their cultures; they cut them off from their past, leaving them without a history, without an anchor in the sea of life.

With the disappearance of the linguistic and spiritual ties that had previously held them together as a people and connected them to their surroundings and the world at large, the surviving Indians became alienated and developed a psychosis of sadness or *triste* (TREES-tay), which was to color their lives and the lives of the Indianized mixed-bloods from then on.

Today there is still a conspicuous element of sadness in Mexican culture, not all of it from the destruction of the world of the Indians. A significant portion of the *triste* part of Mexican life derives from the Spanish sexism that made women subject to the will and peccadilloes of macho men and kept their spirits subdued.

Like the Japanese, who have a similar element of sadness in their culture, Mexicans dealt with the brutality and injustices that were characteristic of their society by turning the sadness in their lives into rituals and art forms.

A disproportionate percentage of Mexican songs, poetry and fiestas are imbued with elements of sadness which is a legacy of the country's authoritarian, brutal, anti-human history.

Beneath many of the happy-appearing blood-heating dances that are synonymous with Mexico, one can easily discern a stratum of sadness. The drinking and violence that is characteristic of many Mexican festivals is fueled by a deep-seated sadness for which there is no immediate cure.

Much of the macho behavior of Mexico's poor urban men is a protest against the helplessness and sadness they feel in not being able to extract themselves from poverty and from the demands of the macho image they feel compelled to maintain.

There has traditionally been an especially profound aura of sadness in the faces and actions of the common people of Mexico, particularly among dispossessed Indians and poor farm workers whose lives were mean and unchangeable.

In fact, most Mexicans on all social levels do not feel complete if they do not regularly experience the sadness of *mariachi* songs, poetry and religious observances. Nothing is quite so sad as the atmosphere of a Mexican church, where the underlying theme is suffering and death.

Even bullfights, with all of their pageantry and orgiastic pleasures, are fraught with elements of sadness. The poignancy of the matador, his slender body poised in front of a deadly bull, and the bull itself, wounded and facing death but still defiant in its last lunge, evoke feelings of sadness as well as admiration.

Foreigners who are not aware of the history or role of sadness in Mexico may find such celebrations as the Day of the Dead, the proliferation of crucified Christs, ritualistic drinking to an alcoholic stupor and other cultural idiosyncrasies a confusing quirk in the Mexican character.

But like all countries that are Catholic on the outside and native on the inside, and which historically have had authoritarian governments, Mexico has two faces, in combination with a split personality. One of Mexico's faces is that of a people who have been victimized and brutalized for centuries and is forlorn, sad and prone to sudden outbreaks of violence. One might call this Mexico's poor face. The other face, the well-to-do and smiling face, is the sunny one that foreigners associate with Mexicans' well-known love of art, singing, dancing, poetry, humor, spritely conversations and sports.

Not surprisingly, Mexicans appreciate other people who are capable of expressing their own emotions and do not feel inhibited about expressing them. The most manly of Mexican men are not above crying, either from sadness or from joy.

Mexicans regard North Americans, both men and women, who control their emotions and stay dry-eyed no matter what, as cold, unfeeling and with little or no passion, which, they believe, is the essence of life.

132

Tu / Usted
(Too / Oo-STED)

"Getting Personal"

Like most old cultures with a highly refined and detailed etiquette based on hierarchical relationships, the "proper" use of language in Mexico requires extensive knowledge of the special nuances of many words, along with skill in using them in the right way at the right time.

While Mexicans will generally forgive the misuse of these words by non-native speakers of their language, whose goodwill and good intentions are obvious, such mistakes nevertheless grate on their cultural sensibilities.

Two of the words that are most often misused by people in the early stages of learning Spanish are *tu* (too) and *usted* (oo-STED). *Tu* is the personal, intimate form of "you," generally used among family members and close friends who have peer relationships.

Usted is the formal word for "you," which is used when talking to a person in general, regardless of their social status, including acquaintances and others with whom one does not have an intimate relationship.

Mexicans (and other Hispanics) are very sensitive to the differences between *tu* and *usted*. It is important that they be used in a culturally acceptable manner, especially in situations that are themselves sensitive.

Usted can be used when talking to anyone under any circumstances, since it is both formal and polite. But *tu* is another matter. Using *tu* to a just-met senior businessperson, for example, could create a very awkward situation.

To further complicate matters, people in superior positions—real or assumed—often use *tu* to people who are "below them," and with whom they do not have an intimate relationship. This is deliberate and meant to put them down by treating them as too child-like to know what is good for them, or in an attempt to imply intimacy that does not really exist.

While this pretended intimacy may be harmless enough when used in neutral situations, some people use it as a subtle ploy to take advantage of others.

A notable example: *tu* has traditionally been used by people buying from or selling to Mexican Indians as a technique for downplaying the fair value of their labor and their products.

One aspect of this malicious treatment of Indians is that it is intended to make the Indians feel that concern with money is immoral, so that they will accept the idea that they should take less. Some unscrupulous people "good-naturedly" accuse their Indian victims of just wanting money in order to buy liquor or fire-crackers for a festival, with the connotation that those are "evil" things and the individual is "saving" the Indians from themselves by paying them less for their goods or services.

Knowing when one is able to begin addressing a new boyfriend or girl-friend as *tu* instead of *usted*, and not appear overly aggressive, requires an especially well-honed intuition—and sometimes a lot of courage.

The best thing to keep in mind if there is any doubt about which word to use is that you can't go too far wrong with *usted*.

Unión Libre
(Ooh-NYON LEE-bray)

"Living in Free Union"

Life in Mexico was historically charged with an extraordinary degree of sexuality. The natural sensuality of both males and females was emphasized in virtually every manner possible.

Young girls were primed to flirt and tease. Young boys were conditioned to aggressively pursue sexual relationships. At the same time, parents in all classes traditionally made a valiant effort to keep sexual knowledge from their daughters and to prevent them from engaging in sex before they were married.

Yet, particularly among lower classes, adults referred to sex constantly in their jokes, threats and discipline. Lower-class fathers and mothers habitually screamed at daughters who showed interest in boys, calling them sluts and whores. Girls in this class therefore tended to be perversely and viciously primed in sexuality. Although forbidden to indulge in sex on the pain of severe punishment, they were drawn to it and were constantly targeted by older boys and men whose advances could hardly be refused.

By the time boys reached the age of puberty they had long since learned that Mexican men considered women outside of their own family as instruments of sexual gratification. They began to emulate older men who looked upon women as material to be molded by their masculinity and imagination.

With the highly volatile sexuality of women sucking at their masculinity like magnets, most young men who did not have sexual access to house-maids, older female relatives or widows began visiting prostitutes by the time they reached their mid-teens.

Lower-class Mexican boys learned early that men regularly humiliated their wives and children as part of their masculine behavior, and that their fathers would abandon them for the slightest reason with no apparent qualms. They also learned to be silent and reserved in their father's presence. The older boys grew, the deeper the gulf between them and their fathers.

Unable to stand up to his father, a boy might begin taking his resentment out on his mother and sisters. Outside the house, young boys tended to have sunny, inquisitive dispositions. But after they passed puberty they began the terrible struggle to prove themselves as masculine men. Their friendly open manner was replaced by reserve, secretiveness, antagonism and sarcasm.

Some sociologists say that the hypersexuality of Mexican men in all social classes was a form of rebellion against the church and, in particular, against the virgin mother of Christ, who was historically presented as the symbolic mother of them all.

In any event, Mexican men have traditionally been contemptuous of the church, which is decidedly feminine—with virgins abounding—and blamed any bad luck they encountered on one or the other of the many female saints. On these occasions, men typically cursed the saints and called them whores.

During the revolution from 1910 to 1921 bands of Mexican rebels fre-quently demonstrated their contempt for female saints and religion in general by using local churches for organized sex parties with prostitutes.

The Catholic Church was also primarily responsible for as many as 50 percent of poor couples in Mexico traditionally choosing to live together in *unión libre* (ooh-NYON LEE-bray) or "free union," rather than marrying legally. The church charged such high fees for marriage licenses and wedding ceremonies that the people couldn't afford them.

There were also compelling social reasons why common-law marriages have been normal among Mexico's poorer classes. Open courtship was tra-ditionally forbidden throughout Mexico, resulting in an unusually large per-centage of marriages beginning as elopements. Unable to get the consent of both sets of parents, young couples often ran off and got married, or simply began living together at the homes of friends or sympathetic relatives if they could not afford a place of their own. Reconciliation with the parents sometimes took place within a few days or weeks, or sometimes never. In extreme cases in the past, the parents of the girls sued the boys.

Still today social authorities estimate that in some villages in Mexico more than half of the couples are in *unión libre*. Predictions are that the custom will remain an important factor in Mexican life as long as a significant proportion of the population exists at or below the poverty level, and the influence of the church and the masculinity cult remain essentially negative.

A sexual revolution has been going on in Mexico since around the 1960s. With the exception of some of the more traditional rural areas, young boys and girls are no longer segregated or watched over by chaperons. But many of the old traditions persist to varying degrees.

As a rule, adult Mexicans still today do not have any guilt feelings about sex. Men typically brag openly about their sexual conquests, and are particularly proud when they are able to seduce a girl or woman.

Mexican women still take delight in teasing men, and women in the lower classes tend to be contemptuous of them. Women in this category are said to look upon men as walking but brainless "male organs." These women, according to Mexican sociologists, fear rather than respect men.

The old idea that men and women cannot resist their sexual impulses is noticeably dying in urban Mexico, but in rural areas it still flourishes. Just as Mexican men in this category do not accept responsibility in sexual matters, they also habitually shift responsibility in other matters, laying the blame on an ephemeral "it" or "they."

Over the decades, a significant percentage of the Mexican men who have gone to the United States to work and stayed for a year or more have ended up establishing "free union" relationships with women in the United States.

134

Un Poquito
(Oon poh-KEE-toh)

"Just a Little Bitty Thing"

Another cultural habit that Mexicans share with Asians, the Japanese in particular, is in diminutizing things, but in this case with a very important twist.

The Japanese diminutize solid, tangible things in order to attract attention to them; primarily to emphasize the importance of the objects themselves, but sometimes to demonstrate their skill as well.

Mexicans diminutize happenings, events, ideas and other intangible things they want to deemphasize; things they want to present as unimportant and not worthy of attention.

In Japan the diminutization of arts and crafts was turned into an art within itself centuries ago. Japanese artists and artisans sought to eliminate all of the extraneous, all of the gaudy, all of the pretension from the things they created, and get down to their essence.

The ultimate goal of Japan's artists and artisans was to represent the whole world in a tiny garden, the heart of beauty in a tea cup or in a single flower, or a lifetime in the face of a clay figurine. In other words, to reveal the essence of things in a miniature and let viewers fill in all of the details from their own experience and imagination.

Japan's miniaturization impulse grew out of Buddhist and Shinto concepts of the cosmos, concepts that were totally humane in both physical and spiritual matters. It therefore contributed to the development of a far more benign cultural than what emerged in Mexico.

In contrast to the Japanese, until recent times, ordinary Mexicans were pawns in a culture—inherited from their Aztec and Spanish forbearers—based on inhumanities that had become institutionalized into religions. For more than 400 years Mexican society was molded by arrogant, oppressive religious leaders and government officials who, like their forbearers, stifled independent thought and action and routinely tortured and killed anyone who opposed them.

In order to survive emotionally and intellectually within this essentially savage society, Mexicans made intimate personal relationships and a highly refined and detailed etiquette the focus of their personal lives.

An important facet of this system was emphasizing style and form rather than substance, keeping things vague and uncertain, and downplaying anything that might attract attention and result in some kind of disharmony. Thus the Mexican impulse to diminutize grew out of a desperate need to humanize personal relationships and actions; to create an intimate world where they, and not the uncertain world at large, had control.

Mexican conversations and references are filled with the diminutives of words, some down to a second level. *Casa* (house) becomes *casita* (little house). *Un poco*, a little, becomes *un poquito* (oon poh-KEE-toh), a little tiny bit, and so on.

Foreigners need to remember this tendency to diminutize when invited to socialize in Mexico, because in a number of situations it has a typically Mexican reverse twist. *Un tequilata, una cervezita* and *un taquito* always mean "lots of!" instead of a "small amount" or a "little bit." Furthermore, when doing business or in everyday life, *un momentito* generally doesn't mean "just a little minute."

The Mexican rationale for using diminutives has two broad goals. One is to bring in a personal touch, to add intimacy to a relationship. The other is to reduce the importance of things, to bring them down to the point where they virtually disappear and one doesn't have to be, or shouldn't be, concerned with them.

It is this latter use that often creates problems for foreign businesspeople and others involved with Mexico. Things that outsiders consider important are routinely downplayed and frequently ignored by Mexicans as a part of their natural behavior, not because of any genuinely malicious intent.

From the North American viewpoint the Mexican tendency to diminutize things is obviously a major handicap, because it impacts directly and negatively on every level of business and politics, the two primary governors of change and progress.

The North American businessperson or politician who goes to Mexico with a proposition typically emphasizes how big, great, important and wonderful it is—as if he or she were looking at it through a magnifying glass.

His or her Mexican contacts, on the other hand, see the proposition through a demagnifying glass. The more money that it would cost them and the greater the risk, the smaller the proposition looks to them.

North Americans magnify things; Mexicans shrink them. The challenge is to find a happy medium.

135

Vaqueros
(Vah-KAY-rohs)

"The First Cowboys"

As the number of part-Spanish part-Indian mixed-bloods grew during the Spanish period in Mexico (1521–1821), some mixtures were allowed to work with and eventually own horses, and it was mixed-bloods, working for Spanish land-grant holders, who became the first American cowboys.

These cowboys, or *vaqueros* (vah-KAY-rohs), wore high crown hats woven from straw, jackets and pantaloons of deerskin and chaps made of goatskin. They carried serapes over their shoulders, and were armed with long, curved knives. This new breed of range men had adapted the fancy hats, trousers and other accessories of their Spanish overlords to fit the needs of a working cowboy, including the broad-brimmed hat, the pommeled saddle, high-heeled boots, tight trousers, gun-belts and bandannas.

Mexico's first "Wild West" was actually its "Wild North," the great Bajio Valley, between Mexico City and the dry Sonoran desert in the present state of Guanajuato,* which was later to play a vital role in the history of the country.

Early Spanish administrators, missionaries and, later, Mexican-born Spaniards started Mexico's first large cattle ranches in Bajio Valley; that is where the *mestizos* of Mexico first found themselves and began creating a world of their own.

The Guanajuato region of Bajio became almost totally cattle country, with hundreds of *ranchos*, some of them established by the despised mixed-blood *leperos* or "social lepers" from Mexico City.

Mestizos used as *vaqueros* by the cattle ranch owners in Bajio became master horsemen and fierce fighters with guns or knives, ready to kill to protect themselves and their honor.

---

*Horses brought into the northern regions of Mexico in the 1590s were stolen by Apache and Comanche Indians, and from there fell into the hands of the Plains Indians of North America, who created a whole new culture around them. The Plains Indians' prowess with horses played a key role in their battles against American settlers and military forces in the 1800s.

As the generations passed, "freelance" bands of these mixed-blood *vaqueros* roamed the cattle ranges of northern Mexico, looking for legitimate work when they could find it, and turning to rustling and banditry when they could not.

It is said that the *vaqueros* had three ambitions in life: to be expert horsemen, heroic bullfighters and great lovers.

On holidays and other occasions, *vaqueros* put on exhibitions of riding and roping, fighting bulls from horseback with long lances, driving their lances through tiny rings while galloping at full speed down a causeway, and racing alongside of bulls and throwing them to the ground by their tails or horns.

The new frontier allowed Indians and *mestizos* to become real men—as relatively free cowboys, shepherds and farmers—for the first time since the beginning of the Spanish period.

Over the generations, the Indians and mixed-bloods in Bajio basin merged, both racially and culturally. And it was these new *Norteños* or "Northerners," who began the creation of a new Mexican, a new race.

When the Spanish conquistadors and priests pushed their explorations into what is now Arizona, California, New Mexico and Texas, they were accompanied or soon followed by ranchers and *vaqueros*, so the first cowboys in what is now the American Southwest were Mexicans.

Catholic missionaries from Mexico taught horse-riding and cattle-raising to the Diegueño, Ipai and Tipai Indians of California in the 1700s.

It was the Valley of Bajio and the Sonoran deserts farther north that gave birth to most of the free-spirited and self-confident men, both *mestizo* and *criollo*, who were to take up the battle against Spain for Mexican independence in 1810; a hundred years later they began and finished a new revolution for political and social reform.

During the late 1800s and early 1900s northern Mexico was overrun by rogue *vaqueros* who had turned to rustling and banditry, and in 1910 became revolutionaries. Chief among them was Francisco "Pancho" Villa† (1877–1923), from the state of Chihuahua.

Villa was so successful as a revolutionary general that for several years the United States backed him with supplies and arms. By 1920 he was the

---

†Rustler-killer turned revolutionary, Pancho Villa's first army was made up of Yaqui warriors, the survivors of a once large tribe that had been hunted for generations by the *federales* and bounty killers. After the railroad workers of northern Mexico joined Villa's campaign, he housed his troops in railway boxcars—along with their wives, mistresses, children, goats and chickens—and thereafter used the trains to move troops around the countryside. A number of foreign journalists also became camp followers of Villa.

most famous revolutionary in northern Mexico (Emiliano Zapata‡ occupied the same status in southern Mexico), and was powerful enough to play a role in the selection of presidential candidates.

When a competing general, Alvaro Obregón, was selected as president in 1920, Villa was given an impressive hacienda estate in Chihuahua in exchange for his retirement from the battlefield.

He was assassinated in 1923 when returning to his hacienda after spending a night with a lady friend.

Mexican *vaqueros* predated by some 200 years the American cowboys who began roaming the West after northern Mexico was annexed by the United States in 1846/48, and especially following the end of the American Civil War in 1865.

The famous North American rodeo, popular in Arizona and other southwestern American states, was an invention of the *vaqueros*. And all those cowboy movies that have entertained the world since the 1930s owe a deep bow to the *vaqueros* of Mexico.

Here is just some of the cowboy terminology that originated with the *vaqueros* of Mexico:

Bronc, from *bronco*, meaning wild or rebel.

Buckaroo, from *vaquero*.

Chaps, from *chaparajos*.

Corral, from *corral*.

Lariat and lasso, from *lazo*.

Mustang, from *mesteno*.

Ranch, from *rancho*.

Rancher, from *ranchero*.

Rodeo, from *rodeo*.

---

‡Emiliano Zapata's life was ended in 1919 by order of President Venustiano Carranza. General Pablo Gonzalez, President Carranza's right-hand man, sent a Col. Jesus Guajardo into Zapata's territory, claiming to be a defector who wanted to join him. Gonzalez arranged for Guajardo and his troops to slaughter 59 government soldiers in a ploy to convince Zapata that the defection was genuine. Zapata agreed to meet with Guajardo in a nearby town.

On horseback, with half a dozen of his men, Zapata rode into an ambush of 600 riflemen concealed in and on buildings around the town square. When Zapata and his small group were well into the square, a squad of soldiers posing as an honor guard suddenly opened fire, riddling him with bullets. Guajardo was promoted and paid 50,000 pesos. The president who followed Carranza had Col. Guajardo executed.

======== 136 ========

Velorios
(Bay-LOH-ree-ohs)

"Laughing It Up at Wakes"

Mexicans have an irrepressibly macabre sense of humor which shows up in the oddest places and ways.

Almost everyone who has spent time in Mexico is familiar with the Day of the Dead Festival when people display, as well as eat, a variety of things representing death. It is a custom that literally mocks death.

Mexicans have traditionally used their peculiar sense of humor in the face of oppression, abuse, pain, hunger, disappointment and other conditions no doubt because they had no control over such events and could not change things. Why they choose humor to mitigate their suffering is not so easily explained, but it seems to be a worldwide human reaction, and not unique to Mexicans.

One occasion in Mexico when humor plays a significant, if rather bizarre, role is during *velorios* (bay-LOH-ree-ohs), or "wakes" for the dead.

Wakes are major events in Mexico and other Latin countries: they have long been famous for their good food, drinks and jokes.

It is customary for the wives of friends and neighbors of the deceased to bring food to the home of the family. Women invariably bring their best dishes. Other mourners bring a variety of alcoholic drinks.

This custom often attracts people who have no connection whatsoever with the deceased, but who make it a practice of crashing wakes to eat and drink. In some areas male college students on slim budgets have been known to attend as many *velorios* as possible in order to eat their fill of the free food.

It is also customary for men and women attending wakes to separate into all-male and all-female groups, and for the men to drink and tell jokes. It is said that the best jokes in Mexico and other Latin American countries are told at *velorios*.

Unlike some cultures in which family members of the deceased weep, scream and otherwise demonstrate their feelings at funerals, Mexicans are much more restrained. But some families do hire *planideras* (plah-nee-DAY-rahs) or "professional weepers," to cry and carry on at funerals.

Foreign businesspeople in Mexico who have been accepted by their Mexican employees or associates as *buena gente*, or "good people," may be invited to wakes and experience this facet of Mexican life directly.

137

Veteranos
(Vay-tay-RAH-nohs)

"The Border Hardcases"

Americans and Mexicans owe much of the image they have of each other to conditions along the U.S.–Mexican border, and from the events that take place there.

The American image of the border cities and their residents is primarily negative. Americans generally see the towns and cities as places to shop and to go for entertainment, including sex. Many of the Mexicans they encounter are hustlers, touts and other sleazy characters, which tends to give Americans a dim view of all Mexicans.

Mexican residents of border cities, on the other hand, tend to regard Americans, especially those who are young and who cross the border to drink, visit whorehouses and generally raise hell, as arrogant, loud-mouthed, ill-mannered, immoral, often stupid and easily duped.

"Neither side reflects long enough to realize that they are both reacting to exaggerated cultural differences rather than character weaknesses, and as a result the relationships are irrational and damaging to both parties," said a Mexican businessman.

He also observed that one of the reasons why the border cities were lagging behind the rest of Mexico in social and industrial development was that the negative impressions of the two sides—the Mexican and the American—tended to be self-fulfilling.

The businessman continued: "Americans think they are going to be cheated when they cross the border to shop, and they often are. Most of them never come back and end up badmouthing Mexico to their friends.

"Many Mexican shopkeepers and others along the border treat Americans like suckers who deserve to be taken. They try to get as much out of them as possible because they presume they will never come back. And the shopkeepers have so far been incapable of cooperating to change this mutually negative situation."

Among the worst elements on the Mexican side of the border are gangs that specialize in robbing both Mexicans and Americans. The Mexican victims of these gangs are usually people from the interior who have come to the border cities to look for work or attempt to enter the United States illegally.

Border authorities say that the biggest concentration of these gangs is in Tijuana, across from San Diego, where annual border crossings by shoppers, workers, sightseers and the curious run into the millions.

San Diego authorities add that the most dangerous and vicious of these Tijuana robber gangs are those called *veteranos* (vay-tay-RAH-nohs), or "veterans." These are young men in their late teens and early twenties who have been on the streets for 10 or more years, and who are noted for brutalizing their victims, sometimes killing them as casually as one swats a fly.

Because of their viciousness, *veteranos* are feared by everyone, including the Mexican police and younger youth gangs.

Insiders say that making eye contact with a *veterano* can be taken as a challenge, resulting in a vicious attack.

Violencia
(Vee-oh-LEN-cee-ah)

"Violence as a Way of Life"

Many societies in the Old World of Europe and Asia have been known for their violence; some of it state-sponsored and some of it growing out of the culture and character of the people themselves.

Some societies were literally based on violence. The people made their living by making war on their neighbors, killing the men, raping and enslaving the women and stealing their treasures, food and goods.

A number of the Indian nations of pre-Columbian Mexico used violence to sustain themselves as nations, to appease their gods, and to maintain conformity and order within their own societies.

The Spanish conquistadors who conquered Mexico in 1521 were also the progeny of a warlike society that was imbued with a penchant for bloody violence and which treated its enemies with the utmost cruelty, often destroying them totally.

To make things worse, the conquistadors who discovered and conquered Mexico looked upon the native inhabitants of the "New World" as literally subhumans, who could be abused and killed without any feelings of guilt or remorse, even though they were not enemies in the usual sense.

The political and economic systems that the Spanish imposed upon the surviving Indians of Mexico were based upon the use of force and brutal punishment. Indians who did not quickly surrender and obey the new Spanish warlords were just as quickly exterminated.

Spain's subsequent 300-year reign in Mexico was marked by policies and actions that dehumanized both the surviving Indians and the mixed-blood Spanish–Indian offspring, which were the result of wholesale miscegenation practiced by the Spanish administrators and thousands of Catholic priests.

Mistreatment of the Indians and mixed-bloods by the Spanish for generation after generation created in them a latent blood-lust which was eventually to engulf Mexico and make it one of the world's most violent countries.

The massive blood-letting and carnage during the long civil war between 1910 and 1921, and the religious uprising shortly afterward, had a cathartic effect on the survivors. But the lust for violence built up by the Spanish–Indian mixtures of Mexico over a period of some 400 years has not totally disappeared.

Mexican historians now label the period from 1910 to 1940 as Mexico's "era of violence." Small-scale uprisings, political murders and senseless killings by drunken men, rural bandits, urban criminals, the military and the police were everyday occurrences during this period.

Violence on a personal and small scale is still endemic in Mexican society but the majority of the people now greet it with outrage rather than a fatalistic shrugging of the shoulders, and it is gradually subsiding.

In the 1990s one of the most notorious new forms of violence was a rash of kidnappings and ransoming of wealthy businessmen, which, in turn, resulted in a rush by ranking industrialists to buy armored cars.

Colombia is another Latin American country in which violence, particularly wanton murder on an immense scale, has been endemic since the days of the Spanish conquistadors.

According to newspaper accounts there is, and has been for centuries, a murder in Colombia every 20 minutes, nearly 10 times the going rate in the United States. Colombia's Nobel laureate writer Gabriel Garcia Marquéz traced this phenomenon to the Spanish conquest, following which violence became a way of life for the surviving Indians and Spanish–Indian mixed-bloods.

Garcia Marquéz went on to say that the penchant for violence in Colombia (known simply as *La Violencia*) preceded the appearance of the Colombian drug cartels in the 1970s, pointing out that between 1946 and 1966 more than 200,000 Colombians were murdered. He blamed the murder rate in Colombia on the failure of the country's mixed-blood population to come to terms with its racial and ethnic heritage.

Mexico's mixed-blood people are coming to terms with their own *mestizo* origins, not only because they are the overwhelming majority in the country, but also because there are fewer barriers to social mobility in Mexico than what exists in other Latin American nations. In today's Mexico, *mestizos* occupy many seats of power and are constantly visible to the public.

Indications are that political and economic reforms initiated by the Mexican government in the 1990s will further purge the country of the tendency of *violencia* that has plagued its culture like an evil virus for centuries.

Zonas de Tolerancia
(ZOH-nahs day Toh-lay-RAHN-cee-ah)

"They Are Prettier at Night"

While in Nogales, Sonora, some years ago, I asked about the city's famous red-light district on Canal Street, located in a narrow hollow a few minutes from the downtown area. I was advised not to go there until after dark because it looked "much prettier at night."

Red light and "blue light" (unlicensed) districts were a conspicuous and popular feature of virtually every Mexican town and city from the days of the Spanish era (1521–1821) down to modern times. (Until recent times, one of the attractions of major *fiestas* and fairs were *carpas* or "tents" set up to house "traveling" prostitutes.)

Prior to reforms in the 1900s, any Mexican female over the age of 15 could apply for a license to work as a prostitute. Records show that during the revolutionary period from 1910 to 1921, the number of licensed prostitutes swelled to around 10 percent of all females in the country who were between the ages of 15 and 30.

By the early 1920s venereal diseases were so common in Mexico that one doctor declared there was no more danger of them spreading further because the whole population was saturated with them. In 1926 the Mexican government estimated that 60 percent of the population had syphilis.

During this period, prostitutes in Mexico City wore images of the Virgin of the Soledad around their necks to protect them from VD. According to regular patrons of prostitutes, every workroom in every red-light district or whorehouse in the country had its religious icons.

White slavery was an ugly fact of life in Mexico throughout its early history, and did not begin to dwindle until the 1960s. One of the more notorious cases that decade involved three sisters who bought and sold more than 2,000 girls and maintained a "death camp" where recalcitrant girls were tortured and killed. The sisters' favorite torture technique was to force a girl to lie down on a board, wrap her in barbed wire and leave her there for several days. They referred to this fiendish device as the "Royal Bed."

Prostitution is legal in most Mexican states and it flourishes in *Zonas de Tolerancia* (ZOH-nahs day toh-lay-RAHN-cee-ah), or "Zones of Tolerance," in areas where it is not legal. In Mexico City the typical whorehouse is a large home in a residential or semiresidential district that, except for the traffic, is indistinguishable from other homes in the neighborhood.

The bulk of the house customers in Mexico City are Mexican businessmen from out of the city and students in from the provinces. The next most conspicuous group of patrons are American and Japanese tourists.

Whorehouses in red-light districts generally operate under the transparent guise of nightclubs with hostesses, where men come to drink, eat and dance. Patrons are expected to drink and sometimes eat as well before making use of one of the rooms in back with the woman of their choice.

Prices of drinks and food are four or five times more expensive in the "clubs" than in regular bars or restaurants—the bar and food bill often cost more than 30 minutes with one of the hostesses.

Despite usually vigorous efforts by the hostesses to stimulate patrons while they are drinking and dancing, by using both their hands and bodies to massage them, not all patrons of the clubs are there for sex. Some go just for the atmosphere, using the clubs as places to meet for business discussions or to titillate visiting friends or businessmen.

One also sometimes sees older men in the clubs with teenage boys. The men are usually uncles or friends of the family, escorting the young men to the districts for their first sexual experience.

Like their Spanish forbearers, modern-day Mexican men consider sex a personal thing that has nothing to do with the church or society at large. To them sex is an expression of their maleness, which must be exercised regularly.

Not only has this attitude resulted in entirely different standards for men and women, it also forces people to maintain a two-faced attitude toward sex for the benefit of their public image.

Everybody knows that the whorehouses are there, but they pretend not to see them. Pornographic magazines cannot be imported into the country, but virtually every Mexican magazine has its seminude or nude photographs.

Women who work as prostitutes range in age from their midteens to their early thirties. Older women are usually widows, divorcees or abandoned wives. Most of them come from provincial villages and towns in the poorer areas of the country.

Younger women working as prostitutes commonly say they intend to return to their villages or towns to get married or start some kind of business after they save enough money.

Women taking up the profession are instructed in how to have safe sex (they also physically examine each patron in advance), and are required to have clinical examinations weekly. But VD remains a constant threat to anyone patronizing the *Zonas de Tolerancia*.

GLOSSARY

Mexican Spanish contains an especially rich collection of both obscenities and slang words, and it is virtually impossible to get inside the cultural skin of the country without knowing many of these terms in their fullest cultural sense.

All segments of Mexican society, from the underworld to teenagers, as well as regionally throughout the country, have their own special slang.

Numerous historical terms that are no longer in daily use continue to be of interest because they refer to attitudes and behavior that are still very much a part of Mexican culture.

There are, of course, hundreds of additional everyday Spanish words that have special meanings in their cultural context and are essential to understanding the character, personality and behavior of Mexicans. Here are some of the most important ones in all of these categories:

A chaleco (ah chah-LAY-coh)—Something that is obvious; that should be, or must be, done. Something that is said more often than it is done; often used in reference to commitments made by businesspeople.

Acordados (ah-cor-DAH-dohs)—A special police force established in the 18th century to battle growing legends of *leperos* ("social lepers") or *mestizo* bandits. The *acordados* were authorized to immediately execute all captured mixed-blood bandits. The special forces soon began crucifying their prisoners rather than killing them outright, nailing them to crosses erected along busy roadways and intersections, so that it took them several days to die. Victims were also executed by being hung from tree branches along roads, their bodies left to rot and to vultures. The *acordados* no longer exist, but some of their attitudes and behavior can still be seen in Mexico's police.

Aficionado (ah-fee-see-oh-NAH-doh)—A fan, an ardent devotee or admirer. International television has made most of the world familiar with the reaction of Latins to sporting events, from soccer and boxing to bullfights. Many Mexican *aficionados* of entertainers, movie stars, sports figures and so on, take their enthusiasm to the point that it virtually becomes a cult. Mexicans take great pride in being *aficionados* of some art or sport, and delight in demonstrating their knowledge. There is also a particular breed of fans called *fanaticos* (fanatics), who regularly resort to violence to vent their anger or joy.

Ahora (ah-ORR-rah)—Dictionaries and Spanish language books translate *ahora* as "now," but old-timers say there is no true concept of "now," meaning at this very instant or moment, in Mexican culture; that in the Mexican context of things, *ahora* means "sometime, maybe soon." *Ahorita* is widely used in the sense of "in a moment."

A huevo (ah WHAY-voh)—A slang phrase meaning "by balls," or "by force." A reference to the propensity for members of the *pachuco* subgroup of young Mexican-American males to use force to get what they want. In colloquial terms, it means "this is the way it is going to be and that is final."

Albur (ahl-BOORR)—Literally, something that has a double meaning. When used in reference to a business venture it means there are no guarantees; that it may go either way, up or down. In a colloquial sense it also means "if you are lucky," a phrase that one often hears in Mexico because so many aspects or factors in life cannot be controlled.

Alcahuetes (ahl-cah-WHEY-tehs)—This old word has several primary uses. In one it refers to women (often widows) who hire themselves out as go-betweens for young boys and girls seeking romantic liaisons. These women may also be known as *correvedile*, which means to "run-see-and-tell." The occupation is not without its risks. A boy rejected by a girl he has never met and whose name he doesn't know may feel so insulted that he will attack the girl to get revenge, or attempt to blacken her reputation by telling lies about her. In another context it refers to pimps or procurers and whoremongers. It may also mean a stupid person, a bad-acting person or a person who covers up the wrong-doing of others.

Alegria (ah-lay-GREE-ah)—Joy—the convivial, ebullient attitude that is characteristic of Mexicans most of the time; a constant festive mood that is typical of people when they are eating, drinking and talking with friends. Unrestrained happiness.

Angeles Verdes (AHN-hay-lehs BAYR-dehs)—These are Mexico's famed "Green Angels," a radio-dispatched fleet of automobile repair trucks with bilingual drivers who patrol sections of the country's most highly traveled tourist highways from 8 A.M. to 9 P.M. daily, except Tuesday mornings. Operated by the Mexican Tourism Administration, the Green Angel mechanics provide free service to motorists in distress, but they charge for fuel and any parts used. They also expect to be tipped. There are roadside emergency phones within the areas covered by the *Angeles Verdes*, with a toll-free 24-hour number to Central Dispatch.

Ánimo (AH-nee-moh)—Courage, fortitude, spirit—the ideal Mexican character—which allows them to survive any challenge. No matter how poor and mean their existence, *ánimo* helps them find pleasure in simple things and be joyful at heart. Hope.

Bajarselo (bah-hahrr-SAY-loh)—To cheat someone out of something by trickery. Often used in reference to shady deals in business when one side loses.

Ballena (bah-YEH-nah)—Men in some of Mexico's southern tribes prefer their women conspicuously plump if not fat, whereas most Mexicans, particularly those in the northern states, like their women shapely but svelte. In northern Mexico and in Mexican-American border communities, a really fat woman is often referred to as a *ballena* or "whale."

Bandoleros (bahn-doh-LAY-rohs)—Bandits. The first bandits in Mexico were *mestizos* (Spanish–Indian mixed-bloods), who took to the jungles and mountains in the 1700s because of their "leper" status, the harsh rule of the Spanish overlords and lack of job opportunities. In the early 1800s bandits turned revolutionaries played key roles in winning Mexico's independence from Spain. Again in the early 1900s, such bandits as Pancho Villa became leaders in the civil war against the entrenched military and clergy that had ruled Mexico for the previous 100 years. There are still occasional reports of *bandoleros* in various parts of Mexico.

Baño (BAH-nyo)—This is a generic word for restroom or toilet. As in English, there are a number of euphemisms for toilet, both refined and vulgar, but this word is all you need to locate one. In hotels and other public buildings, most toilets are labeled *Damas* (Ladies) or *Caballeros* (Gentlemen). Some are designated *WC*, which stands for "water closet." If it is followed by an "M" keep in mind that this does not stand for "Men" but for *Mujeres*, which means "Women."

Barrio (BAH-ree-oh)—Originally a city district (ward or quarter). Now often used in reference to tenement housing, where families of up to 10 or 12 people may live in one or two rooms and share a single toilet, often with other families as well. Also, a ghetto-like Hispanic neighborhood or area where poor people live.

Bilis (BEE-lees)—Literally "bile," *bilis* refers to a variety of ailments that have traditionally been endemic in Mexico—headaches, stomachaches, dizziness and a general feeling of malaise. They are said to have been brought on by unrequited anger, frustration, embarrassment and other strong emotional feelings. The same complaints are still common in Mexico and are still attributed to the same psychological causes. Used in the sense of "becoming angry."

Blanco (BLAHN-coh)—A person who is white or very light-skinned. Despite laws prohibiting discrimination on the basis of skin color, the lighter the skin of Mexicans the greater the social, economic and political advantages they have. Some nine percent of the population of Mexico is regarded as pure "white" or mostly white.

Bodegas (boh-DAY-gahs)—These are warehouse-style volume discount stores that specialize in selling merchandise to the working class and others with low incomes. Some of these stores specialize in selling single categories of merchandise, such as drugs, furniture and toys— the so-called "category killer" stores.

Bola de rateros (BOH-lah day rah-TAY-rohs)—"Gang of thieves," a term often used to describe the police, as well as politicians and bureaucrats. A significant percentage of Mexican police, in particular, have histori- cally engaged in criminal activity, extorting money from people through various pressure techniques such as robbing them at gunpoint, kidnap- ping and killing. It was not until the Salinas and Zedillo administrations (1988–1994 / 1994–2000) that the government began trying to reform the country's police departments, a process that will no doubt take generations to accomplish since it requires a fundamental change in Mexican morality in concert with basic economic and political reforms.

Borrachera (boh-rah-CHAY-rah)—A "drinking binge," something that apparently goes all the way back to the time of the Aztecs when— except for the elderly and ill—public consumption of alcoholic drinks was restricted by law to festivals and other specific events, with death the penalty for breaking the law. This led to men going on *borracheras* during legal drinking occasions. The goal of such binges was to drink as much as possible, usually in a riotous manner, eat copious amounts of food and sometimes have lots of sex—before falling unconscious. The custom, only slightly more "civilized," is still common in present-day Mexico, and foreigners who get caught up in a group hell-bent on engag- ing in a *borrachera* may find it difficult to refuse, especially if they are customers or potential customers. The Mexicans are apt to take such a refusal as a slight. About the only way to extricate oneself from such a situation is to claim a serious medical problem that precludes heavy drinking, and then not give in to the pressure to drink anyway.

Bromas (BROH-mahs)—Jokes. Mexicans are inordinately fond of jokes, and often the more macabre the better. Psychologists relate this to the cen- turies of oppression and violence that made them fatalistic, and inclined to see humor in the hardships they were forced to endure. *Bromistas* are people who like to make fun of others.

Buena presentación (BWAY-nah pray-sen-tah-see-OWN)—This literally means "good presentation," and refers to one of the most important factors in job-hunting in Mexico. It refers not only to one's appearance insofar as clothing and grooming are concerned, but also to overall demeanor, manners and speech. In Mexico one's *presentación* generally takes precedence over other qualifications.

Buena Vibra (BWAY-nah VEE-brah)—Good vibes, good feelings, good mood. Often used in reference to people who inspire such feelings. A very important ingredient in person-to-person relations in Mexico. Mexicans are very sensitive to the "vibrations" given off by others—something that is especially important when they are sizing up a possible business relationship with foreigners, because they have a natural inclination to be suspicious and wary of the character and motives of outsiders.

Buey (bway)—Literally an ox or bullock, *buey* has a number of possible meanings when used in reference to a person, including "eunuch," "dumb ox," "brawn but no brains" and so on. In northern Mexico it is often used among men in a jocular rather than insulting manner. *Buey* is also the Mexican equivalent of "bastard." A man who allows himself to be cheated is often mocked with this word.

Burro (BOO-roh)—Literally, this is the sturdy and stubborn little animal that played a vital role in the history of Mexico as a beast of burden (and in more recent times as something for tourists to take pictures of). It is also a highly descriptive term for someone who is especially dumb. In *pachuco* argot, the group or gang with which one pals around may be referred to as a *burrada*, a drove of donkeys or asses.

Cacique (cah-SEE-keh)—This term originally referred to a hereditary Indian chief. It now refers to a village headman or local boss, including political leaders and leaders of groups or farmers or ranchers. During much of Mexico's post-Cortés history, Mexican-born Spanish *caciques* maintained their own gangs of *pistoleros*, just like later-day rogue cattlemen of the American West. Some large landowners and businessmen still have bodyguards and enforcers who are commonly called *pistoleros*. Local and regional *caciques* control much of the political and economic activity that goes on in their areas. They are especially powerful in the state of Veracruz and in the states making up the Yucatan Peninsula.

Calaveras (cah-lah-BAY-rahs)—Skeletons or skulls; the images and replicas of skulls and skeletons used in Mexico to mark the Day of the Dead. The same word is also used in reference to people who are especially skinny—walking skeletons as it were. Politicians and other public figures are often depicted in cartoons as *calaveras*.

Calentura (cah-len-TUH-rah)—Literally, warmth or a fever; sometimes used when people pretend to be ill just to avoid work, and to con people into pampering them. Also used in the sense of sexually "hot," or horny.

Caliente (cah-lee-EN-teh)—When used in reference to men and women *caliente* means sexually "hot." It has historically been applied to politicians who have traditionally used their official power to consort with many women.

Camarillas (cah-mah-REE-yahs)—Political cliques surrounding a leader who aspires to office. Such groups are especially common in Mexico because power has traditionally been based on surrounding oneself with loyal followers.

Camatear (cah-mah-TAY-ahr)—This is one of some 20 slang words that are the equivalent of "to screw" (have sexual intercourse with) used in various parts of Mexico and the Hispanic community along the U.S.–Mexican border. Others include *cochar, echar, jodar, puchar, coher* and *tronar*. It is also used in reference to someone who is provoking trouble.

Camote (cah-MOH-tay)—A sweet potato. Also a young man who avoids responsibility and thinks only of his own selfish pleasures. Also, the male organ, a person with red hair or a girlfriend. It is also used in reference to a big problem.

Cantina (cahn-TEE-nah)—A relatively low-class bar, with "bat-wing" swinging doors that traditionally catered exclusively to men. Until recently, the only women seen in *cantinas* were prostitutes. Now a few female patrons may be seen slumming in some of the more upscale *cantinas*. In keeping with the whimsical character of the men who patronize *cantinas*, the bars often have colorful and humorous names.

Cantinflesco (cahn-teen-FLEHS-coh)—Cantinflas was a comedian who became a legend in his own time. A combination of the U.S.'s Red Skelton and Danny Kay, Cantinflas had a trademark act in which he put on amazing demonstrations of talking big about something without ever actually saying anything at all. His skits portraying politicians were especially popular. A "Cantinflesco" is a person who talks a lot but doesn't say anything.

Cárcel (CAR-cell)—Jail; a place to be avoided anywhere, but especially in Mexico. In earlier times, people who were jailed for any offense could buy themselves out if they—or their families or friends—had the going price. The custom is still common, although political pressure generally prevents notorious prisoners from buying their way out. Whatever the crime or political circumstances, being able to pay off jailers and guards results in far more lenient treatment and many privileges. On the humanitarian side, long-term Mexican prisoners are usually permitted to have conjugal visits from wives and girlfriends.

Cargos (CAR-gohs)—Village offices—mayor, secretary, treasurer, police officers—that are rotated on an annual basis among residents recommended for the positions. Traditionally, holders of the positions are not paid. One of the most important of these *cargo* offices in Indian and Indianized *mestizo* villages in the state of Chiapas is the one in charge of conducting religious ceremonies. Individuals appointed to this position must spend weeks to months during their one-year tenure preparing for the various events; not only taking time away from their own work, but also paying whatever costs are incurred. *Cargos* is also another word for "charges."

Carteristas (car-tay-REES-tahs)—"Wallet-boys" or "pickpockets." Public events such as bullfights, festivals and religious pilgrimages bring out scores of *carteristas*, many of whom are young boys trained by modern-day Fagins. Pickpockets also work crowded buses and subways. It also refers to burglars who specialize in stealing wallets.

Caudillos (cau-DEE-yohs)—Charismatic military and political strongmen who rise to power by the force of their personalities and arms. For more than a hundred years, politics in Mexico was dominated by such men, including Santa Ana, Porfirio Díaz, Pancho Villa and other self-appointed "generals."

Causa (COW-sah)—The standard meaning of *causa* is cause or origin, as well as movement in a political sense. It is best known as part of the slogan, *Chicanos por la Causa*, which was made famous by Hispanic activists working to improve the social and economic situations of Mexican Americans.

Cayetanas (cah-yeh-TAH-nahs)—This is a "code word" referring to apple cider that is disguised by being sold in a beer bottle. It is ordered by cabaret hostesses, prostitutes and others who get commissions from drinks but who don't want to drink alcohol themselves. If they really want to drink hard liquor they order a *pisto*.

Cementeros (say-men-TAY-rohs)—"Glue addicts." Mostly very young homeless boys along the U.S. border, particularly Tijuana, who are the sons of prostitutes and other women who abandoned them or were killed. Individual *cementeros* specialize in luring tourists into dark alleys, where they are attacked, robbed and sometimes killed by half a dozen or more gang members using knives, sharpened screwdrivers and metal pipes as their weapons.

Cena (SAY-nah)—This is the Spanish word for a full or "heavy" supper or dinner, usually associated with a special occasion such as a wedding or entertaining guests, and normally eaten late in the evening—between 8 and 10 P.M. The normal evening meal is a light "snack" called a *merienda* (may-ree-EN-dah), which may be eaten as early as 6 or 7 P.M. and as late as 11 P.M.

Chaquetero (chah-kay-TAY-roh)—A *chaquetero* is someone who is without scruples or morals. In the past the term was most commonly associated with government officials, bureaucrats and law enforcement agents. Now it is also frequently used in connection with people involved in get-rich-quick business schemes.

Chava (CHAH-vah)—Mexico City slang for girl or girlfriend, used by barrio men.

Chavo (CHAH-voh)—Mexico City slang for kid, boy or boyfriend.

Chavos banda (CHAH-vohs BAHN-dah)—Boys' gang. There are said to be well over half a million gang members in Mexico City alone. Some of the gangs number in the hundreds, and virtually control areas of the city.

Chichis (CHEE-chees)—"Tits" (female breasts). Interestingly, *chi chi* is also Japanese slang for tits. Other slang Spanish terms with the same meaning: *chicheros, pelotas, chichonas*—the latter means "big tits."

Chihuahua (chee-WAH-wah)—One of Mexico's northern states, this word is also used in northern Mexico as an exclamation of surprise or dismay, similar to "Jesus Christ!" "Holy cow!" "Wow!" "Holy shit!" "Damn it !"

Chilangos (chee-LAHN-gohs)—A derogatory term frequently applied to residents of Mexico City by people in other cities, towns and villages, who feel that Mexico City gets an unfair share of all tax revenues and other government benefits. The depth of the feelings toward Mexico City residents is indicated by such bumper sticker slogans as: "Do a good deed; kill a *Chilango!*"

Chiquito (chee-KEE-toh)—Anything small, including a boy. Women, especially bar girls and street girls, wanting to put a man down may refer to his penis as *chiquito.*

Chismoso (cheez-MOH-soh)—A "tattletale." One common use of the word is in reference to students who tell on other students who cheated on their exams. Many Mexicans consider this kind of "ratting" by another student a greater crime than cheating on examinations because of the mindset that no one, under virtually any circumstances, should cooperate with the authorities or the establishment in general, and that anyone who can "beat" the system is to be praised rather than condemned. Mexicans have traditionally gone out of their way to cheat on "the system" because they had so few rights and were powerless to change it.

Cholos (CHOH-lohs)—*Cholo* now generally refers to hoods or street toughs who specialize in intimidating and robbing people, particularly along the U.S.–Mexican border. *Cholo* was originally used in reference to a Spanish–Indian half-breed. Later, it was expanded to include Indians who adopted the "Mexican" way of living. In more contemporary times, it came to be a label for Chicano street-gang members and pimps, and as a derogatory term for "low-riders" and Mexican Americans in general. *Cholos* typically wear a particular style of dress that identifies them.

Chula (CHOO-lah)—A term of affection (and affectation) similar to the way some Southerners and movie stars use the term "darling."

Cinco de Mayo (SEEN-coh day MAH-yoh)—May 5 marks the day in 1867 when the Mexican army defeated the last of the French forces that were occupying the country. It is one of the most important annual holidays in Mexico. The date and its celebration have great emotional significance for Mexicans; it is also widely celebrated by Mexican Americans.

Ciudades perdidas (see-oo-DAH-days per-DEE-dahs)—"Lost cities," it refers to makeshift settlements, some of them huge, on the outskirts of cities. They consist mostly of shacks made of cardboard, scrap wood and tarpaper. (See **colonia**.)

Cocos (COH-cohs)—In its *pachuco* context, *cocos* refers to Mexican Americans who have turned their backs of their native culture—they are brown on the outside but white on the inside. It is also used to mean female breasts or tits, the head, the brain, the mind, someone who is crazy, a sore and a sore scab. In its original Nahuatl form (*cocoliztli*) *coco* had a wide variety of meanings, from coconut to an infection or illness.

Colas (COH-lahs)—A *cola* is not a drink, but a line-up, a queue, of people waiting for transportation, to get some kind of service at a desk or window and so on. The good manners that Mexicans are noted for in social situations often does not apply to *colas*. People who are used to getting their own way, either by gall or muscle, frequently force their way into queues at or near the front.

Colectivos (coh-leck-TEE-vohs)—These are airport and city passenger vans or taxis that act more like minibuses; they run on established routes and carry several passengers with different destinations. *Colectivos* have regular stops but they will generally pick up passengers who flag them down at in-between places, especially if they are not packed full. Many passengers who ride the same *colectivos* every day become known to the drivers and may get special treatment. These licensed but privately operated minibuses are cheaper than regular cabs and city buses. (See **Combis, Peseros**.)

Colgados (cohl-GAH-dohs)—During the 18th and 19th centuries military and police forces in Mexico routinely used terror to intimidate the population and keep people passive. One of the ways they did this was to use the branches of roadside trees to kill people by hanging, leaving their bodies on the trees until they rotted; thus *colgados* or "the hanging ones."

Colonia (coh-LOH-nee-ah)—Originally a subdivision in and around a major city, with full city services and facilities. Now, squatter settlements on the outskirts of towns and cities are sometimes referred to as *colonias*. Like the *cuidades perdidas*, housing in these settlements usually consists of huts made from cardboard, scrap wood, metal and sometimes tarpaper. Many *colonias* are totally without modern utility services or facilities of any kind. They are noted as places of frequent violence and heavy drinking by male residents.

Combis (COHM-bees)—These are mini shuttle buses that operate between airports and city hotels. They charge set fares which are usually lower than taxi fares. There is an extra charge if you call for a personal pickup. In Mexico City such privately owned passenger vans have traditionally been called *peseros*. They have established routes and fares. When passengers want to get off, they push a button, if there is one, or call out *baja* (BA-hah), which means "down" (instead of "off").

Comida corrida (coh-ME-dah coh-REE-dah)—A full-course meal at a fixed price, generally available at both middle- and upper-class restaurants throughout Mexico.

Como Mexico no hay dos!—(COH-moh MAY-hee-coh no eye dohs)— Literally, "Like Mexico, there aren't two!" In other words, "There is no place like Mexico!" A common saying that is quite true, it is an expression of pride in being Mexican.

Consentido (cohn-sen-TEE-doh)—"Favored one:" It refers to a person who has been singled out by the president or some other ranking individual to become his heir; or favored for some other key position that is due to open up.

Cremosos (cray-MOH-sohs)—Used as a slang term in reference to young boys in Guadalajara who act like they are "smooth," "cool" or "cocks of the walk." The literal meaning is "creamies."

Criada (cree-AH-dah)—A female servant. In earlier times male members of most Mexican families assumed sexual rights to their female servants. The custom has not totally disappeared. Foreigners visiting Mexican homes with servants are advised to treat them with formal respect, but not like members of the family. It is bad etiquette for guests to request or order things from a *criada* directly. Proper protocol is for guests to ask the lady of the house for whatever it is they want. (See **Las gatas.**)

Cruda (CROO-dah)—A hangover; also a woman suffering from the effects of one.

Crudo (CROO-doh)—A man with a hangover.

Cuate (KWAH-tay)—Usually translated as "buddy" or "pal" this term literally means "twin," suggesting that the relationship between two men is a deeply emotional one, more on the order of the ancient Indian custom of forming "blood-brother" ties than mere friendship.

Cuaycura (kway-COO-rah)—A liqueur made from the damiana plant, which reportedly has aphrodisiac effects. It is one of the more popular liquor items bought by foreigners in towns and cities bordering the United States. (See **Damiana.**)

Cucaracha (coo-cah-RAH-chah)—In addition to meaning "cockroach," this versatile term was formerly used as a nickname for women with dark complexions and for women who followed soldiers during Mexico's revolution. Along the U.S.-Mexican border it was also used in reference to skinny women, beat-up cars and people who smoked marijuana. It may also be used to mean just "girl" or a "low-life."

This term is also used in reference to the pooling of resources by a group of people, usually not related, to share the cost of renting a single room or residence and buying food. The inference, of course, is that they live like cockroaches in a single nest. It is commonly used by Mexicans who are in the United States illegally and are trying to save as much of their income as possible in order to send more money to their families in Mexico.

Cuilchilete (kweel-chee-LAY-tay)—Literally, a man with a long penis. Figuratively, a man who is stingy and controls all of the family income.

Damiana (dah-me-AH-nah)—A long time ago Indians who live in the Sonoran Desert regions of northern Mexico learned that chewing on a plant, now known as *damiana*, had an almost immediate stimulating effect on the brain, and that it was particularly effective as a treatment for muscular and nervous disorders.

The plant reportedly had a side effect that made it even more popular as a pick-me-up. It was said to produce a rather dramatic surge in both sexual desire and potency, something that was guaranteed to make it a staple in the medicine man's little brown bag. Not surprisingly, this is one old folk remedy that has survived into modern times, and is now the root of a major industry in Mexico—the production of a liquer known as *Cuaycura* or *Licor de Damiana*.

Decente (de-CEN-tay)—This word is translated as "decent." The challenge is to keep in mind that being "decent" in Mexican culture means abiding by all of the social etiquette and obligations that make up Mexican culture, from the "proper" use of speech to fulfilling personal and public obligations in all of their specific Mexican nuances.

Defensora popular (day-fen-SOH-rah poh-poo-LAR)—A paralegal who helps poor women who have been battered and/or abandoned by their husbands, or have other legal problems. Mexican social authorities say that close to half of all husbands in poor families leave their first wives before they reach middle age.

Derechos humanos (day-RAY-chohs hoo-MAH-nohs)—Human rights. History has shown that human rights are recognized and protected only in democracies. Genuine democracy did not begin to appear in Mexico until the 1990s, and it still has a long way to go. The authoritarian nature of Mexican culture is at its worst in the legal and justice systems, and until the culture itself is significantly changed, human rights in Mexico will suffer the consequences. *Derechito*, the diminutive of *derecho*, is commonly used in reference to business deals that are "straight," not "crooked."

Desmadre (des-MAH-dray)—Literally "upheaval" or "chaos," this term is used in reference to the social, political and economic changes—most of which are positive—that are occurring in Mexico. It is also used in everyday language to mean "a mess."

Dia del Grito (DEE-ah dehl GREE-toh)—The "Day of the Cry" for independence from Spain, first sounded in 1810 by the priest Miguel Hidalgo. Mexicans mark the occasion by staging drinking parties and other festivities on the eve of September 16; precisely at midnight they shout *Viva Mexico!* ("Long Live Mexico!"). It is a very emotional event that is celebrated with considerable gusto.

Doble jornadas (DOH-blay hohr-NAH-dahs)—"Double days," which refers to Mexican women who work full time and then have to do the cooking, housecleaning, laundry and other domestic chores at night and on holidays and weekends. Also *jornadas doble*.

Dompe (DOME-apy)—This is border slang for garbage or trash dumps. Larger border cities like Tijuana have one or more *dompes* that are "inhabited," like villages or towns, by people who make their living by scavenging. Some of the large dumps have "bosses" or "mayors" who use hired gunmen to force "residents" into paying fees for working the dumps. There are social "ranks" in some of the dump towns, with those on the bottom being outcasts even among the other untouchables.

El mandamas (ehl mahn-DAH-mahs)—Figuratively, "The man who has the last word," or the man who has the most power. In colloquial speech, Mexicans often use this term instead of the formal title of the individual concerned.

El Norte (ehl NOR-tay)—Literally, "The North." Figuratively, "The United States of America."

El otro cachete (ehl OH-troh cah-SHEH-tay)—Literally, "the other cheek." Also used by people along the U.S.-Mexican border to mean "the other side" of the border.

El otro lado (ehl OH-troh LAH-doh)—"The other side"—the United States.

Enamorado (eh-nah-moh-RAH-doh)—A boy who is girl crazy. It also means to be in love.

Enamoramiento (eh-nah-moh-rah-me-EN-toh)—The "love-look" boys and girls give each other during the *paseo* and on other occasions when they are trying to communicate their romantic interest by facial expressions. It connotes a feeling that is not going to last.

Encerrones (en-ceyr-ROH-nehs)—Literally "lock-outs," this word is also used in reference to group sex parties, something that insiders say are common among employees of *maquiladoras* (foreign-owned companies in Mexico, just across from the U.S. border). It also refers to a private gathering.

Enchufe (en-CHOO-fay)—In standard usage this is an electrical "plug" or "outlet." It also means "connections" in the form of personal relationships with people, something that one must have to get things done in Mexico.

En la onda (en lah OWN-dah)—Cool; with it.

En tramite (en TRAH-me-tay)—This means "in process," and is a term that is constantly used by government officials, bureaucrats and others to explain why something has not been done. The practice of leaving things *en tramite* for long periods of time is so common that it has become an institutionalized part of Mexican life. Until recent decades, few Mexicans dared to protest about the practice because they knew that it would only delay things further, and if they persisted it could have serious consequences.

Entrona (en-TROH-nah)—This is border slang for a women who is conspicuously brave and aggressive in whatever she does, from work to sex. A woman who really puts her heart into things.

Fandango (fahn-DAHN-go)—A community dance held on weekends, usually Sunday evenings; also birthday parties and weddings in some Mexican states, notably Hidalgo, San Luis Potosi and Veracruz. Women often perform this energetic dance without male partners, putting on passion-arousing shows that are certain to enflame the men. In earlier times, it was customary for men to recite poetry aloud at the parties as a way of impressing women with their ardor and talents. *Fandangos* are normally accompanied by a lot of drinking, and frequently end in fights. Another traditional celebration, sometimes confused with the *fandango*, is the *huapango* (whah-PAYN-go), which features singing instead of dancing. *Huapango* is often used in the sense of regional music: *huapango Veracruzano; huapango Jaliciense.*

Fayuqueros (fah-yoo-KAY-rohs)—Dealers in *fayuca* or contraband; usually items smuggled into Mexico from the United States or elsewhere. Prior to the passing of the North American Foreign Trade Agreement in 1994 the U.S.–Mexican border was thronged with *fayuqueros*. It is still an important industry.

Feria (FAY-ree-ah)—Slang for money; also festival, fair.

Fichadoras (fee-chah-DOH-rahs)—Taxi dancers employed by some cabarets and nightclubs. In most of these clubs, the women work as part-time prostitutes. (See **Cantina**.)

Fresas (FRAY-sahs)—Literally, "strawberries" (or "drill bits"). Used in Guadalajara as a slang term to mean young girls who are stuck up and who look down on others. Along the U.S.–Mexican border the word is used in reference to girls who are virgins, unusually pretty or conspicuously dumb.

Frescos (Frays-cohs)—In addition to meaning "fresh" and "cool" as in soft drinks, as well as "sexually voluptuous" and "forward," *frescos* also means "a flirt" and "faggot" (homosexual). It is also applied to men who are disrespectful toward women.

Fueros (FWAY-rohs)—Exemptions. Mexico's *Constitution of 1824,* primarily prepared under the direction of the clergy and military leaders, continued the old Spanish tradition of exempting clergy and military personnel from being subject to civil law, no matter what crime they might commit—a tradition that has yet to be fully purged from Mexican politics. A reference to influence and power.

Gallineros (gah-yee-NAY-rohs)—"Chicken coops." A derogatory term used in reference to single rooms or small houses occupied by several unrelated people to save money.

Gastos (GAHS-tohs)—Housekeeping money, doled out on a daily basis by many lower-class husbands as part of their efforts to control the behavior of their families.

Gente decente (HEN-tay day-CEN-tay)—A "decent person"; that is, someone who is well educated and a member of the middle or upper class. (See **Buena Gente** in text.)

Gente de razón (HEN-tay day rah-ZOHN)—This literally means "people of reason." It is sometimes used in a literary sense by upper-class Mexicans to mean "Mexicans" when they are referring to themselves—a vestige of the early colonial years under Spain, when it was the official policy of the Spanish administrators and the Catholic Church that the natives (Indians) of Mexico were *gente sin razón* or "people without reason." It is also used to mean "people with good judgment."

Guayabera (guay-yah-BAY-rah)—The "national" patch-pocketed, open-necked, pleated shirt of Mexico, worn outside of the trousers. It is considered formal attire, and is suitable for most formal occasions. Fancier versions of the shirt are decorated with embroidered designs and rows of buttons. Politicians often wear *guayaberas,* especially when they are out in rural districts; it is a way of saying they are just one of the people and are therefore strongly interested in their welfare. *Guayabera* shirts originated in Yucatan where the year-around tropical climate made them the ideal wear for men, and the best *guayabera* shirts are still made in that area.

Güero (GWAY-roh)—A light-haired or light-skinned person. There are several terms in Mexican Spanish referring to people with light-colored hair and skin, which attests to the importance of these racial characteristics. This word is also spelled as *huero* (WHEY-roh). (See **Blanco**.)

Halcones (hahl-COH-nehs)—Literally "falcons," this is the name given to paramilitary troops who took part in a massacre of more than 50 students in the Corpus Christi neighborhood of Mexico City on June 10, 1971. The special forces were trained by Mexico City police to "swoop in and kill."

Hijo de puta (EE-hoh day POO-tah)—Son of a whore. The Mexican equivalent of "son-of-a-bitch." One of the most offensive phrases in the language.

Huevos (WAY-vohs)—The standard meaning of *huevos* is eggs. But when it is used with the verb *tener* meaning "to have," the inference is more likely to be to "gonads." *Tiene usted huevos?* "Do you have balls?" This can be a problem when you want to ask for eggs at a store. The problem is avoided by saying *"Hay huevos?"* "Are there any eggs?" In border slang, a *huevon* is someone who is lazy, with the connotation that his "balls" have grown so big from inactivity that he can't get around much anymore.

Inmigrado (een-me-GRAH-doh)—A foreigner who has permanent resident status in Mexico. Investments in Mexico by *inmigrados* are usually considered as domestic rather than foreign investments. Exceptions depend on where the investments are made and other circumstances.

Jarave Tapatio (hah-RAH-bay tah-pah-TEE-oh)—This is the famous Mexican Hat Dance, especially popular in the state of Jalisco, where it is said to have originated. It is more or less regarded as the state anthem.

Jefe (HEH-fay)—Boss or chief. The relationship between a *jefe* and his subordinates is paternalistic, generally going well beyond financial and personal considerations. The relationship is especially feudal among criminal elements. *Jefe* is also used as slang for "the old man," "the old lady," wife, husband or girlfriend.

Jimadores (he-mah-DOR-ehs)—"Field workers," especially those who work on plantations in the state of Jalisco that grow agave for the production of tequila.

Joder (hoh-DAYR)—This is a slang term that means to annoy, bother or bug someone. It is also used to mean "screw up," to take advantage of someone, or to beat them up. A *jodido* or *jodida* is someone (male or female) who is feeling rotten, or is "all screwed up," stressed out or in pain.

Juanita (whah-NEE-tah)—A girl's name; also a nickname for marijuana. Mexican Indians had been using marijuana as a medicine and as a hallucinogen for untold centuries when the Spanish conquistadors arrived in 1519. Over the following centuries, Indianized Spanish-Indian mixed-bloods adopted some of the medicinal uses of the plant, and it is still one of the things used by modern-day *curanderos* in Mexico. In the mid-1900s small numbers of Mexican youths, particularly along the U.S.-Mexican border, began using marijuana as a recreational drug. (See **Marijuana**.)

Jubilación (hoo-bee-lah-cee-OHN)—This word, which means "retirement," tells a great deal about the Mexican attitude toward work. It connotes that retirement is an occasion for joy and celebration. *El retiro* is also used.

La cosita (lah coh-SEE-tah)—Literally, "the little thing." This is a term frequently used by Mexican women in reference to the male sex organ. It is usually derogatory in the sense that Mexican men are more interested in their *cositas* than anything else.

Ladinos (lah-DEE-nohs)—Literally "foxes." This is the term traditionally used by Mexican Indians in reference to all persons of mixed-blood.

Lambiscones (lahm-bee-SCOH-nehs)—Literally, "lickers" or "those who lick," it is used in reference to the people who flock around powerful politicians, supporting them in return for favors of all kinds.

Lamehuevos (lah-may-WAY-vohs)—Sucking up to people by being obsequious or especially good to them; particularly associated with people catering to powerful politicians and bureaucrats. Another commonly used term in the same category is *mamón*, which can be translated as "sucking up" or "boot-licking."

La movida (lah moh-BEE-dah)—A mistress; a one night stand; also a TV program.

Lana (LAH-nah)—Money; literally "wool."

La neta (lah NAY-tah)—This term looks very much like "the net," and it means "the truth"—what is left after all the untruth has been removed.

Las gatas (lahs GAH-tahs)—Literally "cats," this is what maids were traditionally called in Mexico City. The label apparently came into use because the young Indian and mixed-blood girls and women who worked as live-in maids were always there, coming and going silently like shadows, seldom speaking and never raising their voices, particularly when the men of the house joined them in their beds, a custom that was virtually institutionalized during the Spanish colonial period (1521–1821).

Las movidas (lahs moh-BEE-dahs)—"The moves"; tricks of the trade used by taxi drivers (and others) to get as much money as possible out of customers. *Las movidas* include arranging with bars, clubs and whorehouses to get commissions when they deliver customers to these establishments. The process is also known as "hustling fish."

Latifundios (lah-tee-FOON-dee-ohs)—Huge private estates similar to the land grants issued by the Spanish Crown to Hernán Cortés, his men and select friends in the early 1500s. People who own these estates are called *Latifundistas*. Often synonymous with *hacienda*. (See **Campesinos, Haciendas** in text.)

Leche (LAY-chay)—Milk. When asking about *leche*, the meaning of the word changes depending on the verb used. *Tiene usted leche* means "Do you have breast milk?" *Hay leche?* means "Is there (do you have) any (cow's) milk?"

Licenciado (lee-cen-cee-AH-doh)—A person who has a degree from college or university that allows him or her to practice some profession. Until the 1990s, having the title of *licenciado* was one of the most coveted and powerful status symbols a Mexican could have. Now, say insiders, having money is more important than having a degree.

Limpiaparabrisas (leem-pee-ah-pah-rah-BREE-sahs)—"Street kids" who gather at intersections with stoplights; they rush into the streets and wash the windshields of cars waiting for the lights to change, then demand to be paid.

Línea (LEE-nay-ah)—Line. This term is often used in reference to the U.S.–Mexican border. When used in this sense by Mexicans, the word conjures up all kinds of images, mostly negative, of both Mexico and the United States.

Loca (LOH-cah)—A girl who is boy crazy and has several sweethearts.

Loncherías (lohn-chay-REE-ahs)—These are the popular "lunch counters" and food stands that one finds all over Mexico; they are the traditional Mexican version of fast-food restaurants.

Los nombres (lohs NOHM-brehs)—It is important to keep in mind that *los nombres* or "names" are very important to Mexicans and other Latin Americans. Most Mexicans have two "last names," with the second of the two names usually being the mother's maiden name. When both the paternal family name and the mother's maiden name are used the individual should be addressed by the paternal family name. Ruben Alvarez Rivera is Señor Alvarez.

Lucha libre (LOO-chah LEE-bray)—"Free fighting"; it refers to Mexican-style professional wrestling— featuring both men and women—in which teams of wrestlers, some in masks, play roles of good guys and bad guys (with the bad guys looking very much like foreigners).

Bad-guy teams spend a lot of time shouting insults and obscenities at the audience to get the spectators excited, with the verbal matches between spectators and wrestlers reaching new heights of abuse. Women are often the most vociferous of the hecklers among the spectators— one of the rare times when they can shout at men and get by with it.

A highlight of a match is when one wrestler manages to rip the mask off of his opponent's face—a very significant action, since masks have traditionally played a vital role in the spiritual world of Mexico.

Maestro (MY-strow)—Teacher or professor. Also an honorific title used to address people who are skilled in virtually any profession, from carpentry and plumbing to music. This is an important custom, and it plays a key role in dignifying people and maintaining the high level of courtesy that is characteristic of Mexican behavior.

Mal de ojo (mahl day OH-hoh)—The "evil eye." Many Mexican Indians and uneducated Mexicans continue to believe that supernatural powers can affect their lives. These superstitions include the belief that witches and others who are in contact with the spirit world can cast a *mal de ojo* on them. When this occurs, it is necessary to go to a "good" *bruja* (witch) or *curandero* (healer) to have the spell removed. It is also believed that some people have the power of the "evil eye" without being aware of it, and that they sometimes unintentionally cast spells on others.

Malecón (mah-lay-CONE)—This is the "coast drive," "coast road" or "beach-front street" that distinguishes towns and cities fronting on the ocean. The *malecón* in resort cities like Acapulco, La Paz and Mazatlan are invariably dotted with restaurants, night spots, hotels and various recreational facilities, and are favorite gathering places day and night.

Malinchista (mah-leen-CHEES-tah)—A person who has been "corrupted" by foreign influence, or prefers foreign things rather than Mexican things. *Malinchista* is a derivative of the Indian name of the slave girl Malinche who was given to Hernán Cortés, the conqueror of Mexico, shortly after he arrived on the Gulf coast in 1519. She subsequently played a key role as an interpreter and advisor to the Spaniards, which enabled Cortés to capture and destroy the Aztec empire. A traitor.

Mamacita (mah-mah-SEE-tah)—Literally, "little mother," this is a term of endearment frequently used by men, especially when they are addressing sexual partners.

Mamasota (mah-mah-SOH-tah)—The original meaning of this word is mom, ma or mama, and the mammary glands. But in Chicano slang it is also used to mean a women who has an especially sensual figure, as well as an attractive face and a pleasing personality .

Mano dura (MAH-no DOO-rah)—The "heavy hand"; the "hand" of the church, the Spanish viceroys, the dictator-generals, the politicians and others who have traditionally oppressed the people of Mexico and inflicted all sorts of cruelties upon them.

Maricón (mah-ree-CONE)—A homosexual. The more indelicate words, *joto* and *puto*, are also commonly used. In Mexico a homosexual lifestyle is known as "the life." Homosexuals who take the masculine or active role are described as *activo* or "active." Those who take the passive role are referred to as *pasivo* or "passive." Masculine homosexuals are not as publicly scorned as "feminine" homosexuals. Some areas of Mexico are especially tolerant of homosexual behavior. In other areas, beatings are common and city police often extort money from well-to-do homosexuals. *Mariposa* or "butterfly" is also commonly used to mean homosexual. Chicano slang for homosexual is *pájaro*, or bird.

Marijuana (mah-ree-WHAH-chah)—Marijuana (also spelled mariguana and marihuana) or "pot" has been known and used in Mexico for thousands of years, primarily as a medicine. Abuse of the mildly euphoric weed as a "recreational" drug by young people, mostly boys, dates from the mid-1900s, and is most common along the U.S.–Mexican border. Mexican slang words for marijuana include *bote* (referring to one ounce of the weed), *grifas, hierba, juanita, leña, lucas, mota, yesca* and *zacate*. The Mexican equivalents of "pot-head" include *grifo, mariguano* and *yesco*.

Marimacha (mah-ree-MAH-chah)—This term originally referred to a woman who was masculine in appearance and behavior. Chicano youths sometimes use it to mean "lesbian" or "dyke."

Mayordomo (mah-yohr-DOH-moh)—A foreman, manager or overseer in charge of the staff of a large house, a club, a bullring, etc. This title bestows respect upon the individual concerned and is an important facet of the Mexican system of detailed, refined etiquette.

Mezclas (MEHS-clahs)—People who are racially mixed. Mexicans who are racial mixtures, primarily of Spanish and Indian blood, now make up some 60 percent of the Mexican population. Racial mixtures of black Africans, Indians and Spanish are also common in the southeast portions of the country, where large numbers of black slaves were used as plantation laborers during the Spanish period. In earlier times the majority of the larger landowners, successful businessmen and politicians in the northern states of Mexico, particularly Sonora and Chihuahua, were primarily of Spanish blood. After areas along the U.S. border began to develop as sites for foreign-owned factories, large numbers of mixtures flocked in from central and southwestern Mexico. Also, *mestizo*.

Mica (ME-cah)—This is the "resident alien card" issued to immigrants by the U.S. Immigration and Naturalization Service signifying that they have been granted permanent resident status in the United States.

Mica chueca (ME-cah CHWAY-cah)—A false or "crooked" residency card. Many Mexicans and other Latin American nationalities who have entered the United States illegally are able to obtain *micas chuecas* from well-organized underground "suppliers." Insiders say the process of getting a *mica chueca*, a Social Security card and other false documentation takes only three to four days.

Mi lic (ME leec)—This is an abbreviation of *mi licenciado*, which is used when writing to a person who is a university graduate but who has no other title, or when you don't know their professional title. It is more or less the equivalent of putting "My Dear Sir" before a person's name.

Moreno (moh-Ray-noh)—A person with brown or dark skin; a term that was derogatory in the early centuries, but which gradually came to be accepted as either neutral or complimentary as time went by. A *moreno* is not as dark ad someone called or described as *prieto*.

Mosca (MOHS-cah)—An ordinary "housefly"; also used in reference to the helicopters used by the American Immigration Service to patrol the

U.S.–Mexican border in search of Mexicans trying to cross into the United States illegally.

Mota (MOH-tah)—A slang term for marijuana. (See **Juanita, Marijuana**.)

Muina (moo-EE-nah)—A disease marked by the loss of appetite and vomiting, caused by emotional trauma brought on by the repression of aggressive tendencies. In the past Mexicans were often afflicted.

Nacos (Nah-cohs)—"Ruffians," or "thugs"; also sometimes used in reference to Mexico's famous *pelados*, the "plucked ones," who live in urban slums and are noted for their adherence to a strict code of masculinity.

Nahuatl (NAH-whah-tahl)—This was the language spoken by the Aztecs. During the age of the Aztec empire it was the common language spoken by many other Indian tribes and nations in their dealings with the imperial capital of Tenochtitlán (Mexico City). Many of the descendents of the Aztecs, who have survived the Spanish conquest and European diseases, still speak Nahuatl. It is being studied by a growing number of Mexicans as a way of getting in closer touch with the cultural legacy of the Aztec empire.

Negra / Negro (NAY-grah/NAY-groh)—Literally, negress and negro. In some parts of Mexico when used in the diminutive (*negrita* and *negrito*) it is a term of endearment.

Niña (NEE-nyah)—This is a term for girls who have not yet reached their 15th birthday. After her 15th birthday a girl becomes a *señorita*. (See **Quinceañera** in text.)

Norteños (nohr-TAY-nyohs)—People who live in the northern states of Mexico are commonly referred to as *norteños* or "Northerners." They are often singled out as being Mexico's pioneers—people who settled the wild and generally rough northern territories—and as being more direct, more aggressive and tougher then other Mexicans.

No tiene madre (no-tee-EH-nay MAH-dray)—This literally means "it (he or she) doesn't have a mother," and is an expression commonly used to infer that some thing or some idea is no good, not valid, not acceptable and so on, or that some person is not what he or she pretends to be.

Ojo de gringa (OH-hoh day GREEN-gah)—Literally, "the eye of a foreign woman," especially a blonde. Figuratively, a 50-peso note, which is blue (blonde and blue being more or less interchangeable in Indian Mexico).

Padre (PAH-dray)—This, of course, means father, in the sense of biological father as well as priest. It is also used to mean "author" and "source," and in Mexican–American *pachuco* slang it is used as the equivalent of "awesome," "far-out" and "boss."

Palmadas (pahl-MAH-dahs)—These are the "pats on the back" that men exchange during an *abrazo* or "embrace." They are done with the right hand, which is extended over the left shoulder of the person being embraced.

Palomillas (pah-loh-ME-yahs)—Groups or cliques of people who hang out together for social and other purposes. Joining a *palomilla* may be a good way for foreigners in Mexico to widen their circle of friends and contacts.

Pandilleros (pahn-dee-YEH-rohs)—Gang members on the Mexican side of the U.S.-Mexican border, especially noted for their viciousness and wanton brutality. They mostly prey on people trying to cross the border for work (*pollos*) and those who help them (*coyotes*). One of the techniques they have used to immobilize victims is to cut the leg tendons that control the feet.

Papacito (pah-pah-SEE-toh)—"Little father." A term of endearment used by women in reference to their husbands or lovers. *Papi* is another term used in the same way.

Papeleo (pah-pay-LAY-oh)—A mania for formalizing and documenting everything; characteristic of government officials on every level. Red tape.

Paracaidistas (pah-rah-kie-DEES-tahs)—"Parachutists," a nickname given to squatters who appear suddenly on the outskirts of towns and cities, as if they had dropped out of the sky.

Paraestatales (pah-rah-es-tah-TAH-lays)—State-owned industries. When political reform finally took root in Mexico in the latter part of the 1980s, the government began privatizing many of the industries it had owned since the 1800s.

Parranda (pah-RRAHN-dah)—A long drinking party.

Partido Revolucionario Institucional (pahr-TEE-doe ray-bow-loo-cee-own-AH-ree-oh een-stee-too-cee-own-AHL)—The Institutional Revolutionary Party (PRI), founded in 1929, and the ruling party for the next several decades.

Peda (PAY-dah)—A drunken party. Sociologists say that *pedas* have been institutionalized in Mexico for centuries, because poor Mexican men have traditionally resorted to drinking and drunkenness as a means of stifling their frustrations. Machismo has also required that men drink often and heavily to demonstrate their masculinity and as a rebellion against the virgin-oriented church and the political and economic establishment.

Pendejo (pen-DAY-hoh)—The standard meaning of this term is pubic hair but it is commonly used to mean foolish, cowardly, stupid and silly. A *pendejo* is a dummy, a stupid person.

Pensadores (pen-sah-DOH-rays)—Literally, "thinkers," it is used in reference to intellectuals, most often writers whose view of the world is essentially artistic rather than scientific. *Pensadores* are greatly admired in Mexico.

Penúltimo trago (pay-NOOL-tee-moh TRAH-goh)—"Next-to-last" drink. In Mexico, a "last drink" is the one just before you die, so suggesting a "last drink" before breaking up a drinking party is definitely bad form. A last drink is sometimes referred to in terms of a saddle stirrup (*estribo*)—the last step one takes before getting on a horse.

Pepenadores (pay-pay-nah-DOH-rays)—Scavengers who live off of city garbage. For years the Santa Fe dump on a foothill ridge on the outskirts of Mexico City was the largest garbage dump in the world. It covered 150 acres and was well over 200 feet deep. Some 2,500 people lived on the dump, which had its own "king." The king, who had several million dollars in foreign bank accounts, also had a wife, a common-law wife and several mistresses. His common-law wife had him killed, following which city authorities closed the dump. There are now several large dumps around Mexico City, but *pepenadores* are no longer officially permitted to live on them. They are allowed on the dumps only between 7 A.M. and 7 P.M.

Peseros (pay-SAY-rohs)—Vans and cars operated by private owners that cruise up and down some of the main thoroughfares of Mexico City and other major cities, picking up and dropping off passengers anywhere along their routes. In Mexico City they are usually painted green and white. In other cities, especially those along the U.S.–Mexican border, the vehicles are commonly referred to as *combis*. (See **Colectivos**.)

Piñata (pee-NYAH-tah)—Traditionally a large clay pot wrapped in colorful paper and filled with candy, the *piñata* was hung up on a tree limb or rafter, etc., to be broken by children wielding sticks at birthday parties and saints' days. Present-day *piñatas* are made of papier-mâché or cardboard and are shaped like animals, people or other objects. Older kids and youths are often blindfolded to make the ritual more exciting. In ancient times the ritual was part of the celebration of the first Sunday of Lent, with adult guests at masked balls invited to try their hand at breaking the *piñata*. (See **Las Posadas** in text.)

Pistoleros (pees-toh-LAY-rohs)—Gunslingers; bodyguards hired by politicians and others who could afford armed protection from the lawlessness and killings that were commonplace from 1910 until the 1960s. Some wealthy businesspeople who fear kidnapping, as well as prominent politicians, still employ armed bodyguards. In earlier times, bandits who roamed the rural areas of northern Mexico were called *pistoleros*.

Planta baja (PLAHN-tah BAH-hah)—The ground floor in Mexican homes, hotels, office buildings and so on is just that, the *planta baja*, while the first floor refers to the floor above the ground floor (which is the second floor in the United States). On the elevator panels in Mexico the ground floor is generally abbreviated as P.B.

Pocamadre (poh-cah-MAH-dray)—When used in the exclamation, "*Qué pocamadre!*" this refers to a person without shame; someone who behaves in a shameless manner. This term is especially strong because it invokes the goodness of Mexican mothers, as a contrast to those who have no decency or pride. "*Está pocamadre*," however, means "How great it is!"

Porfiriato (pohr-fee-ree-AH-toh)—This refers to the dictatorial rule of Profirio Díaz from 1877 to 1910, figuratively "the Porfirio era." This was the period when the common people of Mexico were little more than slave laborers in bondage to a small elite group of Mexican and foreign (mostly American) industrialists, who dominated the economy. The memory of that time is still strong in the historical consciousness of Mexicans, and is a primary factor in their wariness toward foreign investment in Mexico today.

Porros (POH-rrohs)—Thugs who stand around polling places and intimidate voters. Called "cheerleaders," they are most often hired by local officials who want to make sure their candidate wins. *Porristas* refers to secret agents who are paid to stir up trouble. In 1971 *porristas* posing as students were involved in the killing of more than 50 students in the Corpus Christi section of Mexico City during a demonstration, which they helped start.

Presidios (pray-SEE-dee-ohs)—The standard meaning of this word is "fort," but in recent times it came to be used as a slang reference to tenement-type housing in the United States, where large members of illegal Hispanic aliens live behind closed and locked doors.

Prieta (pree-EH-tah)—A person who is dark-skinned. Also, a vulgar slang term for the male sex organ.

Pueblo (PWAY-bloh)—*Pueblo* is most commonly used by North Americans to mean an Indian village or small town, but in Mexico it also means "people," in the sense that one cannot understand Mexico without understanding the *pueblo.*

Puente (PWANE-tay)—Literally, a "bridge." Also used in reference to the custom of creating four-day weekends by taking an extra day off when national holidays are near weekends. Banks, government offices and schools are normally closed on these *puente* days.

Qué frondosa! (kay fron-DOH-sah!)—The men of Tehuantepec like their women plump and voluptuous. *Qué frondosa* is one of the compliments they pay to women who meet their standards of sensual beauty. Its figurative meaning is, "How fat and luxuriant you are!" (in the sense of a large tree well rounded by a luxuriant growth of leaves).

Querida (kay-REE-dah)—A term of endearment meaning "dear" or "sweetheart" and sometimes "mistress." My Mexican friends warn that caution is necessary when using this word in order to avoid giving the impression that a girlfriend is a mistress.

Quince años (Keen-say AH-nyohs)—Literally "15 years," in reference to the 15th birthday of girls, when they officially become "señoritas." (See **Quinceañeras** in text.)

Rancheros (rahn-CHAY-rohs)—Ranchers, generally referring to owners of smaller, independent ranches. Traditionally, Mexican *rancheros* have looked upon themselves as super cowboys, and they put great emphasis of horses, guns and women. In border slang a *ranchero* sometimes means a "hick," somebody from a rural area who is unsophisticated, naive.

Rapto (RAHP-toh)—A prearranged ceremonial "kidnapping" of a bride, common in the Juchitán area of Mexico, where the local society is said to be matrilineal, with women ruling the men. After the bride has been carried away by the groom, the couple is married in a civil and church ceremony.

Ratero (rah-TAY-roh)—From "rat" (the furry kind), *ratero* is commonly used in reference to hoodlums, gangsters and other law-breakers, including government officials who are on the take. One popular anecdotal story has a politician speaking to a gathering of politicians when he wants to impress upon them that they may be equal but he is more equal than they are. He says, "We are all rats. But I am the biggest rat here!"

Reconquista (ray-cohn-KEES-tah)—The literal meaning of this word is "reconquest." It refers to the nearly 800-year effort of the Spanish to expel the Moors from Spain. (The Moors invaded Spain in 711 A.D. and were not expelled until 1502.) During this long period, virtually all commerce and manual labor in Spain was performed by Moors and Jews, while male Spaniards devoted themselves to the art of war, poetry and the priesthood. Thus by the time Columbus discovered the Americas in 1492, most Spanish men had long since lost all traditions of working with their hands. The Spaniards who colonized Mexico brought the *reconquista* mentality with them, seeing themselves as conquerors, masters of slave kingdoms and representatives of the Catholic Church. The *reconquista* ethic set the tone of the 300-year Spanish reign in Mexico, and left an impact on Mexican culture that is still visible today.

Rentistas (ren-TEES-tahs)—These are foreign residents of Mexico, mostly American retirees, who live on income from outside sources. An immigrant visa in this category is good for one year and may be renewed annually.

Rollero (roh-YEH-roh)—Someone who is talkative; someone who is very convincing but who cannot always be trusted or believed—as in a politician.

Sacadolares (sah-cah-DOH-lah-rays)—A "dollar remover"; a person who "parks" money (usually large sums) in foreign banks as a hedge against deflation and various political dangers.

Salud (sah-LOOD)—This is the simple, ordinary toast of Mexico, ritually but casually said before taking your first drink. There are numerous additions to it which are used for more formal or important occasions. One of the most common is *"Salud, dinero y amor, y el tiempo para gozarlos!"* (Sah-LOOD, dee-NAY-roh ee ah-MOHR, ee el tee-AYM-poh PAR-rah goh-ZARA-lohs!), which means, "Health, money and love, and the time to enjoy them." It is common for this to be shortened to *"Salud, dinero y amor!"* with the rest being understood. One of the variations of this toast that demonstrates the biting sense of humor typical of Mexican men is *"Salud, dinero y amor sin suegra,"* which means, "Health, money, and love without a mother-in-law!" (Notes Geri Canalez de

Jimenez: When serving wine at a dinner or party it is customary to make sure that a guest gets the last drops in a bottle. They are referred to as *Las gotas de felicidad* or "The drops of happiness.")

Sangrita (Sahn-GREE-tah)—A jolting drink made of orange and tomato juice, lime, tobasco and pepper. Normally used as a chaser when drinking tequila.

Santo (SAHN-toh)—This means "saint." Mexicans are assigned a saint at birth, and thereafter celebrate that particular saint's day for the rest of their lives. A child's *dia del santo* is often celebrated with more bang than a birthday. Family members, relatives and friends typically drop by the homes of adults to congratulate them on their saint's day, and are generally treated to drinks and snacks. Some people invite family members and friends out to restaurants to mark the occasion. Every calendar day has its own saint or saints. Children are often named for the saint day on which they are born.

Secretario (seck-ray-TAH-ree-oh)—A male secretary. Traditionally in Mexico male secretaries were educated men who served politicians and government officials, who were often uneducated but had power, including those on the highest level of government. Because of their positions as the "right hands" of these men, *secretarios* often were able to exercise a great deal of power in the names of their bosses, as well as on their own. *Secretarios* are still in powerful positions in Mexico's political world. *Secretario de Estado* is any member of the president's cabinet.

Serranos (syar-RAH-nohs)—Literally, "mountain men." This term was used to describe cowboys, miners and others who, in earlier decades, lived in distant mountains and were known for their wild ways. They still exist in large numbers but are less wild than in earlier days.

Sindicatos (seen-dee-CAH-tohs)—Labor unions. Almost all professions in Mexico are unionized; most Mexicans are members of one union or another, and they take their unions and membership seriously (as a counterbalance against the traditional tyranny of the government). Labor Day, May 1, is one of Mexico's most important holidays. Towns and cities throughout the country hold parades marked by lots of flag-waving, music and patriotic speeches. Leaders of labor unions have traditionally been among the most powerful people in Mexico, sometimes running their unions as if they were private fiefs.

Sinvergüenza (seen-bayr-GWAIN-zah)—This is someone who has no shame; a scoundrel. It is frequently used in reference to government officials and bureaucrats who demand especially large *mordidas*, or "payoffs," before they will approve documents or actions.

Sopilote (soh-pee-LOH-tay)—A vulture. Also Chicano and border slang for an older man who preys on young girls.

Susto (SOOS-toh)—A scare or fright that can cause a variety of illnesses, particularly fever—a folk belief that is still prevalent among some Mexican Indians. One type of illness said to be caused by fright is called *espanto*. Other "folk" illnesses include *empacho*, said to be brought on by eating something that doesn't agree with you, and *caida*, loss of energy and ambition to do anything. A traditional remedy for *susto* is *agua de brasas* or "charcoal water" (water in which a chunk of charcoal had been crushed.)

Tacos (TAH-cohs)—In addition to being something edible, *tacos* is also used in reference to fake voting ballots. People who stuff ballot boxes with fake ballots are *taqueros*. *Taco* also means pool stick.

Tapados (tah-PAH-dohs)—Literally, "veiled ones," which refers to those who want to be president but who remain behind the scenes while their backers are out gathering support from national, regional and local groups. *Tapados* hold private meetings with key high-level individuals and groups, offering deals in exchange for their support. After the reigning president has publicly acknowledged his choice of the candidates, the chosen one is known as *El Bueno*, or "The Good One."

Tapatios (tah-pah-TEE-ohs)—This is a nickname for the local people in Guadalajara and the surrounding area in Jalisco. *Tapatios* are known for being especially laid-back and fun-loving.

Tarjetas de visita (tar-HAY-tahs day be-SEE-tah)—"Calling cards"—the Spanish equivalent of name cards or business cards. Some people in Mexico (and other Latin countries) carry two kinds of name cards, one bearing their home address and phone number for social purposes, and the other one giving their business affiliations. This is a useful custom to follow.

Telenovelas (tay-lay-no-BAY-lahs)—Soap Operas, á la *All My Children, One Life To Live*, et al. Mexican *telenovelas* cover the same armpit of human relations that have made their foreign counterparts a social and economic phenomenon of the century.

Tecnicos (TECK-nee-cohs)—Literally, technicians, but commonly used in a political sense to refer to people (often educated abroad) who favor precise formulas and systems, as opposed to the more personal, open-minded approach that has been traditional in Mexico. Similar to "bean-counters."

Tequios (tay-KEE-ohs)—Municipal projects in towns and villages. Male residents are required to volunteer their labor for the projects.

Tío taco (TEE-oh TAH-coh)—A *pachuco* slang term that is the Mexican equivalent of an "Uncle Tom"—someone who is a traitor to his own people. Primarily used by Chicanos and Mexicans along the U.S. border. From *tío* (uncle) and *taco* (the food).

Tirar sin apuntar (tee-RAHR seen ah-poon-TAHR)—Literally, this means "to shoot without aiming." It is the Mexican equivalent of "to shoot from the hip," that is, to say things without giving due consideration to the consequences. Mexican businesspeople and politicians have traditionally been noted for their propensity to shoot from the hip, but growing numbers are now taking responsibility for their promises. It is especially important for new businesses going into Mexico to document their activities, policies and procedures, thereby reducing the possibility of employees engaging in *tirar sin apuntar*.

Títulos (TEE-too-lohs)—As in other class-and-rank-conscious societies, professional titles are an important facet of Mexican etiquette. It is customary to address people by the title that expresses their occupation: *Arquetecto* (architect), *Doctor*, *Ingeniero* (engineer), *Licenciado* (person with a degree), *Maestro* (master of some skill/art), etc.

Topes (TOH-pays)—Speed bumps. These are cement, and sometimes metal, ridges or humps put across streets and highways to force automobile drivers to slow down. They are most often found on the outskirts of small towns and villages, and are usually indicated by roadside signs. Hitting a series of the bumps, especially late at night, is more than enough to get your attention. They are also called *tumulos, vibradores* and *bordos*.

Tragafuegos (trah-gah-FWAY-gohs)—Literally "firebreathers," these are street performers who put gasoline, kerosene or some other flammable liquid in their mouths, then squirt a stream toward a burning torch held in one of their outstretched hands. The result is a flash-wall of flame between their mouths, the torch and the ground as the burning screen of liquid drops. Performances are staged near street intersections where there are lots of pedestrians and cars, and where tips can be expected from startled and impressed spectators. Firebreathers who continue the profession for a year or more, doing as many as a dozen performances an hour, usually end up with their taste buds dead, their gums rotten and their nervous systems shot.

Mexico's government condemns the practice; sometimes fire-breathers are grabbed off the streets and put into detoxification centers, where it tries to help them get regular jobs. Spokesmen for the government say that as the economy of the country improves the firebreathers will disappear.

Tronar (troh-NAR)—Literally, "to explode" or "to happen." This word is used to describe many of the things or events that occur suddenly in Mexico, without immediately obvious reasons, but which in reality are the result of circumstances that have been building up for decades or ages. It is also in reference to smoking marijuana and taking drugs. "*Te la tronaste!*" ("You smoke pot!")

Ubicación (oo-bee-cah-cee-OWN)—How successful one is in Mexico, in business, politics or social life, is directly related to the connections that one has—family, business and political. The term *ubicación*, which literally means "personnel placement," refers to the level one is "plugged into" in the establishment. The higher your *ubicación*, the better you can make out.

Vecindades (bay-ceen-DAH-days)—Housing projects, primarily for the poor, that typically become slum courts. There are many in Mexico City and in cities along the U.S.-Mexican border.

Vete a la chingada (Bay-tay ah lah cheen-GAH-dah)—"Go to Hell!" In this case, *chingada* means a bad or terrible situation, a bad place, a mess.

Viejo / vieja (bee-EH-hoh / bee-EH-hah)—Something old or worn out; also said of men or women. In Chicano and border slang, *viejo* is also used to mean father, husband or "old man"; and *vieja* is used as the equivalent of mother, wife, "old lady," girlfriend, broad, etc.

Vientos (bee-EN-tohs)—Winds. When this term is used it is generally in the sense of *mal aires* or "bad airs"—evil influences carried by the wind that can cause bad luck and illnesses. Indians and as well as many other Mexicans on all levels of society fear evil winds and take precautions against them.

Virtud (behr-TOOD)—Chastity. Mexico's Spanish-oriented culture traditionally put a high premium of female *virtud* before marriage, with parents going to extremes to prevent their daughters from being alone with teenaged and adult males, including relatives, and then controlling their courting with chaperons. One of the reasons for these extreme measures was that Mexican males were programmed to go to similar extremes in exercising their sexuality, creating an extraordinary amount of sexual tension between males and females. In contrast to this contradictory approach to human sexuality, most of Mexico's Indian nations had a much more casual attitude toward female *virtud*, and some allowed young men and women to practice "free sex" before settling down with mates. Mexican men still tend to be sexually predatory, causing Mexican women no end of problems. But by the 1960s the custom of keeping young women segregated from young men had gone by the wayside, and although virginity in brides is still highly prized by males, it is no longer the rule.

As Mexicans are wont to say: "*La virtud y la honestidad se pierden muy facil*" ("Chastity and honesty are easily lost").

Visitante (bee-see-TAHN-tay)—A "business visitor visa" which is good for six months. Another type of visa for businesspeople, created by the North American Free Trade Agreement (NAFTA), which went into effect on January 1, 1994, is a "Business Visitor" visa, good for up to 30 days. Other types of "NAFTA" visas include Professional, Intracompany Transferee and Investor/Trader.

Zanate (zah-NAH-tay)—Literally a "blackbird." Also used by *pachuco*-type youths along the U.S.–Mexican border in reference to black people and those with dark skin.

Zócalo (ZOH-cah-loh)—The main square in a town or city; traditionally it is the center of evening and holiday activity, when it is filled with vendors, strollers and musicians. *Zocalos* are usually the best places in Mexico for people watching.

Zona rosa (ZOH-nah ROH-sah)—This is a colloquial term for a city's primary entertainment and shopping district. Visitors to a *zona rosa* are advised to be especially wary of pickpockets and purse-snatchers, who congregate in these areas to prey on tourists and foreigners in general. The literal meaning of *zona rose* is "pink zone," recalling the days when it referred to red-light districts.